Lineages
of Revolt

Lineages of Revolt

Issues of Contemporary Capitalism

in the Middle East

Adam Hanieh

Haymarket Books
Chicago, Illinois

© 2013 Adam Hanieh

Published in 2013 by
Haymarket Books
P.O. Box 180165
Chicago, IL 60618
773-583-7884
info@haymarketbooks.org
www.haymarketbooks.org

ISBN: 978-1-60846-325-1

Trade distribution:
In the US through Consortium Book Sales and Distribution, www.cbsd.com
In the UK, Turnaround Publisher Services, www.turnaround-uk.com
In Canada, Publishers Group Canada, www.pgcbooks.ca
In Australia, Palgrave Macmillan, www.palgravemacmillan.com.au
All other countries, Publishers Group Worldwide, www.pgw.com

Special discounts are available for bulk purchases by organizations
and institutions. Please contact Haymarket Books for more information
at 773-583-7884 or info@haymarketbooks.org.

Cover design by Rachel Cohen.

This book was published with the generous support of the Wallace Global
Fund and Lannan Foundation.

Printed in the United States.

Library of Congress CIP data is available.

10 9 8 7 6 5 4 3 2

Table of Contents

Chapter 1: Theories and Perspectives   1

Chapter 2: Framing the Region: Imperialism and the Middle East   19

Chapter 3: Mapping the Neoliberal Experience   47

Chapter 4: Capitalism and Agrarian Change in North Africa   75

Chapter 5: Class and State in the West Bank: Neoliberalism under Occupation   99

Chapter 6: The Regional Scale: Bringing the Gulf Arab States Back In   123

Chapter 7: Crisis and Revolution   145

Appendixes   177

Bibliography   195

Notes   219

Index   267

CHAPTER 1
Theories and Perspectives

M ore than two years since the downfall of Tunisia's president Zine El Abidine Ben Ali, the cries of *al-shaa'b yurid isqat al-nizam*—"the people want the downfall of the regime"—continue to reverberate through the streets of every Arab capital. The region has never before witnessed such an all-encompassing, deeply felt, popular revolt. From the Atlantic to the Gulf, millions of people have confronted authoritarian, corrupt, and feckless rulers, whose contempt for their populations has been matched only by the fear of losing a grip on power. These regimes met the explosion of popular rage with characteristic brutality, killing, maiming, and torturing tens of thousands in a desperate attempt to restore the passivity and obsequiousness that autocrats expected of generations past. Concurrently, Western states scrambled to rearrange their domination of the region and identify new mechanisms of stable rule in one of the most strategically significant areas of the world, responding to the uprisings with their standard amalgam of military intervention, promises of financial aid, and constant political intrigue. Despite this growing specter of counterrevolution, the initial hope manifested by the uprisings persists, witnessed most prominently in the ongoing mobilizations in Egypt and Tunisia. It is, moreover, a conjuncture that has inspired millions across the globe. From demonstrations in Gabon, Nigeria, and Djibouti to the Spanish *indignados*, the Occupy movement, and the dramatic confrontations in Greece, the repertoire of protest tactics and slogans born in the Arab uprisings continues to be generalized, molded, and transformed to fit circumstances and struggles elsewhere. From the vantage point of late 2012 it remains unclear where these revolts will end up—it is certain, however, that the region will never be the same.

Beyond the profound and largely uncharted political implications of these revolts, one of their most enduring ramifications will undoubtedly be the renewed interest they have awakened in the Middle East's political economy. Questions of political economy were clearly paramount in the minds of the demonstrators themselves, as the widespread slogan *aish, hurriyah, 'adalah ijtima'iyah* ("bread, freedom, social justice") testifies. The popularity of this cry points to the numerous social crises that faced much of the region in the decade preceding the uprisings, a period marked by extremely high levels of unemployment, poverty, rising food prices, and the growing precariousness of daily existence. These intense social problems worsened in the wake of the 2008 global economic collapse, further contributing to the deep malaise and frustration experienced by those living under repressive regimes. As many observers have noted, these are the proximate roots of the uprisings, indisputably confirming that the political and economic spheres remain inseparable and intertwined. They remain central to any assessment of the future trajectories of the region.

Yet much of the discussion around these issues of political economy has been frustratingly superficial. Even in radical accounts of the Middle East, analysis tends to remain overly focused on the surface appearances of poverty and relative measures of inequality rather than engaging with the nature of capitalism as a systemic totality that penetrates every aspect of social life. This is a major weakness in the understanding of the region. The unequal distribution of wealth is not an unfortunate consequence of wrong-headed economic policy or a "conspiracy" of elites but rather a necessary presupposition of capitalist markets themselves. The challenge of mapping the essence of this social system remains largely unfulfilled—tracing the patterns of capital accumulation in the Middle East, the structures of class and state that have arisen around it, and their interconnection with capitalism at the global scale.

This book is intended as a contribution to such an analysis. It by no means purports to provide a comprehensive account of all aspects of the region's political economy, a detailed narrative of the uprisings, or an in-depth study of every country in the region. Its goal is to trace in broad outline some of the most significant transformations of the Middle East through the lens of Marxist political economy. Its novelty lies in the emphasis on capitalism and class as crucial pivots of analysis, two categories frequently downplayed in standard approaches to the Middle East. It further attempts to take seriously the nature of the region *as a region*—to trace the changing hierarchies at the regional scale as an integrated unity that shapes social formations at the national level. In this manner, the book hopes to sketch the essential backdrop to the revolts while demonstrating how important political economy is to understanding the Middle East.

Approaching the Middle East

Conventional accounts of political economy in the Middle East tend to adopt a similar methodological approach, which begins, typically, with the basic analytical categories of "state" (al-dawla) and "civil society" (al-mujtama' al-madani).[1] The former is defined as the various political institutions that stand above society and govern a country. The latter is made up of "institutions autonomous from the state which facilitate orderly economic, political and social activity"[2] or, in the words of the Iraqi social scientist Abdul Hussein Shaaban, "the civil space that separates the state from society, which is made up of non-governmental and non-inheritable economic, political, social and cultural institutions that form a bond between the individual and the state."[3] All societies are said to be characterized by this basic division, which sees the state confronted by an agglomeration of atomized individuals, organized in a range of "interest groups" with varying degrees of ability to choose their political representatives and make demands on their political leaders. The institutions of civil society organize and express the needs of people in opposition to the state, "enabling individuals to participate in the public space and build bonds of solidarity."[4] The study of political economy becomes focused upon, as a frequently cited book on the subject explains, "strategies of economic transformation, the state agencies and actors that seek to implement them, and the social actors such as interest groups that react to and are shaped by them."[5]

A conspicuous feature of the Middle East, according to both Arabic- and English-language discussions on these issues, is the region's apparent "resilience of authoritarianism"—the prevalence of states where "leaders are not selected through free and fair elections, and a relatively narrow group of people control the state apparatus and are not held accountable for their decisions by the broader public."[6] While much of the world managed to sweep away dictatorial regimes through the 1990s and 2000s, the Middle East remained largely mired in autocracy and monarchical rule—"the world's most unfree region," as the introduction to one prominent study of authoritarianism in the Arab world put it.[7] A dizzying array of typologies for this authoritarianism has been put forward, characteristically dividing the region between authoritarian monarchies (the Gulf Arab states, Morocco, Jordan) and authoritarian republics (Egypt, Syria, Algeria, Yemen, Tunisia).[8] These authoritarian regimes are typically contrasted with a third category, the so-called democratic exceptions, in which "incumbent executives are able to be removed and replaced."[9] Israel is frequently held up as the archetype of this latter group—with Turkey, Iran, Lebanon, and Iraq (following the 2003 US invasion) also included, each with a varying "degree" of democracy.[10]

An entire academic industry has developed around attempting to explain the apparent persistence and durability of Middle East authoritarianism. Much of this has been heavily Eurocentric, seeking some kind of intrinsic "obedience to authority" inherent to the "Arab mind."[11] Some authors have focused on the impact of religion, tracing authoritarian rule to the heavy influence of Islam, and the fact that "twentieth-century Muslim political leaders often have styles and use strategies that are very similar to those instituted by the Prophet Muhammad in Arabia some 1400 years ago."[12] Similarly, others have examined the source of regime legitimacy in places such as Saudi Arabia, where the "ruler's personal adherence to religious standards and kinship loyalties" supposedly fit the "political culture" of a society whose reference point is "Islamic theocracy coming from the ablest leaders of a tribe tracing its lineage to the Prophet."[13] Other more modern explanations for authoritarianism have been sought in intra-elite division,[14] leaders' skills at balancing and manipulating different groups in society—so-called statecraft,[15] natural resource endowment,[16] and the role and attitudes of the military.[17] All these approaches share the same core methodological assumption: the key categories for understanding the Middle East—and, indeed, any society—are the state, on one hand, counterposed with civil society, on the other.

This state/civil society dichotomy underlies another frequent (although not unchallenged) assertion made in the literature on the Middle East—that of a two-way, causal link between authoritarianism and the weakness of capitalism.[18] According to this perspective, authoritarianism not only means that political and civil rights are weak or absent but also that the heavy hand of state control interferes with the operation of a capitalist economy.[19] Individuals are prevented from freely engaging in market activities while state elites benefit from authoritarianism by engaging in "rent-seeking behavior"—using their privileged position to divert economic rents that pass through the state for their own personal enrichment and consolidation of power.[20] Authoritarian states seek to dominate and control economic sectors through their position of strength, allocating rents to favored groups in order to keep society in check.[21] In the Middle East, as a result, "private property is not secure from the whims of arbitrary rulers . . . [and] many regimes have yet to abandon allocation for alternative strategies of political legitimation, and hence must continue to generate rents that accrue to the state."[22]

Within this worldview, the agency of freedom is neatly located in the realm of the market, while tyranny lurks ever-present in the state. The history of the region is thus characteristically recounted as a long-standing struggle between the "authoritarian state" and "economic and political liberalization." Told from this perspective, the narrative usually begins with the emergence from colonialism in the aftermath of World War II, when various independence movements sought a definitive end to British and French influence in the area. These independence movements were typically led by militaries or other elites, which seized power in the postcolonial period and began an era of "statism" or "Arab socialism." By the 1980s, however, these authoritarian states would come under severe strain due to the inefficiencies of state-led economic devel-opment and the desire of increasingly educated populations for greater economic and political freedom. These pressures for economic liberalization were compounded in the era of globalization by the ethos of "democratization" that swept the globe through the 1990s. There was—as two well-known scholars of the Middle East put it—a "direct correlation between economic performance and the degree of democracy . . . the more open and liberal a polity, the more effective has been its economy in responding to globalization."[23] Authoritarian states that had "waged literal or metaphorical wars against their civil societies and the autonomous capital that is both the cause and prod-uct of civil society" might sometimes choose the "right" economic policies, but these were inevitably "dead letters in the absence of implementation capacity, which only a dynamic civil society appears to be able to provide."[24] Capitalism was, in short, best suited to—and a force for—democracy.[25]

This logic was widely replicated outside of academia through the 1990s and 2000s, forming the core justification for a wide range of so-called democracy promotion pro-grams. Integral to this was the US National Endowment for Democracy (NED), estab-lished in 1983 and funded by the US State Department. NED, in turn, supported other organizations such as the National Democratic Institute (NDI) and the International Republican Institute (IRI)—linked to the Democratic and Republican parties respec-tively—and bodies such as the Center for International Private Enterprise (CIPE) and the Solidarity Center (affiliated to the AFL-CIO). A host of other private corporations and NGOs were also involved. Through these institutions, the US government focused on programs that twinned the extension of neoliberal policies with the democracy pro-motion agenda in the global South. As then president George W. Bush noted in 2004, this policy was based around "free elections and free markets."[26] It was a form of democracy understood in the narrow sense of regular electoral competitions, usually waged between different sections of the elite, which largely aimed at providing popu-larly sanctioned legitimacy for free market economic measures.[27] While organizations such as NED, NDI, and IRI were the most visible and explicit face of this policy orien-tation, all international financial institutions were to employ the same basic argument linking "free markets" and "a vibrant civil society" with the weakening of the author-itarian state.[28]

In this vein, the response of Western governments and institutions to the revolts of 2011 and 2012 was largely predictable. Instead of viewing the Arab uprisings as protests against the "free market" economic policies long championed by Western institutions in the region, they were framed as essentially political in nature. The problem, according to the Western angle, lay in authoritarianism, which stifled markets, and the popular rage expressed on the streets of the Middle East could thus be understood as pro-capitalist in content. US president Barack Obama noted, for example, in a major policy speech on the Middle East in May 2011, that the region needed "a model in which protectionism gives way to openness, the reins of commerce pass from the few to the many, and the economy generates jobs for the young. America's support for democracy will therefore be based on ensuring financial stability, promoting reform, and integrating competitive markets with each other and the global economy."[29] Likewise, the president of the World Bank, Robert Zoellick, argued that the revolts in Tunisia occurred because of too much "red tape," which prevented people from engaging in capitalist markets.[30] This basic argument would be repeated incessantly by Western policy makers throughout 2011 and 2012—autocratic states had stifled economic freedom; "free markets" would be essential to any sustained transition away from authoritarianism.

A Marxist Framework of Class and State

Instead of the state/civil society dichotomy that characterizes these standard approaches, this book adopts a radically different framework for investigating the political economy of the Middle East. Its basic starting point is the notion of class as the key social category from which to comprehend the dynamics of any society, distinct from the catchall notion of civil society (as it is conventionally understood). This focus on class leads to fundamentally contrasting perceptions of the role and nature of the state, the relationship between markets and political democracy, and the assessment of social struggles such as those that spread through the Arab world in 2011 and 2012.

Class, according to the conception developed by Marx, is understood as an expression of the relations that people form between each other around the process of producing society's needs. This differs from the way it is typically viewed by standard sociological approaches, in which class is seen as a category of income or a group of people who do the same type of work.[31] Capitalist society is characterized by the private ownership of the means and products of social production. The essential class division is thus between those who own the means of production (capitalists) and those who have little choice but to sell their capacity to work in order to be able to meet their needs in the marketplace (workers). Capitalists draw their profit from the ability to force workers to produce commodities that can be sold at a greater price than the money spent on production itself.[32] Rather than taking private property and private interests as naturally given, Marx emphasized that they are socially determined, "achieved only within the conditions laid down by society and with the means provided by society; hence . . . bound to the reproduction of these conditions and means."[33] Class, in other words, is always a social relation, which is continually being made and remade in an ongoing process of accumulation and contestation.

An emphasis on class does not mean that other divisions do not exist within a given society. Class formation is a process involving real human beings, and this means that the concrete conditions of class always carry specific characteristics—of gender, race, age, national origin, and so forth—that are given particular social meaning through their process of coming into being.[34] Approaching class in this manner helps to guard against economistic views that tend to set up class as an abstract category shorn of its particularities. It means, for example, that it makes little sense to speak of class in a concrete sense without also acknowledging that it is simultaneously gendered as it forms. Moreover, in the Middle East context, as well as globally, class formation cannot be understood without tracing movements of people across and within borders—it is thus also marked by distinct and concrete relationships between geographical spaces.[35] These processes need to be considered concurrently if a full picture of class formation is to be grasped.

It is also important to acknowledge that there exists a wide variety of labor relations within any capitalist society. In the global South, the working class rarely manifests in the "pure" form that Marx emphasized in *Capital*, made up of individuals, each of whom "as a free individual can dispose of his labour power as his own commodity" with "no other commodity for sale."[36] In reality, capitalism continues to reproduce and integrate into the process of accumulation various "forms of labor exploitation,"[37] including slavery, indentured labor, child labor, sharecropping, dormitory systems for migrant workers, and forms of subcontracting. Workers frequently depend upon non-wage activities in order to reproduce themselves (such as the farming of small plots of land or unpaid family labor). Within both rural and urban spheres, classes are typically stratified according to varying levels of wealth and power. In the Arab world, all of these complexities are crucial to describing the specificities of capitalism and class.

Keeping these subtleties in mind, it is nonetheless accurate to state that conventional accounts of the Middle East generally downplay questions of class, reducing it to just one of many different "interest groups," such as "business elites." This is a fundamental flaw in mainstream conceptions of civil society, which, as Ellen Meiksins Wood has pointed out in her seminal analysis of the notion, is a "conceptual portmanteau [that] indiscriminately lumps everything together from households and voluntary associations to the economic system of capitalism."[38] In this manner, the state/civil society dichotomy serves to "conceptualize away the problem of capitalism, by disaggregating society into fragments, with no overarching power structure, no totalizing unity, no systemic coercions—in other words, no capitalist system, with its expansionary drive and its capacity to penetrate every aspect of social life."[39] Academic approaches that present the ideal of liberal democracy as the desired policy goal—supposedly guaranteeing the same rights and responsibilities for all "civil society actors" regardless of wealth, social status, or accident of birth—act to obfuscate this reality of class power. The economic realm is separated from the political sphere. Capitalism itself is rendered invisible through a juridical scrim of "equal rights" that posits equality where none exists.

An emphasis on patterns of class formation leads, furthermore, to a sharply different notion of the state than that employed in conventional frameworks of analysis. According to Marx, the nature of political institutions such as the state is a historically determined social form—or form of appearance—of the class structure that has arisen around capitalist accumulation. The state serves to represent and defend this class structure while mediating conflicts that inevitably arise between (and within) the ruling class and other classes and strata.[40] It is, in other words, not a separate sphere of politics that stands apart from the economic sphere but a social relation, or, as Bertell Ollman describes it, "the set of institutional forms through which a ruling class relates to the rest of society."[41] Ollman's use of "relate" here has a very specific meaning, based upon his reading of what he describes as Marx's "philosophy of internal relations." Within this perspective, the relations existing between objects should not be considered external to the objects themselves but as part of what actually constitutes them. Any object under study needs to be seen as "relations, containing in themselves, as integral elements of what they are, those parts with which we tend to see them externally tied."[42] Objects, in other words, are not self-contained; they are constituted through the relations they hold in their stance with the whole. The relationships in which all things are embedded do not exist "outside" these objects (or externally) but are intrinsic to their very nature. Utilizing this approach, analytical emphasis moves away from taking for granted the isolated categories presented to us by the empirical world (such as the authoritarian state) toward an attempt to comprehend reality through the totality of internally related parts.[43]

From this standpoint, the state is not an independent, separate feature of society, severed from the class structure that generates its character. The relationship the ruling class holds with the state is actually part of what constitutes it as a class; state and class need to be seen as mutually reinforcing and co-constituted, with the latter providing the conditions of existence for the former. An analysis of the state, therefore, must begin with an "examination of the 'anatomy of bourgeois society,'" that is, an analysis of the specifically capitalist mode of social labour, the appropriation of the surplus product and the resulting laws of reproduction of the whole social formation, which objectively give rise to the particular political form."[44] Seen in this manner, class formation—the ways in which classes coalesce around the production, realization, and appropriation of profit—becomes a central element to understanding social formation and the nature of state power.

The eschewal of this consideration is a major weakness of standard approaches to authoritarianism and the form of the state in the Middle East. By treating the state as

a disconnected, all-dominating "thing" rather than as a social relation formed alongside the development of class, these perspectives treat the institutional forms of society
as determinant rather than determined.[45] In contrast, within the Marxist framework,
the secret behind the state's form is not to be found in contingent factors such as culture, religion, resource endowment, leadership styles, or the institutional arrangements of ruling families but rather in the specific nature of capitalist accumulation in
that particular society. The authoritarian guise of the Middle East state is not anomalous
and antagonistic to capitalism, but is rather a particular form of appearance of capitalism in the Middle East context. The task becomes one of demonstrating how and
why this is the case—not beginning with the appearance of the state and investing it
with determinant explanatory power.

In line with this basic methodological approach, a major goal of this book is to convey some of the principal aspects of the intertwined development of class and state in
the Middle East—tracing where and how various classes in the region (both capital and
labor) originated, what their accumulation is based around, how this has shifted over
time, and the ways in which this process of class formation links to the nature and
changing attributes of the state. With this perspective in mind, there are three key concepts employed throughout this book that require further elaboration: the internationalization of class and state, imperialism, and neoliberalism.

Internationalization of Class and State

Marx himself famously noted that capitalism always acts to "tear down every spatial
barrier to intercourse, i.e., to exchange, and conquer the whole earth for its market . . . [as capital develops] the more does it strive simultaneously for an even
greater extension of the market."[46] This observation has been strikingly confirmed
in the contemporary world economy, where the production of a typical commodity
involves labor and inputs from across the globe. The place where a given commodity
is eventually sold is very likely not the same place as where it is produced. The
largest capitalist firms consider their production and marketing decisions from
the perspective of a global marketplace, not simply from within their own national
borders. These processes indicate, as Christian Palloix noted in the 1970s, that the
commodity is "conceptualized, produced, and realized at the level of the world market."[47] Palloix termed this fundamental characteristic of global capitalism "the internationalization of capital"—a tendency signaling that capitalism was "a social
system driven by the encompassing accumulative imperatives of a world market."[48]

Internationalization takes place through a variety of means, including the establishment of joint ventures, the expansion of foreign direct investments (FDIs), the
listing of companies on overseas stock markets, and the licensing of brands and agency

rights. Moreover, as the geographical scale of accumulation grows, the costs of doing business rise exponentially, generating the need for global financial markets and international banking systems. The development of highly complex global production and marketing chains means dealing with potentially disastrous fluctuations in currencies, interest rates, and other variables. Thus internationalization is also linked to the increasing power of financial instruments, such as derivatives, which enable capitalists to manage the risk associated with fluctuations in value that occur across time and space—and make money by speculating on this risk.[49] All these mechanisms, which increasingly set the production and realization of value at the level of the world market, necessarily signify a growing interpenetration of ownership and control of capital.

Internationalization also necessitates a rethinking of the nature of state functions within the contemporary world market. Accumulation is always territorialized—it demands "a certain 'coherence' and 'materialization' in time and space."[50] This means that internationalizing capital is faced with the challenge of generating the necessary conditions for accumulation in all spaces of the global economy. The traditional functions of the state within a given national territory—disciplining labor, protecting private property rights, ensuring adequate financial conditions, and maintaining contracts, laws, and so forth—are thus increasingly oriented toward the international scale. This does not mean that the state has lost its importance or has been superseded by the global; in fact, the internationalization of capital often means that processes of state formation are strengthened.[51] The national state apparatus has become ever more important "for managing its domestic capitalist order in a way that contributes to the managing of the international capitalist order."[52] The internationalization of the state thus develops in tandem with the internationalization of capital.

These tendencies of internationalization raise significant questions around conceptualizing class and state at the national scale. The vast flows of capital and labor across borders means that processes of class and state formation striate national boundaries; for this reason, the nation-state cannot be understood as a self-contained political economy separate from the ways it intertwines with other spatial scales, namely the regional and global. Following Ollman's notion of "internal relations," the relationships with these other scales are not external to the social relations existing in any particular country but actually part of what constitutes them. It is thus impossible to understand processes of class formation without tracing the way these cross-scale relations develop and interpenetrate—how these relations become part of the very nature of the nation-state itself. It is necessary, in other words, to be wary of "methodological nationalism"[53]—a privileging of "national" social relations without acknowledging the ways these relations are actually constituted through their relationships with other spatial scales.

In his pathbreaking account of global labor history, Marcel van der Linden makes a powerful case for the importance of overcoming such methodological nationalist biases. Van der Linden notes that methodological nationalist approaches "consider the nation state as the basic, self-evident analytical unit for historical research ... Cross-border or border-subverting processes are perceived as distractions from the 'pure' model."[54] While it is clear that "[I]n a global perspective, the existence of nation-states obviously remains an essential aspect of the world system," Van der Linden argues that the existence of these states need "to be thoroughly historicized and relativized vis-a-vis sub-national, supra-national and trans-national aspects."[55] An important aim of this book is to highlight the saliency of this approach to the Middle East. In a region that is so integral to the way that the world system has developed, state and class formation should be reconceptualized through this multi-scalar lens.

One useful way of thinking about these notions was elaborated by the Greek theorist Nicos Poulantzas during an earlier set of debates regarding the relationship between US and European capital in 1970s Europe.[56] Poulantzas argued that internationalization was leading to the growing interiorization of "foreign" capital within the domestic social formation. In other words, in contrast to positions that posited a ceaseless conflict between national and foreign capital, Poulantzas asserted that all capital—regardless of its national origin—was compelled to orient to the global scale and, simultaneously, foreign capital had become internalized as a largely indistinguishable component of the "national bourgeoisie."[57] This did not mean that nation-states had lost their significance, or that there existed a single, transnational capitalist class, but rather that capital needed to be regarded as increasingly existing beyond any locally specific identities.

These debates bear particular significance in the Middle East because, as later chapters will demonstrate, the regional political economy has come to occupy a prime position in national economies over the last two decades. This means that it is necessary to reject the Linnean style of categorization typical of comparative politics, which divides the Middle East into "authoritarian republics" and "authoritarian monarchies" and delineates the differences and similarities of neatly ordered states whose social relations are bounded by national borders and externally related to one another. Most important to this reconsideration of the regional scale is the role of capital from the Gulf Cooperation Council (GCC)—a regional integration project bringing together the six oil-producing monarchies of Saudi Arabia, Kuwait, United Arab Emirates (UAE), Qatar, Bahrain, and Oman. A chief premise of this book is that the internationalization of GCC capital has transformed the political economy of the region, becoming internalized in the class structure of neighboring states.

These trends carry far-reaching political connotations. Most significantly, they bring into question one of the favored concepts of much of the Arab nationalist movement (and parts of the Left)—that of the "patriotic bourgeoisie" (ra's al-maal al-watani), which is viewed as a potential ally against foreign capital. In Egypt, for example, one of the most prominent voices of the uprising, the Nasserist leader Hamdeen Sabahi, has emphasized this notion as an important plank of his political vision. Sabahi's Arabic-language electoral platform in the 2012 presidential elections (in which he came in third, with 20.72 percent of the vote)[58] called for putting "Egypt on the road to comprehensive renaissance, moving from the ranks of the Third World to emerging economic countries, and competing with the strongest economies of the world order."[59] While Sabahi listed a long line of important social-justice goals, including rights to food, housing, health care, education, work, fair pay, comprehensive insurance, and a clean environment, his plan for achieving these goals rested upon—in addition to the state and "cooperative sector"—what he described as "private sector–led national capital." In this electoral program, he called upon national capital to "play the primary role that is expected of it in the Renaissance project." He promised, if elected, to support this orientation with "investment incentives . . . and laws against monopoly that would guarantee the ability of national capitalism to achieve its social duty."[60] One of the aims of this book is to demonstrate the weaknesses inherent to this type of strategy. The conjoined internationalization tendencies of state and capital—particularly as they are expressed in a region such as the Middle East—mean that notions of independent development driven by an alleged patriotic spirit of the capitalist class offer little hope of achieving genuine liberation.

Centrality of Imperialism

The concept of internationalization captures the inexorable drive of capital to scour the globe in the search for profitable markets, raw materials, and production sites, bringing ever-larger spheres of human activity into its ambit. As this process plays out, control of capital becomes held in fewer and fewer hands. There is thus a very close connection between the internationalization of capital and its concentration and centralization.[61] This relentless drive toward the domination of space is a defining feature of imperialism—the division and control of the world market by a handful of rival companies backed by the largest states. The notion of imperialism captures the tendency of dominant capital to increasingly draw the world market in on itself, forcibly extracting profits from all corners of the globe and thereby actively accentuating the unevenness of the system as a whole, while simultaneously deepening the interdependency of states as a necessary prerequisite for this extraction to take place.[62] Imperialism thus consolidates the combined and uneven nature that characterizes the world market in contemporary capitalism—one in which varying temporalities of development are harnessed within the totality of the world market.[63]

In contrast to many conventional approaches to the Middle East—which tend to treat imperialism as synonymous with colonialism and date its end to the close of World War II—this book highlights imperialism as an essential and ongoing theme in the shaping of the region's political economy. As later chapters will discuss in some detail, the Middle East differs from other areas of the globe in that its vast supplies of hydrocarbons confer upon it an immensely significant geopolitical weight. For this reason, the major imperialist states—headed by the United States throughout the contemporary postwar period—have placed the highest priority on exercising power over the region and preventing any challengers from gaining a foothold.

There are two foremost aspects to imperialism emphasized throughout this book. The first of these is the dialectic of rivalry and unity of interests that characterizes the relationship between the major imperialist powers. On the one hand, the internationalization of capital has generated heightened levels of competition between the large corporations that dominate the global economy, and this is refracted through increased interstate competition. Consequently, inter-imperialist rivalry remains a salient feature of the world market. On the other hand, the very nature of internationalization demands greater coordination and cooperation between states in order to maintain the required conditions for accumulation as a whole. This is all the more relevant in contexts such as the Middle East, which has been in a constant battle to free itself from imperialist control—a path that, if successful, would have enormous ramifications for the entire capitalist system. For this reason, the importance of controlling the Middle East not only stems from inter-imperialist rivalry—an attempt to command a "potential chokehold on other leading powers"[64]—but is also driven by a common existential interest on behalf of all imperialist powers in preventing the peoples of the region from determining their own future. These dual tendencies of cooperation and rivalry are vital to understanding the ways that imperialism continues to interact and shape the political economy of the Middle East.

Second, imperialism is too often viewed—even by many theorists on the Left—as solely a question of military or political domination. While this book explores these aspects of imperialism in some detail, it emphasizes the fact that *imperialism is primarily a question of exploitation—one that necessitates, and is principally bound up in, forms of economic domination*. Much of the analysis of this book is concerned with tracing the projection of economic power in the Middle East by imperialist states—the attempt to integrate the forms of accumulation in the region into global production chains and subordinate local classes to the exigencies of capital in the core countries of the world market. This tendency is linked to the dialectic of rivalry and cooperation noted above, but more generally it has had vital implications for class and state in the Middle East. It means—as later chapters will show—that capitalist class formation in the Middle East has become increasingly tied to the ebbs and flows of accumulation at the global scale. One of the effects of imperialism, in other words, has been to generate a domestic capitalist class internal to the Middle East that is to a great extent aligned with the interests of global (imperialist) capital. This observation further confirms the point made earlier—it makes little sense to speak of a "patriotic bourgeoisie" in the Middle East that is somehow counterposed or in confrontation with international capital and in which hopes for a national project for liberation can be invested.

Neoliberalism

The main period that this book focuses on is the neoliberal phase of capitalism, which had its origins in the global crisis of the 1970s, was consolidated during the mid-1980s, and continues through to the current day.[65] Drawing from a range of sources including classical liberalism and Austrian and monetarist economics, neoliberalism's policy prescriptions are now familiar across the globe: privatization, cutbacks to social spending, the reduction of barriers to capital flows, and the imposition of market imperatives throughout all spheres of human activity. The Middle East was no exception to the worldwide embrace of these policies by governments and ruling elites—and a major aim of this book is to consider the profound consequences that they continue to hold for class and state in the region.

As later chapters will outline, however, neoliberalism needs to be seen as much more than the familiar litany of economic policies with which it is typically associated. Its essence lies, as David Harvey points out, in an attempt to reconstitute and strengthen class power in the favor of capital.[66] Its policies emerged out of the systemic needs of capitalist social reality. Specifically, the turn to neoliberalism reflected the accumulation needs of capital in an era of internationalization, i.e., capital with accumulation spaces increasingly spread across a global level. Its logic came to penetrate all national social formations and was specifically concerned with the ways in which these formations were integrated into global circuits of accumulation. By speeding up the rate at which capital moves across and through national spaces, and widening the spheres of human activities subject to the imperatives of accumulation, neoliberalism aimed to ensure the conditions for capitalist reproduction at a global scale.

The widespread adoption of neoliberal policies was facilitated by the restructuring of the world market that took place during the 1980s and 1990s. With the collapse of the Soviet Union and the integration of China into the global economy, capitalist social relations spread throughout the world, compelling all states to comply with norms set at the international scale.[67] In regions such as the Middle East, this process was closely related to the economic crises of the 1980s and the pressure countries faced to earn foreign exchange revenues in order to service their debt obligations. A range of international institutions drove the technical implementation of neoliberal policies—notably the International Monetary Fund (IMF) and the World Bank—while governments from the United States and Europe pursued bilateral trade and financial agreements with the region.

This book traces the neoliberal transformation of the Middle East over the last two decades. Its focus goes beyond the policies themselves to examine the ways in which neoliberalism has underpinned the modalities of class and state formation. Specifically, the penetration of neoliberalism has been a pivotal force in shaping the production and development of working classes as well as the nature of capitalist class formation around the new internationally connected circuits of accumulation. It has also lent a particular dynamic to the nature of the state apparatus, closely connected to the spread of authoritarian regimes. As always, these processes must be tackled across national, regional, and international scales.

A final core feature of neoliberal ideology—echoed in conventional academic accounts of Middle East development—is the claim to an apparent neutrality and "objectivity" of analysis. A key intention of this book is to unpack these claims and to demonstrate that they not only are false but actually conceal a discursive attempt to defend, maintain, and extend the uneven and exploitative nature of capitalism in the Middle East. Assertions of an ideologically detached or impartial methodology (even, as is often the case, when such assertions are only made implicitly) deny the inherently partisan nature of all attempts to comprehend social reality. In contrast, this book is unequivocally framed as a challenge to the status quo. This partisanship is not a weakness of the analysis but rather a potential source of strength. If it is true that capitalism is the root source of the region's problems, then confronting this critically and openly provides the best route to capturing the reality of the contemporary Middle East, precisely because it opens up the right kinds of questions and ways of thinking about the problems posed. If it is not true, and the region's difficulties stem from the antimonies of authoritarianism and the free market, then the analysis will fall. The point is to be explicit about this fact—recognizing that a certain political perspective and standpoint on reality is inevitably embedded in any set of methodological assumptions. There is no claim here to neutrality: the book openly takes sides.

The Structure of the Book

With these initial methodological and theoretical perspectives established, it is now possible to summarize the basic structure of this book. The first point to note is the contested and controversial nature of what constitutes the "Middle East." Different definitions of this area are used both within and outside the region. The book employs a variety of generally synonymous terms—Middle East, Arab world, and Middle East and North Africa (MENA)—depending on the context.[68] Most of

the analysis concentrates on the experiences in the Arabic-speaking countries of
the region—these have been the focal point of the recent uprisings, show strong
similarities in regards to their political economy of development, and are particularly important to understanding the regional scale. Where necessary, references
are also made to Israel, Iran, and Turkey, although the nature of class and state
formation in these countries is not dealt with in detail due to their distinctive historical and contemporary characteristics. In general, however, while different
chapters focus on specific country case studies as appropriate, it is important to
emphasize that the book should be read thematically rather than as an exhaustive
account of any individual country's experiences.

Chapter 2 outlines the development of US and European imperialism in the region
from the end of World War II through the first decade of the twenty-first century. It
examines the strategic pillars of Western rule in the Middle East from the perspective
of military, political, and economic power. Emphasis is placed on the use of financial
instruments such as debt and foreign aid as well as a range of trade and investment
agreements. This process has taken place in confrontation and interaction with indigenous social and political forces in the area, reconstituting patterns of state and
class and opening the way to the penetration of neoliberal reform. It has altered the
patterns of accumulation internal to the region itself while differentially integrating
various zones of the Middle East into the world market.

This global perspective helps to frame the account, in chapters 3 and 4, of the rise
and impact of neoliberalism. The first of these chapters outlines some elements of
neoliberal strategy, including privatization, labor market deregulation, liberalization
of trade and investment, and changes to financial markets. It focuses in particular on
three North African countries—Tunisia, Morocco, and Egypt—in addition to Jordan.
The emphasis is on the logic that drives neoliberal reform and its ramifications for
class development. It also discusses the ways in which neoliberalism has altered the
nature of state power in each of these cases. Chapter 4 examines the impact of neoliberalism on agriculture, tracing the ways in which neoliberal reform has linked capital
formation across urban and rural spaces while dispossessing people from the land and
proletarianizing rural life. Its counterpoint, which is considered empirically, has been
the development of large agribusiness conglomerates, linked to international agro-
commodity circuits and providing a vital point of accumulation for domestic classes.

The book then turns to two important case studies that are deeply connected to the
ways in which the regional political economy has formed through the neoliberal era.
Chapter 5 considers these themes in the Palestinian West Bank, examining the ways
that Israeli occupation has shaped the development of Palestinian capitalism along
highly neoliberal lines. A core argument is that the question of Palestine needs to be
viewed through the prism of capitalist development, linked to the nature of imperialism

in the Middle East, not solely via a rights-based perspective that focuses on the copious examples of human rights abuse that take place under Israeli control. Chapter 6 concentrates on the extremely significant case of the Gulf Cooperation Council (GCC) countries. It presents an overview of class formation in the Gulf, emphasizing the pivotal position of migrant labor alongside the development of large capitalist conglomerates across the GCC. A major consequence of this has been the internationalization of Gulf capital in the Middle East; this phenomenon is examined empirically through the interpenetration of the Gulf with class formation in the representative example of Egypt.

The book ends with a discussion in chapter 7 of the 2011–2012 uprisings and their implications for further political developments in the region. The background and context are laid out for each of the most prominent revolts—Egypt, Tunisia, Yemen, Bahrain, Libya, and Syria—as well as broad outlines of the Western and regional responses. The aim is to situate these uprisings in the context of the previous chapters. Once again, it is important to emphasize that this book does not present an exhaustive account of the politics and blow-by-blow details of any specific case study—and certainly not a definitive assessment of events that are still unfolding. Rather, it outlines some of the commonalities and specificities of the uprisings, demonstrating that their trajectory can be best understood through the evolution of state and class as mapped throughout this book. Taken as a whole, they indicate that the long-standing social crises facing the Middle East—including the prevalence of authoritarianism, the perpetual economic exclusion, and the marginalization of much of the region's population—are not a result of too little capitalism but are direct consequences of capitalism itself. These processes of class and state formation constitute the *lineages of revolt*.

CHAPTER 2

Framing the Region: Imperialism and the Middle East

The contemporary Middle East is shaped by two important and interlinked dynamics. First, since the mid-twentieth century, the region has represented a vital zone within the wider global economy. Its vast supplies of hydrocarbons, coupled with the prodigious financial surpluses that accompany them, mean that control of the Middle East is a source of enormous strategic power and thus a long-standing flashpoint of global conflict. Second, however, the dynamics of the Middle East's own social formation, and the struggles that are inevitably bound up with them, form a crucial counterpoint to the rivalries and collusion of foreign powers. For this reason, the region is much more than simply an object of external domination—the histories and struggles of the region are supremely relevant, existing alongside and within the story of foreign rule. The purpose of this chapter is to consider the interaction of these two dynamics and their implications for contemporary patterns of class and state formation. Subsequent chapters will discuss in detail the character of the region's social relations under the impact of neoliberalism. The aim here is to set the scene for that discussion by providing an overarching account of how the trajectory of imperial domination since World War II has shaped the specificities of the neoliberal era, the means through which this domination has been extended and enhanced, and the ways this has been articulated with—and altered by—particular forms of resistance.

The chapter begins by tracing the extension of US power through the region in the postwar period and detailing its conflict with popular struggles seeking independence and greater sovereignty. US strategy initially relied upon the cultivation of various regional allies, settling in the late 1960s on a strategic partnership with Israel, Iran, and Saudi Arabia as a means to confront the growing strength of Arab nationalist movements. As military defeat pushed back struggles in Egypt and elsewhere, the United States also employed food aid and other forms of assistance to lock development patterns into a dependency on Western imports and financial inflows. In the specific conjuncture of global crisis that racked the world economy in the 1970s, this relationship paved the way for mounting fiscal problems that culminated in the debt crises of the 1970s and 1980s, finally opening the path to the neoliberal reforms that will be explored in later chapters.

This early history confirms that imperialism is not simply a question of military conquest; central to the heightened control of Western powers has been the region's unequal and uneven integration into global capitalism. The second part of the chapter explores this integration in greater detail, examining the trajectory of US and European relationships with the region through the 1990s and 2000s, as well as the rise of new actors such as China and Russia. The various bilateral trade and financial agreements promoted over these decades have profoundly reworked the nature of capitalism in the Middle East. By reconfiguring the patterns of production and consumption, they have acted to subordinate the region to the circuits of accumulation in the advanced capitalist countries. Understanding these varied paths of integration of the Middle East region into the world economy will be an essential element to discussions of the neoliberal era in later chapters.

The Transition to US Power

World War II signaled a major shift in both the nature of capitalist production and the structure of the world market. Most significantly, the end of the war witnessed a qualitative leap in the internationalization of capital. Capitalist firms, led by those headquartered in the United States, expanded overseas and oriented their production toward international exports. Between 1959 and 1964, US companies set up international subsidiaries at the rate of more than three hundred per year, more than ten times the prewar rate.[1] New industrial sectors also emerged at this time, notably the petrochemical industry, led by US multinationals such as Dow, Union Carbide, and Standard Oil. These companies manufactured substitutes for naturally occurring materials—plastics, synthetic fibers, pesticides, fertilizers, and detergents—vastly increasing the scale and scope of commodity production.[2] Internationalization brought with it a fundamental reconfiguration of the transport sector. Central to this was, of course, mass automobile production, which expanded as factories were built throughout Europe under US-backed reconstruction plans. Large-scale commercial land and air transit also grew rapidly in the immediate postwar period as the first "global" markets began to take shape.

All these trends were underpinned by a growing demand for inputs of energy and raw materials. Internationalization—because it was premised upon globally oriented production circuits—demanded large increases in energy use. And here, too, there was a shift—away from the centuries-old use of coal—toward oil, and later natural gas, as the principal sources of energy. Oil had become, in the words of Simon Bromley, a "strategic commodity."[3] Its greater energy density and portability (relative to coal) made it ideal for powering automobiles, airplanes, and modern militaries.[4] Not only did these hydrocarbons supply the necessary energy for industrial production and transportation, they also formed the basic feedstock for the vast array of products generated in the new petrochemical industries.

Through the first few decades of the twentieth century, the bulk of the world's oil production had been located in Europe and the United States. But following a wave of discoveries during the 1920s and 1930s, it became clear that the Gulf region of the Middle East—Saudi Arabia, Kuwait, Iraq, Iran, and the smaller Gulf states—held the world's largest supplies of cheap and easily accessible hydrocarbons. This brought with it profound geopolitical consequences, conferring on the region a potentially decisive role in determining the fortunes of capitalism at the global scale—"a stupendous source of strategic power," as a US Department of State memo described Saudi Arabia in 1945.[5]

But concurrent with this transformation in the nature of capitalist production were sweeping changes to the Middle East state system. The existing nation-state borders were largely a result of British and French machinations, which had divided the region into various colonies and assorted protectorates in the early twentieth century alongside the collapse of the Ottoman Empire. World War II, however, had significantly disrupted these old colonial structures. A deep-seated yearning for independence had been percolating for decades and—with the weakening of British and French hegemony during and after the war—a resurgence of anticolonial struggles shook the established patterns of rule. Squeezed by mounting financial and political crises at home, the former colonial powers were faced with burgeoning movements demanding control over their natural resources and strategic transport routes, and the right to freely determine relations with other countries. The increasing intensity of these struggles raised the specter of popular sovereignty and national independence over what had arguably become the most important zone in the world market. These challenges to British and French rule took place in the context of the new global order that had consolidated in the ashes of war. The United States had emerged as the preeminent capitalist power, its military and economic leadership vastly superseding the older colonial rivals of Europe.[6] At the same time, however, the Soviet Union had won great prestige through its resistance to Nazi Germany and was also seeking to extend its global reach. As a result, many of the Arab leftist and anticolonial movements that had emerged in the postwar period looked toward alliances with the Soviet government as a means to carve out space against their colonial masters.

It was in recognition of these dynamics that shortly after World War II, US president Harry Truman declared, in a famous speech to Congress, that the United States would actively intervene around the world in support of its interests and those of the "free world." Although the Truman Doctrine, as it became known, was framed largely as a response to a growing Soviet influence in Turkey, Greece, and elsewhere, at the root of US foreign policy concerns were the various independence and left-wing movements that had emerged in the wake of Europe's destruction. Truman's speech did not directly reference the Middle East, yet its supreme significance was undoubtedly foremost in the minds of the speechwriters—an earlier draft confirmed the importance of the region's "great natural resources."[7]

In light of the potentially enormous ramifications of any realignment of sovereignty in the Middle East—and clearly cognizant of the importance that the region held for its own position atop global hierarchies—the United States took the lead in attempting to recast the nature of political rule during the postcolonial period. The strategy initially pursued by the United States, in close alliance with Britain and France, was to negotiate the handover of power to leaders who were viewed as amenable to continued foreign domination, albeit in the framework of formal independence. Britain had earlier shown some success with this approach, replacing direct rule in Egypt (in 1922) and Iraq (in 1932) with new governments, led by pro-British rulers who allowed a continued presence of foreign troops and largely acquiesced to orders from London. It was with this logic in mind that Lebanon and Syria were constituted as two separate states with the end of French Mandate in 1943, and the Emirate of Transjordan (later called Jordan) was granted independence from the British Mandate in 1946. In 1951, the UN bestowed upon Libya its independence, under the control of the country's monarch, King Idris.

In most countries, however, this reliance upon pro-Western monarchs and urban elites could not survive long into the 1950s and 1960s. The depth of the problem faced by the Western powers was confirmed in 1951, with the nationalization of the British-owned and -operated Anglo-Iranian Oil Company (AIOC) in Iran. Iran's recently appointed prime minister, Mohammed Mossadegh, had been emboldened by mass mobilizations across the country to expel AIOC and place Iran's oil in state hands.[8] The nationalization of AIOC was followed a year later, in 1952, by a dramatic turn of events in Egypt, where the country's monarch and a principal ally of colonialism in the region, King Farouk, was ousted by a military coup led by the popular officer Gamal Abdel

Nasser.[9] Nasser's coming to power forced the withdrawal of British troops from Egypt in 1954 and led to the independence of the Sudan in 1956. Nasser confirmed the West's worst fears when he turned to the Soviet Union for military support as well as technical and financial assistance for large-scale infrastructure projects such as the Aswan Dam. Egypt's newfound sovereignty was crowned with the nationalization of the British/French-controlled Suez Canal in 1956—an action celebrated by millions of people across the entire Middle East. As Nasser took these steps, anticolonial struggles were also growing elsewhere in the region, most notably in Algeria, where a guerrilla war for independence was launched against the French occupation in 1954. Although French control did not end in Algeria until 1962, the Algerian revolt was a significant factor in propelling France to grant formal independence to Morocco and Tunisia in 1956.

In response to these challenges, the United States elaborated the so-called Eisenhower Doctrine, proclaimed on January 5, 1957, as part of a "Special Message to the Congress on the Situation in the Middle East." Decrying the threat of "international communism," Eisenhower guaranteed US readiness "to employ the armed forces of the United States to assist to defend the territorial integrity and the political independence of any nation in the area."[10] Although Eisenhower's speech was framed, as Truman's had been, by the supposed Soviet threat, much of his speech alluded to events in Egypt, particularly the nationalization of the Suez Canal. Eisenhower noted that the canal "enables the nations of Asia and Europe to carry on the commerce that is essential if these countries are to maintain well-rounded and prosperous economies," and that the Middle East was a "gateway between Eurasia and Africa . . . [with] about two thirds of the presently known oil deposits of the world. . . . The nations of Europe are peculiarly dependent upon this supply, and this dependency relates to transportation as well as to production."[11]

Eisenhower's doctrine was first put to the test in 1957 in Jordan, where a pro-Nasser government, led by Suleiman al-Nabulsi, had come to power and sought to curb the powers of the Western-backed monarch, King Hussein.[12] Building upon the anti-British sentiments that were running high following the nationalization of the Suez Canal, Nabulsi canceled a treaty between Jordan and Britain and called for closer relations with China, the Soviet Union, and Egypt. In response, Hussein dismissed the Nabulsi government, banned all political parties, and placed Jordan under martial law. After Hussein expressed tacit support of the Eisenhower Doctrine, the United States responded with financial and political aid, replacing Britain as the major Western supporter of Jordan.[13]

As this crisis unfolded in Jordan, the United States also moved to support pro-Western forces in Syria by backing conservative politicians and encouraging Turkish and Iraqi plots against the country.[14] Here the attempts failed, serving only to further generate support for Communist and Arab nationalist forces. In 1958, Egypt and Syria formed the United Arab Republic (UAR), a short-lived attempt by Nasser to form a union based on Arab nationalism, which was embraced by Syrian elites in reaction to the strength of the Communist movement in Syria.[15] Responding to the formation of the UAR, Jordan and Iraq formed the Arab Union, a federation of the two monarchies that was set up as a pro-Western counterpoint to Arab nationalism. The unity lasted only six months, however, ending with the assassination of Iraq's King Faisal II in a military coup largely inspired by the overthrow of Egypt's monarchy in 1952. As these Western allies teetered, British troops were dispatched to Jordan to support King Hussein (with the support of Israel and the United States), while US Marines landed in Lebanon to bolster the pro-Western government of president Camille Chamoun.[16]

By the mid-1960s, popular and underground movements claiming fidelity to Arab nationalism and left-wing ideologies were shaking all the pro-Western regimes in the region. A most important and often overlooked part of this history was the range of deep-rooted struggles taking place in the Gulf region, where strikes and worker movements threatened the stability of corrupt and decrepit monarchies. In Bahrain, for example, where the first political party in the Gulf had formed in 1954, militant labor struggles occurred through the 1960s that culminated in a three-month uprising in March 1965 following the sacking of hundreds of workers at the Bahrain Petroleum Company (BAPCO).[17] These struggles were led by Communist and nationalist leaders who fused agitation against the ongoing British presence in the Gulf with demands around worker and social issues. The strikes drew support from wide layers of society, including high school students who walked out in solidarity with the workers.[18] Worker actions and nationalist-inspired movements were also widespread in Saudi Arabia, Kuwait, and the smaller Gulf emirates. Elsewhere in the Arabian Peninsula, an armed struggle was launched in 1963 by the Front for the Liberation of Occupied South Yemen (FLOSY) and the National Liberation Front (NLF) against British control in Yemen.[19] The mood of the time was encapsulated in the formation of the Popular Front for the Liberation of the Occupied Arabian Gulf (PFLOAG) in 1968, which viewed its base of operations as extending throughout all the Gulf states.[20]

The Character of Arab Nationalism

The landscape of Middle East politics from the vantage point of the mid-1960s was thus deeply marked by the chameleonic character of Arab nationalism, which assumed a variety of forms differing radically across time and place.[21] While the Arab nationalist movement was represented most prominently by Nasserism in Egypt and the rival factions of Ba'athism in Syria and Iraq, its ideology and political practices resonated powerfully in every country in the region. At numerous points in its history, Arab nationalism, particularly in its Nasserist variant, would clash sharply with imperialist interests in the region. The overthrow of colonially backed monarchies, the nationalization of the Suez Canal, and the later confrontations around Israel (discussed below) are potent indications of this fact. All these points of resistance generated widespread sympathy and deep-seated feelings of pride among all layers of Arab society. Millions of people hold a genuine nostalgia for this era that remains indelibly inscribed in political and cultural practices to the present day.

Nevertheless, it is important not to fetishize the confrontations with imperialism and ignore the configurations of class power that marked the rise of Arab nationalist ideology. Too often the reasons behind the failures of the movement are attributed to the military and political defeats inflicted by external forces or the contingent actions of individual leaders during the 1960s and 1970s. While these are no doubt a critical part of the movement's history, they can obfuscate the class dynamics that innervated the struggles of the time—most notably the fact that Arab nationalism rested on a contradictory ideology that, although focused on Arab unity, consciously downplayed the reality of class struggle.[22] Indeed, many Arab nationalists, such as the Syrian intellectual Adib Nassur, condemned a focus on class as being divisive to the cause of Arab unity.[23] Likewise, Michel Aflaq, one of the leading founders of Ba'athism, called on Arabs not to "lose their nationalism nor to confuse it with the felonious notion of class interests, so as not to endanger national unity."[24] In its dominant forms, this orientation actually ended up prioritizing the development of national capitalist classes, and was partly enabled by the presence of the Soviet Union. It was this (ultimately unsuccessful) negotiation of Cold War rivalries that generated the possibility for Arab nationalism to square the contradictions stemming from its pro-capital orientation and its apparent confrontations with imperialism.

The state-led fostering of national capital necessitated the elimination of institutional configurations—supported by earlier elites tied to colonialism—that blocked the development of new capitalist groups. Nasser captured this sentiment well in his *Falsafat al-thawrah* [*Philosophy of the Revolution*], in which he argued that the revolution was "a popular progressive struggle not class struggle" that brought together "peasants, workers, soldiers, intellectuals and national capital" as an alternative to "the alliance of exploitative capital and feudalism."[25] This struggle was an important, albeit partial, explanation of the character of the land reform that took place in the 1950s and 1960s (see chapter 4). In practice, it did not necessarily mean the destruction of those old social elites—in many cases they became an important component of the new capitalist classes—but was aimed rather at the institutional forms that represented those older social relations. The development of this local, state-supported bourgeoisie also helps to explain one driving force behind the confrontation with imperialism—an attempt to attain basic sovereignty over resources, state policies, financial systems, and so forth. All these measures explain the ubiquity of the "strong state" that typified Arab nationalist governments through the 1950s and 1960s, which provided the conditions for national accumulation through state-distributed contracts, financial linkages, and trading opportunities. Within this structure the military took a preeminent position as the only state institution with the internal cohesiveness and organizational discipline to direct this transformation.

It is this "pro-capital"/"pro-state" orientation of Arab nationalism that helps clarify a further feature of this history, which is often missed in the hagiography of Nasser and other nationalist leaders. The Arab states that emerged during the 1950s and 1960s were characterized by sharp confrontations with the Left, independent worker movements, and other struggles. These movements were tolerated at points, and their discourses were often absorbed into the language of ruling regimes (as can be seen in the frequent refrain of "Arab socialism"), but all Arab nationalist movements aimed at demobilizing and persecuting any left-wing forces that attempted to strengthen the autonomous mobilization of workers and other social forces.[26] This strategy of demobilization could be seen in another innovation of Arab nationalism—the creation of state-led, corporatist unions and other federations that were billed as representatives of working classes but that, in reality, were frequently used to suppress struggles and prevent them from emerging outside of the state structures. These institutions were seamlessly taken over by the autocratic rulers that followed the first generation of Arab nationalist leaders (such as Mubarak and Ben Ali), and are important to understanding the contemporary form of struggles following the 2011 uprisings.

In short, despite their rhetoric, Arab nationalist regimes acted primarily to strengthen capitalism and an emerging, state-linked capitalist class—they had little to do with socialism, regardless of the nomenclature used to describe the various regimes of the time. This is not to deny the ways in which these regimes did carry out a range of measures that improved living standards and addressed many of the deprivations that populations had faced under colonialism—land reform, job security in the public sector, and, very importantly, provision of food and other subsidies to guarantee food access for the poorest layers of the population. These measures met real social needs, and were utilized by the Arab nationalist regimes—as with their anti-imperialist rhetoric—to bind mass support to governments in the context of sustained pressure from below. But their provision through the state, without any organs of real democratic participation or control (in fact, in a context where mass participation was actively prevented), meant that they were always secondary to the principal goal of capitalist development.

These contradictory dynamics help to explain the evolution of the Arab states in the 1970s and 1980s. By the end of these two decades, the proclaimed goals of the Arab nationalist movement lay in tatters—Egypt had become a key US ally, and virtually all

Arab states were laying the groundwork for strict neoliberal economic programs that would be launched under the auspices of the IMF and World Bank. By the mid-1980s, most of the Arab states had reoriented from a confrontation with imperialism toward a protracted incorporation into US and European power structures in the region. Somewhat ironically, as later chapters will trace, this incorporation actually helped strengthen the development of the national capitalist classes sought by Arab governments for decades. This occurred, however, not through a break with imperialism but through the insertion of this emergent class into the circuits of accumulation developed by the advanced capitalist states over the region as a whole.

1970s and 1980s: The Mechanisms of Counterrevolution

Overcoming Arab nationalism and subsuming it into the structures of imperial rule took place through a combination of political, military, and economic means. The overriding characteristic of this process was the widening of hierarchies and the differentiating of power at both the regional and national scales. By magnifying the region's uneven patterns of development while simultaneously tightening its interdependencies, foreign powers were able to lock certain social forces within the Middle East into a framework of shared interests opposed to those of the vast majority. In spite of significant opposition, the principal consequence of these changes was the tempering of any anti-imperialist features of Arab governments and the sustained rollback of the populist measures on which they rested.

On the political and military front, Western governments—led by the United States—initially pursued this strategy through strengthening alliances with three main regional pillars: Saudi Arabia, Iran, and Israel. Each of these countries was provided with large amounts of financial and military aid, and the specific socioeconomic and political characteristics of these three countries enabled them to emerge as the main articulation of US and European influence in the region. Their position within regional hierarchies was strengthened, and in return, they helped to confront the various radical movements that had developed during the 1950s and 1960s, whether nationalist or left-wing.

In the Gulf, the Saudi monarch, King Saud, had long been reliant on US aid and military support following the arrival of US oil companies to the country in the 1920s. But Saud's anachronistic regime and close relationship with the United States faced the rise of revolutionary and nationalist movements during the 1950s and 1960s, which were severely repressed with the open support of US and British advisors. The influx of huge flows of petrodollars into the Gulf in the 1970s as a result of oil price rises (first in 1973–74 and again in 1979–82) underpinned the growth of a Saudi ruling class that was exposed to profound threats from below and from the wider region (see chapter 6). In this context, an alliance with the United States (and Britain) helped to strengthen the position of the Saudi monarchy and the social forces connected to it, laying the basis for a particular form of regional dominance that has persisted into the present.

In return for Western military and political support, the Saudi regime was all too willing to move to undercut Arab nationalism through the corrupting influence of petrodollars, which could be used to back pro-Western forces in the region without a direct link to Western funding.[27] In line with this logic, Saudi Arabia was encouraged to employ Islam as a regional counterweight to nationalist and left-wing organizations, organizing "Islamic summits" that asserted Saudi influence and challenged Egypt's role as the leading Arab state.[28] A vitriolic propaganda war opened up between the Saudi and Egyptian governments, leading the US Senate to object to broadcasts from the Voice of Cairo radio station calling upon Saudi citizens to "overthrow these lackeys who have sold their honor and dignity and who cooperate with the arch enemies of the Arabs."[29] This proxy conflict with Egypt took its most vivid form during the eight-year North Yemen civil war, where Saudi Arabia was the main supporter of the royalist, pro-British forces that had been overthrown in 1962, while Egypt backed the republican movements arrayed against the ousted monarchy.

In the case of Iran, the United States (and Britain's M16) had engineered a coup against Mossadegh in 1953, bringing to power a pro-Western government loyal to the Iranian monarchy, headed by Mohammad Reza Shah Pahlavi.[30] The United States explicitly conceived of Iran as the principal base of control for the Gulf region, and military funding reached $1.7 billion under the first Nixon administration (1968–72), nearly three times the limit set by Nixon's predecessor, Lyndon Johnson.[31] A 1969 report by the RAND Corporation—a prominent think tank closely connected to Washington policy makers—noted that Iran was a critical feature of US power in the Gulf because it could "help achieve many of the goals we find desirable without the need to intervene in the region."[32] This role was convincingly demonstrated in 1973 with the dispatch of the Iranian military to Oman to assist British troops in the repression of the Dhofar rebellion—a powerful struggle that gave birth to the PFLOAG and was at the heart of left-wing movements in the Arabian Peninsula. The Iranian troops, supplied with US helicopters and other weaponry, succeeded in crushing the rebellion.[33] US military support to Iran skyrocketed from 1973 onward, amounting to more than $6 billion annually from 1973 to 1975. In addition, Iran received the most sophisticated weaponry available from the US military arsenal.[34] As the United States extended military support to Iran, it also helped the Shah build a domestic security apparatus (the SAVAK) that became renowned for its vicious repression of any internal dissent.

The other major pivot of US power in the broader region was the state of Israel. As a settler-colonial state, Israel had come into being in 1948 through the expulsion of around three-quarters of the original Palestinian population from their homes and lands.[35] Due to this initial act of dispossession and its overarching goal of preserving itself as a self-defined "Jewish state," Israel quickly emerged as a key partner of foreign powers in the region.[36] Inextricably tied to external support for its continued viability in a hostile environment, Israel could be counted on as a much more reliable ally than any Arab state. During the 1950s, Israel's main external support had come from Britain and France.[37] But the June 1967 war saw the Israeli military destroy the Egyptian and Syrian air forces and occupy the West Bank, Gaza Strip, (Egyptian) Sinai Peninsula, and (Syrian) Golan Heights. Israel's defeat of the Arab states encouraged the United States to cement itself as the country's primary patron, supplying it annually with billions of dollars' worth of military hardware and financial support.

Israel's victory in 1967 signaled a decisive turning point in the evolution of Arab nationalism.[38] While pro-Western regimes continued to be challenged from below by various radical movements, and new nationalist governments came to power in Southern Yemen (1967),[39] Iraq (1968), and Libya (1969), Israel's victory dealt a devastating blow to the notions of Arab unity and resistance that had crystallized most sharply in Nasser's Egypt.[40] The military defeat was symbolically reinforced by Nasser's death in 1970 and the coming to power of Anwar Sadat, who subsequently moved to reverse many of Nasser's more radical policies. The priority placed by the United States on its relationship with Israel was further highlighted in 1973, following another war between Israel and a coalition of Arab states led by Egypt and Syria. Despite initial Egyptian and Syrian advances in the opening salvos of the war, US airlifts of the latest military equipment led to Israel's eventual victory. This was the framework in which the other front of imperialist strategy unfolded—the region's economic subjugation.

The Economic Front

Alongside these political and military defeats, much of the Arab world was faced at the time with the realities of the global economic slump that had begun in the early 1970s. This downturn had two important ramifications for the Middle East. The first of these was the increase in oil prices in the early 1970s, which produced a sharp rise in the cost of oil for oil-importing countries in the region (while simultaneously feeding the prodigious growth in petrodollars for the Gulf, as noted above). The second impact of the world crisis was a drop in global demand, which hit export levels and created severe balance-of-payments problems for oil-importing countries. This was the context in which two interlinked elements emerged as central features of Western strategy in the region—aid and debt. Both mechanisms strongly reinforced the political and military defeats described above, compelling a reorientation and opening up of local economies to the world market—a move later consummated in the economic program of neoliberalism.[41]

The United States had first begun to employ food aid as a major element of its foreign policy in the early 1960s, under the Kennedy-era Food for Peace program. This was an attractive tool of successive US administrations because not only did it help dispose of US agricultural surpluses, it also locked Arab governments into a dependency on imports in a context where the guarantee of cheap food (particularly bread) was an important element of regime legitimacy.[42] In 1961, for example, US food aid made up 77 percent of Egyptian wheat imports and 38 percent of total supply, increasing to 99 percent and 53 percent, respectively, by 1962.[43] This aid was explicitly political in nature, with the US ambassador to Egypt noting that the intent was to establish a conscious association between Egyptian "policies and attitudes towards the United States and continuation of such [food] assistance in the future."[44] US diplomats openly linked the apparent "moderation" of Egyptian government delegates at a 1962 conference of the Non-Aligned Movement to this food aid dependency.[45] Levels of US aid to Egypt dropped in the second half of the 1960s as the Egyptian government distanced itself from US interests through its support for the republican forces in Yemen and its various political and military alliances with the Soviet Union. But Egypt's defeats in 1967 and 1973 provided an opening for the United States to resume this aid in an attempt to build a closer relationship with Nasser's successor, Anwar Sadat. From 1973 to 1979, Egypt received around one-fifth of all US food aid globally, a powerful indication of US hopes for Sadat and his subsequent embrace of US foreign policy goals in the region. This aid was further supplemented by other policies to encourage the disposal of US agricultural surpluses to Egypt.

Food aid and cheap wheat sales deeply impacted the nature of agriculture and food production in the Middle East and laid the basis for the neoliberal transformation of agrarian relations, which will be explored in chapter 4. Local farmers were unable to compete with the large, cheaper quantities of grains coming from the United States and elsewhere, and as a consequence, agricultural systems were progressively undermined. Instead of relying on farmers to produce food for domestic consumption, countries across the region became increasingly reliant upon imported grain and other food. In 1960, Egypt had a self-sufficiency ratio (domestic production in relation to consumption) for wheat of around 70 percent. By 1980, the self-sufficiency ratio had fallen to 23 percent as imports rose to massive levels.[46] The process was mirrored in Algeria, Morocco, and Tunisia—underpinned in those countries to a greater extent by subsidized grain imports from Europe rather than the United States.[47]

Food aid and grain imports not only signaled a much tighter integration with the world market (and hence exposure to fluctuating global prices), they also paved the way for growing levels of indebtedness as access to foreign currency became a key determinant of whether a country could meet its food needs. In the case of Egypt, these developments were an important part of Sadat's decisive turn toward the United States through the 1970s. The 1973 war was estimated to have cost around $40 billion, and the general fiscal squeeze caused by rising food and energy imports led Sadat to seek loans from US and European lenders as well as regional zones of surplus capital such as the Gulf Arab states.[48] The latter played a decisive role in bringing Egypt into the US orbit, with Saudi Arabia, Kuwait, the UAE, and Qatar forming the Gulf Organization for the Development of Egypt (GODE) in 1976 to provide aid to Egypt. The condition for Gulf financial aid was the abrogation of Soviet influence in Egypt (the Soviet-Egyptian Friendship Treaty was canceled in March 1976) and the strict control of the US Treasury, IMF, and World Bank over a series of economic reforms, including an end to subsidies and a deregulation of the Egyptian pound (which would raise the cost of imports).[49] GODE was initially slow in providing funds, waiting for Sadat to agree to the conditions laid down by the World Bank and IMF, but as the Egyptian government moved to amend laws to allow repatriation of profits, free flows of capital, and tax-free holidays, and attempted to lift subsidies, the money was forthcoming.

Similarly, elsewhere across the region, the combination of global economic turmoil and the rising costs of food and energy imports meant countries were forced to borrow increasing amounts in order to stay afloat. These debt levels accelerated dramatically after the US government sharply raised interest rates beginning in 1979—a move called the "Volcker Shock," after Paul Volcker, then chairman of the Board of Governors of the US Federal Reserve.[50] Because most Arab debt was held in US dollars, the spike in interest rates hit countries in the Middle East very hard (particularly when coupled with the global recession of 1981–82). By the mid-1980s, Algeria, Egypt, Jordan, Morocco, and Tunisia were paying 30–65 percent of their entire export earnings just to service their debt (see table 2.1). At the same time, new loans had to be taken on in order to keep afloat, and so overall debt stock actually rose despite the continual outflows of debt service (see table 2.1). In other words, indebtedness increased each year in tandem with growing debt and interest repayments. Debt thus represented an ever-escalating drain of wealth from the Arab region to the richest financial institutions in the world.

Table 2.1. Debt Service and Debt Stocks
for Algeria, Egypt, Jordan, Morocco, and Tunisia, 1980–1988

	1980–1982		1983–1985		1986–1988	
Country	Average annual debt service	Percent change in total debt stock over 3 year period	Average annual debt service	Percent change in total debt stock over 3 year period	Average annual debt service	Percent change in total debt stock over 3 year period
Algeria	29.5	-8.9	36.2	11.6	65.0	15.1
Egypt	21.7	42.8	33.3	19.5	32.4	15.6
Jordan	13.6	41.9	21.7	20.5	35.4	22.5
Morocco	51.2	27.6	44.7	23.1	41.9	17.8
Tunisia	17	7	24.8	20.3	30.0	14.4

Source: Debt service represents total repayments on debt as a percentage of exports of goods, services, and income. Calculated by author from debt stock and debt service statistics, World Bank database (http://data.worldbank.org).

Trapped in the cul-de-sac of debt and balance-of-payment crises, Arab countries attempted to renegotiate payment schedules with US and European banks through the 1980s. They quickly discovered, however, much like Egypt's earlier experience with GODE loans, that further financial support would be made contingent upon consent from the IMF and World Bank. In order to receive this consent, countries had to agree to lift restrictions on trade, begin the privatization of state-owned enterprises, deregulate labor markets, and demonstrate that they would develop medium-term policy to drop barriers to capital flows (see chapters 3 and 4 for detailed discussions). It was in this context—tied to Western states through a dependency on foreign capital inflows, food imports, and military and economic aid—that Arab countries began to embrace a range of neoliberal restructuring programs in the late 1980s and early 1990s.

By the end of the 1980s, all these changes meant that a range of crucial Arab countries across North Africa and the Mediterranean—notably Egypt, Jordan, Morocco, and Tunisia—were well on the way to being integrated into a framework of US and European interests. Once again, the case of Egypt was particularly striking, as it had been transformed from the leading voice of Arab nationalism to one of the most important allies of the United States. Through the 1980s, Egypt was the second-largest recipient globally (after Israel) of US bilateral foreign assistance, with military aid reaching $1.3 billion a year from 1987 onward.[51] These funds were estimated to cover up to 80 percent of the Egyptian Defense Ministry's weapons procurement costs and one-third of Egypt's overall defense budget each year.[52] As subsequent chapters will examine in detail, the integration of states such as Egypt into the sphere of Western influence represented not just a political realignment, involving a shift in foreign policy alliances, but was above all indicative of a process of class formation—one through which a state-fostered bourgeoisie, strong military elites, and domestic private capital came together as partners sharing a joint interest in the new neoliberal order. In the words of a prominent Egyptian commentator and close confidant of Nasser, "Oil fields began to loom far larger in the public mind than battlefields; *tharwa* (riches), it was said, had begun to take over from *thawra* (revolution)."[53]

The 1990s and 2000s: Imperialism Consolidated

By the early 1990s, US power appeared triumphant. The collapse of the Soviet Union and its satellites from 1989 to 1992 made it much more difficult for those states and political movements that had relied upon Soviet support to pursue independent policies, and the United States utilized the new political context to further extend its influence in the region. The target chosen in this respect was Iraq, which, in the early 1990s, possessed extensive oil reserves (estimated as second only to Saudi Arabia) and the largest unexplored deposits of any country.[54] Through the 1980s, Iraq had been locked in a bloody and self-destructive eight-year war with Iran, following the overthrow of the US-backed Shah in early 1979.[55] The war had been largely funded by the United States and the Gulf monarchies, which saw Iraq as a useful counterweight to the threat of Iranian influence in the Gulf. By mid-1990, Iraq owed a debt of more than $42 billion, on which it was paying $3 billion annually.[56] This was in the context of a major economic crisis—inflation was running at 40 percent annually, and the country's cash reserves were equivalent to only three months' worth of imports.[57] In the face of this dire situation, Iraq's president, Saddam Hussein, attempted to cajole the Gulf states into forgiving the debts Iraq had incurred during the war. Failing in this goal, he invaded Kuwait in August 1990, justifying the invasion with the claim that Kuwait was drilling for oil beneath the Iraqi border and colluding with other Gulf states to keep the price of oil low in order to damage Iraq's parlous finances.[58]

Despite the fact that Hussein had been a primary ally of the United States during the war with Iran, he was considered unreliable and his leadership rested partly on a claim to Arab nationalism.[57] The United States, seizing the opportunity presented by the invasion of Kuwait, quickly mobilized to launch an attack against Iraq. In this endeavor, the political alliances that had developed during the 1980s played a chief role in garnering broader Arab support. Egypt organized an emergency Arab summit in 1990 that endorsed the invasion and also sent troops to take part in combat. Although the Iraqi government was not ousted by the US-led coalition, its military was severely weakened and the country was cut in three by the no-fly zones imposed by the United States and Britain after the war.[58] US president George H. W. Bush utilized the occasion of the war to announce what he described as the "New World Order"—untrammeled US supremacy

across the globe. The war was followed by a decade-long regime of sanctions that dev-
astated Iraq's industrial and social infrastructure, with the United States remaining focused on bringing to power a pliant government.[59] At the end of the war, Egypt was
rewarded for its efforts with a $15 billion write-off of its debt commitments, the largest
cancellation in the history of the Middle East.[60] Likewise, Morocco, which sent 1,200
troops to aid in the attack, received $5 billion in debt forgiveness from the United States
and the Gulf states.[61] In both cases, the relationships of debt bondage were undoubtedly
a major factor in steering the foreign policy choices of the two Arab states.

Once again, however, the extension of US power through the 1990s and 2000s was
not solely military in nature. As Iraq faced invasion and a punishing sanctions regime,
the United States developed a series of highly significant trade and financial initiatives
that radically transformed the relationships between the wider region and the advanced
capitalist core. As subsequent chapters will show in detail, these initiatives—alongside
similar ones from the European Union (EU)—have been a major force in structuring
the context of national neoliberal reforms over the last two decades. But beyond the
national scale, they have also acted to rework the nature of accumulation at the regional
scale—shifting the pattern of financial and trade linkages with Western capital and
consolidating a specific set of hierarchies within the region itself.

As had been the case since the 1970s, US power continued to be articulated through
close military and political relationships with the Gulf, Israel, and client Arab states
such as Jordan and Egypt. There was a shift, however, in the way these relationships
were conceived. The basic approach was to draw these pillars of support together in a
single economic zone under the domination of US capital. A critical pivot of this strategy was thus the normalization of economic and political relations between Israel and
the Arab world. As a consequence of its long-privileged relationship with the United
States—expressed most pointedly in the massive receipts of aid without the conditionalities characteristic of loans to other states—Israel's economy had developed in a qual-
itatively different direction from those of its neighbors. Israel's capitalist class had
emerged with the support of the state apparatus around activities such as construction,
agriculture, and finance. But through the 1990s, direct US financial support helped to
enable the development of high value-added export industries connected to sectors
such as information technology, pharmaceuticals, and security.[62] Unlike its relationship with other states in the region, the United States had run a massive trade deficit
with Israel since the signing of a US-Israel free trade agreement (FTA) in 1985. In this
context, the push to normalization would inevitably strengthen the position of Israel
(and thus the United States) within regional hierarchies.

The first step in this process was the 1993 Oslo Accords, signed between Israel and
the Palestine Liberation Organization (PLO), which led to the establishment of the

Palestinian Authority (PA), with limited self-rule over the Palestinian population in the West Bank and Gaza Strip. As chapter 5 will discuss in further detail, this agreement was a necessary prerequisite for other Arab states to embark on normalization with Israel. Throughout the 1990s, this self-rule evolved into a situation akin to the bantustans of apartheid-era South Africa: Israel retained full control of Palestinian movement, the entry and exit of goods, and economic development in isolated patchworks of territory, while a small layer of Palestinians mediated the occupation on behalf of the occupying power. At the same time, because this process occurred under the rubric of "peaceful negotiations" and the blessing of the United States and EU, Oslo and subsequent agreements helped to open the way for Israel's normalization into the broader Middle East.

At a regional level, the trend toward normalization was confirmed in the MENA Economic Summits, a series of intergovernmental meetings held annually between 1994 and 1998. As the Jordanian Foreign Ministry noted, these summits were "intended to create economic interdependencies between Arab states and Israel, promote personal contacts between the two sides and foster trade, investment and development."[65] The first MENA summit was held in Casablanca, Morocco, in 1994 and, in addition to the Arab states, was attended by then Israeli prime minister Yitzhak Rabin, foreign minister Shimon Peres, and 130 Israeli businesspeople. The participants agreed to take measures to lift the regional economic boycott of Israel and also to establish a Middle East chamber of commerce—with then US secretary of state Warren Christopher effusing that "the Middle East is open for business . . . the conference could be the beginning of a beautiful friendship."[66] The second summit was held in Amman, Jordan, in October 1995, and aimed at facilitating "the expansion of private sector investment in the region, [and] to cement a public-private partnership which will ensure that end and to work to enhance regional cooperation and development."[67] As part of the Amman summit, it was decided to establish the Economic Summit Executive Secretariat, which would work to advance "the public-private partnership, promoting contacts, sharing data and fostering private sector investment in the region."[68] The neoliberal ethos guiding these gatherings was continued in the third MENA summit, held November 12–14, 1996, under the theme of "Building for the Future, Creating an Investor Friendly Environment" in Cairo. The final resolution of the Cairo conference noted, "The region's economic, commercial and trade potential . . . is being greatly enhanced by important economic reform programs currently being undertaken by many states in the region. These reforms, which include privatisation, structural reform, and removing trade barriers, have provided for a more business-friendly economic climate throughout the region."[69]

The MENA summits explicitly linked normalization to the consolidation of neoliberal reform, with the integration of Israel into the region predicated upon the dropping of barriers to trade and investment flows under the auspices of US power. Perhaps the most revealing confirmation of these linkages was the establishment of the so-called Qualified Industrial Zones (QIZs) in Jordan and Egypt. The first of these zones came about as a result of economic agreements signed between the United States, Israel, and Jordan in 1997. Under the QIZ agreements, goods produced in the zones were given duty-free access to US markets, provided that a certain proportion of inputs were Israeli (8 percent in the case of Jordan, 11.7 percent in the case of Egypt). Soon after the first agreement was signed, an additional twelve QIZ sites were established in Jordan. These agreements were intended to weld together Israeli and Arab capital in the joint exploitation of cheap labor, with exports aimed at the US market. They have since come to dominate bilateral trade between the United States and Jordan (and, to a lesser extent, Egypt). By 2007, the US government was reporting that exports from the thirteen QIZs established in Jordan accounted for a massive 70 percent of total Jordanian exports to the United States.[70] In 2004, Egypt also launched its first QIZ in an agreement with Israel and the United States. Six more QIZs were approved in subsequent years, and from 2005 to 2008 exports from these zones grew at an annual average rate of 58 percent, ten times that of total exports from Egypt to the United States.[71] By 2008, close to one-third of Egypt's total exports to the United States would be coming from QIZs.[72]

The moves toward normalization appeared to stumble following the onset of a Palestinian uprising against Israeli rule in 2000 (see chapter 5) and a second US-led invasion of Iraq in 2003.[73] But the link between normalization and neoliberal reform continued to drive US strategy in the region despite renewed military conflict. In mid-2003, these goals were encapsulated in the George W. Bush administration's announcement that it sought a Middle East Free Trade Area (MEFTA), spanning North Africa to the Gulf, by 2013. In June 2003, then US trade representative Robert Zoellick (later to become World Bank president) gave a speech to the World Economic Forum in Jordan in which he outlined the basis of the MEFTA plan. Zoellick's speech blamed poverty, unemployment, and terrorism on Arab "autarky" and "failed socialist" models. He described the war on Iraq as "an opportunity for change—an opening for the people of the Arab world to ask why their region, once a nucleus of trade, has been largely excluded from the gains of this modern era of globalization."[74] In a bizarre teleological reading of history that traced an alleged pro-business "spirit of the Levant," stretching from the time of the Quran through eighteenth-century Arab merchants to the supposed commercial zeal of Arabs living in the contemporary United States, Zoellick argued that if the Middle East liberalized and opened to foreign capital within a regional trading bloc, then the problems stemming from "closed national borders, centralized economic controls, the heavy hand of government, and nationalized industry" would be solved. The goal of US policy was "to assist nations that are ready to embrace economic liberty and the rule of law, integrate into the global trading system, and bring their economies into the modern era."[75]

The US strategy was to negotiate individually with "friendly" countries in the region using a graduated six-step process and eventually leading to a full-fledged FTA between the United States and the country in question. These FTAs were designed so that countries could "moor" with neighboring states, thereby expanding agreements into sub-regional agreements that could be linked over time, until the entire Middle East came under US influence.[76] Importantly, these FTAs were also used to reinforce the notion of normalization with Israel, with each agreement containing a clause committing the signatory to normalization with Israel and forbidding any boycott of trade relations.

US government representatives openly conceived MEFTA and these bilateral FTAs as a counterpoint to other rivals in the region. Zoellick noted, for example, in a 2003 editorial for the *Wall Street Journal*: "The Bush administration's reinvigoration of America's drive for free trade—globally, regionally, and with individual countries—has created a momentum that strengthens US influence . . . [they] level the playing field for US businesses because others—especially the EU—negotiated a host of agreements in the '90s while the US stood on the sidelines."[77] A month later, a widely referenced article from the Washington-based Cato Institute made essentially the same point, stressing the market for services as a particularly important prize for US capital: "The major potential benefit of the Bush administration's proposed Middle East free-trade area is the market opening in the Muslim world that it would entail—and the impetus to broader economic reforms in the region that it would provide. . . . The biggest prize in FTA negotiations—the hardest to attain, but offering the richest rewards—is liberalization of trade in services."[78]

Immediately after announcing the MEFTA initiative, US representatives began a rapid succession of FTA negotiations with countries across the Middle East. Talks had begun with Morocco in early 2003 (prior to the war on Iraq) and concluded successfully following a year of discussions. The agreement was approved by the US Congress in July 2004 and the Moroccan parliament in January 2005, coming into force at the beginning of 2006. The FTA severely reduced Morocco's ability to restrict US goods from entering the country by eliminating tariffs on 95 percent of all bilateral trade, with all tariffs to be eliminated within ten years.[79] Prior to the agreement, the average tariff on US exports to Morocco had been more than 28 percent. The tariff reduction was particularly beneficial to US agribusiness as the main provider of Moroccan grain imports. It immediately eliminated, for example, tariffs on US sorghum and phased out duties on US corn over five years and, as a result, reinforced the earlier trends of food import dependency.[80] For this reason the FTA was strongly supported by US agribusiness interests, such as the US Grain Council, which noted that they had been "striving to build demand for U.S. feed grains in Morocco for many years . . . promoting U.S. feed grains to ensure our producers and agri-businesses will reap maximum benefit from this agreement."[81] The agreement also enabled US capital to benefit from Morocco's agreement with the EU (see below), with tariff reductions applying to US goods produced in Morocco and then exported to Europe.

The US-Moroccan FTA took place concurrently with negotiations with individual Gulf Arab states. An FTA was signed with Bahrain on September 14, 2004, and legislation to approve and implement the agreement was passed by Congress in January 2006. This agreement was also aimed at increasing market share for US corporations. Additional rules within the US-Bahrain FTA meant that government procurement of goods and services had to be opened to US companies on the same basis as a local company, and the state could not restrict the number, type, or residency conditions of US companies.[82] Similar conditions declared virtually all goods from the United States duty-free, opening the route for US commodities to enter the Bahraini market. In services, the FTA forced Bahrain to allow private US medical, educational, legal, and other corporations to enter the marketplace. The market-opening goal of the FTA was explicitly applauded by the Advisory Committee for Trade Policy and Negotiations (ACTPN), a peak body of large US companies and industry representatives, which noted that its provisions "meet or exceed the best that have been negotiated in any other US trade agreement and . . . is a truly impressive achievement."[83]

These trade and financial agreements have helped underpin a shift in the US economic relationship with the Middle East.[84] As appendix 1 details, through the 2000s exports to the United States from Israel, the Gulf Arab states, and Jordan overtook, in value terms, those to the EU. Israel should be highlighted in particular here—from 2000 to 2010, Israel's trade surplus with the United States ranged between $5 billion and $7 billion annually—a remarkable contrast to all other non-oil-producing states, which were running large deficits through the same period.[85] Moreover, while European exports have remained dominant throughout the Middle East (see below), the gap between the US and EU market share has narrowed significantly in the cases of Morocco and Egypt following the various FTA and QIZ agreements. Appendix 2 demonstrates the pattern of the region's trade with the United States, which consists largely of technology, aircraft, and other high value-added machinery imports in exchange for low-wage textiles and garments (in the case of Egypt, Jordan, Morocco, and Tunisia) or hydrocarbons (in the case of the Gulf states and Algeria). The proportion of cereals, soybean, and corn products in US exports to the region, however, is also marked. In the case of Morocco, Tunisia, and Egypt, for example, US agricultural products have constituted between 30 and 50 percent of all US exports through the 2000s—indicating that the North African dependency on the food imports noted above has changed little.

These same patterns are also reflected in the sphere of capital flows. Although foreign direct investment (FDI) originating from the United States is generally much lower in the Middle East than that from European or Gulf countries (see chapter 6), the United States has developed a dominant financial relationship with the two central poles of the regional economy—Saudi Arabia and Israel. In the case of Saudi Arabia, the United States has long been the largest source of FDI, holding 13.7 percent of FDI stock in the country in 2010, significantly more than the other countries in the top five (Kuwait holds 9.9 percent, France 9.0 percent, Japan 8.5 percent, and the UAE 7.4 percent).[86] This is particularly important because Saudi Arabia became the largest host economy for FDI in the MENA region during the 2000s.[87] Most FDI in Saudi Arabia is targeted at the petroleum refining, petrochemical, contracting, and real estate sectors. In the case of Israel, US companies were responsible for a remarkable 82 percent of all FDI in Israel from 2003 to 2008, equivalent to €23 billion.[88] Reflecting the unique characteristics of the Israeli economy, most of this investment was aimed at sectors such as software, electronics, biotechnology, and advanced research and development.

The European Union: Imperial Rivalries and Consensus

As these American initiatives progressed through the 1990s and 2000s, the European Union also sought to strengthen its trade and financial influence in the Middle East, moving to draw the region—particularly the countries surrounding the Mediterranean—closer to European production and trade networks. The EU's orientation to the region demonstrated the dualities of rivalry and shared interests vis-à-vis the United States—both zones looked to extend their penetration of the region while participating in the further consolidation of the Middle East's neoliberal trajectory through the common mechanisms of debt, aid, and the promise of increased market access. The EU's goals were initially codified in the Euro-Mediterranean Partnership (EMP), also known as the Barcelona Process, launched at a meeting in Barcelona in November 1995 between the EU and foreign ministers from Algeria, Cyprus, Egypt, Jordan, Israel, Lebanon, Malta, Morocco, the PA, Syria, Tunisia, and Turkey. The final communiqué of the Barcelona meeting was quite open about its intentions, highlighting "the promotion and development of the private sector . . . [and] the establishment of an appropriate institutional and regulatory framework for a market economy" as a principal aim of the new partnership. The EU admitted its longer-term objectives frankly, noting that its overall purpose was "to create open economies by the opening-up of markets . . . [and] the elimination of trade barriers." This would require the acceleration of "Fiscal, administrative and legal reforms as well as deregulation of public services . . . in order to raise the level of foreign direct investment in the southern Mediterranean economies."[89]

In line with these objectives, two major themes dominated the ongoing Euro-Mediterranean negotiations. The first of these was an attempt to establish a free trade area through a stepping-stone of individual FTAs between Mediterranean countries and the EU, with 2010 set as the target date for concluding a final region-wide agreement. The second theme was "the progressive elimination of obstacles to [EU] investment"[90] through the passage of new laws aimed at privatizing state-owned firms in industry, agriculture, and banking.[91] Over the next decade, these twin themes of free trade and foreign investment were consolidated in individual bilateral treaties, called Association Agreements, signed between the EU and the EMP countries.[92] Association Agreements committed countries to restructuring their policy environments in return for financial incentives and promised access to EU markets. Arab partners had little room to maneuver in negotiating these agreements, given their high levels of indebtedness and the fact that the EU was the largest trading partner for most countries in the region.

In regards to trade, the Association Agreements demanded significant reductions by EMP countries in customs duties, tariffs, and taxes on imports. Regulatory change went well beyond trade in goods to affect services as well—compelling countries to open up sectors such as finance, telecommunications, transport, energy, and more to foreign companies and ownership. These reforms required dramatic revisions of government laws. To facilitate this process, two financial programs, MEDA I and MEDA II,[93] were set up, with close to €5 billion earmarked for distribution between 1995 and 1999. The amount of funding that countries received was explicitly linked to how much they agreed to change their domestic laws—with the EU noting that the basic principle of the MEDA program was that it "makes economic transition and free trade the central issue of EU financial cooperation with the Mediterranean region."[94] MEDA grants were supplemented by additional loans from the European Investment Bank (EIB), with all these funding mechanisms designed to provide "incentives for economic transition and the development of open, competitive markets" and to foster "political and social reforms in the Mediterranean partners . . . as a catalyst to macroeconomic structural adjustment."[95]

In the first round of MEDA funding (1995–1999), €3.435 billion in grants was distributed with another €4.808 billion provided in loans from the EIB. Around 45 percent of the MEDA funds were directly linked to structural adjustment programs, including more than €500 million in direct grants to national budgets so that countries could carry out neoliberal reforms in partnership with the IMF and World Bank, and another €1.035 billion aimed at policies to help "the creation of an environment favourable to the development of the private sector."[96] To a great extent these grants resembled little more than a bribe, with the EU noting that "national budgets of the Mediterranean partners receive a cash injection in return for the implementation of structural reforms."[97] Projects backed by MEDA in this initial round included trade liberalization (Algeria, Jordan, Tunisia), privatization of state-owned companies (Algeria, Jordan, Tunisia), and financial sector opening (Morocco and Tunisia).[98] By 2003, the EU assessed that funding had achieved "significant progress . . . towards the liberalisation and the regulating of the economy, in particular in the banking system where progress towards competition has been achieved. Progress was done [*sic*] towards the restoration of the balance between the public and private sectors [i.e., privatization], though unequally. Evaluators noted that the liberalisation of the capital market went further than the labour market."[99]

In 2003, the European Commission outlined an updated vision of the relationship with the EMP countries, which became known as the European Neighbourhood Policy (ENP). The ENP also applied to non-Mediterranean neighbors of the EU such as Armenia, Azerbaijan, Belarus, Georgia, Moldova, and Ukraine, and was intended to complement the Barcelona Process. It set up a framework for intensifying negotiations with EMP countries through a series of three-to-five-year action plans drafted by the EU, which laid out what steps countries would need to take in return for continuing European aid. The ENP differed from the EMP in that it involved a much more explicit focus on integrating Mediterranean countries into European markets, although, importantly, it ruled out the possibility of accession to EU membership.[100] Moreover, it placed heavy emphasis on the goal of closer economic integration between the countries of the Mediterranean.[101] The justification for this was unambiguously framed in the interests of European capital, with the EU commissioner for external relations, Chris Patten, noting that South-South integration "will create larger markets, which will serve as a strong incentive to make the region more attractive for foreign direct investment."[102] One of the mechanisms by which this was encouraged was a decision to establish so-called "rules of cumulative origin"—meaning that goods made up of a variety of inputs from different Euro-Med countries could be treated as having the same origin, provided the producing countries held trade agreements between one another.[103] In this manner, the EU hoped to encourage countries in the region also to sign FTAs between one another. "Cumulative origin" would, in the words of Patten, encourage "economic operators from different countries to get together and perform the different stages of their production in the country where it produces greatest profit. It would have a significant effect on encouraging joint ventures in the region, and it would enable all to take advantage of the specific economic structure of each partner."[104]

Around 2007, differences emerged within the EU regarding the best way to advance the ENP process. These differences were reflected in a proposal put forward by Nicolas Sarkozy during the French presidential campaign of 2007, in which he suggested the establishment of a Mediterranean Union (MU), modeled on the EU. Sarkozy's proposal envisaged the MU as consisting of countries surrounding the Mediterranean, and thus excluded EU member countries such as Germany. The European Commission and German chancellor Angela Merkel came out against the MU for this reason, as did proposed members, such as Turkey, who feared the MU would be used as an alternative to full membership in the EU itself. Other EU member states such as Italy, Spain, and Greece gave their support to the suggestion. At the beginning of 2008, Sarkozy modified his suggestion to include all EU member states, not just those bordering the Mediterranean. It subsequently became part of the Barcelona Process, and was presented as a new phase of the EMP at a conference in Paris in July 2008.

By the end of the decade, the consequences of these agreements for the Middle East region were clear. Most importantly, European control over export markets was consolidated (see appendix 1). The EU was consistently the largest exporter to every Euro-Med partner country through the 2000s—for Algeria, Morocco, Tunisia, Libya, and Lebanon, the EU was supplying around half of all imports; for other EMP states, the EU share was consistently over 25 percent. These EU-produced goods were generally high value-added, technically advanced items—machinery and equipment, vehicles, and aircraft (see appendix 2). Concurrently, the various regional agreements acted to tie the productive activities of EMP countries to European markets as exporters of low-wage manufactured goods, agricultural products, and natural resources. These trade patterns were particularly stark in the case of Morocco and Tunisia, where around 75–80 percent of all exports were going to the EU through the decade—mostly textiles/garments and agricultural goods (appendixes 1 and 2). Textile and garment exports were also significant for Jordan and Egypt, although a larger proportion of these tended to go to the United States as a consequence of the various bilateral agreements noted above. The defining characteristic of this trade for many ENP countries—the exchange of technologically advanced goods produced in the EU for labor-intensive clothing and agricultural goods manufactured in the Middle East—is indicative of one mechanism of the transfer of value from the Middle East to European capitalism.[105] This has been reflected in persistent and widening trade deficits with Europe.

Moreover, this orientation of trade developed concurrently with policies of privatization and the opening up of ownership to foreign investment. From 2003 to 2008, French, Spanish, and Italian investors were particularly prominent in the region—buying up newly privatized assets in the utilities, real estate, banking, and industrial sectors.[106] North African countries—notably Morocco, Tunisia, and Egypt—were a major target of these investment flows. Through these investments, industrial and agricultural activities in EMP countries were frequently incorporated in early production stages of vertically integrated conglomerates that straddled the Mediterranean itself—again, particularly in textiles/garments and the food industry (see chapters 3 and 4). For this reason, any growth in exports that might have accompanied increased access to European markets actually ended up flowing to firms that were linked to European conglomerates through joint ventures or, in some cases, direct ownership.

Rising Powers?

While the European Union and the United States continue to dominate the political economy of the Middle East, rising powers have increasingly built separate and competing alliances with states in the region.[107] This has been reflected in a partial reorientation of the region's trade and financial flows. With the exceptions of Morocco and Bahrain, all countries in the Arab world have seen a declining share of their imports coming from the EU or United States over the last decade. For Egypt, Jordan, Syria, and the Gulf states, this proportion has fallen below 50 percent (see appendix 1). In place of these traditional exporters to the region, an increasing proportion of goods are coming from countries such as China, Russia, Turkey, South Korea, and India. In 2010, China was one of the top three sources of exports to the region for twelve out of seventeen countries (see appendix 1). In regards to exports from the Middle East, India, East Asia, Brazil, and Turkey rank as significant markets for goods produced in the region.

China and Russia have been the leading actors in this entry of emerging powers into the region. Not surprisingly, these two countries have looked at forming linkages in the region through those states that remained largely outside of the orbit of Western power over the last two decades—notably Iran and Syria. By the end of the 2000s, China had become Iran's biggest trading partner and the largest purchaser of Iranian oil.[108] Russia's links with Iran were focused on the sale of military hardware, although these came under pressure due to sanctions imposed on Iran as of the mid-2000s. The closer links among Russia, China, and Iran were confirmed in 2005, when Iran was granted observer status at the Shanghai Cooperation Organization (SCO), a regional security grouping of Russia, China, Kazakhstan, Kyrgyzstan, Tajikistan, and Uzbekistan founded in 2001. Iran applied for full membership in the SCO in 2008, although this has not been granted due to the ongoing UN sanctions. Some observers have suggested that the potential consolidation of the SCO into a tighter military and political alliance could form a possible counterweight to NATO influence in the Middle East/Central Asia region.

Russia and China have also formed strong relationships with Syria. In 2008, Syria's president, Bashar al-Assad, agreed to allow Russia to convert a naval port located at the Syrian town of Tartous into a permanent military base for Russian warships. It would be Russia's only such base in the region. The agreement signified that Syria had become Russia's most important ally in the Middle East, a fact reflected in Russian arms exports to Syria, which accounted for about 10 percent of Russia's total weapons sales during the 2000s.[109] China is likewise tightly linked to Syria as the largest exporter to the country and its biggest source of FDI. The latter investments have been concentrated in Syria's Al Furat Petroleum Company—Syria's main oil producer, which was partially privatized over the 2000s—as well as in construction and utility projects.

The close Chinese relationship with Syria reflects the importance of the Middle East to the balance of global power. Nearly half of China's crude oil imports were coming from the Middle East by 2006, with Saudi Arabia the largest source of imports (around 16 percent) and Oman and the UAE also significant sources; this was despite the fact that China itself was the sixth-largest oil producer in the world that same year.[110] These levels continued to increase, and in early 2010 a spokesperson for Saudi Arabia's oil producing company, Aramco, revealed that Saudi oil exports to China had surpassed those to the United States—a profound shift that marked a new era in the patterns of Middle East oil trade.[111] The eastward shift of Gulf trade was not restricted to crude oil and gas; it was also reflected in petrochemical exports that provide a critical feedstock for Asian factories. In 2004, China imported about 42 percent of globally traded polyethylene, 44 percent of polypropylene, 45 percent of polyvinyl chloride (PVC), and 48 percent of polystyrene.[112] Much of these basic petrochemical products were sourced from the Gulf region; the Saudi Basic Industries Corporation (SABIC), the most important petrochemical firm in the Middle East, was sending half its exports to Asia by the end of 2009.

China's dependence on Middle East oil presages a deepening rivalry with the United States—not only over oil supplies per se, but due to the fact that US hegemony in the Middle East provides it with an important source of leverage over China, a fact amply demonstrated in regards to the conflicts over Iran. Any long-term contestation of a US-centered world order presupposes a shift in the form of external domination of the Middle East, which, as the history of the last five decades decisively confirms, will necessarily be accompanied by a range of political, military, and economic initiatives that attempt to draw the region away from US domination. Nonetheless, while both China's and Russia's increasing involvements in the region undoubtedly present a challenge to US and broader Western hegemony, some care needs to be taken in interpreting the nature of these rivalries. Precisely because of the highly internationalized structure of the world market, all major states—including China and Russia—are deeply enmeshed in mutual trade and capital flows, sharing a common interest in the stability of global capitalism. This means they have little interest in seeing a qualitative break with the patterns of uneven development in the Middle East, or with the region's embrace of neoliberal reforms. Indeed, the entry of China and Russia into Middle East markets—much as with Europe and the United States—has been predicated upon the intensification of neoliberalism in places such as Iran and Syria. For these reasons, it is mistaken to see these countries as any sort of progressive force for liberation (chapter 7 provides further discussion of this issue).

Conclusion

The protracted domination of the Middle East by Western states has developed through a variety of different means, but the underlying themes have been consistent: deepen the uneven and combined development of the region, widen the hierarchies of states and their interdependencies, and utilize the resulting differentials of power to consolidate control. The forms and patterns of these arrangements have shifted over the last five decades, but their result has been the same. This strategy has not only acted to realign the specific relationships between different zones in the region and the major capitalist powers, but—most significantly for the analysis throughout this book—has also generated a specific set of relationships internal to the region itself. There are six core characteristics to this realignment that can be initially sketched here and will be further developed in subsequent chapters:

1. *The European Union has brought closer to itself the key Euro-Med countries, most notably those of North Africa.* The productive and commercial activities of these countries have been tightly linked to the Eurozone as neoliberal reforms have proceeded apace. This has meant a reorientation of North African economies toward the needs of European capital—fixing the Mediterranean as a subordinated and dependent adjunct of its larger neighbor through trade and foreign direct investment flows.

2. *The integration of Mediterranean productive sectors with European capitalism has acted to deepen social differentiation both within individual nation-states as well as between the region as a whole and Europe.* In other words, the relationship with the EU has helped to shape the trajectory of class formation (again, most notably in North Africa), by simultaneously enriching (and drawing closer to the European project) a tiny layer of the region's elites. As subsequent chapters will confirm in detail, the intertwining of trade and investment through the EMP has played an important role in reinforcing the concentration and centralization of capital in the hands of large domestic and foreign capital through key sectors such as textiles/garments and agriculture.[113]

3. *Simultaneously, the United States has constructed privileged relationships with two core pillars of its power in the region—Israel and the GCC (specifically Saudi Arabia).* These two pillars are distinct from other countries in the region in that they form the apex of hierarchies in the regional space. Their relationships with the imperialist core differ from the rest of the region in that they are both able to retain a greater share of the value generated in the region (Israel through its advanced industrial exports and the GCC through its control of hydrocarbon supplies). The United States reinforces these regional hierarchies through aid (military and financial) and political support to these two poles, while also being deeply enmeshed in their economies through flows of FDI and other financial relationships.

4. *The United States has also attempted to use these two poles as the axis for its drawing together of the wider region under its hegemony.* Jordan and Egypt have played a specific

and highly important role in this process through the QIZs and other agreements
with Israel. The European Union has also emphasized this point through the
framework of the Euro-Med negotiations. This means that the question of normalization with Israel has a specific centrality to resisting imperialist influence in the
region, as does the wider Palestinian movement against ongoing dispossession.
This also helps to explain the specificity of class formation in the Palestinian territories (see chapter 5).

5. *The deepening of neoliberal reforms, which has been the necessary corollary of both the EU
   and US restructuring of the region, has also acted to widen the hierarchical relationships
   within the region as a whole.* Most notably, this has meant the strengthening of the
   position of the Gulf Arab states within the Middle East and North Africa. This has
   been most sharply expressed through the internationalization of Gulf capital and
   the enmeshing of Gulf conglomerates with domestic capitalist classes in the region
   (see chapter 6).

6. *These realignments also need to be placed in the context of potential challenges to US/
   European hegemony at the global scale.* While the EU and the United States continue
   to dominate the political economy of the region, rising powers—notably China and
   Russia—have increasingly built separate and competing alliances with states in the
   region. This has been reflected in a partial reorientation of trade and financial
   flows across the region, but its most important feature has been the alliance of Russia and China with those states that remained largely outside of Western hegemony
   through the 2000s (notably Iran and Syria).

These six features of the regional scale confirm the deep interconnection of imperialism with the political economy of neoliberalism in the Middle East. Imperialism
is not principally a military project—despite the significance of force to the way it operates—and to conceive of it in this way is to mistake the outward appearances of Western intervention for its essence. Rather, imperialism is primarily about ensuring the
ongoing subordination of the region's political economy to the forms of accumulation
in the core capitalist states of the world market. Seen in this light, neoliberalism is
much more than simply a menu of "free market" economic policies; it represents a
radical restructuring of class relations that acts to facilitate and reinforce the region's
domination by external powers. In so doing, it generates a set of social forces that are
internal to the region itself, and that have an objective stake in supporting the new status quo. This restructuring has not just involved the transformation of class and state
within individual nation-states but has also produced a new set of hierarchies and in-
termeshing of social relations across the regional space as a whole. These observations
form the basic analytical lens through which to approach the different aspects of the
region's political economy, as explored in the following chapters.

CHAPTER 3
Mapping the Neoliberal Experience

The previous chapter outlined the context and origins of neoliberal development in the Middle East. As these policies spread through the region over a period of decades, Arab countries were compelled to radically rework their economies. Trapped in a cycle of debt and the conditionalities that accompanied loan packages, they saw patterns of social reproduction shift dramatically—the ways in which people met their basic needs, the kinds of work they did, and their relationship to the market and the state broke sharply with the forms of accumulation that had earlier characterized the Arab world. This chapter investigates the core policies connected to this transformation, focusing on the experiences in Egypt, Morocco, Tunisia, and Jordan—four states with similar economic profiles and histories. All are largely non-oil economies in which agriculture has traditionally played a major role (albeit to a lesser extent in Jordan), and manufacturing activity is dominated by low value-added activities such as the production of textiles and garments. Following the debt crises of the 1980s and the adoption of IMF-sponsored Structural Adjustment Packages (SAPs), these states have been at the forefront of neoliberal reform, with international institutions consistently lauding their economic policies as a model for neighboring countries to follow. Their integration into the world market has also followed similar routes—each holds membership in the World Trade Organization (WTO) and Association Agreements with the European Union, and has a close relationship with the United States.

This chapter, however, does not purport to present a detailed account of the neo-liberal experience in these four states. Its goal is to map more broadly the principal motivations of the neoliberal project and the ways this has been expressed through policies that share all their essential features regardless of the country involved. The first section examines some of these key policies, including privatization, labor market deregulation, liberalization of trade and investment, and changes to financial markets.[1] Emphasis is placed on understanding the logic by which these policies have been jus-tified and their consequences for the broader political economy. But this chapter also demonstrates that neoliberalism is much more than simply a set of economic policies. The second part turns to a further important component of the neoliberal project, the institutional reconfiguration of the state—specifically, the ways in which the form of state power itself has shifted, radically modifying its key functions, the character of decision-making, and its fiscal operations. Taken together, this examination of both the policy logic and institutional characteristics of neoliberalism provides an essential insight into how state and class were reconstituted in the region in the decades leading up to the 2011 revolts.[2]

Privatization and the Discourse of Crisis

From the early 1980s onward, all major international financial institutions (IFIs) typically began their reports on the Middle East by warning of the specter of im-pending crisis. Economic disaster was fast approaching, according to the IFIs, due to the combined effects of a rapid expansion in the region's labor force and the lack of employment growth. From 2000 to 2010, average annual growth in the labor force was predicted to reach over 3 percent a year, double that of any other country in the global South.[3] Forty-two million additional people would be looking for work by the end of the decade. Without faster economic growth, the region would face massive social costs in the form of spiraling levels of unemployment, the proliferation of urban slums, and the growth of informal labor markets. Hard-est hit would be youth and women. In this context, the region would soon suffer a tsunami of urban decay and social discontent unless there was an urgent volte-face in economic policy.

Predictably, this talk of crisis completely sidestepped the history of imperialist in-tervention as outlined in the previous chapter. Two centuries of occupation and war, the forced dependency on external markets for food and technology, and the ongoing drain of wealth through debt and other capital flows were simply disappeared from the terms of the debate or posited as a consequence rather than as a cause of the region's predicament. But with the scale of the problem established and its framing neatly cir-cumscribed, IFIs took the lead role in articulating a direction out of the potential crisis.

Indeed, "some kind of crisis"—as the World Bank noted in 2003—was seen as very much an opportunity because it would help compel policy makers to make a "firm commitment" to a new economic trajectory.[4]

The solution advanced by the IFIs to this imminent employment crisis was seductively simple. The way to avert the looming social explosion was through a rapid acceleration of economic growth. This growth could best be achieved by unfettering the private sector and connecting with the world market, allowing capitalism to "meet the growth in jobs required in the region . . . to absorb the new entrants to the labor force and to address the stock of unemployed."[5] The private sector would become, in the words of the World Bank, the "engine of strong and sustained growth."[6] Most important, it was necessary to be cognizant of the shift in the international context that made this private-sector-led growth an imperative. The choice was clear: the "new global economy" meant a world market that was "a winner-take-all environment," where "rewards . . . go to the most hospitable environments [for capital investment]."[7]

Animated by this logic, all subsequent IFI-led policy reform has been principally oriented toward the "enabling" of market relations and the removal of barriers to private sector investment. Central to this project, of course, was the goal of reducing the size and scope of the public sector through privatization. State-run enterprises were said to be less efficient, act as a drain on fiscal resources, and reduce growth because of the "perverse incentives and contradictory demands" placed on managers of state-owned enterprises.[8] Privatization of state-owned firms would improve the efficiency of markets and help attract new investment. Indeed, as one prominent Arab advocate of privatization argued, it was "the most important initiative Arab governments can take to encourage foreign direct investment."[9]

Privatization thus became a centerpiece of the SAPs that were developed through the 1980s and 1990s. Its subsequent history can be divided into two clear phases. The first begins in the late 1980s with the laying down of a legislative and institutional framework for selling state assets as a requirement of structural adjustment, and extends to the end of the 1990s.[10] A total of 271 companies were divested from state ownership across seven countries through this period, with the total proceeds reaching over $8.1 billion (see table 3.1).[11] Although a range of countries were involved in privatization deals during this decade, Egypt, Morocco, and Tunisia dominated the sell-off. From 1988 to 1999, Egypt's privatization receipts reached $4.172 billion, while Morocco and Tunisia recorded $3.1 billion and $0.59 billion respectively—together, these three countries constituted 97 percent of total revenue from privatization in the region and were also the clear leaders in sheer number of deals.

Table 3.1: Privatization Proceeds in Selected Countries, 1988-2008, US$ million

	1988-1999	2000	2001	2002	2003	2004	2005	2006	2007	2008	Total 2000-2008
Algeria	55.05	7	369	0	360	421	384	0	161	0	1,702
Jordan	63.81	568	20	112	173	2	55	208	556	104	1,798
Lebanon	122	0	0	0	0	0	236	0	0	0	236
Morocco	3,099.13	2,110	0	0	1,551	2,616	147	650	552	0	7,626
Egypt	4,172.62	300	82	0	0	52	2,173	7,583	311	681	11,182
Yemen	0.79	20	0	0	0	0	0	214	0	0	234
Tunisia	593.78	230	0	227	0	247	121	2,282	61	480	3,648
Total	8,107.18	3,235	541	339	2,084	3,338	3,116	10,937	2,891	1,265	27,746

Source: Calculated by author from World Bank Privatization Database (http://go.worldbank.org/W1ET8RG1Q0).

The second phase began in the early 2000s, with a marked acceleration in the pace and scale of privatization. Total proceeds from 2000–2008 exceeded $27 billion, with Jordan joining Egypt, Morocco, and Tunisia in registering a very large uptick in the value of sales. Alongside this increase in privatization revenue was a notable shift in the nature of the companies being sold. During the previous decade, most privatized entities had been connected to manufacturing (112 companies) and service (70), with relatively few in the finance (23) or infrastructure (16) sectors.[12] By 2008, telecommunications and finance had become much more significant in both the number and overall value of these deals—the two largest privatization sales in each of the seven countries listed in table 3.1, aside from Jordan, were from these two sectors.

Despite the generalized increase in privatization through the 2000s, Egypt stands out as the region's clear leader. The country's privatization program was launched as part of the SAP agreed between the Egyptian government and the World Bank and IMF in 1991. The major focus of this SAP was Law 203 of 1991, which designated 314 public sector enterprises for sale. By 2008, Egypt had recorded the largest number of firms privatized out of any country in the region and the highest total value of privatization ($15.7 billion since 1988). Unlike other states, in which just one or two deals made up the majority of privatization receipts, Egypt's sell-off was very broad-based—covering flour mills, steel factories, real estate firms, banks, hotels, and telecommunications companies. By contrast, in Morocco, the country with the second-largest receipts from privatization, the top three sales constituted 78 percent of the total sales over 2000–2008.

To prepare state-owned companies for privatization, the Egyptian government terminated subsidies and ended their direct control by government ministries. In doing so, these companies were forced to compete on the market and their management was given relative autonomy in terms of decision-making. Company managers could reduce the size of the workforce prior to privatization, thereby making the company more attractive to a potential buyer and potentially gaining a stake for themselves following the sale of the firm.[13] In many cases, loans from international institutions were used to assist in the restructuring and upgrading of facilities prior to sale—burdening the state with debt while investors received newly retooled and modernized factories.

One important innovation in Egypt's privatization process was the use of so-called Employees Shareholders Associations (ESAs). ESAs involved the distribution of an ownership share to workers and were framed to the public as a "democratization" of capital ownership—with one government official even claiming that they represented the "summit of socialism."[14] Behind closed doors a much more candid assessment prevailed, with a leading US conservative think tank noting at the time that such schemes were an "ideal vehicle for the privatization of government-owned enterprises" because, by offering workers a share in the company, it could turn "worker opposition to privatization into strong support."[15] The leading push for ESAs came from USAID, which noted in 1985 that an ESA represented "a method of transferring a parastatal to private ownership."[16] ESAs were even linked to debt-for-equity swaps—the US government would swap the debt that a country owed to it for equity in a newly privatized company, and then sell this equity to workers. In this manner, the country's debt burden was directly offloaded onto workers while they were simultaneously enlisted to help in the privatization of their own company.

Egypt was the first country in the global South to trial the ESA approach. The experiment involved a USAID-backed project to privatize the Transport and Engineering Company (TRENCO), a publicly owned tire producer supplying 31 percent of the market in Egypt.[17] USAID's Center for Privatization provided the project loan to the Egyptian government through its Commodity Import Program—a scheme through which the US government granted loans on the provision that they be used to import US-made goods. Four basic "pillars" underpinned the project, according to USAID: restoring free markets, restoring private property in the means of production, limiting government power in the economy, and promoting widespread access to capital ownership. The project established a new company, Alexandria Tire Company (ATC), which was owned by TRENCO and a group of investors including the Italian tire company Pirelli and a number of local and regional banks. In addition to these investors, workers from TRENCO and, later, those employed at ATC itself would receive shares in the company.[18] The number of shares that each worker received, however, was proportionate to salary—ensuring that the majority of shares actually went to the top management of the company, as did the positions on the board that ran ATC.[19] USAID noted that the advantage to this method was that it "unites the interests of workers with other interests, foreign and domestic . . . reduces likelihood of strikes and other stoppages" and created a "broader political constituency against redistributive taxation and over-regulation of business."[20] This frank and honest appraisal was confirmed in 1999, when ATC was fully privatized and transferred to Pirelli's majority ownership. Later, in 2005, TRENCO itself was sold to French-based Michelin.

During the 1990s, virtually all privatization in Egypt made at least partial use of employee ownership as a stepping-stone to divestment by the state.[21] By 1999, 137 out of the 314 companies declared eligible for privatization had been sold.[22] This pace accelerated dramatically in 2004, however, following the appointment of the "government of businessmen," headed by Ahmad Nazif, who announced his intentions to privatize most state-owned firms, including in sectors that had previously been off-limits. Nazif was strongly endorsed by the IMF, which noted that his economic program was "commendable [and] attaches top priority to modernizing government and to reducing government interference in market mechanisms, necessary conditions for accelerating Egypt's transformation into a dynamic, private sector-driven economy."[23] While the number of workers in public sector enterprises had fallen by more than half from 1994 to 2001, the IMF was optimistic that there would be an even faster pace of privatization under Nazif, commenting that asset sales over 2005–2006 had already "surpassed expectations."[24]

The IMF's hopes were not disappointed. The period from 2004 to 2008 saw Egypt's privatization program turn sharply toward telecommunications, banking, and real estate, sectors that had seen little attention in the earlier decade. The method of privatization also shifted to direct offerings to potential investors, sometimes without even publicly announcing the sales of assets.[25] Buyers were generally international firms, Gulf-based conglomerates, or large domestic capital—often acting in joint partnership (see chapter 6). Many of the privatized firms were sold at below their market value—an issue that was to become important to the social struggles that emerged in the post-Mubarak period. Egypt's total receipts from privatization in the 2004–2008 period constituted a remarkable 70 percent of all privatization revenues since the inception of its structural adjustment in 1991, and the World Bank recognized Egypt as the "region's top reformer" in each year from 2006 to 2008. Indeed, in 2008, the country was crowned the "World's Top Reformer" by the World Bank and the International Finance Corporation.

Labor Market Deregulation

Closely connected to the acceleration of privatization in the 2000s was an attack on labor and the conditions of work more generally. According to the argument advanced by IFIs, if wages were lowered and social protection measures rolled back as much as practically possible, investment would then become more attractive to the private sector. It was a logic that led to some perverse conclusions; the World Bank plainly argued, for example, that maternity leave in the Middle East was a *cause* of female unemployment and that stronger labor codes actually led to increased levels of unemployment and informalization.[26] In line with this perspective, loan packages through the 1990s and 2000s identified "labor market deregulation" as a top priority—explicitly targeting minimum wage laws, severance pay, regulations over hiring and firing, and payroll tax. In place of these regulations, governments were urged to promote the casualization of the workforce—described by the World Bank as a shift to "more flexible hiring and dismissal procedures."[27]

This deliberate erosion of working conditions was tightly interwoven with the push to privatize. As the previous chapter noted, the public sector was the dominant employer in many MENA countries, and popular support for the Arab nationalist regimes rested partly upon their ability to provide workers in the public sector with secure jobs, relatively high wages, and the promise of a pension following retirement. Workers naturally found these conditions attractive, but from the perspective of the private sector it was highly problematic—better conditions in the public sector meant that real wages across *all* sectors could not be reduced because "the dominant role of government as employer introduces rigidities in the wage structure that distort labor market incentives."[28] A core feature of the neoliberal project was to take aim at these "rigidities," attempting to reduce real wages and conditions in the public sector in order for a "realignment of incentives toward work in the private sector" to take place.[29] By reducing the costs of labor, those companies slated for privatization would become more attractive to investors and, moreover, would not have to compete with better work conditions in the public sector once they were sold. In this sense, privatization and labor market deregulation were two sides of the same process—a generalized degradation of working and social conditions aimed at making the private sector more profitable.

The practical policy implications of this logic were soon made clear. Working conditions in the public sector had to be significantly worsened in order for private sector employers to be able to pay lower wages and still attract workers. Alongside privatization, governments needed to "reduc[e] government employment and the wage bill [through measures such as] lowering remuneration for new entrants, adjusting the pay scale to strengthen the link between compensation and productivity, and focusing on nonwage benefits that distort labor decisions, such as generous pension systems and family allowances that add to the lure of employment in the public sector."[30]

To help this process along, the World Bank established its annual *Doing Business* index in 2003, which, among other indexes, ranked countries on their "Rigidity of Employment." Countries were rated on a series of measures, including the following: make it cheap and easy for companies to fire people, employ workers on temporary contracts rather than permanent ones, require employees to work for more than fifty hours a week, give the shortest possible time for paid annual leave and any notice of redundancy, and pay the lowest possible minimum wage. These rankings came to be widely utilized by businesses and governments for assessing the pace of reform, serving as a benchmark for the region or, as the World Bank described it, a "cholesterol test for the regulatory environment for domestic businesses."[31]

Labor market deregulation moved relatively slowly through the 1990s, but by the early 2000s it had become a major focus of loan packages between IFIs and Arab governments. Throughout the decade, Egypt, Jordan, Morocco, and Tunisia all passed major laws that saw the introduction of temporary contracts in place of permanent ones, lifted limits on the repeated use of these contracts, and made it easier to fire workers in the public sector.[32] These measures were highly controversial and met with significant resistance due to the huge social consequences they carried. It is perhaps for this reason that the language used to describe deregulation became increasingly obtuse—perfectly illustrated in the World Bank's endorsement of new labor legislation in Tunisia in 2010 as a policy that "enables firms to react to economic realities by adjusting their factor inputs, including labor, and thereby lowering the transaction costs for open-ended employment."[33]

PPPs and the Infrastructure Target

The wave of privatization during the 2000s represented most fundamentally a direct transfer of wealth to domestic and foreign capital (see appendix 4 and chapter 6 for more detailed discussion of the beneficiaries of this process). But despite this fact, many essential services across the MENA region continued to be provided and run by governments. Energy, transport, and water stand out in this regard; the complex infrastructure networks necessary to maintain these utilities have seen relatively low levels of private sector involvement and remain generally state-owned. For this reason, the privatization of public utilities and associated infrastructures—with their promise of potentially huge profits for private investors—became a major target of neoliberal governments from 2005 onward.

The push to privatize service provision in these key sectors focused on the use of Public-Private Partnerships (PPPs)—a means of encouraging the outsourcing of previously state-run utilities and services to private companies. In a PPP, a private company provides a service in contract with the government—typically, this may include activities such as water distribution, waste disposal, running ports, or building and operating infrastructure such as highways and power plants. For this, they receive payments from the government or through the users of the service (such as highway tolls). A PPP is a form of privatization, which, in the words of one of its foremost proponents, Emanuel Savas, is "a useful phrase because it avoids the inflammatory effect of 'privatization' on those ideologically opposed."[34]

PPPs differ from typical privatization deals in that they often involve the partitioning of economic sectors into a large number of integrated functions, each of which is contracted out separately. PPPs in the electricity sector, for example, may involve separation of the generation, transmission, and distribution of power among a variety of companies or contracual arrangements. In the water sector, the tasks of water production, treatment, storage, retail distribution, sanitation collection, treatment, and disposal are often unbundled and contracted to different providers. This separation institutionalizes a market-driven logic into the everyday reproduction of the economy that is difficult to combat because the precise responsibility for various functions can be hard to identify. Moreover, the state may retain a role in one or more of these functions, socializing the risk and cost of less profitable activities while profit-making functions are shifted to the control of private capital.

A number of PPP deals have been signed across the MENA region. Perhaps the country that has moved fastest in this regard is Jordan, which has PPPs for power generation, water provision, and management of the Amman airport terminal. By 2006, Jordan had 40 percent of its population receiving drinking water from a private provider.[35] PPPs have also been launched in Morocco (water), Tunisia (desalination, electricity, and airports), and Egypt (wastewater). But despite this range of sectors and countries, the development of PPPs remains at an early stage. Laws to govern the use of PPPs are still being drafted in Jordan, while Morocco and Tunisia have no specific legislation to deal with PPPs. Egypt passed a PPP law on July 1, 2010, but the government unit in charge resigned for fear of retribution following the ousting of Mubarak.[36]

PPPs carry with them important implications for the broader neoliberal project. As with privatization in general, PPPs are heavily reliant upon the removal of any ownership regulations and barriers to investment, such as currency-exchange controls or restrictions on the repatriation of dividends. They also require the liberalization of market prices, which generally increase with the privatization of the service. But because of the large amount of funding typically needed for infrastructure, and the complexity of PPP-type projects that can extend over decades, the development of PPPs is much more dependent than normal privatization deals upon the deepening of domestic financial markets. If PPPs are to be funded domestically and in local currency, they require a wide range of domestic and foreign-owned banks to provide lending, bond markets where governments and corporations can take on debt, and active equity markets.[37] Frequently, PPPs will see firms borrow from financial institutions in a number of different countries—they thus promote deeper regional interlocking of financial markets (this has been noticeable in the case of Europe). International institutions often provide loans for PPPs and have been closely involved in devising policy around the sale of infrastructure and services. Of note here is the EIB, a financial institution particularly active in promoting privatization in the Mediterranean region as part of the EMP process discussed in the previous chapter. PPPs thus help to further embed leading neoliberal institutions in state decision-making.[38]

For all these reasons, the growth of the PPP market is contingent upon, and helps to catalyze, a broader set of policy changes, which can sometimes be difficult to identify (and combat) due to their diffusion across a range of different state institutions. Major international financial institutions such as the European Bank for Reconstruction and Development (EBRD) and the EIB fully understand these linkages, and for this reason have explicitly identified PPPs as a strategic leverage to the further deepening of neo-liberalism. Furthermore, they have targeted the relatively low level of PPP deals in the region as the next major area of policy intervention—a goal that has continued following the 2011 uprisings (see chapter 7). As such, PPPs need to be regarded as the new face of privatization in the MENA region—one that carries enormous significance for both labor and capital.

Opening to the World Market

A range of international agreements signed by MENA countries from the mid-1990s onward provided the context for these conjoined processes of privatization and labor market deregulation. Tunisia, Egypt, and Morocco joined the World Trade Organization (WTO) in 1995 and were followed shortly by Jordan in 2000. As the previous chapter noted, all four countries established Association Agreements with the EU between 1995 and 2001, and Morocco and Jordan signed FTAs with the United States in 2004 and 2009, respectively. The implication of these agreements was laid out in a major World Bank report issued in 2003, *Trade, Investment, and Development in the Middle East and North Africa*, which prescribed a fundamental shift in trade and investment policies as the anchor of a broader neoliberal restructuring. The three-hundred-page report noted that changes in the nature of international production networks meant that there were "finer gradations of specialization" within the value chains of most industries. The MENA region had a comparative advantage in this new global marketplace because of its relatively cheap labor, which gave it "virtually unlimited" prospects within the world market.[39] By opening the region to trade and capital flows, foreign investment would be drawn to this cheap labor, and the increased competition would force changes in the "productivity" of domestic capital.[40] This would help to catalyze a transformation in the region's economy "from public, state-dominated to private, market-oriented activities; and from protected, import-substitution to competitive, export-oriented activities."[41]

In line with this logic, policy makers in the four countries were urged to quickly cut tariffs, eliminate nontariff barriers, depreciate the real exchange rate, reduce regulation, and open up to foreign investment in both industry and services.[42] Import tariffs were slashed by 30–50 percent through the 2000s.[43] Governments moved to abolish any legal distinction between foreign and domestic investors in most economic sectors, permitted the free repatriation of profits, and drastically shrank state support to domestic industries.[44] Special economic zones sprang up across the region—aiming to attract foreign investment by offering incentives such as reduced or zero corporate tax rates, cheaper prices for land rental, and subsidies for hiring.

These policies were conceived very much as a single package. Opening up to the world market did not just mean the reduction of tariffs or the liberalization of foreign capital flows but was also predicated on the privatization and deregulation of telecommunications, transport, and financial services—described as "behind-the-border trade and investment constraints" by IFIs.[45] In this sense, the agenda of trade and investment liberalization helped to lock in an overall policy trajectory across the entire economy. Moreover, this combination of policies clearly constituted a self-reinforcing cycle. Countries became increasingly dependent upon capital inflows, domestic industries were unable to compete against foreign-produced commodities, and a further stage of liberalization was required to incentivize the investment climate in competition with neighboring countries or regions. Taken in conjunction with the privatization of state-owned firms, the combined effects meant that the general character of a country's production and consumption was ever more determined by the patterns and needs of capital accumulation beyond the national scale.

The substantial impact of these changes on the structural characteristics of both capital and labor is well illustrated in the textiles and garments industry—one of the most important non-oil industrial sectors in the region. In 1993, textiles and garments constituted 37.8 percent of all manufacturing employment in Morocco, 38.9 percent in Tunisia, 29 percent in Egypt, and 10 percent in Jordan.[46] For Morocco and Tunisia, textiles and garments remained the leading employment sector throughout the 2000s. In Egypt, the industry ranks second only to food manufacturing, with the country's Misr Fine Spinning and Weaving representing the largest textile company in Africa and the Middle East, employing more than twenty-five thousand workers. In addition to the industry's huge workforce, textiles and garments also constitute a significant proportion of nonagricultural exports—for Tunisia, around 40 percent of the country's entire exports during the first half of the 2000s.

Despite the ongoing importance of the sector to each country's political economy, the last twenty years have seen a sweeping decline in wages and conditions and a major restructuring of ownership patterns and industrial structures. This began with accession to the WTO, which meant that cheaper clothes and textiles entered domestic markets as import barriers came down, placing enormous pressure on domestic companies. In Egypt, sales of clothing by local producers fell by half between 2000 and 2004, as foreign competitors drove Egyptian firms out of the domestic market.[47] Textile and clothing imports grew by around 500 percent from 2000 to 2008 while domestic production stagnated.[48] As import barriers dropped, larger companies began to shift toward export-oriented production. Often these export industries were located in specially created economic zones, where labor and environmental laws were lax and foreign investments were granted preferential tax and other investment incentives.

Initially exports grew rapidly, to Europe for Morocco and Tunisia, and to the United States for Egypt and Jordan through the QIZs. But in the mid-2000s all four countries were severely hit by the end of a key GATT protocol, the Multi Fibre Arrangement (MFA). The MFA had set quotas on the amount of textiles and garments that countries in the global South could export to the North; it was the central agreement governing world trade in textiles and garments from 1974 to 2004. Its termination on January 1, 2005, meant that the most important markets for textile and garment exports, the EU and the United States, were opened to Chinese and other, potentially cheaper, exports. The increased competition placed further pressure on MENA producers. According to the World Bank, textile and clothing exports to the European Union fell by 5.8 percent in Tunisia, 7.4 percent in Morocco, and 13 percent in Jordan in the year after the MFA agreement expired. In Tunisia, job losses were estimated between thirty-five thousand and fifty thousand between 2000 and 2005, the higher figure equivalent to 20 percent of the sector's workforce. In Morocco, the number of people employed in the clothing industry fell by 10 percent from 2003 to 2007, with one in ten of the country's clothing and textile companies closing during that period, according to the Moroccan Textile Producers Association (AMITH).[49]

In the lead-up to the end of the MFA, the World Bank called on Morocco, Tunisia, Jordan, and Egypt to "lower labor costs, increase productivity, and improve access to cheap inputs" in an attempt to remain competitive.[50] This was necessary, the Bank commented, despite the fact that costs of labor in the textile and garment sectors of Egypt and Jordan—$0.82/hour and $0.46/hour, respectively, *inclusive* of all social costs—were already "lower than or comparable to those of most Asian exporters." Morocco and Tunisia had costs less than "some Eastern European countries and Turkey" ($2.56/hour and $2.05/hour, respectively).[51] In order to achieve a reduction in costs, the Bank urged countries especially to draw in the large, underemployed population of women into the textile and garment labor force—not because of concerns about gender equality, but because the very large wage gap between women and men could provide a comparative advantage to the MENA region.[52] The World Bank put forth Mexico as the model to emulate—low-wage manufacturing zones where foreign-owned factories produced for export markets (*maquiladoras*) and women constituted more than half of total employment.[53]

These exhortations to drive down conditions were largely fulfilled. Governments moved to privatize major textile and spinning mills (particularly in Egypt) and passed laws that further deregulated the labor market. The net result was a severe deterioration in labor rights and wages, facilitated by the growth in informal work conditions and the increasing exploitation of women in "micro" or small enterprises where minimum wage, social security, and other legal rights were not in effect. Female employment in the textile and garment industry grew particularly high in Tunisia, Jordan, and Morocco—reaching 65, 70, and 80 percent, respectively, of total employment in the industry. Egypt had relatively fewer women working in textiles and garments—approximately 15 percent in 2008, although this figure does not accurately capture the large informal sector in which women are predominant.[54]

These trends of feminization and poor working conditions helped to reinforce particular forms of integration into the world market. Each country became essentially a platform for cheap labor, in which clothing was "cut, made, and trimmed" according to the specifications of international firms. Morocco and Tunisia were tightly affixed to European markets and investment, with large Italian, Spanish, French, and German companies setting up in their export zones to produce for the European market. Both countries now send around 90 percent of their apparel exports to the EU and are the top two MENA exporters to the area. In Tunisia, where 2,100 firms employed more than 200,000 workers in 2008, an ILO report noted that an estimated 68 percent of the contracts in the textile industry were temporary and 19 percent were nonstandard—confirmation of how important labor market deregulation was to the industry.[55] In Morocco, 150,000 workers are employed in registered firms with equal or greater numbers estimated to work in the informal sector, including a significant number of children. One study found women workers in factories supplying Spanish companies working fifty-four hours per week for less than \$1/hour.[56] European foreign investment in the sector typically takes place in joint ventures with large domestic conglomerates, indicative of the way that a domestic North African bourgeoisie has been adjoined to foreign capital, with each benefiting from the general downgrading of wages and conditions.

Jordan differs somewhat from Morocco and Tunisia in that 93 percent of textile exports are shipped to the United States through factories located in QIZs. The majority of these factories are foreign-owned, mostly by Asian and Indian investors, and are "full package suppliers"—sourcing fabric, designing, and assembling clothes for sale to the United States. Unlike in North Africa, the vast majority of workers in the QIZs are migrant women from Asia (Bangladesh, China, and Sri Lanka, and to a lesser extent India and the Philippines). According to reports from the mid-2000s, working conditions in many of these QIZ factories were akin to involuntary servitude, in which workers were placed in debt bondage, compelled to continue working in order to pay off money owed to recruiting agents. The US National Labor Coalition alleged in 2006 that more than ten thousand migrant workers had had their passports confiscated by factories in the QIZs. Despite claims by the Jordanian government that these abuses would be addressed, a 2010 report by the US Department of State noted that cases of forced labor, physical violence, and the withholding of wages were still present in the QIZs.[57]

Egypt's clothing exports are more diversified than the other three cases, and the country also has a much larger domestic market. About 40 percent of Egypt's clothing exports go to the United States, largely produced in about five hundred factories located in QIZs. Another 30 percent is sent to the EU and is manufactured in non-QIZ industrial zones. International companies such as Marks & Spencer, GAP, Walmart, Levi Strauss, Target, and Calvin Klein source their clothes from Egyptian factories. The structure of the industry is marked by a pronounced vertical integration—ranging from cotton harvesting, spinning, and weaving to manufacturing and distributing clothes. Traditionally, state-owned companies were dominant, but this shifted dramatically following the privatization wave initiated in the mid-2000s. In 2003, public firms held a 90 percent share of spinning and 30 percent of apparel production; by 2009 this had shrunk to 50 percent and 10 percent, respectively.[58] Privatization corresponded with a severe deterioration in work conditions. Egyptian garment workers experienced a 4 percent drop in real wages between 1999 and 2007 and the workforce plummeted from 343,000 in 2000 to 244,646 in 2008.[59] One of the largest producers in the country, Shebin El-Kom Textile Company, privatized in 1997, laid off more than 50 percent of its workforce over the latter half of the 2000s.[60] As privatization proceeded, foreign investors entered the sector in a major way, with FDI increasing by nearly 300 percent during the thirteen years from 1995 to 2007. Much of this has been from Asian countries and the Gulf region, with Arab investments increasing from 2 percent of total investment in textile and clothing in 1995 to 14 percent in 2007.[61] The net result has been the consolidation of large, vertically integrated capital in the industry—both domestic and foreign-owned.[62]

The Power of Finance

A final, critical element of the neoliberal package has been the development and restructuring of financial markets. This restructuring was characterized by a series of standard steps advocated by IFIs, notably (1) the removal of government controls or influence on credit allocation, lending policies and interest rates; (2) opening up the banking sector to foreign competition and privatization of state-run banks; and (3) introduction of a range of non-bank financial markets such as stocks, mortgage, insurance, and bond markets. These measures were broadly begun in the mid-1990s as conditionalities of World Bank and IMF loans as well as requirements connected to WTO accession.

Interest rates and lending were liberalized in Tunisia (1987), Jordan (1990), Morocco (1990–1996), and Egypt (early 1990s), which meant that governments no longer controlled the distribution of credit and commercial banks were able to lend with minimal restrictions. Prior to this point, banks had been compelled to lend to the state, and private firms tended to rely upon short-term loans or medium-term lending provided to strategic sectors by state-owned development banks. The liberalization of credit meant a very rapid increase in lending to the private sector—the ratio of domestic credit to the private sector as a proportion of GDP more than doubled in Egypt from 1992 to 2002 (22.3 percent to 54.7 percent), and also increased significantly in Morocco (26.4 percent to 43.4 percent in 2002), and Jordan (55.9 percent to 72.7 percent).[63] Only in Tunisia, where earlier government lending had led to large levels of surplus liquidity, was there a slight decrease (66.2 percent to 62.3 percent).

This increased credit to the private sector was directed to a small number of borrowers associated with influential businessmen and large conglomerates, and thus was an integral part of the state-led support of the capitalist class. In the case of Egypt, one commentator calculated that in early 2000, 42 percent of the 206 billion Egyptian pounds extended to the private sector went to only 343 clients, with 28 of them taking 13 percent of the total.[64] By 2002, nearly 18 percent of nonperforming loans were held by only 12 clients. He points out that well-connected business groups were generally able to borrow with insufficient collateral and no formal procedures. In many cases, these borrowers were tightly connected to the Mubarak regime and the state—the so-called *nuwab al-quroud* (Loan MPs) were indicted in the 1990s for running a loan distribution network connecting public banks, businesses, and the political system.[65]

As banks increased their lending to the private sector, the banks themselves underwent changes of ownership. In 2001, state-owned banks had held 79 percent of banking assets in Egypt. By 2007, following a wave of banking privatizations, this had dropped to 55 percent. Similarly large reductions were seen in Morocco (79 percent to 38 percent) and Tunisia (53 percent to 42 percent). Jordan does not have any state-owned banks.[66] Foreign banks also entered local markets following the entry into force of the General Agreement on Trade in Services (GATS) as a WTO treaty in 1995, which obligated states to open up their financial sectors to foreign investment. From 1995 to 2009, foreign banks as a proportion of total banks increased from 36 to 50 percent in Morocco, 6 to 52 percent in Egypt, 11 to 40 percent in Jordan, and 36 to 50 percent in Tunisia.[67] Assets controlled by these foreign banks also increased—reaching 23 percent of total banking assets for Egypt and Jordan in 2009, 34 percent for Morocco, and 28 percent for Tunisia.[68]

In addition to opening up branches, foreign banks also moved to buy up domestic banks. In Jordan, by 2007, the three largest banks were all majority foreign-owned.[69] In Tunisia, four of the top ten largest banks were foreign-controlled and three had significant minority ownership.[70] Four of the seven largest Egyptian banks were foreign-owned in 2008, although the top three remained state-owned.[71] Alongside the growing domination of private capital over the banking sector, there developed a very pronounced concentration of control: in Jordan, the three largest banks held 47.8 percent of assets, in Egypt 53.88 percent, in Tunisia 28.64 percent, and in Morocco 64 percent (figures for 2007; 2006 for Morocco).[72]

This growing power of finance was further strengthened by the expansion of equity markets. Although stock exchanges already existed in Morocco (est. 1929) and Tunisia (1969), these had remained largely dormant (with market capitalization less than 1 percent of GDP) until reforms in the early 1990s made it easier for companies to buy and sell shares.[73] Stock markets were reactivated in Egypt in 1992 and set up for the first time in Jordan in 1997. With wealth increasingly circulated and amassed through shareholdings, the stock market became a prime mechanism for facilitating the accumulation of the largest corporate groups. In Egypt, the average size of a company listed on the country's stock exchange grew more than twelve-fold from 2001 to 2007—total market capitalization rose by 700 percent to reach 86 percent of GDP, up from 30 percent in 2001.[74] In Jordan and Morocco, the size of the stock market increased by similar amounts (600 percent and 500 percent growth in market capitalization, respectively). Concurrently, market capitalization became concentrated in a tiny number of companies. In Tunisia, for example, 10 percent of market capitalization in 2007 comprised just one company, the Poulina Group (discussed further in the next chapter).[75] Concentration was even more pronounced in Jordan and Morocco, with one privately owned bank, the Arab Bank, constituting more than one-third of the Amman Stock Exchange, and Maroc Telecom, a state telecom privatized in 2001, making up 20 percent of Morocco's market capitalization.[76] In Egypt, companies controlled by just seven families represented more than one-fifth of the country's entire stock exchange capitalization in 2008.[77]

The exponential growth of equity markets was closely linked to the liberalization of real estate and the increasing significance of capital flows through the built environment. This was particularly notable in Egypt, where the government launched an urban development strategy in 1997 focused on the establishment of new cities and the "reclamation" of desert areas. Laws were passed that slashed property taxes and permitted foreign ownership of real estate for the first time. Seventeen cities were planned as part of the new development strategy, with the construction, development, and marketing of these cities managed by private real estate companies involved in a diverse range of sectors such as residential housing, shopping centers and malls, tourism, and hotels. These companies were typically controlled by large private capital groups in partnership with state investments, and included government-owned entities that were soon privatized (e.g., Nasr City Housing and Development, Heliopolis Housing Company), massive construction and industrial companies that expanded into real estate development (e.g., Bahgat Group, Talaat Moustafa Group, Oriental Weavers), new companies established for particular projects (Sixth of October Development and Investment Corporation, Palm Hills Development), and large regional developers, usually GCC-based (Emaar, Solidere, Barwa, Damac). To support these companies, the Egyptian government embarked on a vast sell-off of urban areas by auctioning land at cheap prices or negotiating closed-door agreements with individual companies. Allegations of corrupt transfers of land to private interests were widespread and became a prominent feature of court battles post-January 2011. As private ownership of urban land expanded, real estate companies listed themselves on the Cairo Stock Exchange, thereby attracting additional capital flows from those hoping to benefit from the growing market and contributing to the upward trend of equity prices. From the mid-2000s onwards a flood of capital from the GCC into Egyptian real estate and stock markets markedly reinforced these tendencies, as pools of surplus funds arising from record oil prices sought profitable avenues for investment.

This expansion of Egyptian real estate was critically dependent upon further innovations in finance, notably the establishment of mortgage and bond markets. As the supply of housing grew, banks and other financial institutions were particularly keen to diversify into mortgage lending as the next lucrative component of their credit portfolios. A mortgage law that provided the legislative framework for real estate lending was passed in 2001, and a few years later, leading financial institutions formed the Egyptian Mortgage Refinance Company (EMRC) to provide mortgage refinancing for banks and finance companies. The EMRC bundled together mortgages sold by these companies in bonds, which were offered for sale on Egypt's emerging bond markets. Through this process, the lending base for property development could expand, while the risks arising from these loans were shifted away from the financial institutions themselves. The stock and bond markets thus facilitated the liquification of land and property, turning the bricks and mortar of the built environment into a financial instrument that could be securitized and commodified. In this manner, the mutually reinforcing effects of credit liberalization, the privatization of land and other state assets, and the deepening of bond and equity markets constituted a principal nexus of accumulation for large domestic and foreign conglomerates.

Across the region, financial markets thus underpinned a transformation in the structure and power of the capitalist class itself. The markets permitted a qualitative leap in the scale and scope of capital accumulation, pooling funds from local and regional investors, including those from the state itself. Liberalization of credit, often circulated through real estate markets, fed the growing investment in financial instruments. Large, family-owned conglomerates listed their subsidiaries on the stock markets and thereby expanded their capital base. They also took shares in banks and privatized companies, which were sold through Initial Public Offerings (IPOs) on the new exchanges.[78] In this manner, financial institutions became increasingly interconnected with industry through complex webs of ownership that tied together conglomerates involved in a range of different business activities. In short, financial markets helped to bridge all the components of the neoliberal project—strengthening the power and influence of the largest domestic and foreign conglomerates over every aspect of social life.

Centralization and Authoritarianism—A New Institutionalization of State Power

The policies described above were met with repeated waves of popular protest, including large-scale demonstrations, labor and student strikes, and the emergence of new political forces. Overcoming this resistance was a necessary element to successful implementation of the neoliberal project, and it was accomplished through the consolidation of dictatorships and authoritarian regimes. In Tunisia, the coming to power of Ben Ali in a 1987 coup marked the real commencement of neoliberalism, and foreign governments across Europe and the United States backed his long rule in large part for this reason. For example, the World Bank noted enthusiastically in 1993 that Ben Ali appeared "eager to encourage and accelerate the restructuring and privatization process."[79] Egypt's Mubarak, who succeeded Sadat in 1981, expanded the *infitah* ("opening" or "open door" policy) of his predecessor and was warmly endorsed by the IMF and World Bank with the signing of the 1991 Structural Adjustment Plan. In Morocco, King Hassan II unleashed repeated crackdowns against labor and political movements resisting the Structural Adjustment Plan inaugurated in 1982, repression that came to be known as the "years of lead." Jordan's King Hussein presided over two decades of martial law, authorizing military and security crackdowns on students and others protesting the beginnings of liberalization in the 1980s.

These kings and dictators led the rollback of the limited social gains made in the immediate postindependence period because they were willing to turn their security and military forces against those resisting the new liberalization. They were embraced by IFIs and Western governments alike, who clearly understood their pivotal role in the success of the new economic diktats and knowingly endorsed repeated acts of repression. Of course this relationship between authoritarianism and neoliberalism is not unique to the Arab world (as the examples of Chile, South Korea, and Turkey illustrate), but these essential facts of history remain an inconvenient truth for those who today attempt to link neoliberal reform with "democracy."

At the same time as governments meted out repression against those who resisted the neoliberal turn, the new policies also very much depended upon the cultivation of a domestic social base. A myriad of institutional actors were involved in this process. These included presidents, ruling families, key government ministries (notably ministries of finance), central bank personnel, leading academics, industry lobby groups, and chambers of commerce. Their policy choices helped to advance a shift in the structures of the state itself, acting to protect and foster a powerful bourgeoisie that grew in the interstices of the changing economy. Among this mélange of state and business leaders, the role of international institutions was—as the World Bank put it in a major 2004 study on MENA employment—one of "bringing together the best knowledge, expertise, and experience" in order to establish "priorities and directions for a comprehensive and structured policy reform agenda."[80] This coordinative function, centered on articulating an ideological justification for policy choices, was just as critical to the internal construction of neoliberalism as any external compulsion or conditionalities.

The success of this project depended upon a sharp realignment in the institutional character of the state apparatus itself. This was the other side to authoritarianism, placing the increasingly centralized nature of political decision-making in the hands of a single individual or small, unaccountable committees. By enabling economic policy to become progressively the purview of a tiny few, consciously sequestered from the broader institutions of the state, this institutional restructuring circumvented any opposition from within the bureaucracy or broader society to the new economic measures. It also acted to render obscure exactly what decisions were being made until long after the fact, reducing public debate around the trajectory of neoliberal reform and making it more difficult for labor and social movements to mount successful resistance to these decisions.

An excellent example of this can be seen in the case of Tunisian privatization. Law 89–9, passed soon after Ben Ali came to power, established the framework for the institutional restructuring that would underpin the sell-off of state firms (although, as a World Bank analyst drily noted, "for political and social reasons" the Tunisian government intentionally omitted the word "privatization" from the law itself).[81] With the passing of the new law, decisions about which companies to privatize were concentrated solely in the hands of the prime minister, following the recommendation of a small committee that he chaired, CAREPP (Commission d'Assainissement et de Restructuration des Entreprises à Participation Publique).[82] Another body, the Technical Commission for Restructuring Public Enterprises (CTAREPP), led by an individual appointed by the prime minister, was tasked with developing the overall strategy and "nuts and bolts" for privatization. In this context, it was hard for anyone within or outside the state to oppose or slow down privatization—a feature approved by the World Bank, which noted that Law 89–9 gave a "clear direction . . . and an efficient organizational vehicle to implement the privatization program"[83] and that centralization of decision-making at a high level "defused jurisdictional disputes and rivalries . . . and streamlined the process."[84] As part of its strategy to obfuscate the sale of state firms, CAREPP deliberately chose not to announce in advance which companies were the preferred candidates for privatization, making it difficult for workers to mount any sort of resistance because they were unaware of steps toward a sell-off until late in the process.[85] The World Bank also praised this goal of avoiding the "social consequences of such an announcement [of privatization]" as one that worked "reasonably well" and was "important to create momentum to boost the whole process."[86]

International institutions were not simply external observers that applauded the tight centralization of state power in Tunisia from the sidelines. The IMF included "public sector reform" as a conditionality of the 1986 Structural Adjustment Package and assisted in developing the structures necessary for its implementation. The World Bank provided a $130 million loan in 1989 to aid the functioning of CAREPP and prepare companies for sale. As part of this loan, key elements of legislation—such as the "performance contracts" that public firms were expected to adopt as a prelude to privatization—needed to be agreed to by the World Bank prior to their approval by CAREPP.[87] Even more directly, a paid consultant of USAID served as a member of CTAREPP and as an advisor to CAREPP from 1988 to 1990.[88] The Japanese government helped with funds to privatize cement factories and the dairy industry. The United Nations Development Program (UNDP) provided technical assistance to help with the listing of privatized firms on the stock market. All these organizations were thus consciously complicit in fostering the authoritarianism and centralization of political power that accompanied the development of the neoliberal project.

This restructuring of state institutions was replicated across the Middle East. In Morocco, telecommunications privatization was driven by King Hassan II and his son, Mohammed VI, who established a group called G14 to push the case for liberalization. G14 included the chief executives of the state telecom carrier and the main new private telecom, and essentially wrote the legislation for privatization that was later enacted through a series of royal decrees.[89] Likewise, Jordan, Egypt, and Lebanon have units or ministerial committees dedicated to fast-tracking the decisions around privatization, writing legislation, and proposing targets for sale. In all cases, the development and execution of economic policy has been distanced as far as possible from any control or influence of legislative bodies within the state.

Decentralization and Autonomy

The growing centralization of political power confirms that neoliberalism is very much a state-led project, not, as is commonly assumed, one that has meant the undermining or eroding of the state apparatus. But the centralization of decision-making has occurred concurrently with an opposite trend of decentralization, in which increasing autonomy is given to government departments in their planning and, most importantly, their budgetary decisions. This decentralization has been ideologically driven by the ethos of "new public management," through which government departments are forced to compete against one another for central funding, and market-based incentives increasingly become part of budgetary calculations. Departmental success is measured through a "performance budgeting" schema that is ultimately concerned with the financial cost-effectiveness of outputs. It is a strategy that can be marketed as being "more efficient," "less bureaucratic," and "more flexible," but essentially compels individual government departments to take greater responsibility for fiscal matters (both expenditure and revenue). Given the vast needs and the general lack of resources, this displacement of fiscal control helps facilitate the implementation of fees-based service provision, in other words, to accelerate the commodification of public sector activities.[90]

In Jordan, the third stage of the World Bank's 2001 Public Sector Reform Loans (PSRL) provides a good example of this centralization/decentralization dialectic. Under pressure from the Bank, control over the Jordanian budget was tightly centralized in the General Budget Department, while, simultaneously, different ministries and departments were given considerable operational autonomy. Instead of funding these departments on the basis of annual estimations of input costs, "performance budgeting" was implemented in each sector and department, with funding tied to the cost-effectiveness of the outputs achieved. Coupled with the decentralization of operational control at the local level, the emphasis on cost-effectiveness created a continual pressure to reduce costs, cut services, and find other means to lower departmental budgets. This structural configuration meant that the government could pass a central decision—as it did in March 2004 when it issued a blanket directive requiring all ministries to cut utility bills by 20 percent—and leave each department to determine how it could best meet the new fiscal requirements.[91]

Likewise, in Egypt, a major feature of the institutional restructuring of the state was the agglomeration of state-owned enterprises into single, sector-wide holding companies, usually through the simple decree of Mubarak, that were progressively cut off from state subsidies and forced to compete on the market. Although they remained "state-owned," this restructuring was consciously understood as the first step toward privatization. Holding companies were required to adopt the basic principles of performance budgeting and profit maximization, with management given substantial autonomy in workforce matters and fiscal decisions. In the case of water, for example, a presidential decree in 2004 rationalized institutions involved in the sector into a single holding company, the Holding Company for Water and Wastewater (HCWW). The company's budget was no longer under the control and supervision of the People's Assembly (the Egyptian parliament), but a separate board of directors who were encouraged to seek joint ventures with private companies, offer shares, and make a profit through the distribution and sale of water.[92] Around the same time, the Egyptian Water Regulatory Agency was established with a mandate—alongside controlling service delivery and ensuring policies and regulations were followed—of promoting PPPs in the water sector.[93] In its first few years of operation, the HCWW underwent an institutional restructuring that reduced the size of its workforce and doubled the price of water for domestic users. From June 2007 to January 2008, more than forty demonstrations around water—dubbed the "thirst protests"—were noted across Egypt in response to the increasing inaccessibility of water as a result of these measures.[94] These included protests against an HCWW-affiliated company in the Kafr al-Shaikh province, in the north of Egypt, because it was diverting water away from their town to investors in a nearby summer tourist resort.

These examples show that the process of neoliberal reform is driven by the ability of a highly centralized political core to frame the context of decentralized implementation of its policies. This dialectic of centralization and decentralization has been the distinguishing feature of the institutional restructuring of the neoliberal state in the Middle East region—rhetorically founded upon "good governance" and "accountability," while simultaneously strengthening the tendencies toward authoritarianism. By creating this form of decentralized, horizontal competition between different parts of the state, vertically constrained through the concentration of political power at the center, neoliberal governments naturalize the reduction of state activities as a normal part of everyday operations. This obfuscates the locus of power within state structures, shaping the reform process as a multitude of decentralized management decisions that are difficult to oppose and organize against because of their diffuse nature, and whose ultimate source of power is hidden by the sequestration of undemocratic and unaccountable committees within the state itself.

The State as Conduit of Wealth

In line with these changing political and institutional forms of neoliberal rule, the state has also undergone a transformation in its fiscal structure. A key aspect of this has been a generalized cutback in social spending as more services are shifted to the private sector. Government expenditure as a proportion of GDP fell sharply in Egypt, Morocco, Jordan, and Tunisia through the 2000s. The main reason for this was the shrinking public sector wage bill—the share of wages and salaries in government expenditure declined 10 percentage points in Tunisia (65 percent in 2003 to 55 percent in 2008), 8 percentage points in Egypt (26 percent in 2001 to 18 percent in 2007), 4 percentage points in Morocco (51 percent in 2005 to 47 percent in 2008), and 4 percentage points in Jordan (20 percent in 2001 to 16 percent in 2008).[95] This trend reflected both the success of ongoing privatization efforts and the downward pressure on public sector wages. Social services were particularly hard hit by these cuts. Education spending, for example, fell by large amounts in Jordan (15 to 12.1 percent of government expenditure), Egypt (7 to 5.7 percent), and Morocco (27 to 25.7 percent) between 2004 and 2010.

A major target of cuts to social spending has been the state subsidy system—in particular, government subsidies for food and fuel. These subsidies, as noted in chapter 2, were an important feature of regime legitimacy in the postindependence period and provided a measurable level of access to basic food staples for the poor. From the 1980s to the early 2000s, subsidy levels were slashed across the MENA region as part of structural adjustment packages. In Egypt, for example, spending on subsidies dropped from 14 percent of government expenditures in 1980–81 to 5.6 percent in 1996–97.[96] The Egyptian government adopted a variety of strategies to achieve this reduction: removing meat, fish, chicken, and rice from the list and dropping the number of subsidized food items to just four—*baladi* bread,[97] coarse flour, edible oil, and sugar; reducing the number of people entitled to receive subsidies; allowing the price of sugar and bread to rise; and reducing the quality and portion size of subsidized items.[98] In Jordan, food subsidies were essentially eliminated in the 1990s and replaced by cash transfers to particular sections of the population.[99] Tunisia and Morocco also saw a substantial drop in the number of subsidized commodities and changes to entitlement schemes, which excluded much of the urban and rural poor.[100]

Not all government spending, however, has been equally targeted for reduction. Confirming the ongoing linkages between authoritarian rule and neoliberalism, the share of government spending on the military and internal security has tended to remain very high and in some cases has actually increased. In 2010, the military and internal security constituted 34.1 percent of Jordanian government expenditure, 12.9 percent in Egypt, 11 percent in Morocco, and 5 percent in Tunisia (Tunisia's figures only include military spending).[101] In Jordan and Egypt, expenditure on the military and public security exceeded the combined education and health budgets every year from 2005 to 2010 and, in contrast to these social services, assumed a growing share of government expenditure over the same period. Moreover, these figures likely understate the true extent of military and security budgets, as the region's authoritarian governments rarely provide transparency in this area.

Occurring alongside these shifts in expenditure has been a transformation in the nature of state revenues. There are two important aspects to this. First, in line with supporting domestic and foreign capital, governments have moved to reduce corporate and income taxes and replace these with a value-added tax (VAT), which disproportionally affects the poor.[102] These changes to tax regimes were often directly initiated and written by international institutions. In Egypt, for example, a $60 million USAID project was launched in 1989 to restructure the Egyptian tax system. This project saw the introduction of a general sales tax in 1991 to replace the previous consumption tax, considered to "discriminate against imports" because it charged higher amounts on goods brought in from outside the country. The income tax structure was also changed, with the highest corporate tax rate reduced from 78 to 48 percent.[103] In early 2005, a new law was passed that dropped the highest corporate rate down to 20 percent, with no differentiation between family businesses and large foreign corporations. The same law slashed the highest personal income bracket from 40 to 20 percent.[104] With only four brackets defined by the law, someone earning around $550 a month was in the same category as a billionaire.[105] In Morocco, a VAT system was also introduced, with changes in 2005 and 2006 increasing the rates on items that had previously been exempt, including basic food items such as butter and salt. Revenue from the VAT grew at 20 percent a year from 2005 to 2008, reaching 33 percent of the government's total fiscal revenue in 2008.[105] While Morocco moved to adopt the VAT system, the top marginal personal income tax rate was slashed—dropping by half between 1985 and 2002.[106] Likewise, in Jordan and Tunisia during recent years, corporate tax rates have been severely cut at the same time as a VAT system was introduced.[107]

The second major shift in the way the state funds itself has been an increasing reliance on debt instruments such as government bonds. However, in contrast with the 1980s, during which debt obligations to external lenders reached the astronomical levels detailed in the previous chapter, the recent period has seen a move away from external borrowing toward the issuing of government bonds to domestic investors. Egypt, Jordan, Morocco, and Tunisia have been at the forefront of this change, which requires the deepening of bond markets, as noted above. All four countries now issue domestically traded debt on their financial markets and have come to depend heavily on these markets for state financing.[108] One of the consequences is that interest repayments on public debt have become a major drain on government spending. Egypt stands out in this regard, with interest repayments on domestic debt as a proportion of government expenditure reaching 22.8 percent in 2010—more than total spending on education, health, and food subsidies combined.[109] Most of Egypt's debt payments (58 percent) flow to banks, financial institutions, and other investors operating in domestic markets. In this sense, the state has become even more plainly a conduit for the transfer of wealth to large financial institutions through the mechanism of the state budget. The chains of debt remain very much in place, only reconstituted in a different form.

Conclusion

In every sense, the last three decades have seen the sustained erosion of basic economic and social rights as a direct consequence of neoliberal policies. Hardest hit is an entire generation of youth, particularly young women, who have been condemned to a future of unemployment, low-wage work, and social exclusion. This situation is the logical and predictable endpoint of neoliberal reform, one that has been socially engineered in a highly conscious manner by local elites and international institutions—not an accidental outcome of policy mishaps or the arbitrariness of authoritarian rulers. These patterns are not unique to the four countries that have formed the focus of this chapter; all countries in the MENA region have followed the same basic trajectory, albeit at differing pace and scale.

Policies of privatization and labor market deregulation had a dramatic impact on wages and the security of employment. Companies found it easier to fire people at will, and the use of temporary contracts vastly increased the overall precariousness of work. These characteristics were reflected in consistently high unemployment figures, with Jordan registering an average of 14.1 percent over the 2000s, Tunisia 14.6 percent, Morocco 11 percent, and Egypt 10 percent.[110] As bad as they are, these official figures hide the much worse situation faced by youth; around 30 percent of young people have consistently been out of work in Tunisia, Jordan, and Egypt throughout most of the last decade. Prior to the global economic crisis, this figure was among the highest of any region in the world and is even more striking when placed alongside the extremely low labor market participation of youth, with only around one-third of youth in work or actively seeking employment (it should be emphasized that those individuals not seeking work are not counted in employment figures).[112] Not only are most young people jobless or not in the labor market, but the majority of the unemployed are also often youth—in Egypt, for example, about three-quarters of the unemployed are young.[113] This has significant social implications for countries where the governing elites are frequently aged in their seventies.

Moreover, in contrast to patterns typically observed elsewhere in the world, unemployment is particularly bad among university graduates. The public sector traditionally provided jobs for young people graduating from tertiary education, women in particular, and with the cuts to the public sector this avenue is no longer available. For Egypt and Jordan, nearly half of all females between fifteen and twenty-four are unemployed, double the rate of young men.[114] In Jordan, where the private sector went from employing 42 percent of the workforce in 1995 to employing 71 percent in 2006, university graduates constitute the second-largest group of unemployed people.[115] The majority of these jobless are women graduates, who had an unemployment rate of 26.1 percent in 2006—nearly three times that of male graduates. In Egypt, the largest numbers of any category of unemployed people are those with a university education, with female university graduates making up nearly one-quarter of all unemployed females in 2006. In all MENA countries, rates of female unemployment are among the worst in the world.[116]

These painful figures, however, are themselves a substantial understatement of the extent of joblessness and job precariousness. The definition of "employed" in the region typically covers those working just a handful of hours and, most importantly, is a questionable descriptor for the huge numbers of people working in the informal sector. In Egypt, Morocco, and Tunisia, between 40 and 50 percent of all nonagricultural employment is in the informal sector, a figure that is among the fastest-growing of any place on the planet.[117] One researcher has found that three-quarters of new labor market entrants in Egypt from 2000–2005 joined the informal sector, up from only one-fifth in the early 1970s.[118] Work in this sector is highly precarious, unpredictable, and lacking in effective social protection. The enormous scale of this informality is the direct consequence of three policies in particular: the commodification of land (see chapter 4), the privatization of state-owned firms, and the deregulation of labor markets. It is paralleled spatially in the proliferation of large peri-urban settlements of dilapidated housing that surround most of the large metropolises in North Africa, zones of existence that carry critical political and social meaning (see chapter 7).[119]

Levels of unemployment and the expansion of the informal sector are themselves indicative of the growing scale of poverty. In the two countries where longitudinal wage statistics are available, Egypt and Jordan, real wage levels have worsened as a result of informalization and precariousness. In Egypt, median real hourly wages declined by 6.7 percent between 1988 and 2006. The decline in private sector wages over the same period was 16 percent.[120] In Jordan, real wages in manufacturing declined by 1.5 percent from 2001 to 2008.[121] Figures from a 2006 national survey in Jordan found that the poorest 30 percent of the population earns only 11 percent of the total income.[122] According to the most recent statistics, the number of people living below the poverty line is around 40 percent in both Egypt and Morocco and 23.8 percent in Tunisia.[123] Combined with cuts to public spending, this has had a disastrous impact on social conditions—between 2000 and 2006, 20 percent of children in Egypt and Morocco demonstrated stunted growth as a result of malnutrition,[124] and illiteracy remains at astonishingly high levels in Morocco (44 percent of the adult population), Egypt (34 percent), and Tunisia (22 percent).[125]

These bleak social trends, however, are only one side of the story over the last two decades. With the region inserted into the world market on the basis of its cheap labor and a flexible, informalized workforce—fully subordinated to the needs of accumulation in the EU and the United States—neoliberal policies have acted to nurture the growth of large domestic capital and provided enormously profitable opportunities for foreign investors. This is powerfully confirmed by the region's rapid economic growth—Morocco, Egypt, Tunisia, and Jordan all experienced a real annual GDP growth rate that averaged over 5 percent from 2003 to 2008, with GDP per capita rising between 20 and 30 percent over the same six-year period.[126] As this has proceeded, ownership of the major economic sectors has become increasingly concentrated in the hands of the tiny few who have been enriched by neoliberal reform.

These trends point to an incontrovertible conclusion: the transformation of the last period has not simply been one of growing poverty, unemployment, or social exclusion; it has also involved, at its most fundamental level, the growth and consolidation of a domestic capitalist class, tightly linked through myriad channels of accumulation to the state and foreign companies. Immiseration and accumulation are forcefully connected—neoliberalism has effectively acted to redistribute wealth from the region's poor to the wealthiest layers of society by subsuming every aspect of social life under the logic of capital. This radical reconstitution of class power remains at the core of the neoliberal project in the MENA region—and is an essential element to any assessment of the revolutionary dynamics of 2011.

CHAPTER 4
Capitalism and Agrarian Change in North Africa

Agriculture has long been a central feature of life in the Middle East. It was in Mesopotamia that one of the first settled agriculture societies arose, spreading westward across the coastal areas of the Mediterranean Sea and Europe and then eastward to the Indus River Valley. The region's immense agricultural resources sustained successive empires across ancient Iraq, Egypt, and Persia. Thousands of years later, the Romans spent nearly six centuries occupying the coastal area of North Africa, drawing annual tributes of grain and olive oil to feed their population back in Rome. In the 1800s, colonial occupations were established that aimed at subordinating the region's plentiful reserves of wheat, wine, and oils to European control. The Fertile Crescent, stretching from Iraq through Syria to the coasts of the Mediterranean, was named as such by a nineteenth-century American archaeologist because of these vast agricultural riches.

By the end of the twentieth century, however, the region was firmly mired in a decades-long agricultural disaster. Poverty among the rural populace had reached levels much worse than that in urban areas, with endemic landlessness and a dispossessed rural proletariat making up a large proportion of the population in the countryside. Most significantly, a region that had once supplied food to the world was now deeply reliant upon food imports for basic survival. Indeed, as of 2009, imports accounted for half of the region's food consumption, making MENA the most food import–dependent region in the world.[1] The increasing linkage with the world market meant, moreover, that food price rises—a lasting feature of global agriculture in the twenty-first century—would profoundly affect living standards in urban and rural areas alike. Yet the outcomes of these trends were wildly uneven. While the Gulf states were embarking on a worldwide grab of fertile farmland, Yemen, the poorest country in the Middle East, was battling one of the worst famines in its history.

How did this agricultural decline come about? This chapter analyzes the transformation of the region's agricultural sector, with a particular focus on the North African countries of Morocco, Egypt, and Tunisia. These three countries are among the most agriculture-dependent countries in the Arab world and provide excellent case studies for the wider region. As table 4.1 indicates, each has a large proportion of its total population living in rural areas (ranging from 33 to 57 percent). Although production levels can fluctuate widely from year to year because of periodic drought (particularly in Morocco), agriculture is a major component of overall economic production. In Egypt and Morocco, agriculture made up around 14 to 15 percent of GDP in 2010; in Tunisia the ratio was smaller but still significant (8 percent). In regards to trade, agricultural produce ranged from 9.2 to 11 percent of the value of overall exports in each of these states from 2005 to 2009.

Table 4.1: Selected Agricultural Characteristics: Egypt, Morocco, Tunisia

	% Total land that is arable (2010)	% Agricultural land equipped for irrigation (2010)	Agriculture as % of GDP (2010)	Agricultural exports as % of overall merchandise exports (2005–2009)	Rural population as % of total population (2010)
Egypt	3	99	14	9.7	57
Morocco	18	4.8	15	11.0	42
Tunisia	17.4	4.5	8	9.2	33

Source: Calculated by author from Food and Agricultural Organization of the UN (FAO) statistics. Egypt figures for rural population need to be treated with caution (see discussion below).

The significance of agriculture to these North African countries stretches back through the colonial period. Under colonialism, Morocco and Tunisia were characterized by a bifurcated agricultural system—most domestic farmers worked small plots of land, depended upon rain, and grew cereals or tended livestock.[2] Importantly, much of the land in this sector was subject to collective or tribal forms of ownership and use. Alongside this "traditional" sector there existed an irrigated zone of large-scale commercial farming, controlled by European settlers and a handful of large domestic farmers, who produced crops—typically fruit, vegetables, olives, or wine—for export to

Europe. With most land across North Africa arid and unsuitable for farming, this division between export-oriented irrigated crops and rain-fed local agriculture has remained a clear marker of wealth and power into the contemporary era. Egypt differed from this bifurcated system and was integrated into the world market during the colonial period through its large exports of cotton. It remains the only country in North Africa where virtually all agriculture is irrigated. Moreover, in contrast to the forms of collective ownership in the rest of North Africa, most agricultural land in Egypt has been privately owned following laws passed in the mid-nineteenth century.[3]

With the end of formal colonial rule and occupation in the mid-twentieth century, newly independent governments in North Africa were faced with the legacy of sharp inequalities in land ownership. In Egypt, British colonialism had rested upon large domestic landowners linked to a ruling monarchy—0.4 percent of landowners held 33 percent of the country's agricultural land, and 44 percent of rural households were landless on the eve of the 1952 revolution.[4] Morocco and Tunisia also suffered severe inequalities in landownership, although, as settler colonies, their land was divided between foreign and domestic owners. A small number of European settlers controlled roughly 20 percent of the arable area in Tunisia and 13 percent in Morocco. Large domestic landowners held a further 15 percent and 21 percent, respectively.[5]

These extreme inequalities meant that land reform was a critical feature of decolonization. New governments took over much of the agricultural land that had been controlled by European settlers or large landowners, redistributing parts of these areas to poorer, landless farmers or turning them into state-owned and collective farms. Land reform was particularly far-reaching in Egypt, where independence necessitated the weakening of an established landed class that had mediated colonial rule. Between 1952 and 1970, Nasser redistributed land to around 350,000 families, setting a maximum ceiling on landholdings in an attempt to reverse the extreme concentration of landownership. Moreover, tenants were given much stronger rights to the land—they could not be evicted as long as they paid rent, tenancy was inheritable, and rent levels were capped at nominal levels.[6] In contrast to the Egyptian experience, independence in Morocco and Tunisia took a more propitiatory path, with power gradually transferred to an indigenous ruling class of large rural landowners who had prospered during the colonial period.[7] Nevertheless, despite the sustained strength of indigenous landowners in the two countries, a significant proportion of land that had been controlled by Europeans was taken over as state property by the newly independent governments. In addition, much of the land in both countries remained under traditional, communal forms of ownership.

The question of agriculture was placed at the heart of the neoliberal project because of these powerful experiences of land reform and the ongoing centrality of rural life to social structures in North Africa. Fundamental changes in the use and ownership of land, food production, and the existing patterns of rural existence were all necessary prerequisites to neoliberalism's wider consolidation. As always, this process was deeply embedded within the development of the global economy. From this vantage point, the aim of this chapter is to trace the ongoing changes in the rural class structures of North Africa—developments that are pushed by capitalist accumulation and link flows of capital and labor across different geographical scales (rural/urban, regional/global). The chapter begins by describing the basic thrust of neoliberal policy in agriculture, focusing in particular on the reversal of land reform and the commodification of land and other key inputs. It then turns to the ways in which this transformation has underpinned the proletarianization of rural life and simultaneously fostered the development of large agribusiness that now dominates much of agricultural production.

Structural Adjustment and the Agribusiness Revolution

The changes in North Africa's agriculture and farming systems have occurred at varying paces but are nonetheless marked by a common logic and consistent array of policies. This consistency points to the fact that—perhaps more than any other sector—external institutions have heavily steered the development of agricultural policies. One of the most important of these institutions is the World Bank, whose overall strategy for rural development has been incorporated almost seamlessly into government plans across the region. This strategy has been expressed and developed through a series of lengthy policy documents, including *Rural Development: From Vision to Action* (1997), *Reaching the Rural Poor* (2003), *Agricultural Growth for the Poor: An Agenda for Development* (2005), *World Development Report 2008: Agriculture for Development*, and *Agricultural Innovation Systems: An Investment Sourcebook* (2012). Other international institutions, notably the UN's International Fund for Agricultural Development (IFAD), the African Development Bank (AfDB), USAID, and similar bilateral organizations, have largely followed the lead of the World Bank in this respect.

The guiding thread of the World Bank's orientation has been to shift agricultural activities toward forms of private ownership that are tightly linked to the world market. The Bank has expressed this logic clearly and frankly, noting in its 1997 *Rural Development: From Vision to Action* that rural development requires "competitive agriculture and agribusiness as the main engines of growth" in which "rural people are linked to well-functioning markets for products, inputs, and finance."[8] According to the Bank, the policy conclusion is self-evident: "Wherever possible, the private sector must be mobilized to provide investment capital, production, and most services [in agriculture] . . . [and] the state must shift away from heavy intervention in the economy toward promoting enabling macroeconomic, fiscal, and sector policy environments."[9]

Foundational to this private sector–led vision of agriculture was the commodification of land—dismantling systems of tribal or collective property rights, removing any ceilings on rent or rights to tenancy, and turning state land into a privately owned commodity that could be easily bought and sold. For the World Bank, a "good land policy" was one "that establishes land rights and the complementary mechanisms of titling, registration, transfer, dispute resolution, and revenue collection, in addition to supporting the development of land markets."[10] According to the Bank's logic, clear property rights over land would give "smallholders incentives to improve productivity and manage natural resources more sustainably . . . [facilitate] access to credit and other services . . . [and allow] farmers to engage temporarily in off-farm employment."[11] On the other hand, "Unclear property rights spark conflict, promote resource degradation, and discourage investment."[12]

Somewhat ironically, the World Bank described this program with the same language of "land reform" used by Nasser and other postindependence governments, carefully noting, however, that their use of the term did not imply redistribution of land through the confiscation of large holdings but rather "a decentralized, participatory, and market-assisted approach."[13] Indeed, the example of a successful "land reform" program highlighted by the World Bank in its 1997 *Rural Development: From Vision to Action* document was the privatization of land in the former Soviet Union during the early 1990s.[14]

This orientation was a counterrevolution against the measures taken in the wake of decolonization. The first phase in this process began during the 1970s and was most thoroughgoing in Morocco and Tunisia. In these states, large landowners who had prospered during the colonial period formed the primary social base of the ruling regimes in the postindependence period. After the limited land redistribution of the 1960s, both governments began to pass laws that privatized state farms or collectively owned land. In Morocco, regulations set a minimum five-hectare size for private land carved out of previously collectively owned land—thus privileging the very wealthy and strengthening the tendency toward concentration and centralization of landownership.[15] Another law enabled the state to expropriate religiously endowed land, which was then transferred to private hands. Likewise, Tunisia passed a law privatizing collectively managed tribal lands, called *habous*, which often housed public facilities such as hospitals and schools. From 1970 to 1986, the Tunisian government embarked on a program to sell state farms to private owners.[16] In this manner, the consolidation of landownership was later to underpin the growth of large companies and capitalist groups linked to the agricultural sector.

There were, however, pertinent differences in the way this reversal of landownership took place in each country. In Morocco, there were two main beneficiaries of the transfer of land to private ownership—the monarchy, which became the largest landowner in the country, and rural elites, whose activities were primarily focused on the agricultural sector. By contrast, in Tunisia, the rural landowners who bought up state land tended to have much closer urban ties than their Moroccan counterparts. They had earlier expanded their base of accumulation through construction, transport, and tourism (particularly hotel management) at a time when imports were restricted and they benefited from easy access to government credit.[17] One of the later consequences of this difference is that the large agribusiness groups that formed in Tunisia tended to be segments of holding companies that were predominantly nonagricultural, whereas in Morocco the monarchy and agriculture-based capital became dominant.

In both Morocco and Tunisia, the power of these large landowners was significantly strengthened by the increasing mechanization of agricultural production and the expansion of irrigation systems. Technological improvement required capital, which was generally unavailable to smaller farmers. Both states deliberately pursued strategies that enabled large landowners to benefit from increasing productivity while making it more difficult for smaller farmers to remain on their land. Thus the Tunisian government selectively provided credit to less than 20 percent of the largest landowners (those holding more than fifty hectares of land) in order for them to purchase machinery and farm inputs.[18] This credit was essentially provided as a grant, as the interest rates on loans were lower than the rates paid by banks on deposits. It had a rapid impact on landownership and agricultural wealth—in livestock, for example, the very largest landowners (those holding more than one hundred hectares of land) held 5.9 percent of cattle and 10.8 percent of sheep in 1975–76. Just four years later, these figures had shifted to 13.9 percent and 16.2 percent.[19] At the same time, landlessness and rural unemployment levels increased—according to one analyst, the level of unemployment in rural areas in the northwest had risen by 50 percent by the mid-1980s and was concentrated in areas where mechanization was most developed.[20]

In Morocco, policies related to the expansion of dams and irrigation—on which the government spent more than 4 billion dirhams between 1968 and 1980—were particularly important in enabling large landowners to accumulate land at the expense of the poor. Indeed, one scholar has noted that Morocco's irrigation plan essentially replicated that of the colonial era and "benefitted the landowning elite . . . expand[ing] the modern export sector composed of large private holdings and the state-controlled former colonial owned farms now being privatized."[21] A 1973 law, for example, obligated Moroccan landowners to "improve" irrigated agricultural land or otherwise have their land expropriated. Thus, poor farmers who could not afford the necessary equipment to take advantage of irrigation would be threatened with losing their land. Another law set a minimum size of five hectares for farms in the vicinity of dams; this meant farmers were forced to sell their lands in order to consolidate holdings into sufficiently large areas.[22] When a new dam was announced, speculators would move to purchase land around the area to take advantage of the inevitable rise in prices. In one example of this, just three individuals bought 40 percent of the land around the Massi Dam in the Souss region before the dam was constructed.[23] An observer of this process wrote in 1981: "A mere four percent [of farmers] own farms of over 20 hectares. These large farms, running up to the hundreds of hectares, occupy half of the total irrigated land. Their revenue is an average of 500 times that of the small traditional farm in a non-irrigated area."[24]

These types of changes occurred at a more gradual pace in Egypt, where land reform had taken a much sharper and deeper turn under Nasser. The coming to power of Anwar Sadat in 1970 saw some first steps toward reversing these policies. Sadat passed a decree in late 1970 aimed at returning land redistributed under Nasser to its original owners. The highest court in Egypt, the Council of State, ratified the decree in 1974 and awarded financial compensation or restitution of property to those who had lost their land.[25] Laws still remained, however, limiting the size of holdings to fifty feddan (one hundred feddan per family).[26] Sadat also removed elected farmer representatives from their positions in rural cooperatives, thereby strengthening the power of larger landholders over rural decision-making. By and large, though, tenants continued to have stable, low rents and retained the right to remain on the land.

These initial steps toward reversing the postindependence land reform were to dramatically intensify as part of the Structural Adjustment Programs (SAPs) of the 1980s and 1990s (see appendix 3). There were two main aspects to these programs as they pertained to agriculture. First, governments moved at varying paces to liberalize agricultural markets. Prices for essential inputs such as fertilizers were allowed to rise to the price of international markets, governments no longer provided guaranteed purchase of crops or set producer prices, and private companies were allowed to operate in the provision of agricultural services, supplies, and distribution.[27] These measures put extreme pressure on those who could no longer afford inputs—in Morocco, for example, fertilizer prices increased threefold from 1985 to 1991—and many small farmers ended up either in debt or compelled to sell land to larger, wealthier landowners.[28] Moreover, because most farmers worked small, marginal plots of land, they were generally net consumers of food—for this reason, even the increase in producer prices that often accompanied liberalization was detrimental to small farmers.[29]

The second main feature of these SAPs was the continuation of policies aimed at commodifying state-owned or collective land. In Morocco and Tunisia, state-owned agricultural land fell to negligible levels by the early 2000s as land was transferred to private hands (78 percent of agricultural land in Morocco is now privately owned; 90

percent in Tunisia).[30] It was Egypt, however, that saw the most radical transformation in land tenure, following Mubarak's coming to power and the 1992 passage of Law 96, which revoked Nasser's Agrarian Reform Law and gave landlords the right to evict tenants from the land. Rents were liberalized as part of the law (subsequently increasing four- or fivefold) and landlords were able to buy and sell land without informing or negotiating with tenants.[31] Rental lands constituted just over one-third of all Egyptian agricultural areas, and following the passage of the law, more than 1 million people—representing an astonishing one-third of all Egyptian farming families—lost their rights to the land.[32] Law 96 was strongly supported by the World Bank and IMF and was particularly promoted by USAID as a core element to establishing a land market and private property rights—indeed, a USAID-sponsored study praised the law for doing away with what it described as "more than 40 years of an imbalanced relationship between landlords and tenants."[33] What these institutions usually neglected to mention was the profound violence that accompanied the law's implementation. According to Egyptian NGOs, there were 119 deaths, 846 injuries, and 1,409 arrests from January 1998 to December 2000 connected to attempts to evict tenants from their land.[34] This violence has since become an institutionalized part of rural life. According to an Egyptian agricultural NGO, Sons of the Soil Land Center, 270 people were killed resisting dispossession from their land in 2010—up from 197 in 2009.[35]

Dispossession, Migration, and the Growth of the Rural Poor

The main outcome of this generalized reversal of land reform has been the reconstitution and intensification of the bifurcated agricultural system that existed under colonialism.[36] The commodification of land and liberalization of agricultural pricing created the possibility for large landowners to strengthen their position by buying up land and consolidating landholdings. Laws that set a minimum size for farms near irrigation (such as in Morocco), or lifted caps on land rents (Egypt), helped to strengthen these tendencies of concentration. This was an entirely predictable outcome. Indeed, in the early 1990s, an OECD (Organisation for Economic Co-operation and Development) analyst—and strong advocate of liberalization—noted that the likely result of commodifying land and other inputs was "a redistribution of scarce resources, particularly land and water, in such a way that the more productive farmers will operate the available resources."[37] In other words, the wealthier, more powerful farmers would benefit from the changes introduced, while the "numbers of farmers and farms decline in the process of economic growth."[38]

By 2004, the MENA region was the second most unequal region for landownership in the world, just behind Latin America and the Caribbean.[39] In Morocco, for example,

70 percent of rural farmers came to own only 24 percent of the land, at an average of less than 5 hectares per farm, while less than 1 percent of farmers controlled 15 percent, with more than 50 hectares each.[40] In Tunisia, 53 percent of farms are less than five hectares and make up 11 percent of the land, while the top 3 percent of farms make up 37 percent of land. Only 1 percent of farms are greater than one hundred hectares, but these constitute an extraordinary 26 percent of the total agricultural land.[41] In both countries, a very large proportion of farmers tend to subsist on rain-fed marginal lands (typically growing grain or tending livestock) and depend upon nonagricultural sources of income for their survival. Alongside these small-scale farmers exists an irrigated sector of large-scale commercial producers who supply both domestic and international markets.

Egypt has a similar division between small family farms and a large commercial sector, but since nearly all agriculture is irrigated, the types of crops grown in each sector are not necessarily demarcated by farm size or mode of irrigation. Landownership, however, is as concentrated as in the rest of North Africa, with 45 percent of the smallest farmers owning only 10 percent of the land, at an average size of less than one feddan. In contrast, just 3 percent of landholders own farms of more than ten feddan, yet these large holders control a remarkable one-third of Egypt's entire agricultural area.[42] Indeed, in 2000, the Egyptian Ministry of Agriculture noted that only 0.05 percent of landholders (2,281 individuals) held 11 percent of Egyptian land, a distribution more unequal than that existing prior to the 1952 revolution.[43] The inequality in landownership is even more pronounced when disaggregated by gender, with female holders representing only 5.72 percent of the total number of landholders in the country.[44]

These dramatic extremes of landownership across each North African country go a long way to explaining the severe deterioration in the standards of rural life. In all three countries, the levels of rural poverty are significantly higher than in urban areas. This is most apparent in Tunisia, where the poverty rate is five times greater in the countryside than in cities (see table 4.2). In Egypt and Morocco, the majority of the country's poor are found in rural areas where safe water and sanitation are much less available. In Egypt, half of all poor Egyptians live in the rural areas of Upper Egypt; these are mainly agricultural laborers, landless farmers, and farmers owning less than half a hectare.[45] One reflection of this poverty is the striking level of child malnutrition—in Egypt, Morocco, and Tunisia, close to one-third of all children living in rural areas suffer from stunted growth due to malnourishment. Poverty gaps between rural and urban areas, moreover, have generally worsened over time. According to World Bank statistics, the number of people living in poverty in the rural areas of Morocco was 3 times greater than that of urban areas in 2008, up from 2.5 times in 1999. In Egypt, rural poverty was 2.6 times greater than urban poverty in 2008, up from 2.4 times in 2000. Recent accurate figures are not available for Tunisia.[46]

One of the consequences of this heavily polarized development is that millions of people have been compelled to leave the land for urban areas. In Morocco and Tunisia, the proportion of the population living in rural areas dropped by more than one-third from 1970 to 2010 (see table 4.3). In the one case that appears to contradict this trend, Egypt, the statistics are highly deceptive, as the category "urban" is defined administratively, without regard to the number of people actually living in the town or city. This results in a huge underestimation of the urban population—if Egypt used the same definition as India, over 80 percent of its population would be considered urban. Indeed, the World Bank noted in 2008 that Egypt's "gross underestimation of urbanization" is "progressively . . . out of touch with reality."[47] Across North Africa, the uniform trend has been one of massive rural-to-urban flight over the last three decades.[48]

Table 4.2: Poverty Indicators in Rural Areas: Egypt, Morocco, Tunisia

	% Living on less than US $1/day (PPP) (rural/urban)	% of poor living in rural areas	% Access to safe water (rural/urban) (2004)	% Access to sanitation (rural/urban) (2004)	Stunting prevalence in children under five (rural/urban)
Egypt	23.3 / 22.5	60	97 / 99	58 / 86	30 / 27
Morocco	22.0 / 7.9	64	58 / 94	27 / 87	29 / 16
Tunisia	8.3 / 1.6	33	62 / 95	47 / 95	27 / 14

Figures from FAO, *The Status of Rural Poverty in the Near East and North Africa* (Rome: Food and Agriculture Organization of the United Nations, 2007); Poverty data is from 2000, except for Morocco, 2003–2004. Child nutrition figures from UNICEF, www.childinfo.org/. PPP = purchasing power parity.

Table 4.3: Population and Employment, Rural Areas: Egypt, Morocco, Tunisia

	Rural population as % of total population	% of EA population in agriculture	% of EA population in agriculture who are male	% of EA males who work in agriculture	% of EA females who work in agriculture
Egypt	58 (1970)				
	56 (1985)	47 (1985)	68 (1985)	40 (1985)	72 (1985)
	57 (2010)	25 (2010)	60 (2010)	20 (2010)	39 (2010)
Morocco	66 (1970)				
	55 (1985)	47 (1985)	68 (1985)	41 (1985)	68 (1985)
	42 (2010)	26 (2010)	52 (2010)	18 (2010)	49 (2010)
Tunisia	57 (1970)				
	46 (1985)	32 (1985)	70 (1985)	28 (1985)	47 (1985)
	33 (2010)	21 (2010)	67 (2010)	19 (2010)	25 (2010)

Calculated by author from FAO and World Bank databases. EA = Economically Active.

Moreover, the share of the population engaged in agricultural labor has declined significantly alongside these internal migration flows. This is not just a function of urban growth—from 1985 to 2010 the proportion of people working in agriculture dropped at a much faster rate than the overall rural population. This trend points to a marked shift in the nature of rural life. Fewer people in rural areas are able to survive through agriculture and instead seek alternative forms of work (in some cases, by commuting daily to nearby factories or towns). This shift, moreover, has been highly gendered. Table 4.3 shows that the proportion of agricultural workers who are male—although still a majority in all three countries—has declined appreciably since 1985. In Egypt and Morocco, the rate of decline of males who work in agriculture has been notably faster than that of females who work in agriculture. Male family members move off the land to find employment in urban areas or nearby factories, while women work on farms. Care needs to be taken in interpreting this "feminization of agriculture,"[49] but it likely points to a deterioration of working conditions in the sector.[50] One indication of this is the fact that women's agricultural work is frequently unpaid—in Egypt, it has been estimated that 85 percent of women's informal employment consists of unpaid agricultural labor on family farms.[51]

Those leaving rural areas do not simply move to nearby cities and towns. The severe pressure placed on rural dwellers as a consequence of neoliberal reform has also been a crucial contributing factor to regional and international migration flows.[52] Egypt and Morocco stand out in this regard, as the largest and third-largest recipients of remittances from overseas workers of all countries in the MENA region between 1970 and 2008, respectively.[53] During the 1970s and 1980s, Egypt provided the largest stock of migrant workers in the Gulf Arab states (see chapter 6) as well as Iraq (which hosted the largest number of Egyptian workers until the 1990–91 Gulf War) and Libya.[54] It was no accident that these flows of labor coincided with Sadat's infitah and the intensification of neoliberalism under Mubarak, with the Egyptian government consciously encouraging migration as a strategy to ameliorate the social crises generated by these economic changes. In 1976, a remarkable 10–14 percent of the Egyptian labor force was estimated to be working overseas; a decade later, the number of Egyptian workers abroad had doubled.[55] Egyptians did not just depart to oil-rich countries; many migrants—particularly from rural areas—worked as agricultural laborers elsewhere in the region.[56] One estimate, for example, claims that as of 1986, 87 percent of agricultural workers in the Jordan Valley (east of the Jordan River) were Egyptian.[57] The number of Arab migrant workers (mostly Egyptian) reached one-fifth of Jordan's workforce by the late 1990s.[58]

Many families in Morocco have also utilized international migration as a strategy to cope with the degradation of rural life.[59] Unlike Egypt, however, these migration flows are directed to Europe rather than the Arab world. In the initial decades following

World War II, Moroccans tended to migrate through "guest worker" programs to France. But since the 1990s, Moroccan migration has been characterized by undocumented flows into low-paid agricultural and construction jobs in Southern Europe. Most of these migrants leave from rural areas throughout Morocco, and this has created enormous dependency on remittance flows in many villages.[60] In 2000, the 1.4 million Moroccans in Europe made up more than half the residents from Arab Mediterranean countries—a figure that certainly understates the true scale of Moroccan migration flows, as it does not include undocumented arrivals.[61]

These migration patterns indicate that the neoliberal transformation of agriculture is deeply connected to class formation beyond the national scale. Neoliberalism has helped generate a mobile army of low-wage and deeply exploited Arab workers throughout Europe and the Middle East: class formation needs to be increasingly viewed from this regional perspective if national dynamics are to make any sense.[62] Furthermore, these flows of labor and the concomitant dependency that many families now have on remittances are central to interpreting the possible ways that economic crises can be transmitted and displaced across different spaces.[62] As chapter 7 will discuss, this particular form of linkage with the world market bears important implications for understanding the impact of the most recent global economic turmoil on the region.

Class Formation in the Countryside: Agribusiness and the Rural Bourgeoisie

Alongside this rural degradation, agricultural development strategies have increasingly emphasized the production for export of fruits, seasonal vegetables, olives, flowers, and other niche/gourmet products. Investment in these crops multiplied through the 1990s, with funds being spent on irrigation, market research, branding, and R&D. Most of these export crops were aimed at European markets, with the ebb and flow of market access deeply dependent on developments in European agricultural policies and negotiations with the EU (see chapter 2). In this sense, the patterns of North African agricultural production were ever more structured by—and vulnerable to—the needs of the European market rather than any domestic provisions.

Food export volumes did grow (see table 4.4), with some key commodities registering increases of up to six or seven times their export levels in the 1990s. Not only did the absolute quantity of exports rise, but (with the partial exception of Morocco) so did the proportion of each crop's production that was exported. This growth, however, was restricted to a handful of crops with generally little value-added processing. For Egypt, the top five food exports (cheese, rice, grapes, potatoes, and oranges) constituted 38 percent of all food exports in 2009.[63] The levels of concentration were even more pronounced for the other two countries—Morocco at 48 percent (oranges, beans, tangerines, tomatoes, olives),[64] and Tunisia at 52 percent (olive oil, dates, tomatoes, sugar confectionary, soybean oil). This has meant that many farmers are highly dependent on the fortunes of a single crop—in Tunisia, for example, olive cultivation occupies 30 percent of the agricultural land area and involves nearly one-third of the farmer population (around one hundred thousand farmers).[65]

Table 4.4: Key Agro-Export Food Crops, Export Quantity (Metric Tons) and Percent Change, 1990 to 2009

Country	Crop	Export Quantity (tons)		Percent Change 1990–2009	Percent of Crop Exported	
		1990	2009		1990–1994	2005–2009
Egypt	Fruits	182,415	1,376,542	655	2.6	7.7
	Rice	75,718	648,815	757	4.1	13.3
	Vegetables	148,682	532,352	258	2.2	2.6
Morocco	Fruits	538,731	584,031	8.4	25.8	21.1
	Olives (preserved)	47,231	64,758	37	11.0	8.1
	Vegetables	224,877	777,852	246	8.7	11.2
Tunisia	Fruits	48,521	132,396	173	5.7	9.6
	Olive oil	49,717	141,688	185	100.0	99.0
	Vegetables	24,214	136,787	465	2.9	6.6

Source: FAO, http://faostat.fao.org

This focus on export-oriented growth has not benefited all farmers but acted to exacerbate the uneven development and relative impoverishment of the rural areas. First, it must be remembered that the majority of farmers in the countries under focus are not involved in the export sector and tend to exist on marginal and, with the exception of Egypt, rain-fed farms. In Morocco, for example, cereal production (largely not for export) accounts for about 70 percent of all agricultural lands and is 90 percent rain-fed.[67] Likewise, in Egypt, the last national survey found that only 16.7 percent of the rural population was involved in cultivating the key export crops of fruits, vegetables, or rice.[68]

Second, even where farmers are involved in growing export crops (such as Tunisian olive farmers), trade has come to be dominated by a small minority of large farmers and export companies—principally those that benefited from the land policies described above. In Morocco, for example, just seven companies account for 70 percent of Morocco's fresh fruit and vegetable exports—mostly citrus and tomato sold to Europe. These companies control individual farms in addition to the marketing and export routes for their products.[69] In Tunisia, a handful of companies control the major export crops of citrus (ten growers with 80 percent) and olive oil (six exporters with 65 percent).[70] For Egypt, just seven companies lead the export trade of fruits and fresh vegetables—for potatoes, Egypt's largest vegetable export, one company supplies around 30 percent of total exports; for oranges, the largest exporter provides 10 percent of total sales.[71] In the case of processed food from Egypt, data from 2005 indicated that 26 percent of all exports were manufactured by just five companies, most of them Gulf-owned.[72] Two of these companies provided 18 percent of total exports.

These dominant companies grab a growing share of agricultural value at the expense of small producers. Table 4.5 shows the ratio of the value of agricultural production at the farm gate to the value of agricultural exports. It is a proxy measure, in other words, of the price paid to farmers as a ratio of the price paid to exporters. In all cases, there has been a massive increase in the proportion of agricultural wealth captured by exporters. By 2009, the value of agricultural exports was more than one hundred times that of farm-gate value—a powerful indication of the differential outcome of export-led growth.

Table 4.5: Ratio of Agricultural Export Value to Value of Agricultural Production at Farm Gate

	1991–1994	2006–2009	2009
Egypt	51	95.6	169
Morocco	99	142.3	134
Tunisia	168	345.1	290

Source: FAO, calculated by author

The shift to export-oriented production has thus helped to facilitate the growing power of large capital groups linked to both domestic and international markets.[73] This is the other side to the nature of class formation in the rural areas, representing the subsumption of agriculture to the wider circuit of capital. Indeed, discussing the North Africa region in the late 1990s, the World Bank presented a candid assessment of the ways in which structural adjustment had helped facilitate the growth of a capitalist class, noting that reforms had "opened up domestic food markets to competition from imports, and stimulated changes in consumer demand."[74] These policies had worked against "years of antientrepreneurial policies" to help "the emergence of a class of rural entrepreneurs, whose initial point of market entry has been into food marketing and the agribusiness chain."[75]

This process of class formation is characterized by a pronounced trend toward vertical integration, in which a single agribusiness conglomerate will control (or contract) the production of the crop or livestock, the provision of inputs such as machinery and fertilizers, the processing of the crops, its marketing, and then final export. Long an explicit goal of neoliberal agricultural policy, agribusiness, the World Bank argued in 1997, should form the primary link "between the rural economy and the urban and export economies" and ought to provide "the inputs to the farm sector and services, such as handling, processing, transportation, financing, and marketing of farm-based products."[76] This has become all the more important, the Bank stated fifteen years later, because "Agriculture increasingly occurs in a context where private entrepreneurs coordinate extensive value chains linking producers to consumers, sometimes across vast distances."[77]

As such, the promotion of vertically integrated agribusiness has been explicitly incorporated into North African agricultural strategies. This is perhaps best symbolized in Morocco, where the 2008 Plan Maroc Vert (Green Morocco Plan, PMV), lays out the country's agricultural plan for the period 2008–2020. The PMV aims to quintuple the value of export-oriented crops (citrus fruits, olives, fruits, and vegetables) as one of its three main goals (the other two being to promote private investment in agriculture and to dismantle the "segmented framework" that stands in the way of private property rights).[78] As part of this massive expansion of exports, the PMV endeavors to shift land away from staple cereal crops toward citrus and tomato cultivation. The core vision behind this strategy is "to promote the vertical integration from production to commercialization of one agri-food chain."[79] According to the consulting firm McKinsey & Company, three hundred thousand hectares were initially earmarked for this transition, and more than half have already been switched to export crops.[80] The method for achieving this shift is instructive—the Moroccan government began a plan in 2009 to lease land in fifty-hectare lots to commercial farmers, who would then outsource production to surrounding small farmers while controlling credit, seeds, and marketing of output.[81] In this manner, the PMV continues to promote an agricultural system that prioritizes production for foreign markets rather than satisfying domestic needs—while concentrating the control of land in large commercial farming operations.

A further important aspect of the development of this vertically integrated agribusiness is the increasing penetration of foreign firms. Although in all three countries foreign investors are legally prohibited from buying agricultural lands, long-term leases are available in Tunisia (forty years) and Morocco (ninety-nine years), and Egypt permits foreign investors to buy so-called reclaimed desert land.[82] Moreover, foreign investment is pronounced in food-related manufacturing for both export and domestic markets. The investments of these conglomerates are partly driven by the changing nature of the agricultural industry globally, in which, as FAO has noted: "The dispersal or 'slicing up' of agricultural value chains on an international basis involves vertical trading chains spanning a number of countries, each specializing in a segment of the supply chain."[83] North Africa has been a prime target of this "nearshoring" by Western

European firms because of its "relatively low-cost qualified workforce, cost-efficient transportation, communications access and location in similar time zone."[84] Egypt stands out in this regard, with large food companies regarding the country as a cheap and effective base for the processing of agricultural exports aimed at Africa, the Middle East, and Europe itself.

The growth of foreign agribusiness investments and the development of vertically integrated production chains carry implications not just for exports but also for the provisioning of domestic markets. Table 4.6 shows the division of market share for some important consumer food sectors and food retail across North Africa. In each country, major segments of these key food markets are controlled by a handful of firms whose activities stretch across entire supply chains. Frequently, the same group has interests in various segments of food production and also controls supermarkets or other retail outlets. While these firms generally control production from the farm through to marketing and retail, this type of vertical integration does not necessarily mean the disappearance of small farmers. In several of the examples listed in table 4.6, the agribusiness groups contract smaller farmers through the provision of seeds, animal feed, and fertilizers. Foreign companies are also prominent players across most markets, acting through either joint ventures, subsidiaries, or licensing agreements.

Table 4.6: Concentration and Centralization of Control in Key North African Agribusiness Sectors

Country	Dairy	Poultry	Edible oils	Other	Supermarkets and food retailers
Morocco	Centrale Laitière, a joint venture between the French multinational Danone and the monarchy-linked group ONA, controls 60 percent of industrially produced milk (Danone has majority control). It controls farms as well as production sites that manufacture a variety of dairy products, dominating production of yogurt, ice cream, and other dairy products. The other major player in the dairy sector is Nestle, which holds about 7 percent of market share.	Two companies, Atzal Holding (Chaouni family) and Koutoubia Holdings (Bimezzagh family), control the poultry sector; both are involved in raising poultry, breeding, slaughtering, and meat distribution. They also contract smaller farmers and supply feed and other services.	A single company, Lesieur-Cristal, previously linked to the monarchy but sold in 2011 to the French company Sofiproteol, controls about 41 percent of market share.[85]	In the case of sugar, there is a single producer, Consumar, which is controlled by the monarchy and employs more than eighty thousand farmers spread across ninety thousand hectares of land.	There are three large retailers in the country: Marjane, controlled by the monarchy's ONA Group; Carrefour, a joint venture between Carrefour and the Moroccan company Label Vie; and Aswak Assalam, owned by the Ynna Group (Chaabi family).

Country	Dairy	Poultry	Edible oils	Other	Supermarkets and food retailers
Egypt	Two companies, Dina Farms (54 percent of fresh milk) and Juhayna (69 percent of packaged milk), control the market. Both are highly integrated along the supply chain, controlling tens of thousands of hectares of farmland, transport and warehouse facilities, and processing plants for dairy products. Dina Farms is the largest privately owned farm in Egypt, stretching for ten thousand hectares with ten thousand cattle.	Three companies, Cairo Poultry Company (Kuwaiti-owned), Misr Arab Poultry (owned by Saudi-based Dallah Al Baraka), and Wataniya Poultry (owned by Saudi-based Rajhe group), control more than 50 percent of commercial poultry production. [86]	One producer, Afia International, controls 42 percent of the market. [87]	One company, Farm Frites, dominates the majority of frozen vegetable sales, with 90 percent of the frozen potato market. [88] Around 40 percent of the carton juice market is controlled by Juhayna.	Carrefour, a joint venture between Majd Al Futtaim (UAE) and Carrefour (France); Makro Cash and Carry Chain (German); Spinneys Hypermarket (Abraaj Capital, UAE); Hyper One (Hawary Group, Egyptian); plus a range of smaller, locally owned supermarkets.

Country	Dairy	Poultry	Edible oils	Other	Supermarkets and food retailers
Tunisia	Delice Danone, a joint venture between Danone and the Tunisian company Delice (part of the TTS Groupe), is the dominant force in the dairy market. A Spanish dairy firm, Kaiku, is the second-largest dairy producer after its purchase of Tunisia-based CLM-Vitaliat in December 2011.	Half the turkey market and one-fifth of the chicken market are controlled by the Poulina Group.	Most domestic needs are met through imports that are controlled by the state-run ONH.	The Poulina Group controls 60 percent of the import of wheat, barley, and other cereals, 60 percent of the ice cream market, 53 percent of the margarine market, and 15 percent of the yogurt market. Bayahi Groupe is the major producer of tomatoes, tinned vegetables, and jams. TTS Groupe (1,400 hectares of land for cattle, sheep, and cereal farming). Groupe Ellami controls 100 percent of the frozen fruit market for yogurt and ice cream. Groupe Soroubat (1,000 hectares of vegetables, cattle, and sheep, and 550 hectares of fruit).	Three retailers control the market: Group UTIC (Carrefour hypermarket, Champion supermarket, and Bonprix supermarkets), owned by the Chaabi family, has a 34.9 percent share of the modern retail sector. Group Mabrouk (Geant hypermarket and Monoprix supermarket brands licensed by the French retailer, Casino), owned by the Mabrouk Group, has a 33.3 percent share of the modern retail sector. Magasin General, a joint venture of the Poulina Group and Bayahi Groupe, has a 30.6 percent share of the modern retail sector.

Source: Company websites and news reports unless otherwise indicated.

Table 4.6 provides useful insight into the common features of class formation across the agricultural circuit in North Africa. There are, however, important specificities to be found in each country.

Class formation in the Egyptian agricultural sector shows highly concentrated ownership structures. But, alongside this concentration, Egyptian agriculture has been a target of foreign investment to a much greater extent than the other two North African countries. The country has both a large domestic market and is seen as a potential regional production base and export hub to Africa and the Middle East. Some of the FDI in the agricultural sector originates from large US and European food companies such as Heinz, Tetrapak, Unilever, Cadbury, Danone, and Coca-Cola.[89] What is striking about the Egyptian case, however, is the very pronounced involvement of Gulf-based conglomerates. Many of the leading companies mentioned in Table 4.6—Dina Farms, Juhayna, Farm Frites, Afia International—are either fully owned by or joint ventures with Gulf-based capital (see chapter 6). Companies owned by Gulf-based conglomerates control more than half of Egypt's total poultry production. The largest of these, the Cairo Poultry Company (CPC), has been a subsidiary of the Kuwaiti-based Americana Group since 2007.[90] CPC controls 30 percent of commercial poultry production and 45 percent of the frozen chicken market in Egypt and is involved in all stages of the industry: manufacturing feed, raising chicks, hatching eggs, processing meat, and selling poultry products through a chain of fast food restaurants.[91] The entry of CPC and other Gulf-based companies into Egypt's agricultural sector was consciously fostered by the Mubarak regime, which marketed the country as a production base for the Gulf and also sought investments in massive Egyptian "megafarms" (see chapter 6 for further discussion). These flows of Gulf capital are critical to understanding the changing regional alignments under neoliberalism.

In Morocco, corporate groups linked to the country's monarchy are particularly prominent, often in partnership with foreign investors. Unlike in Egypt, the majority of this foreign investment is French or Spanish. The significance of foreign investment in Moroccan agribusiness is likely to increase with the PMV, which intends to open up some twenty-one thousand hectares of agricultural land to foreign lease.[92] Morocco has also pushed to attract FDI through the creation of special economic zones specializing in food, known as agripoles, linking together crop, livestock and/or fish production, food processing, suppliers of inputs such as machinery and fertilizers, research and training, and services.[93] There are six agripoles and two fish processing hubs operational or under development in Morocco, mainly focusing on the processing and export of citrus fruits, vegetables, and olive oils. These agripoles, like special economic zones (SEZs) more broadly, operate under different laws and regulations than the rest of the country—the government promises, for example, a 20 percent subsidy for land costs, no corporate or personal taxes for five years, and unrestricted repatriation of profits.[94]

Tunisia shows a high level of corporate concentration across the agribusiness sector. Due, however, to the particular weight of construction and tourism in the earlier development of the Tunisian bourgeoisie, agribusinesses have tended to form as units of larger holding companies rather than as stand-alone conglomerates (e.g., TTS Groupe, Groupe Ellami, Groupe Loukil, Groupe Soroubat).[95] These holding companies are active across a diversified range of sectors and often have their main business activities in a nonagricultural industrial field. As with the Moroccan case, they frequently show a high degree of vertical integration across entire production chains and tend to be owned by wealthy Tunisian families who built their business through the patronage and support of the Ben Ali regime.[96] Although there are several important examples of foreign joint ventures in agribusiness, this is less pronounced than in the Moroccan or Egyptian cases. In 2012 there were 1,037 companies involved in the food industry (191 of which were solely export-companies) and, of these, only 85 were joint ventures with foreign companies (35 in solely exporting activities).[97] The Poulina Group, the largest Tunisian industrial conglomerate, provides an excellent illustration of the general patterns in Tunisia. The Group was founded in 1967 by the Ben Ayed family through the merger of seven poultry contractors. The company benefited from the acceleration of neoliberalism in Tunisia under Ben Ali's dictatorship, growing to become the dominant poultry manufacturer in the country, among its many other business interests.[98] By 2007, half the turkey market and one-fifth of the chicken market in Tunisia were controlled by the group. In addition to directly owning the largest poultry abattoir in Africa (ten hectares in size), the company also contracts small farmers to raise chickens, providing them with feed, incubation, and veterinary services. These chickens are sold to Poulina, which is able to exert power over the price paid to small farmers because of its extensive chain of warehouses, refrigerated trucks, and shops through which it distributes eggs and meat. In addition to agribusiness, the group is involved in real estate, construction, steel, transport, aluminium, and banking.

In each case, the pattern that emerges is striking. The liberalization policies of the 1990s and 2000s have driven a dynamic of capitalist class formation in agriculture. Commercial agricultural production has come to be dominated by large, vertically integrated firms controlled by an interlinked ownership structure of key families, foreign agribusiness, and the state. These firms have extensive business interests outside of agriculture. Small farming persists and is widespread, but it is fully subordinated to the needs of these firms and their control over both export markets and domestic distribution chains. This process is the counterpoint to the dispossession and proletarianization of large parts of the rural population.

Conclusion: Reframing Agriculture in the Middle East

Several themes emerge from this account of North African agriculture that provide broader insights into the recent trajectory of the Middle East. Foremost among these is the way in which claims to neutrality act to obscure the relations of power that structure neoliberal reform. This can be seen, for example, in the admonishments of the World Bank and other international financial institutions to "modernize" agriculture because the food economy is now "globalized"—arguments that effectively naturalize the global system as an external, inevitable, and almost irresistible force. Any sense of how the world market has been purposively designed or constructed—and by whom—is lost. By framing agriculture in this manner, these institutions conceal the relations of power that hide behind capitalism, portraying policy as simply a technocratic and necessary response to changing external circumstances. Their own role as architects of these relations of power is hidden behind seemingly banal activities such as policy research and government technical support. In reality, their claims to "expertise" and "neutrality" have acted as a smokescreen for their efforts on behalf of the most powerful actors—both local and international.

In a similar manner, the introduction of technological changes to North African agriculture provides a further illustration of how relations of power hide behind claims to neutrality and technocratic policy-making. Modes of irrigation, technical improvements, and measures to increase land productivity are not neutral—their outcome depends on the social relations in which they are situated. If these measures are promoted in the context of deepening market relations they likely mean the extension of debt relations and the consolidation of a layer of very wealthy landowners and agricultural companies on one side, and a mass of poorer farmers and rural laborers on the other. In this context, "productivity," "modernization," and "land improvement" emerge as an ideological trope whose primary effect is to catalyze shifts in patterns of landownership and control.

These issues point to the necessity of unpacking homogenizing claims about a supposed "national good," often preferred through the use of aggregate statistics, and ask who benefits from the current social configuration and the policy choices made. Very frequently, neoliberal logic treats the nation as a single unit and calculates the cost and loss of agricultural change on the basis of price efficiency and quantities of foreign currency earned, ignoring the counterposed interests of various social groups. It may well be true, for example, that an export-oriented policy will earn more foreign currency through the sale of agricultural produce on the world market. But this does not mean these profits end up ensuring that people are adequately fed. The likely outcome, as the evidence from North Africa confirms, is that a handful of wealthy producers are able to profit from increased high-value exports (frequently linked to large agribusiness firms in the advanced capitalist countries), while the ability of local farmers to survive on the land, or to provide food for their populations, is severely undermined.

It is this powerful drive toward uneven accumulation that marks agriculture as the nexus of a broader process of class formation—the spatial location underpinning the consolidation of a domestic bourgeoisie. In this sense, the "rural" is inseparable from the "urban." Regardless of its origins, the North African capitalist class solidly straddles moments of accumulation across both spaces. Moreover, as the heavy predominance of Gulf and European capital in North African agribusiness indicates, the nature of this class formation is necessarily pan-regional. The transformation of agriculture is not solely a domestic affair but one that more closely ties together the fortunes of capital across the Middle East and the Mediterranean as a whole.

Dependent on and counterposed to this development of capital is the expulsion of the rural population from their lands and livelihoods. This dispossession has been at the heart of the massive expansion of both urban communities and the incessant flows of migrant labor across the region—a form of class development that is by no means unique to the three countries examined in this chapter. It is a transformation that touches all aspects of life. The spread of urban slums, the unchecked proliferation of informal work, the potential outcomes of a looming ecological crisis, the grinding exploitation of women, the questions of debt, famine, and recurrent food crises—all are directly connected to this process. Moreover, the transformation of rural existence has not ended, as is confirmed by the ongoing push to increasingly liberalize land markets (opening them up further to foreign ownership) and privatize agricultural resources (notably water).[99] In all these respects, agricultural change remains at the core of the neoliberal project in the Middle East.

CHAPTER 5

Class and State in the West Bank: Neoliberalism under Occupation

S
upport for Palestine has long been a deeply held principle of radical political movements in the Middle East. Throughout much of the 1970s, Palestinian refugee camps in countries such as Jordan and Lebanon formed the axis of struggle against pro-Western regimes in the Arab world, providing a fertile ground for political and military training for much of the region's Left (and, indeed, globally). These movements forced even the most reactionary governments in the region to pay lip service to the cause of Palestinian rights. In later decades, the successive uprisings of Palestinians living under Israeli military occupation provoked an outpouring of street demonstrations and other forms of protest across the Arab world—demanding regimes sever political and economic ties with Israel and provide real support to the Palestinian struggle. The political networks that formed in these solidarity movements, often the most palpable expression of resistance to autocratic governments in the Middle East, would later play an important prefigurative role in the uprisings of 2011 (see chapter 7).

Given the preponderant weight of the question of Palestine to Middle East politics, it is striking how little substantive discussion there has been around issues of its political economy. In stark contrast to other parts of the region—where sharp analyses of capitalist development and the strategies adopted by states and ruling elites are regularly dissected and debated—Palestine remains largely viewed as a "humanitarian issue."

Much solidarity work (both in the Arab world and further afield) typically emphasizes the violation of Palestinian rights and the enormous suffering this entails, rather than Palestine's connection to the wider region and its articulation with forms of imperialist power. Placed in a category of its own, Palestine has become an exception that somehow defies the analytical tools used to unpack and comprehend neighboring states.

This chapter presents a counternarrative to this exceptionalism, arguing that the political economy of Palestinian class and state formation is an essential feature to understanding Israel's ongoing colonization and dispossession of the Palestinian people. This process has unfolded through what is akin to "bantustanization," a term referring to the areas of "self-rule" for the rural Black population in 1950s apartheid South Africa.[1] The utilization of spatial zones like the South African bantustans, which provide a veneer of autonomy but can be easily controlled from the outside, has been a feature common to most colonial projects.[2] Although the nature of these bantustans in the Palestinian case is significantly different from South Africa—notably in the role that Palestinian labor plays vis-à-vis the Israeli economy—their political implications are very similar. They have involved the creation of isolated spaces in which limited autonomy is permitted but movement between them is dependent upon Israeli authorization. This spatial separation tends to foster a dynamic of cultural and national disintegration as identities become centered around the local. It also leads to the development of distinct social formations, as different trajectories of class and state formation take root in each isolated enclave.

The discussion below focuses on the nature of class and state formation in one of these zones—the West Bank. The overriding theme since the onset of Israeli occupation of the West Bank in 1967 has been the transformation of Palestinian society from a predominantly rural existence—with social reproduction centered around agriculture and the traditional authority structures of village life—to an incorporated, dependent, and subordinated appendage of Israeli capitalism. This mode of incorporation has underpinned a change in the social relations of the West Bank, characterized, on the one hand, by the proletarianization and dispossession of much of the West Bank population, and, on the other, by the development of a tiny layer of Palestinian capital that articulates Israeli rule and whose accumulation is dependent on this mediating position. This outcome has been achieved through the progressive seizure of Palestinian land and resources by the occupying power and the encirclement and regulation of Palestinian movement through the political, bureaucratic, and military apparatus constituted by the occupation.

The first half of the chapter presents a historical account of this process from the beginning of Israel's colonization in 1967 until the end of the Second Intifada, or Palestinian uprising, around 2005. It traces Israel's strategic attempts over these four decades to formalize a system of bantustanization and to establish Palestinian culpability for how this system operates. The second half of this chapter turns to an examination of what this ongoing territorial disintegration looks like under neoliberalism. It shows how a capitalist class has formed in the West Bank, closely linked to the structures of the ruling Palestinian Authority (PA), which has embraced a neoliberal vision with the same basic assumptions and consequences as those discussed in previous chapters. This neoliberal turn has recently been codified in the Palestine Reform and Development Program (PRDP), an economic development plan strongly supported by the World Bank and other donors, which holds major implications for the nature of the Palestinian struggle.

These transformations of Palestinian society form the corollary to the arguments advanced in chapter 2, which indicated how Israel's alliance with US power—acting through both military means as well as the normalization demanded by neoliberal trade and investment agreements—was central to the political subordination of the wider Arab region. An element necessary to this process has been the cultivation of a Palestinian leadership that is fully incorporated into patterns of Western domination, one that has been willing to provide the "green light" for other Arab regimes to end the isolation of the Israeli state. This Palestinian leadership is largely headquartered in the West Bank (hence the geographical focus of this chapter), but the explanation for its acquiescence is not simply found in "corruption" or misplaced strategic decisions. Of course this should not be taken as an endorsement of the West Bank as the "future Palestinian state" or as limiting the nature of the Palestinian struggle to the territories occupied in 1967. By contrast, this chapter is firmly situated in the perspective that the Palestinian people have the right to return to their homes and lands from which they were driven out in 1947–49, a historical moment that Palestinians refer to as *al-nakba* (the catastrophe). The point, however, is to understand the processes that have led the West Bank–based Palestinian leadership to become the core of accommodation with US strategy for the region.[3] Rather, this chapter aims to show that the weakness of leadership is causally tied to the dependency and subjugation that characterizes Palestinian class and state formation in the area. In this manner, the political economy of the West Bank can be seen to form an essential link to imperial rule and the patterns of capitalist development throughout the rest of the Middle East—one that extends far beyond a purely rights-based focus on Palestinian suffering.[4]

The Occupation of 1967

From 1948 until the Israeli occupation in 1967, the West Bank was under Jordanian rule.[5] During this period, Palestinian society was, for the most part, rural and often described as Jordan's "food basket."[6] The West Bank constituted around one-quarter of Jordan's arable land, generated over 60 percent of its fruit and vegetable crops, and accounted for more than one-third of its grain and livestock production.[7] Christian holy sites also underpinned the Jordanian tourism industry, with the West Bank responsible for 90 percent of the country's tourism revenues.[8] The Jordanian government deliberately restricted investment and rejected any attempts at land reform, perpetuating the same types of landownership and social structures that had existed since Ottoman times. In the rural areas, life was organized around patriarchal village heads known as the *mukhtar* and landownership was highly concentrated—8.6 percent of landholders, those who had farms more than 10 hectares in size, held 38 percent of the land; nearly half of landowners were forced to survive on land of less than 2 hectares.[9] Around 70 percent of land in the West Bank was privately owned and farmed by its owners; tenant farmers cultivated the other 30 percent.[10] In this context, family structure was dominated by a central patriarchal authority, and socioeconomic life focused on agricultural production. Sharecropping—an arrangement in which a landless farmer would be provided with a share of the crop in return for its cultivation—was fairly common in larger farms of fieldcrops and vegetables.[11] Many of these sharecroppers were drawn from the three hundred thousand Palestinian refugees made landless following their expulsion to the West Bank in 1948.

The Israeli occupation of the West Bank that began in July 1967 broke up and disrupted these traditional patterns of social existence. During the war itself, Israel expelled around one-fifth of the Palestinian population, targeting in particular residents of the Jordan Valley and a ring of villages in and around Jerusalem.[12] Much English-language analysis tends to reduce this mass population transfer to a historical footnote of little consequence—one that is largely irrelevant to contemporary politics.[13] The reality is that the areas depopulated during the war came to form the backbone of the Israeli-only spaces that today divide Palestinian towns and villages in the West Bank from one another. They were not always devoid of Palestinian population or agricultural activity but were consciously emptied and then colonized: first by the Israeli military, then by settler militias organized in movements such as the messianic religious group Gush Emunim,[14] and finally by the Israeli citizens who came to view the leafy suburbs of Israeli settlements as comfortable middle-class neighborhoods. This represents the dehistoricization of place and space—in which the recurrent thread of expulsion is disappeared from history and the "facts on the ground" are cast as normality.

In the immediate aftermath of the war, Israeli political leaders held two counterposed views on what to do with the Palestinians they had conquered in the West Bank—a population that, along with Palestinians in Jerusalem and the Gaza Strip, constituted the equivalent of nearly one-third of the Israeli population at the time.[15] The first view considered the occupied areas as an indivisible part of the Zionist homeland that should be incorporated into Israel. The second view, which eventually won the debate, rejected any granting of citizenship rights to Palestinians in the West Bank (and Gaza Strip) because of the implications this held for the Jewish character of the Israeli state.[16] Instead, a military government was established that would come to control every aspect of life in the West Bank; Palestinians did not become Israeli citizens but carried ID cards and were subject to Israeli military law (based on a system similar to the military laws applied to Palestinian citizens of Israel until 1966).[17] The military governor, a high-ranking officer in the Israeli military accountable only to the prime minister, would be the final arbiter regarding all decisions in the territories.

These demographic debates were closely connected to what to do with the land itself. Having decided that the Palestinian population would not be incorporated with citizenship rights into Israel, the Israeli government began to confiscate Palestinian land and build settlements in the areas that had been depopulated in 1967. The initial strategy guiding this settlement project was the Allon Plan, named for Yigal Allon, an Israeli general and deputy prime minister of the Labour Party following the 1967 war.[18] Allon's logic was straightforward: Israeli settlements would be placed between major Palestinian population centers and on top of water aquifers and fertile agricultural land.[19] An "Israeli-only" road network would eventually connect these settlements to each other and also to Israeli cities beyond the West Bank. In this manner, Israel could seize the land and resources, divide Palestinian areas from each other, and avoid as much as possible direct responsibility for the Palestinian population. Based on the population transfer that occurred during 1967, the Allon Plan aimed at the annexation of around 40 percent of the West Bank into Israel proper.[20] From 1967 to 1977 the Allon Plan was followed faithfully by the Labour-aligned Israeli governments of this period. By the beginning of 1977, twenty Israeli settlements had been established in total—75 percent of them in areas identified by the Allon Plan.[21]

With the coming to power of the Likud government in 1977, the construction of settlements fell under the auspices of Ariel Sharon, then minister of agriculture and chair of the Ministerial Committee on Settlements. By 1981, the visions advanced by the Likud government had evolved into a coherent strategy known as the Sharon Plan, which shifted geographic focus away from the areas successfully colonized under the Allon Plan toward the western highlands of the West Bank.[22] The central feature of this plan was a belt of settlements east of the Palestinian towns of Qalqilya and Tulkarem (located in the northwest of the West Bank), which were highly significant to Israeli control for two reasons. First, they were the location of the most important Palestinian agricultural areas in the West Bank following the disappearance of Jordan Valley lands in 1967. After Israel took control of these areas, Palestinians became almost completely dependent on Israeli food imports for day-to-day survival. Second, the western mountain ridge straddled the site of the major water aquifer in the West Bank. Command over this gave Israel access to large quantities of water—equivalent to about one-third of Israel's water consumption—that could be pumped to the 2.5 million Israeli citizens in Tel Aviv and the central areas of the country.[23]

Combined with restrictions on the movement of farmers and their access to water and other resources, these massive waves of land confiscation and settlement building during the first two decades of the occupation transformed landownership and modes of social reproduction. From 1967 to 1974, the area of cultivated Palestinian land in the West Bank fell by around one-third.[24] The expropriation of land in the Jordan Valley by Israeli settlers meant that 87 percent of all irrigated land in the West Bank was removed from Palestinian use.[25] Military orders forbade the drilling of new wells for agricultural purposes and restricted overall water use by Palestinians, while Israeli settlers were encouraged to use as much water as needed.[26] With this deliberate destruction of the agricultural sector, poorer Palestinians—particularly youth—were displaced from rural areas and gravitated toward working in the construction and agriculture sectors inside Israel. In 1970, the agricultural sector represented over 40 percent of the Palestinian labor force in the West Bank. By 1987 this figure was down to only 26 percent. Agriculture's share in the Palestinian GDP fell from 35 percent to 16 percent between 1970 and 1991.[27]

As the weight of agriculture declined, Israel increasingly took control over Palestinian markets. Local Palestinian industries were destroyed as Israeli-produced foods and manufactured goods flooded the West Bank. Industrial activities that did emerge, notably textiles and leather, were usually subcontracted from Israeli companies and concentrated in very small workshops of fewer than five people.[28] Palestinians involved in these activities were provided with raw materials (for example, cloth) that they then distributed to small firms or households, earning a commission once they returned the final product to the Israeli owner. At the same time, select merchants were granted import and export rights by the Israeli authorities and permitted to distribute Israeli products within the West Bank. Frequently these merchants were individuals who also collaborated politically with the Israeli military. Others worked as labor subcontractors, earning commission by providing Israel with a daily supply of Palestinian workers. In all cases, the Palestinian capitalist class that emerged alongside the occupation was characterized by its dependent but allied relationship as a key interlocutor with Israel.[29]

Alongside this creeping strangulation of the Palestinian political economy, Israel erected a complex bureaucratic apparatus aimed at creating a layer of Palestinians who were dependent upon the Israeli military.[30] Employing the carrot-and-stick technique, this layer presented a Palestinian face to Israel's occupation.[31] There were various mechanisms through which this mediation took place. In 1981, Israel established the Civil Administration, which saw thousands of Palestinians employed as front-line police in Palestinian cities and villages in the West Bank and Gaza Strip. In addition, Israel moved to strengthen a network of so-called Village Leagues as an alternative to the outlawed PLO, which largely operated outside of the country and had adopted a sharp orientation toward a Palestinian-led struggle in the wake of the defeats suffered by Nasserism and Arab nationalism in 1967. The Village Leagues were permitted to carry weapons and arrest and interrogate people; they also dispensed family reunion permits, travel permits, and licenses to build or open businesses. Many essential tasks were impossible to accomplish without Village League consent, which ultimately depended upon obeisance to the Israeli military. Funds from the Israeli government for "development" projects were channeled through the Village Leagues in an attempt to undercut support for other bodies affiliated to the PLO. Nonetheless, despite the fact that Ariel Sharon attempted to portray the Village Leagues as the "moderate leadership" of the Palestinians—a term he used in talks in 1982 with the US secretary of defense, Caspar Weinberger—they were widely rejected by Palestinians.[32] Village League representatives were assassinated by activists, and most of the Palestinian population continued to regard the PLO as their sole, legitimate representative, despite its illegality.[33]

These developments had a profound effect on both the Israeli and Palestinian social formations. For Israel, the incorporation of the West Bank into its economy significantly increased the size of Israel's domestic market, providing a captive consumer base and a source of cheap and highly exploitable labor. The resulting Israeli economic expansion was dubbed the "Palestinian boom." By the mid-1980s, Palestinians from the West Bank and Gaza Strip made up around 7 percent of the Israeli labor force.[34] Around one-third of the West Bank labor force worked in Israel in 1985,[35] with around half this number working in the construction industry—a vital sector that was at the core of Israel's capitalist class, composed of large conglomerates tied to the state, private capital, and the labor Zionist movement. In this manner, Palestinian labor filled the lowest rungs of the labor market and covered some of the demand shortfall caused by prolonged Israeli military service for Jewish citizens.[36]

Simultaneously, in the West Bank and Gaza Strip, the dramatic shifts as a result of these developments meant that traditional authority structures began to break down as a generation of Palestinian youth were proletarianized and received independent sources of income. In 1970, only 43 percent of the employed labor force in the West Bank was made up of wage earners. By 1987 this had increased to 63 percent.[37] Money from Palestinians employed in Israel represented around one-quarter of Palestinian GNP between 1975 and 1985.[38] A coterminous process of urbanization took place as families were forced off the land and sought work and residence in Palestinian cities. Wealthier Palestinians from urban areas migrated to the Gulf, where they worked as teachers, as engineers, and in other skilled positions (see chapter 6).[39] The political implications of these changes were reinforced by the growth of the Palestinian national movement outside the country—most notably the Palestinian resistance movements that had shaken the Hashemite monarchy in Jordan through the 1970s and then fought the Israeli occupation and their domestic collaborators in Lebanon. Palestinian political factions brought this politicized atmosphere to the West Bank and Gaza Strip, particularly among the generation of youth attending university for the first time in their families' history.

These social changes were important factors underlying the eruption of a popular mass revolt by Palestinians in 1987. The First Intifada (literally, "shaking off") was a prolonged and large-scale uprising that lasted into the early 1990s and rapidly stamped itself on popular consciousness as a turning point in the Palestinian struggle. Israel's initial response to the uprising, summed up in prime minister Yitzhak Rabin's exhortation to "break the bones" of stone-throwing youth, was violent and characteristically brutal.[40] Despite the generally unarmed character of the uprising, Israeli soldiers and civilians killed around 1,500 Palestinians, including an estimated 300 children.[41] Thousands suffered severe injuries and tens of thousands were locked away without charge or trial. Violence, however, was not the only means that the Israeli state used in its attempt to quash the uprising. No less important to the Israeli response was the rapid development and deployment of a new institutional architecture that helped to entrench bantustanization. Most significantly, this included the widespread introduction of movement restrictions—particularly curfews, zoning restrictions, and the use of permits, passes, and military checkpoints to control entry and exit from Palestinian areas.[42]

By February 1988, travel between the West Bank and Gaza Strip had become almost impossible due to Israeli restrictions. On March 15 and 17, 1988, these restrictions were officially codified in two Israeli military orders that prevented movement between the West Bank and Gaza Strip.[43] This separation was to become a permanent and normalized feature of Palestinian life during the 1990s. In 1989, for the first time, colored ID cards were issued to Palestinians in the West Bank and Gaza Strip that identified whether the bearer was a former political prisoner or considered politically active.[44] The cards also identified place of residence. In the Gaza Strip, a regulation was passed on May 15, 1989, requiring magnetic ID cards for Palestinians wanting to enter Israel for work.[45] All these various institutional innovations laid the basis for the pass system that developed through the 1990s and 2000s, fully controlling not only entry and exit from the West Bank and Gaza Strip but also the movement of Palestinians within these areas.

Oslo Accords

The uprising came to an end with the signing of the Oslo Accords in 1993. Oslo built heavily upon the logic of the preceding decades, raising once again the notion of Palestinian "self-rule." This time, however, it was to take place under the leadership of the PLO, which had returned from exile proclaiming that a Palestinian state would soon be established in the West Bank and Gaza Strip. The returning cadre of the PLO helped to constitute the Palestinian Authority (PA), a Palestinian government with limited powers that were elaborated in Oslo and further agreements signed during the 1990s.[46]

The impetus for the Oslo signing was strongly connected to the processes discussed in chapter 2. Following the Gulf War (1990–1991), US strategy had turned toward the attempt to link its various regional allies into a single economic space, characterized by free trade and investment flows. A precondition for this was the dropping of Arab economic boycotts against the Israeli state. From the Israeli perspective, these boycotts were estimated to have cost a cumulative $40 billion from 1948 to 1994.[47] But even more important for Israeli capital than the direct cost of being isolated from the Arab world were the barriers the boycott presented to the internationalization of Israeli capital itself. In the mid-1980s, Israel had been hit by an economic crisis addressed in the neoliberal 1985 Economic Stabilization Plan (ESP), which saw the privatization of many state-owned companies and allowed the large conglomerates that dominated the Israeli economy to make the leap into international markets.[48] The ESP also opened the Israeli economy to foreign investment. Many international firms, however, were reluctant to do business with Israeli firms (or inside Israel itself) because of the secondary boycotts attached to the policies of Arab governments.[49] In this sense, Oslo was very much an outcome suited to the capitalism of its time—the expansion of internationalization that characterized the global economy of the 1990s.[50]

More important than any substantive resolution of the Israeli occupation, however, was the perception cultivated by the actors involved that negotiations would lead towards some kind of "peace." This perception permitted Arab governments—led by Jordan and Egypt—to embrace normalization with Israel under US auspices, while obscuring the fact that Oslo actually represented a continuation of the strategies underpinning the preceding forty-five years of occupation. In reality, there was no contradiction between Oslo-style "peace" and colonization—one was the prerequisite of the other.

The mechanics of this dialectic were amply illustrated by the details and outcome of the Oslo process itself. Oslo divided the West Bank into Areas A, B, and C. The PA was given autonomy in Area A, a tiny 3 percent of the West Bank in which around 20 percent of the Palestinian population lived. Another 70 percent of the Palestinian population lived in Area B, over which the PA and Israel shared joint authority, with 24 percent of the territory. Israel fully controlled Area C, with more than 70 percent of the territory. Through this division, the Oslo Accords and subsequent agreements essentially codified the intention of the 1967 Allon Plan—to transfer frontline responsibility for Israeli security to a Palestinian face, in this case the PA, while all strategic levers remained in Israeli hands. In the classic colonialist sense, Palestinians were to be given autonomy and limited self-government, carefully circumscribed within the context of Israel's continuing domination.

The means of this control had been largely set down in the preceding decades. While settlements were designated a "final status" issue under the accords, i.e., to be negotiated over a longer period of time, the Labor government immediately launched a massive settlement expansion after signing Oslo. Sharon had planned this expansion in 1991, offering large economic incentives to settlers to relocate to the West Bank and Gaza Strip.[51] The number of settlers doubled between 1994 and the beginning of the 2000s.[52] Focusing on the strategic locations established under the Allon and Sharon Plans, large settlement blocs were cut across the West Bank, preventing the natural growth of Palestinian population centers. The settlements were to be connected by another Oslo-era innovation, the so-called bypass roads—restricted-access highways that connected settlement blocs with one another and with Israeli cities, expanding upon the roads built under the Allon and Sharon Plans.[53] The 1995 Oslo II agreement outlawed Palestinian construction within fifty-five yards of either side of the bypass roads, rendering hundreds of Palestinian houses vulnerable to demolition. By mid-1996, nearly 230 kilometers of the planned 650 kilometers of bypass roads had been built on confiscated land.[54]

The net effect of all these measures meant that the 90 percent of the Palestinian population living in Areas A and B were confined to a patchwork of isolated enclaves— with the three main clusters in the northern, central, and southern sections of the West Bank divided from one another by settlement blocs. Travel between these areas could be shut down at any time by the Israeli military. All entry to and from Areas A and B, as well as determination of residency rights in these areas, was under Israeli authority. Israel also controlled the vast majority of water aquifers, all underground resources, and all air space in the West Bank—with Palestinians thus relying on Israel's discretion for their water and energy supplies. Whereas Israel by the late 1990s used close to 500 million cubic meters of water annually, drawn from aquifers in the West Bank, Palestinians in the West Bank used only 105 million.[55] A similar structure existed in the Gaza Strip, with the PA given "autonomy" and Israel retaining control over settlements and military bases. Permits were even required for Gazan fishermen to use the sea. Likewise, the entry and exit of goods and people from the Gaza Strip came under Israeli control. Movement between Gaza and the West Bank was made virtually impossible, with Israel rendering the two areas separate entities. It was, as the Palestinian author and activist Ahmad Qatamesh described in a prescient 1999 article, a PA that had "authority without any sovereignty over segmented areas, which saw the return of hundreds of thousands of PLO cadre and their families and the establishment of a Palestinian bureaucracy with governmental powers—over 120,000 strong and making up more than 20 percent of the labor force."[56]

A Disposable Reserve Army of Labor

As these movement restrictions took hold, the nature of Palestinian class forma-tion began to shift again in tandem with the evolving system of control. Beginning in 1993, Israel consciously moved to replace the Palestinian labor force that com-muted daily from the West Bank with foreign workers from Asia and Eastern Eu-rope.[57] This substitution was partly enabled by the declining importance of construction and agriculture as Israel's economy shifted away from construction and agriculture toward high-tech industries and exports of finance capital in the 1990s. Foreign workers were more costly than Palestinian labor, as they had to be housed and were brought to the country by labor-hire firms set up in Thailand, the Philippines, and Romania. But they were highly exploitable, with Israeli em-ployers frequently confiscating passports of foreign workers on arrival, employing them under very poor conditions, and often withholding pay.

The foreign workers who arrived in the hundreds of thousands following Oslo meant that the Israeli economy no longer relied so heavily upon the exploitation of cheap Palestinian labor. As these changes proceeded apace, Palestinian labor became a "tap" that could be turned on and off, depending on the economic and political sit-uation and the needs of Israeli capital. Between 1992 and 1996, Palestinian employ-ment in Israel declined from 36.2 percent of the West Bank/Gaza Strip total labor force to 14.9 percent.[58] Earnings from work in Israel collapsed from 25 percent of Palestinian GNP in 1992 to 6 percent in 1996.[59] Between 1997 and 1999, an upturn in the Israeli economy saw the number of Palestinian workers increase to approximately pre-1993 levels, but the proportion of the Palestinian labor force working inside Israel had nonetheless been almost halved compared with a decade earlier.[60] These patterns con-firm that Palestinian labor had increasingly become a marginal but highly flexible re-serve army for Israeli capitalism.[61]

Instead of working inside Israel, Palestinians became increasingly dependent on public sector employment within the PA or on transfer payments made by the PA to fam-ilies of prisoners, martyrs, or the needy. Public sector employment made up nearly 25 percent of total employment in the West Bank and Gaza Strip in mid-2000, a level that had almost doubled since mid-1996.[62] More than half the PA's expenditure went to wages for these public sector workers. The other major area of employment was the private sec-tor, particularly in the area of services. This was overwhelmingly dominated by very small, family-owned businesses (over 90 percent of Palestinian private sector businesses em-ploy fewer than ten people) as a result of decades of Israeli de-development policies.[63]

The population's heavy dependency on the PA for basic subsistence took place alongside the Palestinian economy's increasing subordination to Israel. Israel's complete control over all external borders—codified in the 1994 Paris Protocol, an economic agreement between the PA and Israel—meant that it was impossible for the Palestinian economy to develop meaningful trade relations with a third country. The Paris Protocol gave Israel the final say on what the PA was allowed to import and export.[64] The West Bank and Gaza Strip became highly dependent on imported goods, with total imports ranging between 70 and 80 percent of GDP.[65] By 2005, the Palestinian Central Bureau of Statistics estimated that 73.9 percent of all imports to the West Bank/Gaza Strip originated in Israel while 87.9 percent of all West Bank/Gaza Strip exports were destined for Israel.[66]

With no economic sovereignty, the PA was completely dependent on external capital flows of aid and loans, which were again under Israeli control. Between 1995 and 2000, 60 percent of the total PA revenue came from indirect taxes collected by the Israeli government on goods imported from abroad and destined for the occupied territories. This tax was collected by the Israeli government and then transferred to the PA each month according to a process outlined in the Paris Protocol.[67] If the Israeli government chose to withhold payment of this money for political reasons—as it was to do from December 2000 to 2002—then the PA faced a major fiscal crisis.

The other main source of PA income came from aid and foreign disbursements by the United States, Europe, and Arab governments. Indeed, figures for aid measured as a percentage of gross national income indicated that the West Bank/Gaza Strip was among the most "aid dependent" of all regions in the world.[68] This aid did not just flow to the PA; literally thousands of development organizations also received and distributed foreign funds, including local and international NGOs, multilateral agencies such as the World Bank and the UNDP, and other bilateral funders such as USAID, Canadian International Development Agency (CIDA), and the UK Department for International Development (DFID).[69] In addition to the direct funding provided by these organizations, they came to employ a significant number of Palestinians and thus, in their own right, formed a central component of the Palestinian economy.[70]

Not only did the very high dependence on these flows of external capital further cement Palestinian dependence on Israel, it also helped to facilitate the transfer of wealth to Israeli companies. The West Bank was a captive market for many Israeli goods—and because Palestinian consumption was essentially funded through external capital flows it was extremely profitable.[71] Foreign aid to the PA, in other words, was as much aid to Israel as it was to Palestinians. There were additional aspects to Israel's economic control, for example, the fact that there was no Palestinian currency meant that the monetary system was tied to decisions of the Israeli central bank. One consequence was a very high inflation rate in the West Bank, which benefited Israeli companies that sold to Palestinian consumers but simultaneously had a severe impact on the average Palestinian household.[72]

In this situation of weak local production and extremely high dependence on imports and foreign capital, the economic power of the Palestinian capitalist class did not stem from local industry but rather from proximity to the PA as the main conduit of external capital inflows. Through the Oslo years this class came together through the fusion of three distinct social groups: (1) "Returnee" capital, mostly from a Palestinian bourgeoisie that had emerged in the Gulf and held strong ties to the emerging PA (see chapter 6); (2) families and individuals who had traditionally dominated Palestinian society, often large landowners from the pre-1967 period (particularly in the northern areas of the West Bank); (3) those who had managed to accumulate wealth through their position as interlocutors with the occupation since 1967. The membership of these three groups overlapped considerably, but this new configuration of the capitalist class tended to draw its wealth from a privileged relationship with the PA, which assisted its growth through means such as granting monopolies for goods including cement, petrol, flour, steel, and cigarettes; issuing exclusive import permits and customs exemptions; giving sole rights to distribute goods in the West Bank/Gaza Strip; and distributing government-owned land at below market value.[73] In addition to these state-assisted forms of accumulation, much of the investment that came into the West Bank from foreign donors through the Oslo years—e.g., road and infrastructure construction, new building projects, agricultural and tourist developments—was also typically connected to this new capitalist class in some form.

In the context of the PA's fully subordinated position, the ability to accumulate was always tied to Israeli consent and thus came with a political price—one designed to buy compliance with ongoing colonization. It also meant that the key components of the Palestinian elite—the wealthiest businessmen, the PA's state bureaucracy, and the remnants of the PLO itself—came to share a common interest with Israel's political project. The rampant spread of patronage and corruption were the logical byproducts of this system, as individual survival depended upon personal relationships with the PA. The systemic corruption of the PA that Israel and Western governments regularly decried through the 1990s was, in other words, a necessary and inevitable consequence of the very system that these powers had established.

The Second Intifada

The ramifications of this system of control were to become fully apparent with the outbreak of a second uprising in September 2000. The Second Intifada, as it became known, lasted approximately five years and transformed the nature of life in the West Bank/Gaza Strip. The root causes of the uprising were very much a consequence of the preceding decade: the disastrous deterioration in Palestinian living conditions and the ongoing consolidation of Israeli suzerainty. In July 2000, US president Bill Clinton had invited Israeli prime minister Ehud Barak and Palestinian president Yasser Arafat to Camp David to conclude negotiations on the Oslo Accord's long-overdue final status agreement, which aimed to bring to an end all the outstanding issues, including refugees, Jerusalem, borders, and settlements. Barak proclaimed his "red lines": Israel would not return to its pre-1967 borders, East Jerusalem with its 175,000 Jewish settlers would remain under Israeli control, Israel would annex settlement blocs in the West Bank containing some 80 percent of the 180,000 Jewish settlers, and Israel would accept no legal or moral responsibility for the seven million Palestinian refugees. The negotiations collapsed, with Arafat unwilling to sign away these basic rights. The failure of the Camp David negotiations was followed soon after by Ariel Sharon's provocative visit on September 28, 2000, to Haram Al Sharif (the Noble Sanctuary) in Jerusalem. His visit to a Muslim holy site, accompanied by one thousand armed guards, provoked large Palestinian protests.[74] Israeli soldiers killed six unarmed protesters during these demonstrations—igniting the Second Intifada.

The Second Intifada, in contrast to the First, was militarized relatively early on. After hundreds of Palestinians were shot dead by Israeli troops during protests, Palestinian factions increasingly began to launch armed attacks against soldiers and to conduct bombings inside Israeli towns. Israel responded with widespread collective punishment, assassination of Palestinian militants, and mass arrest campaigns. As repression grew, the Israeli military reentered Palestinian areas and enforced extended curfews on the population. Between December 18, 2002, and January 19, 2003, according to an estimate of the Palestinian Red Crescent, an average of 430,910 people were stuck in their houses each day.[75] Alongside this army-enforced lockup, the constant bombardment of cities and infrastructure by helicopter gunships and tank fire generated a humanitarian disaster, with almost 75 percent of the population living on less than the UN official poverty line of two dollars per day through 2003. Up to eighty thousand Palestinians lost their jobs inside Israel or the settlements due to border closures and Israel's refusal to issue permits. According to a study prepared for the World Food Program, the official level of unemployment in the West Bank almost tripled between 1999 and 2002, reaching 28.2 percent of the population.[76] In some areas of the Gaza Strip, the unemployment rate climbed to over 70 percent.[77] The human toll was also unprecedented, with over 3,700 Palestinians killed and 29,000 wounded throughout the uprising—the vast majority civilians attempting to go about their daily lives.

All these measures confirmed the degree to which the preceding decades of bantustanization had enabled Israel to rapidly subjugate an entire population through the simple restriction of movement. This process intensified further with the announcement in November 2000 of Israel's plan to build a sprawling barrier through the West Bank, dubbed the Apartheid Wall by Palestinians. Construction began in June 2002, consisting of a network of concrete walls and electric fences, eventually extending to 730 kilometers, which demarcated three principal Palestinian ghettoes in the West Bank and locked thousands of Palestinians inside their towns and villages. Its route closely corresponded to the maps elaborated in the Allon and Sharon Plans, confirming that it was envisaged as a final step in the bantustanization of the population. Its effects were demonstrated most sharply in the West Bank city of Qalqilya, which was completely surrounded by the wall in July 2002—an eight-meter concrete barrier, cutting off the 41,600 residents from the outside world.[78] An Israeli military checkpoint marked the only exit and entrance in and out of the city. The unemployment rate in Qalqilya rose to 67 percent in the wake of the wall's construction and 10 percent of the population were forced to leave the city in order to find livelihood elsewhere.[79]

The effects of the wall and the unremitting repression against the civilian population meant that the Second Intifada began to lose steam in 2004–2005. Arafat, who had willingly signed the Oslo Accords and had generally acquiesced to Israeli diktats through the 1990s, proved reluctant and unable to play the role of Israeli gendarme. Despite the efforts of Israel and the United States—backed by Egypt and Jordan, which promised assistance in training an internal Palestinian security force to repress the uprising—Arafat continued to refuse a complete crackdown on the population. Following a long Israeli siege that held him captive for more than two years in his Ramallah headquarters, he died in November 2004.

The Gaza–West Bank Split

Arafat was succeeded by Mahmoud Abbas, otherwise known as Abu Mazen. Abu Mazen had been a founding member of Fatah, the major Palestinian political faction, and one of its major financial backers in the late 1960s. Since 1983 he had been a central proponent of normalizing relations with the Israeli government, and his accession to the Palestinian leadership was strongly supported by Israel, the United States, and the EU. His coming to power brought a definite end to the Second Intifada—to which he had been strongly opposed from the beginning—but it also cast into sharp relief the nature of Israel's control over the West Bank/Gaza Strip. Bantustanization was fully consolidated in the years following his accession to power, with all the various threads developed in the preceding years brought to bear on the nature of the PA and its policies in the areas it controlled. A principal element of this was the full embrace of neoliberal policies by the PA.

Following the death of Yasser Arafat, Palestinian politics began to fragment inside the bantustans. Fatah splintered into localized, small groups. Arafat's Fatah had been organized through a complicated network of individuals, each with their own localized bases of support. Arafat had sat atop this pyramid structure, controlling the distribution of funds, and each group held different allegiances to individuals within Fatah, which provided for little overall clarity in political program. With Arafat's death this system fractured along local and familial lines. Abu Mazen himself held a tenuous grip on power and spent much of his time traveling overseas. His government was split between competing centers of power and was unable to deliver any improvement in the economic situation or a semblance of order. There was widespread popular anger with the PA over the disorder and chaos in the cities, corruption, the worsening economic condition, and the lack of attention given to the thousands of Palestinians held in Israeli prisons.

In this context, Fatah was strongly rivaled by a second political faction, the Islamic Resistance Movement (Hamas). While a large number of its activists had been killed or arrested by occupation forces, Hamas had built a strong network of social institutions on which many Palestinians relied for survival. Its leadership was widely respected in the immediate aftermath of the Second Intifada and was viewed as untainted by the corruption of the PA, in which it had refused to participate. Hamas sought to convert the gains made during the Intifada into its own political power—and came out strongly against the path of Oslo-type negotiations with which Abu Mazen was so closely associated. The organization chose not to contest presidential elections for the PA in 2005 and, as a result, Abu Mazen won these comfortably. But Hamas did decide to contest the elections for the Palestinian Legislative Council (PLC), which were held in January 2006 after being initially postponed by Abu Mazen. Election results indicated a massive swing toward Hamas. Hamas won 74 out of the 132 seats, compared to 45 for Fatah. The secular-left Popular Front for the Liberation of Palestine (PFLP) managed 3 seats, and 2 seats each went to three smaller parties.[80] The popular vote for Hamas was a clear rejection of the Oslo process as well as the corruption, nepotism, and profiteering of the ruling party, Fatah.

In the months after the Hamas victory, a national unity government was set up between Hamas and Fatah. Abu Mazen dissolved this apparatus for joint rule, however, shortly after Hamas seized control of the Gaza Strip on June 14, 2007. Separate authorities formed in Gaza (Hamas-controlled) and the West Bank (Abu Mazen/PA–controlled). The complete separation of the two territories was sealed by an unprecedented Israeli blockade of Gaza, controlling all border crossings and the entry of goods and fuel supplies to the more than 1.4 million inhabitants of this "open-air prison."[81] In December 2008, Israel launched a twenty-two-day war against Gaza that killed more than 1,100 residents and left 50,000 homeless, up to 500,000 without running water, and one million without electricity.[82] The cost of the damage was estimated to be around $2 billion.[83]

The Neoliberal Turn

The 2007 division of the West Bank and Gaza Strip into two completely separate entities merely consumated the long-standing trajectory of bantustanization that began with the occupation in 1967 and reached its zenith in the Oslo Accords. Despite claims to the contrary, the negotiations of the previous two decades had never aimed at achieving a genuinely independent state but were rather a mechanism designed to achieve Palestinian consent to the ongoing colonization of the West Bank and Gaza Strip. Israel's goal was a PA that would police the Palestinian population while allowing the encirclement and isolation of Palestinian towns and villages through the network of settlements, bypass roads, and checkpoints.[84] Palestinian transit between these isolated areas would be controlled by a complicated system of permits and movement restrictions. These population islands would be given the trappings of autonomy, but effective control would remain in the hands of the Israeli state.

Following the split between Fatah and Hamas in 2006–2007, Israel and other foreign states moved quickly to shore up their support for the PA in the West Bank. On December 17, 2007, at a one-day conference in Paris, more than ninety international representatives from various countries and donor organizations gathered to pledge aid to the PA government, headed by Abu Mazen as president and a former IMF official, Salam Fayyad, as prime minister. The conference was the largest of its kind since 1996, and was chaired by the French and Norwegian governments, then British prime minister Tony Blair (as representative of the Middle East Quartet),[85] and the European Commission. Following speeches by representatives of various EU member states, the PA, the IMF, and the Israeli government, attendees pledged over $7.7 billion to the PA. The main impetus for this financial support was the new PA economic strategy, the *Palestine Reform and Development Plan for 2008–2010* (PRDP), which powerfully confirmed the realignment of class power that had occurred over the last decade.

The outlines of the PRDP were first presented in November 2007 and drew upon a detailed series of proposals written by the World Bank and other international financial institutions.[86] Since that time it has become the guiding framework for economic policy in the West Bank areas where the Abu Mazen–led PA has effective control. Its logic was explicitly neoliberal, pledging the PA to undertake a series of economic reforms in order to reach a "diversified and thriving free market economy led by a pioneering private sector that is in harmony with the Arab world, [and] is open to regional and global markets."[87] Echoing a worldview based upon the mutually reinforcing and necessarily compatible relationship between democracy and free markets, it noted that "The eventual Palestinian state . . . will protect human rights, religious tolerance and the rule of law, promote gender equality, create an enabling environment for a free and open market economy, and serve the needs of disadvantaged and vulnerable groups, enabling all citizens to fulfill their potential."[88] In this vision, the unhindered operation of the market, coupled with the formal trappings of political democracy, would produce the best possible outcome. Rich and poor, Palestinians and Israelis—all would benefit from the increasing spread of market relations.

There were three main policy components to the PRDP: public sector fiscal reform, private sector–led development, and security. The reform component committed the PA to a program of fiscal tightening that exceeded measures imposed by the IMF and the World Bank on any other state in the region. This included a sharp reduction in the size of the public sector (where the PA committed itself to a 21 percent reduction in jobs by 2010[89]; a promise not to increase public sector salaries, which in effect meant a sharp decrease in the real wage due to the high inflation in the West Bank; as well as an end to the subsidization of electricity and water bills through the requirement that citizens present a "certificate of payment" in order to receive any municipal or government services. This last measure had a dramatic impact on the poor because the subsidization of electricity and water bills (i.e., allowing these services to continue despite the nonpayment of bills) was a central means of survival for many people in an environment of rapidly spiraling poverty levels. Vital municipal services—including requests to obtain movement permits—could be denied if debts were outstanding. As the vast majority of these payments were destined for Israeli companies controlling the supply of water, electricity, and telephone access, the PA was, in essence, agreeing to become a debt collector for the Israeli occupation.

For the impact of these measures to be fully comrehended, they need to be placed in the context of the economic situation at the time. During the period 1999–2007, Palestinian GDP per capita declined by approximately two-thirds and personal savings were wiped out as a result of Israeli attacks on Palestinian areas. Poverty levels reached the worst on record, with around three-quarters of households in Gaza and 56 percent in the West Bank living under the poverty line. As poverty levels increased, so did inequality. One study noted that in 2007 the richest 10 percent of households in the West Bank accounted for 25.8 percent of total monthly consumption, up from 21.6 percent in 2006.[90] Combined with the high dependency on PA employment (around 20 percent of the labor force in the West Bank/Gaza Strip),[91] the PRDP's plan to gut the public sector labor force, impose a wage freeze as prices skyrocketed, and compel the poor to immediately pay millions of dollars in debt spelled out a profound attack on the living standards of the population.

The same neoliberal logic was expressed in the PRDP's development component. The plan sought to utilize cheap labor in industrial zones and parks, located at the edges of the patchwork of Palestinian territories in the West Bank. Reminiscent of the QIZs in Egypt and Jordan, these zones would bring together Israeli, Palestinian, and regional investments in sectors such as traditional low value-added goods (such as textiles and garments) as well as high-tech sectors that could complement the Israeli economy.[92] This development strategy confirmed how the structures of the occupation had been normalized and legitimated within the model pursued by the World Bank and the PA. Land for an industrial zone in Jenin, for example, had been twice confiscated from Palestinian farmers: in 1998, when the PA first proposed the idea for the industrial zone, and then again in 2003, when the Israeli military confiscated the land as part of construction for the Apartheid Wall "buffer-zone."[93] By 2010, there were four industrial zones under construction in the West Bank, with funding from a range of international donors.[94]

Alongside these economic measures, the PA also began rebuilding its state apparatus in the West Bank. Essential to this was the reconstitution of its security forces, which took place with the open support of Western military and intelligence agencies. The PA security budget was allocated the largest portion of all funding in the PRDP ($257 million), with money going to the training of new police and intelligence forces as well as the construction of new prisons. A US Army officer, Lieutenant General Keith Dayton—fresh from his position as head of the search for alleged "weapons of mass destruction" in Iraq, following the 2003 US-led invasion—was the key point person for the training of Palestinian police. Headquartered in Tel Aviv and supported by British, Canadian, and Turkish personnel, Dayton's mission involved running two training compounds in Jordan and the West Bank for Palestinian security forces.[95] Under Dayton's watch, these security forces were responsible for the torture of hundreds of Palestinian activists (often borrowing from techniques utilized in Israeli prisons), which led to the deaths in custody of at least three prisoners in 2009.[96]

Absenting Power and the Neutrality of Markets

Much like the experiences in neighboring countries, the Palestinian neoliberal turn was accompanied by the close entwining of IFIs with the institutions of the PA. This is most starkly illustrated by the fact that the distribution of donor funding to the PA was made contingent on the implementation of the PRDP, and this would be administered through a trust fund that was headquartered in Washington, DC, and managed by the World Bank.[97] In this sense, IFIs came to fully oversee Palestinian economic development and policy making. Indeed, some Palestinian grassroots organizations have gone so far as to describe these financial institutions as "a de facto 'shadow government' in the West Bank, dictating the development programme of the Salam Fayyad government."[98]

This penetration of the Palestinian state was enabled by a particular discursive framing that posited IFIs as neutral, objective "experts" on economic issues, simply aiming to provide sound advice on matters of policy and institutional governance. To this end, the term "technocrat" was frequently used to convey this sense of neutrality, describing someone allegedly disinterested in "politics" and therefore a supposedly more responsible leader. Fayyad was heralded as an outstanding example of such a technocrat—and his former employment with the IMF was actually used to endorse his economic program as one that was objectively the best course of action and in the interests of the Palestinian people. In this manner, the responsibility of institutions such as the IMF and World Bank for the disastrous social outcomes elsewhere in the region (as described in previous chapters) was largely erased from popular discourse.

This notion of being "apolitical" runs consistently through the PRDP and subsequent economic programs, emptying any consideration of colonization or Israeli power from Palestinian economic strategy. A 2010 World Bank report argued, for example, that "sustainable growth and robust institutions for the future Palestinian state" requires "a joint undertaking of the PA, GoI [Government of Israel], as well as the international community . . . all three have played their role in the recent growth that has taken place in WB&G . . . For the GoI, further actions to improve the conditions on the ground and allow a real take-off in private sector development are necessary."[99] In this vision, policy-making by the PA and policy-making by Israel are treated as two distinct and autonomous spheres, and Israeli settler-colonialism is portrayed as merely a set of administrative regulations that may (or may not) "hinder" Palestinian development, rather than as a form of power that necessarily penetrates all aspects of Palestinian society. The occupation is framed *as a partner* of Palestinian development rather than its antithesis.

This absenting of power leads directly to the incorporation of Israeli colonialism into the process of development itself. Thus the World Bank was able to state that Palestinian development required an "easing of continued [Israeli] economic restrictions"[100]—a phrasing that does not challenge Israel's *right* to control movement as such but, in contrast, effectively asks Israel to exercise that power by deciding to what extent Palestinian goods and people are able to move. The absenting of Israeli power is also evident in the World Bank's call for the PA to "continue to work with its Israeli counterparts to try and return Palestinian customs personnel to the Allenby Bridge where they can once again work alongside Israeli Customs and practice actual customs border procedures and gain needed experience."[101] Here, Israeli border personnel are portrayed as neutral experts in customs control rather than functionaries of a colonizing power. This process is even more explicit in the World Bank's open acceptance of Israel's Apartheid Wall—declared illegal by the International Court of Justice in 2004—for which it has helped to fund Israeli checkpoints (as it also did throughout the wider West Bank).[102]

The end result of this obfuscation of power is simple—those who hold it stand to benefit. Concurrently, as is typically the case with the neoliberal program, the bulk of the population suffered a worsening of living standards and increasing inequality. Much like the rest of the Middle East, the Palestinian territories experienced high levels of growth in the latter half of the first decade of the 2000s—averaging between 7.1 to 9.3 percent annually from 2008 to 2010.[103] In the West Bank, real per capita GDP increased from just over $1,400 in 2007 to around $1,900 in 2010, the fastest growth in a decade.[104] At the same time, however, the unemployment rate remained essentially constant in the West Bank—at around 20 percent, it was among the highest in the world.[105] One of the consequences of this was a profound level of poverty—around 20 percent of Palestinians in the West Bank were living on less than $1.67 a day for a family of five in 2009 and 2010, and more than 10 percent on less than $1.30 a day for a family of five.[106] Despite these poverty levels, the consumption of the richest 10 percent increased from 20.3 percent of total consumption in 2009 to 22.5 percent in 2010.[107]

In these circumstances, growth has been based on prodigious increases in debt-based spending on services and real estate. According to the United Nations Conference on Trade and Development (UNCTAD), the hotel and restaurant sector grew by 46 percent in 2010 while construction increased by 36 percent.[108] At the same time, manufacturing decreased by 6 percent.[109] The massive levels of consumer-based debt are indicated in figures from the Palestinian Monetary Authority, which show that the amount of bank credit almost doubled from May 2008 to May 2010 (from $1.72 billion to $3.37 billion).[110] Much of this involved consumer-based spending on residential real estate, automobile purchases, or credit cards—the amount of credit extended for these three sectors increased by a remarkable 245 percent from 2008 to 2011.[111] These figures are reflected spatially in the visual landscape of West Bank towns such as Ramallah, where advertisements for new condominiums, housing developments, and car loans have replaced the ubiquitous political graffiti of the last decade.

These forms of individual consumer and household debt had a deep impact on how people viewed their capacities for social struggle and their relation to society. Increasingly caught in the web of financial relationships, individuals are taught to satisfy needs through the market—usually through borrowing money—rather than through collective struggle for social rights. This also transforms the individual sense of self-worth, which is no longer measured by community solidarity or collective struggle but by individual possessions. The growth of these financial- and debt-based relations acted to individualize the nature of Palestinian society. It had a deeply conservatizing influence on the Palestinian political project over the latter half of the 2000s—with much of the population becoming more concerned with "stability" and the ability to pay off debt rather than the possibility of popular resistance.[112]

Nonetheless, despite the relative success of this neoliberal project in the period immediately following the Second Intifada, it would be wrong to assume its permanent ability to pacify the Palestinian population. In many ways, these neoliberal structures act to undermine their own conditions of existence. Most notably, they have clarified the role of the PA to a degree not previously witnessed in the West Bank. The significance of this was confirmed in 2011 with the emergence of a range of new youth movements, which, although scattered, directly confronted the complicity of the PA and decried the deterioration of economic conditions. The development of such movements—connected to the growing success of global campaigns to isolate the Israeli state through boycotts and divestment, along with calls to reinvigorate the structures of the PLO—illustrate that the Palestinian people have not been defeated.

Conclusion

Since the first waves of colonization in Palestine there has been a conscious intent to splinter the Palestinian national identity into a patchwork of fragmented, dispersed territories that evolve as distinct social formations. This is clearly illustrated in the various categories that comprise the Palestinian people: Palestinian refugees, now the largest body of refugees in the world; Palestinians who remained on their land in 1948 and later became citizens of the Israeli state; those scattered in the cantons of the West Bank; and, most recently, others isolated in the Gaza Strip. All these groups of people constitute the Palestinian nation—but the denial of this unity has been the overriding logic of colonization since before 1948.

This fragmentation has been made possible by military power. Israel forcibly prevents Palestinian refugees from returning to their land, divides the West Bank and Gaza Strip from each other, places administrative restrictions on the movement of Palestinian citizens of Israel into the occupied territories, and completely controls movement in the West Bank itself. At the same time—and this is a crucial point that often goes unstated—dispossession and expulsion of Palestinians from their land continues in a slow-motion manner, confirming that al-nakba is ongoing.[113] But fragmentation is not solely a spatial process; it necessarily rests upon a temporal disruption. The assault on history itself becomes an integral feature of how colonization functions, with the Palestinian experience dehistoricized and reduced to a recent narrative that accepts the results of fragmentation as permanent and given. It becomes possible to speak of "Gazans," for example, around 70 percent of whom are actually refugees from 1948, with no reference to how this category was constructed through the forcible fragmentation of the Palestinian people as a whole—first during al-nakba, and then through the separation of the West Bank and Gaza Strip. Or to speak of "empty spaces" in the West Bank with no mention of the dispossession of one-fifth of the population in 1967. Because these categories are accepted as given—legitimized as the focus of political negotiations, financial aid packages, and development strategies—they continue to be reproduced. This process is normalized and sustained through the operational practices of foreign governments, NGOs, and a myriad of development agencies, thus providing a materiality to Israeli power.

At the same time as Israeli colonization was a military project aimed at the fragmentation and destruction of Palestinian identity, it also changed the Palestinian economy. In the West Bank, this has meant a type of "hothouse capitalism," in which the power of the occupation generated many of the same processes of social transformation noted in previous chapters. Rural inhabitants were dispossessed from the land and forced to join migrant labor markets. A capitalist class developed through subcontracting and privileged trade relationships with the occupation. In more recent years, Palestinian policy makers eagerly embraced a neoliberal model of development in close partnership with IFIs. This is neoliberalism under occupation, one driven by an identical logic and reinforcing the same coincidence of poverty and enrichment as seen elsewhere in the region. In this sense, there is very little that is unique in the types of economic policies that are today being implemented by the PA—they have been the standard fare of governments across the Middle East for at least two decades.

Palestinian acquiescence to this process did not come about simply due to the corruption of individual leaders, misplaced political decisions, or an unfavorable international context. Indispensable to explaining the trajectory of the last forty-five years are these shifts that took place in the Palestinian political economy, in which the development of capitalism in the West Bank and Gaza Strip was accelerated by the whip of Israeli colonization, ensuring the ancillary integration of these areas into the Israeli economy. The profound transformation of Palestinian class structure that occurred in lockstep with Israel's colonization underpins Palestinian submission to Oslo and the nature of the PA.

The specificity of the neoliberal experience in Palestine lies in the total subjugation of the population by an occupying force and the attempts of more than six decades to fragment and disperse a nation of people from their homeland. Neoliberalism works to reinforce this atomization—turning people away from collective struggle and toward individualized consumption, as mediated through finance. It has produced mass impoverishment alongside the enrichment of a tiny layer of Palestinians that acts as the interlocutor with Israeli and foreign capital. A society constructed along these principles weakens the capacity of the Palestinian people to resist. Most importantly, it means that the question of Palestine cannot be reduced to a purely "humanitarian" issue or simply an issue of national liberation; it is an essential component of the broader struggle against the uneven development and control of wealth across the Middle East. Capitalist development has always acted to consolidate and deepen Israel's power over Palestine, generating a layer of Palestinian society that stands against the interests of most of the population. In this sense, understanding and confronting the political economy of Palestinian capitalism is very much entwined with a struggle of national liberation and return—the success of one fully depends upon the success of the other.

CHAPTER 6

The Regional Scale: Bringing the Gulf Arab States Back In

arlier chapters have outlined the ways in which the Gulf region, and by extension the entire Middle East, emerged as a vital zone within the world market following World War II. Two important features of contemporary capitalism—the internationalization and financialization of capital—gave the Gulf's commodity exports and financial surpluses enormous strategic weight within the global political economy. These tendencies consolidated the Gulf as a region of the world market—integrating it into the architecture of the US-led global capitalism that arose during the postwar era. For these reasons, control and domination of the Middle East has remained an essential goal of Western powers well into the twenty-first century.

Nonetheless, despite the primacy of the Gulf states to the strategic calculations of imperialism, a thorough analysis of the region's social relations has been largely absent from radical accounts of the region. Too often the Gulf is simply reduced to a giant oil spigot, somehow distinct from the processes discussed in previous chapters. The Gulf may indeed be made up of the archetypal "oil-rich monarchies" so favored as an analytical category of mainstream Middle East political science, but fetishization of the oil commodity can lead to a kind of methodological exceptionalism that obscures serious examination of the questions of capitalism and class. The aim of this chapter is to refocus attention on the characteristics of the Gulf's own class and state formation—to show how the Gulf states have developed a particular form of political economy that remains, regardless of its specificities, fully capitalist and subject to the same dynamics as other neighboring states.[1]

The chapter begins by tracing the ways in which the working classes of the Gulf came to be constituted through an extremely heavy reliance on temporary migrant labor. Class boundaries were largely demarcated by citizenship rights, with migrant workers forming a highly exploited and easily deportable population that underpinned the privileged layers of citizenship (itself also stratified depending on proximity to the ruling family). The chapter then moves to mapping the concurrent growth of the Gulf's capitalist classes around the three main circuits of accumulation—the productive, commodity, and financial. These routes of accumulation were mediated through a myriad of family and business ties to the state apparatus and ruling families, producing a capitalism structured around massive conglomerates that form a class in their own right—not simply a mechanical expression of any "rentier state."

The final part of the chapter recasts these dynamics of class and state at spatial scales beyond the national level. The large Gulf conglomerates that emerged in earlier periods increasingly conceive their accumulation at a pan-Gulf scale, supported by the development of the regional integration project embodied in the Gulf Cooperation Council (GCC). Moreover, the spread of neoliberalism throughout most Arab states has progressively opened these countries to capital flows from the Gulf—a phenomenon that is discussed in some detail below for the case of Egypt. These processes confirm a growing influence of Gulf capitalism that has arisen concurrent with the neoliberal processes traced in previous chapters—giving the configuration of state and class in the Gulf a vital place within an understanding of the broader region.

The Weight of Migrant Labor

Many of the key characteristics of the contemporary Gulf states originated in the five decades stretching from the 1930s to the 1970s. During this period, the slow decline of the British Empire—punctuated most graphically by India's independence in 1947—occurred alongside the growth of the Gulf's oil industry and the ensuing transition from British to US hegemony.[2] The expansion in oil revenues raised pointed questions as to how the region's prodigious wealth should be distributed. Rivalries emerged between different factions of the ruling families in the Gulf, merchant classes, and other social groups. Simultaneously, the mood of independence reverberating throughout the Middle East was also felt in the Gulf sheikhdoms of Kuwait, Bahrain, Oman, Qatar, and the seven "Trucial States" that were to become the future United Arab Emirates. In the context of these unprecedented changes, the United States and Britain—and the local monarchies on whom their power rested—were faced with considerable challenges in ensuring that the region remained secure and tied to Western interests.

Initially, the ruling families of the former British dependencies (and Saudi Arabia, which was closer to the United States) attempted to subdue any internal dissent through the judicious deployment of oil wealth. Much of this money went to merchant classes (particularly in Kuwait, Bahrain, and Dubai, where this layer had a history of protest and agitation through the 1930s) and to different factions within the ruling family (Qatar, where the internal divisions of the ruling al Thani family were most acute, stands out in this respect).[3] Ruling families distributed construction contracts for infrastructure, security, and other oil-related activities; gave exclusive licensing, agency, and distribution rights for foreign-produced imports; and provided cheap (and, in some cases, free) land to merchants from which they benefited handsomely following price inflation as urbanization proceeded. All of these mechanisms of redistribution helped ensure loyalty to the ruling family and were critical to the initial formation of capitalist classes in the Gulf (see below).

Challenge to the ruling families did not just come from merchant classes. Through the 1950s and 1960s, as earlier chapters have noted, the Middle East witnessed the emergence of powerful mass struggles in Iran, Egypt, Iraq, and elsewhere. These nationalist, leftist, and anticolonial movements were also reflected within the Gulf Arab states, which were shaken by strikes led by oil workers who sought greater control over oil resources and an end to the extreme exploitation often found in the work camps of British and US oil companies.[4] These early worker movements were particularly inspired by the struggles in Egypt and Palestine, and were thus strident in their condemnation of the Gulf monarchies and their collaboration with the colonial powers. Moreover, other social struggles in the Gulf often overlapped with these worker and anticolonial movements—notably the situation of Shi'a in Bahrain, Saudi Arabia, and Kuwait, and the guerrilla struggles in the Dhofar region of Oman. All these struggles faced the heavy hand of repression, including the arrest, exile, and killing of political activists.

These violent measures, however, were only one side to the Gulf states' response to strikes and political agitation. Accompanying state repression, each of the Gulf monarchies pursued a distinctive form of labor relations as a means of ensuring subordination to the ruling family. Class came to be constituted through an acute reliance on temporary migrant labor flows, with citizenship restricted to a minority of the population. From the 1970s onward, the temporary migrant worker population grew to a remarkable 50–70 percent of the labor force in Saudi Arabia, Oman, and Bahrain, and to 80–90 percent in the remaining Gulf states.[5] Denied rights of citizenship or permanent residency, migrant workers formed the lower ranks of a two-tier system dominated by a narrow layer of "nationals" who had access to public sector jobs, grants of land, free or cheap housing, and social services such as health and education. This highly stratified structure was above all a *spatial* process—class materialized through the set of relations established by labor flows between different geographical spaces, mediated through the institutional arrangements of citizenship and differential laws. In this manner, ruling families wielded a powerful system of control over the vast majority of the resident population while ensuring citizen allegiance to this highly unequal status quo.

Understanding the Nature of Migrant Work in the Gulf

This "spatial structuring of class" is an essential feature of understanding class formation in the Gulf and the Middle East more generally.[6] Very often analyses of the Gulf explain the large reliance on migrant workers as a consequence of a "lack of skills" in the region, or from shortages of population in small countries such as Qatar or the UAE, which are matched by the large populations of nearby countries such as Egypt or India.[7] In this sense, migration is presented as a "positive-sum game," which matches labor supplies and demand across the region. Labor-sending countries are said to benefit from migration through the sending home of remittances, while the Gulf gets workers who are able to keep their economies functioning. Any difficulties faced by migrant workers are explained as a result of the inadequacy of regulations and laws—an administrative issue that can be solved with the right policy mix.

A key problem with this approach is that it ignores the inherently exploitative nature of the labor-capital relation. Wages are not a "just reward" or "fair compensation" for the labor performed by workers but an expression of their exploitation; wages hide the fact that there is a difference, which Marx called surplus value, between the value of the labor power a worker expends during the workday and the value of the commodity they produce.[8] While a worker is paid a wage for their labor power that is, on average, equivalent to its value, the surplus value is "unpaid labor" that is appropriated by the owner of capital.[9] The greater the difference between the value of the commodities workers produce and the value of the commodities it takes to reproduce them as a class (the latter of which is expressed by wage levels), the greater the exploitation. This exploitation is inherent to the capital-labor relation under capitalism—"capitalists *must* exploit their workers if they are to remain in business; the workers *must* concur in order to satisfy their immediate needs; and exploitation is the fuel that moves capitalist production and exchange."[10]

There are three main consequences of using this framework for understanding the nature of migrant work in the Gulf. First, it means that migration to the Gulf needs to be viewed as a type of class formation that links the development of social relations across different spaces in the region and thereby casts the labor-capital relation in the Gulf as internal (in Ollman's sense) to the social relations of neighboring countries. This implies, in one aspect, that the Gulf benefits from the degrading of conditions of life elsewhere in the region, because this deterioration cheapens the value of reproduction of workers and thereby increases the value appropriated in the Gulf itself. A construction worker in the Gulf coming from the Egyptian countryside can be paid a very low wage because the value of their labor power is measured relative to conditions in Egypt; the worse those conditions are, the lower the amount they will be willing to accept. Seen in this light, the neoliberal processes described in previous chapters form one of the mechanisms through which the Gulf's dominant position in regional hierarchies is strengthened. Remittance flows from the Gulf are thus not a form of "aid" or "regional solidarity," as they are often portrayed, but exactly the opposite—a register of exploitation.[11]

Second, the various laws and regulations that govern the conditions of migrant work in the Gulf are the legal expression of this spatial structuring of class. They are a necessary condition for the value of the migrant worker's labor power—the average cost of reproducing the worker—to be measured relative to conditions in the home country rather than in the Gulf itself. If all workers in the Gulf were granted equal labor and citizenship rights, then the intensified exploitation of migrant workers enabled under this system would disappear.[12] Seen in this light, precisely because the differential laws that demarcate citizens from "noncitizens" are constitutive of the spatial structuring of class, the problems that exist with these laws are not merely legislative weaknesses or policy oversights—they cannot be solved without challenging the inherent structure of the system itself.

Finally, these processes are not only a means of exploitation but also a mechanism of class discipline. This needs to be situated in the specific location of the Middle East (and the Gulf) within the global hierarchies discussed in earlier chapters. The centrality of the Gulf to the development of both contemporary capitalism and US power places the nature of the Gulf's working classes at the heart of the global system. The emergence of a strong and militant labor movement in the Gulf—the likelihood of which would be greatly increased upon the extension of equal rights to *all* workers regardless of origin—could profoundly challenge the position of Gulf rulers and their Western supporters. For this reason, the exclusion of labor is embedded within the characteristics of state formation itself—the spatial structuring of class is a form of social control that is a necessary corollary to the Gulf's ascension as a core zone within the global economy.[13] Confirmation of this can be seen by looking to two of the Gulf's oil-rich neighbors—Iraq and Iran—where large indigenous working classes exist and have built important and powerful movements throughout the last century. The presence of a precarious, easily deportable, and highly exploited migrant working class—demarcated through the institution of citizenship—is a major difference between the Gulf monarchies and these neighboring states.

Patterns and Conditions of Migrant Work in the Gulf

With these three theoretical propositions in mind, it is now possible to consider the concrete forms of the spatial structuring of class in the Gulf and the actual conditions faced by migrant workers. In the 1970s, more than 70 percent of migrant workers in the Gulf were Arab—primarily Egyptian, Yemeni, Palestinian, Jordanian, Lebanese, and Syrian. Many of these workers were involved in construction activities (in 1975, 75 percent of Yemeni migrant workers, 50 percent of Egyptian workers, and 40 percent of Jordanian workers).[14] Arab migrants—particularly Palestinian, Egyptian, and Jordanian—also took up positions as teachers, engineers, doctors, and other professionals. These flows of labor were reinforced by various political crises throughout the Arab world. In the case of Palestine, for example, the Israeli occupation of the West Bank and Gaza Strip led to nearly 40 percent of the available Palestinian labor force migrating for work through the mid-1970s.[15] By 1975, Palestinians were the largest nonnative population living in Kuwait, constituting around 40 percent of all non-Kuwaitis.[16] As a consequence of these flows of labor migration, there was a tripling in the level of remittances from the Gulf to the rest of the Arab world from 1973 to 1980,[17] with many governments proffering remittances and the export of labor power as a potential solution to foreign currency shortfalls and high unemployment levels.

A particularly important source of these early flows of labor was Egypt, which provided more workers to the Gulf than any other Arab country. As rural families were squeezed by the liberalization of tenancy laws initiated by Sadat and deepened under Mubarak (see chapter 4), many sought their chances in the Gulf. The right to seek work overseas was enshrined in the Egyptian constitution in 1971, and Egyptian law was modified in 1974 such that no exit visas were required to leave the country. The Egyptian government's 1978–1982 Five Year Plan established vocational centers aimed at training citizens to work overseas, offered special bonds to workers in the Gulf, and set a favorable exchange rate to encourage investment of earnings back in Egypt. By 1979 remittances to Egypt from its overseas workforce amounted to $2 billion, equivalent to the total earnings from cotton, the Suez Canal, and tourism.[18] These processes also led to labor flows to neighboring countries where the departure of workers for the Gulf had created labor shortages in agriculture and construction.[19] As noted earlier, for example, the vast majority of Jordan's agricultural workforce was made up of Egyptian migrants by 1986.[20]

By the mid-1980s, noncitizen Arab workers in the Gulf were increasingly seeking to bring their families with them and to win greater political and civil rights. It was partially in response to these demands that Gulf states reworked the spatial structuring of class: shifting migrant labor flows away from Arab countries toward the Indian subcontinent. Laws were passed that made it more difficult for Arab families to settle for long periods in the Gulf (in the UAE, for example, noncitizen Arabs were prevented from sending their children to public schools). In the wake of the 1990–91 Gulf War, massive numbers of Arab residents were expelled under the pretext that the PLO and Yemen had supported Iraq's invasion of Kuwait. It is estimated that in the four months after the invasion more than 2 million migrant workers left Iraq, Kuwait, and Saudi Arabia.[21] In Kuwait, the number of Palestinians fell from four hundred thousand in 1990 to about fifty thousand by the mid-1990s, and the number of Jordanian workers fell to 10 percent of the 1980 level.[22] The impact of this repatriation on the Middle East was severe. Returnee Jordanians constituted 8 percent of the entire Jordanian population, and the combined effects of these returning workers and the associated decline in remittances contributed to Jordanian unemployment sreaching 25 percent in 1991.[23]

From 1975 to 2000 the number of migrant workers in the Gulf states increased from 1.1 million to 8.5 million workers. During this period, however, the Arab proportion of migrant workers in the Gulf had fallen from 72 percent to around 25–29 percent, replaced with cheaper labor from South Asia.[24] By 2005, the proportion of Arab workers in Gulf migrant labor forces had fallen to 40 percent in Qatar, 31 percent in Saudi Arabia and Kuwait, 12.42 percent in Bahrain, 8.7 percent in the UAE, and 5.6 percent in Oman.[25] In turn, the shift to South Asian labor meant that many neighboring countries were dependent on upon the Gulf as a destination of labor and source of remittances. In the mid-1990s, for example, around 60–70 percent of Bangladeshi overseas workers could be found in the Gulf. By 2002, this proportion had risen to 95 percent.[26] In Sri Lanka, from 2003 to 2007, around 85 percent of all Sri Lankans departing overseas for work went to the Gulf. For India, 95 percent of all labor outflows in 2007 were destined for Gulf countries—the source of 40 percent of India's total remittance inflows.[27] Pakistan and the Philippines were similarly tightly integrated into the labor needs of the Gulf.

Deepening Exploitation

As noted above, the spatial structuring of class is maintained through a set of laws and regulations that demarcate citizens from noncitizens and help to enable particularly intense forms of exploitation and social control. This begins with the process of migration itself. Workers are generally recruited through private agencies in their home country and are charged large fees that can take years to repay. Their visa is tied to a particular sponsor (*kafeel*) and is for a limited duration (usually a few years), which can sometimes be renewed by paying an additional fee.[28] Workers frequently complain that they are paid less than what was initially offered to them or that extra fees are deducted from their salaries.[29] In some cases they are forced to surrender their passport to the employer who controls their salary, ability to change work, and even right to leave the country. This dependency upon the employer creates a system of control akin to bonded labor, in which the worker is essentially trapped in a set of highly exploitative working conditions that are very difficult to challenge.

The majority of migrants are employed in the private sector, where conditions (at lower rungs) are generally much worse than those found in the public sector—there is, for example, no minimum wage in the private sector, and working hours tend to be much longer. In both the UAE and Saudi Arabia, migrant workers constitute close to 100 percent of the private sector workforce. In Bahrain, Qatar, and Kuwait the figure is around 80 percent. Much of this work is in construction and manufacturing—in Saudi Arabia and Qatar, for example, these two sectors were employing nearly half of all private sector labor by the mid-2000s.[30] The weight of these sectors explains the large proportion of male migrant workers in the Gulf (about 70 to 80 percent of the total migrant population), although large numbers of women (mostly drawn from Sri Lanka, Nepal, Bangladesh, and the Philippines) are also employed in the region as domestic and health-care workers. In 2005 more than two-thirds of the total UAE population was male, despite the fact that the gender ratio of the Emirati national population was evenly balanced.

Even within the same sector, wages and working conditions vary considerably depending on the worker's citizenship status. A survey by the Saudi Arabian Ministry of Economy and Planning has documented a threefold difference in pay between Saudi and non-Saudi workers in the manufacturing sector and a fourfold difference in transport and communication.[31] In Qatar, a foreign manufacturing worker received one-sixth the average compensation of a Qatari worker in 2003.[32] In Bahrain, according to the General Organization for Social Insurance, the general average wage for 2006 in the private sector was BD377 for Bahraini workers and BD170 for foreign laborers.[33] Notably, these statistics do not take into account the various forms of nonwage compensation available to citizens, such as provisions for housing, education, and health care. Moreover, foreign workers themselves find their wages differentiated on the basis of nationality. One study has noted, for example, that domestic workers with comparable skills received widely different wages depending on where they were from—Filipina domestic workers received $364–$390 per month, while Sri Lankan workers received less than half that amount.[34]

In addition to low wages, workers frequently complain of severe physical and mental abuse. This can include beatings by employers, sexual assault (especially in the case of domestic workers), overcrowded and dirty living spaces, and substandard health or safety provisions at work. In 2009, Human Rights Watch (HRW) interviewed workers at the Abu Dhabi Saadiyat Island project, a massive multi-year construction project that is envisaged as becoming the "cultural district" of Abu Dhabi and aims to host the world's largest Guggenheim Museum, a Louvre Museum, a branch of New York University, twenty-nine hotels, golf courses, and luxury villas. Workers on the project reported being paid "an average daily salary of around US$8.00 per day, for ten paid hours per day including overtime, although they often spent twelve hours at the jobsite and up to two additional hours traveling to and from the island."[35] HRW estimated the average yearly salary, including overtime wages, of these migrant workers to be just over $2,500. Almost all workers reported having late or unpaid wages. Many also said that their passports had been confiscated and they were lied to about their contracts. Their employers forced them to remain on the island so they could not seek any redress. As a consequence of conditions such as these, workers suffer severe psychological stress. One NGO working in the UAE estimated an average of three suicides per week among construction workers in the country.[36] In Kuwait, migrant workers were committing or attempting suicide every 2.5 days in 2010, according to Migrant Rights, an advocacy organization for migrant workers in the Middle East.[37] In the first half of 2012, suicide rates among migrant workers in Bahrain reached one a week.[38]

These conditions are enabled largely because workers' residency status is directly tied to holding employment, and if they lose their job they must leave the country. This precarious and easily deportable status places enormous barriers in the way of collective action. The perpetual rotation of workers in and out of the country makes it difficult to form long-term relationships or bonds of solidarity, and any protest can be met with deportation. Legal restrictions codify these obstacles to class-based action, with unions banned in Saudi Arabia and the UAE and severely restricted elsewhere.[39] In the case of women domestic workers, these barriers are even more pronounced because of the severe isolation these women experience. One researcher has reported, for example, that nearly half the domestic workers she interviewed in the UAE had never left the houses of their employers by themselves in the two years in which they worked in the country.[40]

Of course, the specificity of this class structure diverges across the Gulf and should not be taken to mean that differences do not persist within the citizen population itself, or that the system is sustainable into the future. The proportion of the population holding citizenship varies from 20–35 percent in the UAE, Kuwait, and Qatar to between 60–80 percent in Bahrain, Saudi Arabia, and Oman.[41] Significant numbers of these citizens experience poverty, and inequality levels have increased alongside rising wealth for some. Saudi Arabia and Bahrain, in particular, are marked by deep poverty levels among some parts of the citizen population. These trends need to be placed alongside preexisting religious and geographic divisions (e.g., Shi'a within Bahrain, Saudi Arabia, and Kuwait; the northern Emirates vis-à-vis Abu Dhabi and Dubai in the UAE; and the poorer industrial town of Sohar relative to the capital Muscat in Oman). A partial exception to note here is Bahrain, where the citizen population experienced quite significant proletarianization (due to the much lower levels of oil wealth and the smaller levels of migration). This overlapped with the entrenched sectarian discrimination against the Shi'a population, and explains why labor and left-wing movements continued to be a prominent feature of the country's political makeup—and why the country was the principal location of the uprisings in the Gulf in 2011 (see chapter 7).

Development of Capitalist Classes

At the same time as Gulf states shifted to this reliance upon temporary migrant labor, capitalist classes began to form in the Gulf.[42] These classes originated in large family-based groups drawn from merchant elites or allied (and often directly related) to the ruler. The ruler had absolute authority over how oil revenues were spent and, as a result, the initial phases of "primitive accumulation" for the family-based groups occurred essentially through gifts—of land, houses, high-ranking jobs in the state apparatus, and so forth, which the ruler provided to his allies to help shore up support for the monarchy. Over time, however, accumulation came to be underpinned by the elaboration and development of a wider circuit of capital stretching across a variety of productive activities, control over imports, the sale of commodities, and finance.

Oil and natural gas are naturally at the center of the productive circuit in the Gulf. The value of these activities ranges from around one-quarter of GDP in Bahrain to close to two-thirds in Qatar. Prior to the 1970s, upstream production (the exploration and extraction of crude hydrocarbons) was mainly controlled by foreign multinationals that paid royalties and other rents to the ruling monarch. As the Gulf states gained independence, state-owned oil companies took over this sector and have (in most cases) dominated it since. State control became most complete in Saudi Arabia and Kuwait, where a direct role for foreign companies in extraction and exploration was virtually eliminated. In the other Gulf countries, foreign oil multinationals continued to play a role (albeit a weakened one) in the production of crude oil.[43] The Gulf's private sector has generally not been directly involved in the upstream sector of the oil industry.

Excluded from upstream production, accumulation opportunities for private capital occurred around other industries connected to oil or were initiated with state assistance from accrued oil revenues. Initially, the most important of these were service and construction contracts granted to local companies by governments and foreign multinationals, either in the oil sector or for broader development purposes. These included activities ranging from building accommodation, laying roads, supplying food and transportation, the manufacture of pipes and other basic infrastructure requirements, and provision of security. Laws were passed that required foreign companies to partner with local capital in development projects, thus ensuring that all state expenditures helped to underpin the growth of domestic capital.[44] The weight of crude oil and gas also shaped the character of other industrial activities interlocked with hydrocarbon production. Specifically, access to large and relatively cheap energy sources in the Gulf states helped encourage the development of those industries—such as aluminium, steel, and cement—that were highly dependent on the cost of electricity.[45] Companies that produced these commodities were established in the 1970s, often through initiatives from state-owned oil companies and other government funds. In subsequent decades, private companies expanded into the manufacture of rolled steel, wires, cables, aluminum extrusions, and so forth that utilized these energy-rich products as their principal feedstock.

A further significant component of the productive circuit has been the expansion of the downstream petrochemical sector (e.g., production of chemicals, plastics, fertilizers, and so forth). Historically, this had been dominated by foreign multinationals that purchased crude oil (or gas) from the Gulf states and then located their downstream activities in Western Europe or North America, where they produced gasoline or more complex petrochemicals. Over the last decade there has been an increasing relocation of this sector to the Gulf to take advantage of cheaper feedstocks of raw material and energy. The focus of the Gulf's petrochemical production has been ethylene, which is a basic building block for more complex plastics such as polyethylene, polystyrene, and PVC, and fibers such as polyethylene terephthalate (PET) and polyester. The average ethylene capacity per production site in the Middle East nearly doubled from 1993 to 2005, surpassing the average for Western Europe by the mid-2000s.[46] By 2011, the Gulf Arab states held just under one-quarter of the world's ethylene production capacity, up from 5 percent in 1993.[47]

Although most of this petrochemical production continues to be dominated by state-owned companies such as the Saudi Basic Industries Corporation (SABIC), the largest ethylene producer in the world, private Gulf capital has begun to enter as a junior partner in petrochemical projects. This has occurred principally through the mechanism of the stock market, with large petrochemical companies opening up ownership to the private sector through share listings. In Saudi Arabia, for example, there are eight publicly listed petrochemical companies (Saudi Arabia Industrial Investment Co., Tasnee, SIPCHEM, Alujain, NAMA, Sahara, APPC, and Saudi Kayan) that are owned by investors from the largest private conglomerates (both Saudi and other Gulf countries). In addition to these companies, SABIC itself is listed on the Saudi stock market and has become the most profitable publicly listed non-oil company in the

Middle East. SABIC's shares can only be held by Gulf investors, providing an important means to redistribute wealth through the Saudi stock market to regional domestic capital groups.

The predominance of oil and petrochemical activities in the Gulf economies has led to a relative underdevelopment of the non-hydrocarbon sectors and a significant dependence on imports. Simultaneously, the large amount of available liquidity and the needs arising from the region's rapid industrialization has meant that the Gulf is viewed by leading international exporters as an important potential market for luxury goods, machinery and heavy equipment, and services. The scale of these imports has closely tracked the movement of the price of oil and grew by more than 20 percent annually from the early 1970s to 1980.[48] Although imports fell in the wake of the 1982 global recession, they began moving upward again in 1987, growing at an average of 10 percent annually until 1993. By the mid-2000s, Gulf import growth rates exceeded that of China, a country frequently held up as symbolizing the new era of globalized trade.

Control over this import trade has formed another important axis of accumulation for the leading Gulf conglomerates. As Gulf states gained their independence in the 1970s, laws were passed that required foreign importers to partner with a local company as their agent and distributor. Many of the same conglomerates involved in construction and other productive activities were also granted exclusive control of these agency rights—importing and distributing automobiles, electrical items, food and beverages, and household consumer goods. In many cases, a group's agency and franchise rights encompassed a variety of different commodities and sectors. In this manner, domestic capital captured a portion of the surplus value realized through the sale of foreign goods. As the import trade grew and urbanization proceeded apace, some of the large corporate conglomerates involved in these activities came to own the retail venues in which imported goods were sold, including large supermarket and hypermarket chains that sell a wide range of commodities ranging from food items to clothing, gold, and electronic appliances within a single store. In some cases, these groups operate franchises for foreign retail giants such as Geant and Carrefour, with their rights extending across all Gulf countries.[49]

This import trade has developed to include another point of accumulation: malls and shopping centers. Large conglomerates—often active in the earlier phases of the commodity circuit (that is, as agents and distributors of foreign imports, or as owners of supermarkets and hypermarkets)—typically own these malls.[50] Here, retail capital captures a portion of the total commodity surplus value through the rent charged for bringing together a large number of retailers in one space. The expansion of this form of commodity capital was a striking feature of Gulf development through the 2000s—

symbolized in the massive malls built during the decade. Malls in the Gulf were estimated to generate around $30 billion in sales annually by the middle of the 2000s,
constituting the majority of the Middle East's total shopping area (84 percent in
2006).[51] The UAE took the lead in this respect, with shopping festivals heavily promoted as a means to encourage tourism in the country.[52] By the end of 2008, three of
the largest malls in the world were located in Dubai, including The Dubai Mall, the
largest shopping mall in the world, which opened in November 2008 and currently
houses more than one thousand retail stores.

The final important activity for the region's largest conglomerates is finance.
Class formation around the Gulf financial circuit has been strongly shaped by the region's location within global financial markets. Prior to independence, oil revenues
from the Gulf were largely directed into foreign banks headquartered in financial
centers such as London. British colonialism used privately owned British banks to
issue currency and act as central banks, reaping enormous profits in the process. In
1959, for example, Kuwaiti deposits, along with the deposits of Kuwaiti residents in
London, represented 47 percent of total deposits of the British Bank of the Middle
East—the first bank established in Kuwait (1941), Dubai (1946), Sharjah (1953), Abu
Dhabi (1959), and Oman (1948).[53] With the growing moves toward independence
through the 1960s, this colonially backed structure began to come under pressure,
and merchant families sought to establish their own banks in order to capture part
of the circulation of oil wealth.[54] By the 1970s, large domestic banks had developed
that were firmly based in the Gulf itself. Many of the same large conglomerates that
benefited from accumulation opportunities in the productive and commodity circuits
came to be heavily invested in this part of the financial circuit—represented on the
boards of the large banks and holding significant shareholdings in them, alongside
state capital.[55]

Other financial institutions have also formed in the recent period to further consolidate the leading corporate groups. Of particular note is the proliferation of private
equity (PE) and other investment firms that pool the wealth of "high net worth" individuals to purchase equity and bonds, make investments in international markets, and
directly buy companies with the intention of obtaining a controlling (or major) interest
that could be sold for a profit after restructuring.[56] PE firms have complex institutional
forms that may involve a variety of holding companies, offshore banking units, and
shell companies. There was a very rapid growth in the size of Gulf private equity through
the mid-2000s, with the total size of PE funds increasing from $78 million in 2001 to
$14 billion in 2006.[57] Between 2004 and 2007, the average investment per fund in-
creased from $10 million to $103 million.[58] This rapid growth was closely tied to the
wave of privatization that occurred across the Middle East during the 2000s, with Gulf

PE companies purchasing telecoms, banks, real estate companies, and other assets that were privatized in this period (see below).[59]

It is around these three circuits of capital—the productive circuit (construction, energy-rich commodities such as aluminium, steel, and concrete); the commodity circuit (agents and distributors of imported commodities, malls and shopping centers); and the financial circuit (banks, investment and PE companies)—that the largest conglomerates in the Gulf have formed over the last three decades.[60] These conglomerates, and the dozens of similar ones operating across the Gulf, constitute the Gulf's capitalist class. Their huge business empires span a wide range of activities and are also tightly linked to the state itself, benefiting from state-directed contracts, agency rights, land grants, and positions within the government bureaucracy. This close interpenetration with the state—with members of the ruling family forming part of this class itself—indicates that it makes little analytical sense to draw a sharp line of division between state and private capital as two separate spheres.

There is one further aspect of class formation in the Gulf important to note—the region's location as a major zone of accumulation for capital originating elsewhere in the Middle East. Particularly illustrative in this sense are the Palestinian and Lebanese examples, where wealthy individuals have become adjoined to Gulf ruling families and domestic conglomerates, establishing their main business activities in the Gulf (e.g., the Masri and Khouri families in the case of Palestine; the Hariri family in the Lebanese example).[61] This diaspora bourgeoisie needs to be seen as a component of the capitalist class in the Gulf itself, playing an important role in their home countries while continuing to base their core business activities in the Gulf region.[62] In some cases, this close integration with Gulf capitalism has even been formally acknowledged through the granting of citizenship (as in the case of the Hariri family, in Saudi Arabia).

The Internationalization of Gulf Capital

Over the past decade, the development of these Gulf conglomerates has been further marked by the pronounced internationalization of capital flows beyond national borders. This is true at two scales. First, the regional integration project embodied in the formation of the GCC[63] has encouraged the interpenetration of the Gulf's own circuits of capital, with conglomerate activities becoming internationalized through the GCC space. This is shown in many sectors: cross-border activities of Gulf construction companies, cross-border investments in petrochemical projects, ownership of franchise and agency rights that extend through numerous GCC countries, the expansion of UAE- and Saudi-owned malls across the Gulf, ownership structures of media and telecommunications companies, growing levels of cross-border purchases on regional stock markets (particularly

Bahrain), and—most markedly—the development of private equity and other financial companies that bring together the largest GCC companies within single
ownership structures. The increasing levels to which accumulation is conceived
and articulated at a regional scale reflects the emergence of a pan-Gulf capitalist
class, Khaleeji Capital, structured around a Saudi-UAE axis and consisting of those
large Gulf conglomerates that tend to operate within these internationalizing circuits.[64] In the words of a leading GCC private equity fund: "We look at the whole
GCC, we believe that there is a customs union, a monetary union almost with a
very close peg to the dollar, there is a cultural union and anything that sells in Saudi
Arabia would sell in Dubai. So for us, we don't look at these markets as being separate entities, we look at them as being one."[65]

But the internationalization of Gulf capital has also occurred throughout the Middle East as a whole. There is a great deal of empirical evidence that confirms this expansion of Gulf capital, particularly following the rapid rise in the price of oil that
began in 1999 and peaked in 2008. According to ANIMA, an EU institution that mon-
itors FDI in the Mediterranean region, the value of projects announced by Gulf Arab
investors in the region exceeded those from any other country or region in the world
for the entire 2003–2009 period.[66] More than 60 percent of all Gulf investments in
the Mediterranean area went to Jordan, Lebanon, Egypt, Palestine, and Syria, and in
these five countries the value of the Gulf's investments was more than three times that
of the EU and twelve times that of North America.[67] For Syria and Lebanon, GCC FDI
constituted more than 70 percent of the country's total FDI in 2008. In Egypt, the
country's minister of investment reported that the share of GCC capital in Egypt's FDI
rose from 4.5 percent in 2005 to over 25 percent in 2007.[68] In Jordan, GCC FDI was
35 percent of the country's total FDI in 2007. The weight of these Gulf investments
continued even after the 2008 global crisis. From 2008 to 2010, the Gulf as a whole
was the top-ranked source of total FDI for Egypt, Jordan, Lebanon, Libya, Palestine,
and Tunisia—surpassing investment flows from the United States, United Kingdom,
China, or any European country—and ranked second in Morocco and Syria (see appendix 4). In 2010, Gulf-based capital was responsible for the largest FDI projects
announced in Algeria, Lebanon, Libya, and Tunisia. These are very striking figures—
all the more so in that they do not include portfolio investment flows in the region's
stock markets or other forms of "development loans" extended to the region from institutions in the Gulf.[69]

As the region's leader in liberalization over the 2000s, Egypt provides a particularly
vivid illustration of how these flows of Gulf capital are closely tied to the dynamics of
neoliberal transformation discussed in chapters 3 and 4. One indication of this is
shown in data for privatization deals. From 2000 to 2008, Gulf investors were involved

in just over 22 percent of all privatization deals recorded by the World Bank for Egypt, representing around 37 percent of the value of all privatization over that period.[70] These purchases ranged across a variety of sectors, including finance (by 2010, Gulf-based conglomerates and sovereign wealth funds were major shareholders of or directly controlled nine of the twelve largest non-state Egyptian commercial banks),[71] real estate, telecommunications, and major industries. In all of Egypt's key economic sectors, privatization acted to facilitate the displacement or merging of Egyptian capital with that of the Gulf—giving the latter a central position in the reproduction of capitalism at the national scale.

The extent of the Gulf's involvement in Egypt's economy is strikingly indicated by ownership patterns in the agribusiness sector—a feature encountered already in chapter 4. Table 6.1 extends the earlier analysis of this sector, demonstrating how Gulf-related investors and companies have come to dominate Egyptian food production, processing, and retailing. Saudi and Kuwaiti firms are particularly noteworthy, specifically the massive conglomerates Americana (controlled by the Al Kharafi Group, a prominent Kuwaiti business family involved in construction, aluminium, cement, banking, and trade) and Savola (a Saudi company established in 1979 by twenty-five founding shareholders drawn from the Saudi state capital and the largest private business groups). These ownership patterns confirm that the transformation of Egyptian agriculture over the last two decades has been accompanied by the increasing weight of Gulf capital throughout all key moments of the sector's commodity chain.

Table 6.1: Gulf Involvement in the Egyptian Agribusiness and Agricultural Sectors

Sector	Company	Ultimate Ownership
Dairy and Juice	Dina Farms (54 percent of fresh milk), largest dairy farm in Egypt	Citadel Capital (PE firm) Saudi group, Olayan, is represented on board of directors UAE sovereign wealth fund, Emirates International Investment Company is represented on the board Qatari royal family member is on the board Suleiman Bin Abdul Mohsen Bin Abdullah Abanumay, Saudi businessman, owns 7 percent of the company and is represented on the board

Sector	Company	Ultimate Ownership
	Beyti (7 percent of dairy market)	Al Marai Group (Saudi Arabia)
	Juhayna (69 percent of packaged milk and 40 percent of carton juice market)	25 percent Saudi owned
Poultry (three companies listed control 50 percent of commercial poultry market)	Cairo Poultry Company	Americana Group (Kuwait)
	Wataniya Poultry	Al Rajhi Group (Saudi Arabia)
	Misr Arab Poultry	Dallah Al Barak Group
Cheese	Greenland (largest producer of white and mozzarella cheese)	Americana Group
Starch and Glucose	Egyptian Company for Starch and Glucose (25 percent of starch, 45 percent of glucose markets)	Americana Group
Pasta	Al-Malika and Al-Farasha (largest pasta producers, with 30 percent of market share)	Savola Group
Edible Oils	Afia International, controls 42 percent of the market	Savola Group
	Ajwa for Food Industries (second-largest edible oil producer) also major producer of frozen vegetables	Saudi-owned Jaber Group
Fruit and Vegetable	Farm Frites, largest frozen vegetable producer, holds 90 percent of the frozen potato market and 22 percent of the frozen vegetable market. Also a major vegetable exporter	Americana Group
	Egyptian Canning Company (major producer and exporter of top-grade olives)	Americana Group
Flour and Bread	Upper Egypt Flour Mills (largest publicly listed flour mill)	10 percent owned by Arab Cotton Ginning, itself controlled by Amwal Al Khaleej (Saudi private equity firm)
Hypermarket and fast food restaurants	Carrefour	Joint venture between Majd Al Futtaim (UAE) and Carrefour (France)
	Spinneys Hypermarket	Abraaj Capital, UAE
	Franchises for KFC, Pizza Hut, Baskin Robbins, TGI Friday's, Costa Coffee, Hardees	Americana Group

Source: Company annual reports and websites

One of the main routes of Gulf capital's interpenetration with Egypt's class structure has been through investments by PE and other financial firms. Egypt was the most popular destination in the MENA region for PE investments throughout much of the 2000s, registering $3.5 billion in investments from 2005 to 2009, one-third of all PE investments in the MENA region through that period.[72] Gulf-based companies were responsible for most of this investment, with two firms in particular standing out—the UAE-based Abraaj Capital and the Saudi firm Amwal Al Khaleej.

Abraaj provides a very clear example of pan-Gulf integrated finance capital. The company brings together investors from across the Gulf region and thus confirms that the internationalization of Gulf capital has taken place at the level of the Gulf region itself.[73] In 2007, Abraaj made the biggest PE investment in the MENA region's history at the time with its $1.4 billion purchase of Egyptian Fertilizers Company (EFC).[74] The company had been privatized by Mubarak and was one of the largest private sector fertilizer companies in the country—operating as an export-oriented producer in the Northwestern Suez Economic Zone, near Egypt's Sokhna Port. Abraaj's purchase of EFC was followed soon after by investments in the country's leading construction firm, as well as real estate, a medical laboratory chain, information technology, food production, and the rollout of the Spinney's Supermarket chain across Egypt (fully owned by Abraaj).[75] These purchases made Abraaj one of the largest foreign companies operating in Egypt throughout most of the 2000s.

Much like Abraaj, Amwal Al Khaleej (AAK) also integrates pan-GCC capital in a single ownership structure and has taken controlling positions in several of Egypt's most important industrial sectors.[76] In 2007, the Saudi-based firm took ownership of the Arab Cotton Ginning Company (ACGC), the largest textile firm by market value in Egypt, which had been privatized in 1996. ACGC gins about 25 percent of Egypt's locally produced cotton, controls about 25 percent of Egyptian cotton exports, and is involved at all stages of the textile chain, including manufacturing and retail.[77] AAK's control of ACGC also gave it ownership of the Upper Egypt Flour Mill, the largest publicly listed flour mill in the country, which had been privatized by Mubarak in 2008. AAK also purchased a stake in Oriental Weavers, the world's largest machine-woven carpet maker, as well as a 15 percent stake in the Egyptian Propylene and Polypropylene Company, an important petrochemical exporter.

In addition to these direct investments, private equity has been a key institutional form through which Gulf capital has become tightly integrated to local Egyptian elites. This has occurred through partnerships in local Egyptian PE firms. The most important example of this is shown by EFG-Hermes, the biggest investment firm in Egypt. EFG-Hermes was born of a merger between the Egyptian Financial Group, the first investment bank in Egypt, and Hermes, a firm that was responsible for setting up the first equity index in Egypt. In 1996, the two companies merged, with ownership initially held by Egyptian investors. It quickly grew to become the largest financial company of its type in Egypt and was intimately connected to neoliberalism in the country; the company was responsible for advising the Egyptian government on privatization and acted as the lead manager for the majority of privatization IPOs in the mid-1990s.[78] In 2006, Abraaj Capital took the largest stake in EFG-Hermes following a $500 million investment. Abraaj exited EFG-Hermes in 2007 through a $1.1 billion sale of its investment, but Gulf capital remained the dominant force within the company after Abraaj's stake was purchased by two UAE-based investment funds, the Dubai Group and the Abu Dhabi Investment Authority. Representatives of these two funds joined prominent Egyptian investors on the board of EFG-Hermes, with the company taking control of some of the largest and most strategic sectors of the Egyptian economy—including companies responsible for the construction and operation of water desalination plants and power generation plants, cattle import and meat processing, offshore oil services, steel production, agribusiness, and infrastructure investments across the Middle East.

Two other important Egyptian PE firms, Citadel Capital and Beltone Financial, display similar integrative roles for Gulf and Egyptian capital. Citadel was noted in Table 6.1 for its ownership of Egypt's largest private farm, and it brings together leading Egyptian capitalists with representatives from two large Saudi private business groups (the Olayan and Abanumay families), a UAE sovereign wealth fund (Emirates International Investment Company), and a member of the Qatari royal family. Likewise, Beltone Financial has a member of the UAE royal family on its board of directors and established a joint investment fund, Beltone Capital, 17 percent owned by Amwal Al Khaleej, with the explicit aim of buying into privatized companies.[79] Both Citadel and Beltone are highly significant institutions, not only for their control of key Egyptian companies but also because they have recently become the principal vehicles for the seizure of farmland in Africa, most notably in Sudan.[80] In this manner, Egyptian private equity has formed a stepping-stone for the expansion of Gulf-based capital into the wider Africa region.

Another major sector of the Egyptian economy that illustrates the intersection of neoliberalism and the internationalization of Gulf capitalism is land and real estate development. The privatization of state-owned land that occurred under Mubarak through the 2000s was a principal route for inflows of Gulf capital into Egypt. This was accomplished through two basic channels—direct purchases of land and development projects by Gulf companies and indirect participation through stakes in Egyptian-based real estate companies. With regard to the first of these entry routes, Gulf-based investors were the chief beneficiaries of land auctions conducted by the Egyptian government to transfer state land to private hands (most notably in 2006 and 2007). One of the largest of these auctions in Egyptian history, in May 2007, saw 90 percent of the 18.5 million square meters of Cairo land that was up for sale go to Saudi, Qatari, and UAE companies.[81]

Despite the downturn in real estate activity globally, Gulf investors continue to dominate this sector in Egypt. According to figures from January 2012, of the twenty-six current real estate developments worth more than $100 million that were ongoing in Egypt at the time, thirteen were fully owned by Gulf-based conglomerates.[82] In terms of project value, fully owned Gulf real estate projects constituted just under 80 percent of the value of all real estate projects under development in Egypt in early 2012 ($80.362 billion out of $102.86 billion). These figures are all the more striking when the second route of Gulf involvement is considered—Egyptian-based companies that have significant Gulf ownership levels (defined as more than 20 percent share ownership or representatives on the board of directors). If these companies are included in the comparison of real estate projects in Egypt—and they certainly confirm an intermeshing of social relations among the regional bourgeoisie—a remarkable twenty out of the twenty-six projects worth more than $100 million are related to Gulf investors.

Two Egyptian-based real estate companies stand out for their close relationship with Gulf investors—the Talaat Mustafa Group and the Sixth of October Development and Investment Company (SODIC). These companies are the largest private landholders in Cairo, and they profited handsomely from land that was distributed by the Mubarak regime in apparent contravention of Egyptian law and at below-value prices.[83] Although they were registered in Egypt and established by prominent Egyptians with close links to Mubarak and the state apparatus, their subsequent development was essentially driven by Gulf capital flows. The Taalat Mustafa Group (TMG), for example, is the largest real estate developer in Egypt, with 50 million square meters in its land bank.[84] Alongside its Egyptian founders, the Talaat Mustafa family, TMG is jointly controlled by the Saudi Binladen Group, whose position was consolidated as part of a change in the company's ownership structures following a 2006 IPO. Two members of the Binladen family are represented on the board of directors.[85]

Likewise, SODIC is closely linked to Gulf-based capital. The company was formed in 1996 to undertake real estate projects in Sixth of October City (to the west of Cairo). It holds 4.8 million square meters of land in the west of Cairo and 0.9 million square meters in the east of Cairo, where it is building downtown centers.[86] During the mid-2000s a controlling stake in the company was acquired by EFG-Hermes, whose largest shareholders, as noted above, are currently UAE investment funds. In 2006, the company underwent a major expansion through the acquisition of two pieces of land in Kattameya, near the American University of Cairo Complex in New Cairo. This expansion increased SODIC's total landbank by more than one-third and was funded by a capital increase, which, according to a SODIC board director, came largely from Gulf investors.[87] In this sense, SODIC's expansion was enabled by the incorporation of Gulf investors into the company's ownership structure. Today, alongside EFG-Hermes's controlling share in the company, another 22 percent of SODIC is owned by the same two private Saudi investors involved in Beltone Financial (the Olayan conglomerate and Suleiman Bin Abdullah Abanumay).

Conclusion

The Egyptian example confirms that the internationalization of Gulf capital was not simply a matter of access to oil revenues and the deployment of petrodollar flows, but was contingent upon the intensification of neoliberalism across the Middle East as a whole.[88] Key sectors of Egypt's economy—agribusiness, finance, industry, and real estate—became directly tied to Gulf capital. These sectors are not only economically significant but they also constitute strategic pivots of the broader neoliberal project. Indeed, the process of liberalization in Egypt was to a great extent predicated upon the westward internationalization of Gulf capital and its incorporation into the anatomy of Egyptian class structure. Viewed from the perspective of the regional scale, the Gulf Arab states were a principal beneficiary of the restructuring of class relations that occurred in the neoliberal period. In this sense, neoliberalism needs to be understood as a project of class power that strengthened the position of national elites while simultaneously consolidating the Gulf's influence over the region as a whole.

The Gulf's position at the core of an increasingly imbricated set of social relations operating across the regional scale contrasts sharply with any "container-like" models of the nation-state. The region's capitalist classes have become tied in a fibril web of finance to the reproduction of capitalism in the Gulf. As a consequence, the Middle East needs to be seen as more than just a simple agglomeration of nation-states, rather as a set of internally related social relations that striate national borders. Class and state formation at the national scale both reflect this interlacing of social relations while simultaneously helping to produce the "regional." Echoing Nicos Poulantzas's rejection of a clear demarcation between "domestic" and "foreign" capitals, the Gulf can be understood as an "internal bourgeoisie" that has become interiorized within the class and state structures of national social formations.[89] Furthermore, these trends also indicate why analyses that reduce the Gulf economies to simply oil rents and fanciful real estate projects in Dubai and Riyadh are misplaced. Gulf capitalism does not operate solely within the borders of the Gulf states but involves all manner of profit-seeking investments beyond the GCC region.

The weight of the Gulf in the Middle East political economy points to the fact that any reversal of the patterns of neoliberal development in the Middle East requires challenging capitalism in the Gulf itself. For this reason, political struggles in the Gulf—some of which will be discussed in the following chapter—are immensely significant, and form a direct continuity with those elsewhere in the Middle East. These struggles have received far too little attention (and solidarity) both within and outside of the region. Moreover, a vital element to challenging capital and state in the Gulf must be the defense of the region's migrant workers. The exploitation of these workers is an integral part of how working classes have formed in the Middle East and is essential to the ways that Gulf capitalism continues to project its power. There needs to be a serious attempt to build cross-regional campaigns with workers who come from beyond the Middle East, based around the rights of citizenship, the right to organize, and working conditions. Workers from India, the Philippines, and so forth need to be seen as *part* of the region's working class—not as foreigners, "guest workers," or "domestics." There are huge barriers in the way of such campaigns (linguistic, cultural, and political—not to mention the entrenched racism found throughout much of the Arab world), but to abstain from this struggle means to further reinforce the fracturing of class solidarity across the region.

These patterns of state and class in the Gulf are inseparably bound to the ways Western power has developed over recent decades. The neoliberal opening of the region over the last two decades has not only been imperialist in nature—facilitating the entry of large European and US companies and the broader subordination of the region to US interests—but it has also been a political project closely aligned to Gulf capitalism. This provides one explanation why imperialism is now articulated to a large extent through the Gulf states in both a political and economic sense. This does not mean that there are no rivalries between the Gulf and the Western states, or, indeed, within the Gulf itself. Nor, of course, does it mean that imperialist states do not continue to hold dominance over the region. Rather, it is a recognition that the Gulf states form the core of the regional political economy, and that their paramount position in superintending imperialism flows directly from an existential concern in maintaining the patterns of uneven and combined development that have characterized the region as a whole over the last two decades. The Gulf's location at the apex of these regional hierarchies is a consequence of precisely those same processes that have generated, in another form, the conditions for the mass revolts. This bears important implications for understanding the possible future trajectories of revolution and counterrevolution.

CHAPTER 7
Crisis and Revolution

T he financial crisis that fully erupted in 2008–2009—spiraling quickly into a global slump deeper than any previous post–World War II downturns—has been utilized by governments across the world to launch a wave of savage attacks on living conditions and wider social rights. Despite the severity of this crisis, its ramifications in the Middle East were frequently misread by commentators in the immediate aftermath of the collapse. In part this was due to a fixation on GDP growth rates as a measure of economic health. These remained relatively high in the MENA region compared to other areas, and many analysts issued upbeat assessments based on this fact. But these high growth rates disguised the polarized outcomes of the preceding neoliberal period; embedded in these assessments was the unspoken assumption that a growth trend at the aggregate scale was good for the population as a whole—a statistical expression of the "trickle-down effect." Indeed, high growth rates were frequently employed as a means of justifying the preceding neoliberal policies. Following a visit to Egypt in February 2010, for example, the IMF claimed that the country had been "resilient to the crisis" because "sustained and wide-ranging reforms since 2004 had . . . bolstered the economy's durability and provided breathing space for appropriate policy responses."[1] Exactly one year later, the country would be wracked by strikes and demonstrations protesing the consquences of the "sustained and wide-ranging reforms" for which the IMF was directly culpable.

One of the reasons that institutions such as the IMF could entirely misinterpret the effects on the Middle East of the 2008 global collapse is that they chose to ignore the social devastation predating the crisis itself. For decades, much of the Middle East had faced a state of permanent crisis—high levels of poverty (particularly in rural areas); a lack of decent, stable work; the massive spread of labor informality in urban areas; and the erosion of various social support mechanisms that had resulted from neoliberal reform. War and displacement had been the frequent accompaniment and—as the experience in Iraq demonstrated only too clearly—often the means of implementation of these neoliberal reforms. In this manner, the 2008 global crisis was not a sharp break with what went before it, a sudden collapse of a healthy, functioning system. Rather, the global slump overlay and deepened the multiple, preexisting forms of social crises that had been long extant in the region.

The escalating cost of food was one of these precursors. Food prices had been on a general upward trend from the early part of the 2000s, but 2007 and the first half of 2008 saw a sharp increase in global prices. As a consequence, inflation in the MENA region rose at a rate greater than double that of world inflation in 2007–2008.[2] Although global prices dropped in mid-2008 as the crisis unfolded, prices in MENA continued to increase. From July 2007 to July 2009, the food consumer price index rose a remarkable 53 percent in Tunisia, 47 percent in Egypt, 42 percent in Syria, 22 percent in Morocco, and 20 percent in Jordan.[3] This placed great fiscal pressures on governments attempting to maintain already reduced subsidy levels. It also meant that poor families, who tend to spend a very large proportion of their income on food, were severely hit.[4] Partly as a consequence, a total of 1.11 million additional people had fallen below the poverty line in Egypt, Jordan, Palestine, Syria, and Yemen immediately prior to the global crisis itself.[5]

Further confirming the region's permanent crisis were the very high levels of joblessness. As noted earlier, the official (and thus highly understated) unemployment rates in Egypt, Jordan, Lebanon, Morocco, Syria, and Tunisia averaged 11 percent in 2008, the highest rate of any region worldwide.[6] This was most heavily concentrated among youth aged fifteen to twenty-four, whose unemployment rate was also the highest in the world—up to 30 percent in Tunisia and 32 percent in Morocco.[7] Not only were large numbers of youth unemployed but they also represented a very large share of the total unemployed, exceeding 40 percent in each of these five countries and reaching around 60 percent in Egypt and Syria.[8] Unemployment, in other words, was largely a phenomenon of youth.

But neoliberal policies had not only undermined the ability of millions to survive on a day-to-day level prior to the crisis, they also shaped the ways in which the crisis itself was transmitted to the region. This took divergent paths depending on the specificities of individual countries and their forms of integration into the world market, but, regardless of these differences, neoliberalism generally acted to leverage the effects of the global crisis and widen the patterns of uneven development across the region. Three key routes of this transmission should be highlighted:

- First, the shift to export-oriented production, coupled with the heavy reliance on Eurozone markets for many countries, meant export levels were hard hit by the decline in global demand that followed the onset of the crisis. Between 2008 and 2009, Tunisia saw the value of its exports drop by 7.6 percent, Morocco and Egypt around 14.5 percent, Syria and Yemen 19 percent and 22 percent, respectively.[9] These falls came on the back of multi-year growth in exports through the 2000s—Egypt, for example, had experienced annual growth rates in exports of over 20 percent for every year between 2004 and 2008.[10]

- A second transmission mechanism of the global crisis was the curtailment of worker remittances. As noted in earlier chapters, one of the results of government policies over the last two decades had been a very high level of out-migration that left many families reliant on remittances. This was particularly true in the case of North Africa—for Morocco and Tunisia, the number of citizens living abroad grew at an average annual rate of 8.1 percent and 5.5 percent, respectively, from 2001 to 2008.[11] By 2008, more than 10 percent of the populations in both countries were living abroad—more than 80 percent of these in Europe.[12] Although Egypt had a smaller proportion of its total population living abroad,[13] a considerable number of families were extremely dependent upon money sent from overseas (remittances accounted for around 4 to 5 percent of national GDP).[14] Many of these North African migrants worked in precarious sectors such as agriculture, construction, and low-skilled manufacturing; as a consequence, remittance levels fell sharply as these sectors were hit by the crisis.[15] Most affected were Egypt and Morocco, which experienced a drop of 17.7 percent and 9 percent, respectively, in officially recorded remittance flows.[16] A plunge in remittances also struck Yemen and Jordan, although this was largely due to problems faced by migrant workers in the Gulf rather than Europe (see below).[17]

- Finally, the opening up of economies during the 2000s had made many countries in the Middle East and North Africa dependent on foreign capital inflows as a source of foreign currency. The global crisis reduced these inflows significantly, notably in tourist spending and FDI. Morocco and Tunisia saw spending by tourists—a key source of foreign currency—fall by around 10 percent from 2008 to 2009. Egypt and Jordan also saw small declines. FDI flows fell precipitously in Yemen (92 percent), Tunisia (39.5 percent), Egypt (29.3 percent), and Morocco (20.1 percent). Only Syria and Lebanon saw increases in FDI inflows, due in large part to their long-standing, large, and relatively prosperous diaspora communities who moved capital back home in the wake of crisis elsewhere.[18]

Many of these same transmission mechanisms also struck the Gulf Arab states. Here, however, the form of social structure outlined in earlier chapters—and the region's specific mode of incorporation into the world market—helped to generate outcomes significantly different from those witnessed in the rest of the region. Initially, the rapid drop in oil and other hydrocarbon prices from July to December 2008, accompanied by a reduction in the volume of oil sold, sharply reduced government revenues. Account surpluses at the time plunged by half in most Gulf Arab states and became deficits in the UAE and Oman. The value of foreign-held assets dropped as stock and real estate markets in the United States and elsewhere collapsed. Paralleling the rest of the Middle East, there was a reversal of the financial flows that had gone to the Gulf in the years preceding the crisis. The impact of these (now) outflows was exacerbated, as asset bubbles, particularly in real estate, began to deflate and investors attempted to move funds to safer and more stable investments outside the region (symbolized most graphically by the puncturing of the Dubai real estate bubble in 2008–2009).

In response, Gulf states pursued an economic strategy that aimed chiefly at supporting the position of the large Gulf conglomerates mapped in the previous chapter. As global oil prices turned upward in the second half of 2009, governments directed surpluses to assist these conglomerates and state entities. A range of massive construction and real estate projects were launched (particularly in Saudi Arabia) that—because of the internationalization of capital through the GCC—acted to support construction companies from all Gulf states. Companies that had previously been active in the UAE, for example, shifted their focus to Saudi Arabia to take advantage of expected projects in the Saudi market. These plans encompassed $1.4 trillion worth of projects from 2009 to 2015—more than the combined GDP of the Gulf countries in 2008.[19] At the same time, all Gulf governments moved to support financial institutions against exposure to bad loans and the withdrawal of capital flows.

Alongside these measures, the Gulf's heavy reliance on temporary migrant labor allowed firms to reduce their workforces (and slow the hiring of new labor) without concern for the possible impact of increased unemployment. Because residency rights in the GCC were explicitly linked to employment, it was very difficult for workers to remain in the GCC for any significant amount of time once they lost their job. As a consequence, thousands of temporary migrant workers returned home in the wake of the crisis, precipitating fears of a devastating drop in remittance flows to surrounding peripheries. One indication of this was the drop in remittances to Yemen (17.7 percent) and Jordan (5.2 percent) during 2009, countries that were both highly dependent on Gulf labor markets. Those workers remaining in the Gulf frequently found that their working conditions deteriorated, as cuts in wages and benefits disproportionally targeted migrant labor.

Concurrent with the Gulf's relatively robust emergence from the crisis was the deepening of problems in the rest of the region. Consumer food prices continued to increase in many countries throughout 2010, notably Egypt (an 18 percent rise) and Yemen (17.5 percent), and were compounded by climbing oil prices from mid-2009 onward. Syria, Morocco, Jordan, Lebanon, and Tunisia all saw their oil expenditure bills rise between 21 and 63 percent over the 2009–2010 period.[20] Coupled with continuing stagnation in tourism and remittance receipts, these trends put severe strain on many government balance sheets.[21] The net result of these processes was a widening economic differentiation within the region—not only the relative strengthening of the GCC elites within the Gulf itself but also the widening gap between the GCC and other Middle East states. The Gulf's dominant position within the region as a whole was thus greatly magnified in the wake of the crisis.

These varied paths of transmission of the global crisis—overlaid on the preexisting social crises in the region—were the context in which popular revolts were to erupt in December 2010; first in Tunisia, then a few weeks later in Egypt, and consequently spreading across the entire region. The global crisis did not *cause* the revolts, but it was an essential ingredient. The patterning of crisis and accumulation at the regional scale helped shape the form of these revolts and the nature of the counterrevolutionary response. Mediated through the particular histories of political struggle and the nature of state rule in each country, these revolts would threaten the entire edifice of Western power that had been so carefully constructed during the preceding decades.

From North Africa to Syria: The Contours of Revolt

The main narrative of the Arab uprisings is by now well established. On December 17, 2010, a twenty-six-year-old man, Mohammed Bouazizi, set himself on fire in the central Tunisian town of Sidi Bouzid. Earlier in the day, police had confiscated his vegetable stand because he lacked a permit. When he complained he was merely trying to make a living, the police taunted him and beat him severely. As news spread about the young man's treatment at the hands of the police, protests erupted across the country demanding jobs and freedom. Bouazizi died nineteen days later in the midst of the uprising that his self-immolation had triggered.

Initially, Ben Ali's regime confronted the unrest with a standard repertoire of repressive tactics, including beating protesters and firing tear gas and live ammunition into crowds of demonstrators. This repression, however, did not deter the demonstrations that continued to spread across the country. On December 28, Ben Ali declared the protests were the actions of a "minority of extremists and terrorists," but by the start of 2011, tens of thousands of people—including workers, students, and the unemployed—were mobilizing across the country. A series of strikes were organized by trade unions, and the judiciary system was shut down following a walkout by eight thousand lawyers. Over the first weeks of January the regime oscillated between repressive measures and the promise of democratic concessions. But despite Ben Ali's pledge of free legislative elections in six months (coupled with the issuing of a state of emergency), the protests continued to escalate. When the head of the army refused to follow a shoot-to-kill order against the demonstrators, Ben Ali was forced to step down from power and eventually fled to Saudi Arabia. His wife, Leila Trabelsi, left for Dubai—although not before removing over a ton and a half of Tunisia's gold from the central bank.

Ben Ali's ousting spurred similar demonstrations in nearby Egypt, with protests against the Mubarak regime escalating across all major towns throughout January. Borrowing a script from Ben Ali, Mubarak attempted to defuse the situation through a combination of promised concessions and brute force. The latter was symbolized most starkly in the "Battle of the Camels" on February 2, 2011, when armed thugs riding camels charged a main demonstration in Cairo's Tahrir Square—only to be repulsed by the extraordinary self-organization of thousands of protesters armed with little more than sticks. Much like Tunisia's, Egypt's military eventually refused orders from the president—in this case, orders to fire on the demonstrations from aircraft assembled above the protests. Following three weeks of continuous popular mobilizations—and with thousands left dead and wounded—Mubarak was forced to relinquish power on February 11.

The ousting of both Ben Ali and Mubarak had an electrifying effect on the Middle East, revealing the fragility that lay behind the networks of secret police (*mukhabarat*) and thugs (*baltajiya*) upon which all regimes in the region depended heavily. In a few short weeks, the elaborate mechanisms of authoritarian control collapsed as millions of people shed their fear and moved onto the streets. Although all countries were profoundly shaken by the subsequent events, four stood out for the depth of their popular mobilizations—and the determination of Western powers to shape the eventual outcome: Yemen, Bahrain, Libya, and Syria.

Yemen

While Egyptian protests were in full swing in January and February 2011, similar actions had also begun to take place in Yemen. These initially focused on the country's economic situation and high levels of unemployment. But following the overthrow of Mubarak on February 11, the demonstrations grew to encompass a wider sense of anger and frustration with the thirty-three-year reign of the country's president, Ali Abdullah Saleh, who was widely believed to be preparing to hand power over to his son, Ahmed Abdullah Saleh.[22] Since at least 2007, street protests against the state-led violence of Saleh's regime had been a frequent occurrence in Yemen.[23] As Yemen is the poorest country in the Middle East, most Yemenis live a desperate existence. Even more reliant on food imports than countries in North Africa, 44 percent of the Yemeni population lacks access to adequate nutritious food, and more than one-fifth depend on food aid for survival.[24] In some areas, acute malnutrition reaches over 30 percent. Almost half the population lives on less than $2 per day and 10 percent of children do not reach the age of five.[25]Yet alongside these acute levels of poverty, the country is the immediate neighbor of the wealthiest states in the Gulf—a juxtaposition that graphically captures the un-evenness of capitalist development in the region.

These issues are compounded by large regional disparities and enduring armed conflict. In the south, where much of the country's oil and many fisheries and port re-sources are located, a secessionist movement has been active since 2007 in protest against the central government's appropriation of south Yemen's wealth.[26] In the north, a rebellion of the Houthi—a Shi'a group that controls significant swaths of territory and is seeking autonomy—has been ongoing since 2004. It has faced severe repression from the Yemeni government (backed by Saudi Arabia), with thousands killed and more than four hundred thousand people displaced in the conflict.[27] An Islamic fundamentalist movement is also active in the country, receiving a hugely disproportionate amount of foreign media attention relative to its size and influence, and utilized more by the Saleh and US governments as a means to distract from the real issues facing the country.[28] In addition, a range of important social movements—including women's organizations that were to play a prominent role in the uprising against Saleh—have long been mobi-lized against the regime.[29]

Under Saleh, the Yemeni state increasingly became an institutional mechanism used to strengthen his extended family's wealth and power. Saleh family members ran key army and security units, held important ministerial posts, and controlled major shares in a network of the country's largest business firms, including petroleum, agri-cultural, and trading enterprises. As this control over the country's political and eco-nomic levers expanded, particularly in a context of declining oil production since 2001, rival families (notably the al-Ahmar family) and important sections of the country's two largest tribal federations (the Hashid and Baqil) have felt increasingly excluded from accumulation opportunities in Yemen.[30]

By the end of February 2011, many of these different groups had come together in protests numbering over one hundred thousand and employing the same types of slo-gans seen in North Africa—al-shaa'b yurid isqat al-nizam (the people want the regime's downfall!); irhal irhal (Leave! Leave!); khobz, hurriyah, 'adalah ijtima'iyah (bread, free-dom, social justice). Through March and April, Saleh responded to the growing mo-bilizations with violence—including unleashing pro-government militias that shot dead at least forty-five people at a demonstration on March 18.[31] Clashes continued through May and June between opposing army factions, tribal groups, and protest-ers—culminating in an assassination attempt on Saleh on June 3 that left the president severely injured and forced to fly to Riyadh in Saudi Arabia for treatment. Despite much speculation that he would step down, Saleh eventually returned to Yemen in late September. Following two more months of mass protests, armed rebellions, and defections from the military and his ruling party, Saleh agreed on November 23 to transfer power to his vice president, Abd Rabbuh Mansur al-Hadi, in return for immunity. A presidential election on February 21, 2012, saw al-Hadi win power.

The end of Saleh's rule, however, did little to dampen the anger of the population or seriously address the problems faced by the country. Unlike in Tunisia and Egypt, where mass protests had left leaders with little choice but to relinquish power, the political transition in Yemen was largely steered through a deal brokered by the GCC with the country's elite. Saudi Arabia, which negotiated with Saleh and his tribal/political supporters, and Qatar, which has a strong relationship with the country's main opposition party, the Al-Tajammu'u Al-Yamani Lil-Islah (the Yemeni Congregration for Reform, commonly known as the Islah Party), both hold a major influence over the country's politics.[32] As a result of this deal, Yemen's elite remained largely unchanged, with the same few families and tribal groups controlling the country's resources, patronage networks, and political structures. Prominent military leaders of the Saleh regime continued to hold the same positions under the new regime, including the former leader's son, Ahmed Saleh. Moreover, the United States used the transition to deepen its military alliance with the Yemeni government; US drone strikes killed more than 110 people in Yemen in March 2012, the month following the election of al-Hadi.[33] The essential continuity in the regime's foreign alliances and political structures portends further battles ahead for Yemen's social movements.

Bahrain

Demonstrations in Bahrain were first called for February 14, 2011—three days after the overthrow of Mubarak—at the Pearl Roundabout, a central traffic junction in the capital city, Manama. The "day of rage," as it was called, saw tens of thousands of Bahrainis come out in protest. The large crowd called for political reform but did not directly criticize Bahrain's monarch, King Hamad, focusing instead on the high levels of unemployment, skyrocketing inflation, and ongoing political repression. These issues cut across the country's Shi'a and Sunni populations—although the Shi'a population faced specific discrimination, were barred from serving in the security forces, and had long claimed that they were denied access to government jobs. Shi'a also raised accusations that the government was bringing in Sunni Arabs and Pakistanis to work as police and security forces in the suppression of protests, granting these Sunni migrants citizenship in order to alter the sectarian balance of the country.[34] These claims reinforced a widespread belief that migrants were being used by the regime as part of a deliberate policy to foment sectarian divisions through its divide-and-rule policy.

Bahrain's uprising confirms the importance of patterns of class and state to the forms of political action, as well as the immense geostrategic significance of the country to the calculations of Western imperialism. The previous chapter noted that Bahrain is distinct from the rest of the GCC states in important respects. Although the country relies heavily upon migrant labor—in 2005, around 58 percent of the Bahraini population was made up of noncitizen migrant workers[35]—the more proletarianized character of the Bahraini citizen population has produced a rich history of labor struggles in the country. This class structure overlaps with the entrenched sectarian discrimination against the majority Shi'a population, with many Shi'a mired in poverty and joblessness. Through the 2000s the country decisively embraced neoliberal reforms, widening the gaps between poorer citizens and the private sector and state elites, who benefited from Bahrain's position as the "freest economy in the Middle East" (according to the Heritage Foundation's 2010 Index of Economic Freedom).[36] One indication of this was the very high unemployment levels, with unofficial estimates ranging from 15 to 30 percent among Bahraini nationals.[37] Unemployment disproportionately hit Shi'a citizens, with many Shi'a villages resembling "suburban shanty towns from which residents have little hope of escape."[38] In 2004, the Bahrain Centre for Human Rights estimated that over half of Bahraini citizens were living in poverty and yet, simultaneously, the richest 5,200 Bahrainis had a combined wealth greater than $20 billion.[39]

Alongside this dramatic polarization of wealth, the Bahraini monarchy remains a principal ally of the United States in the Gulf. In 1983, a regional unified US military command known as US Central Command (CENTCOM) was permanently stationed on US Navy ships in Bahrain and liaised with US embassies and nations across the Middle East. Although CENTCOM was moved to Qatar in 2003, Bahrain continued to play a fundamental part in the projection of US power in the region. A sixty-acre US Navy base is located in Bahrain's capital, Manama, with 2,250 personnel and civilians connected to the base. The US Navy's Fifth Fleet, responsible for naval forces in the Gulf, Red Sea, Arabian Sea, and coast of East Africa, operates from the base and was a focal point of the US-led invasions of Afghanistan in 2001 and Iraq in 2003. Bahrain's importance to US power is further reinforced by its proximity to Saudi Arabia, to which it is linked by a narrow, twenty-five-kilometer bridge. A successful overthrow of the Bahraini monarchy would undoubtedly shake the Saudi regime, due in no small part to the large number of poor Shi'a who live in Saudi Arabia's eastern provinces, just a short drive from Bahrain's capital.

Despite the participation of thousands in the Bahraini protests—a significant proportion of the country's six hundred thousand citizens—the movement suffered from weaknesses that were closely related to the social structure of the country. Although the initial demonstrations were united across sectarian lines, disagreements over demands and friction between competing religious and political forces allowed the government to drive a wedge between the Sunni and Shi'a populations. The tactic of divide-and-conquer had long been part of the arsenal of the Khalifa monarchy, and the king frequently used the rhetoric of sectarianism to foster divisions between Shi'a and Sunni. A prominent part of the monarchy's strategy, common to all governments in the Gulf, was to accuse the regime's opponents of being a fifth column backed by Iran. Moreover, with the majority of the population comprising a highly exploited working class without any citizenship rights, significant barriers were placed in front of any joint working-class action. Indeed, the Bahraini regime deliberately fomented divisions between migrant workers and protesters during the uprising, even organizing "pro-regime" demonstrations to which migrant workers were bused during work hours.

The developing sectarian discourse helped to legitimize one of the key developments in the regime's response to the protests—the military intervention of other GCC states on March 14. The Bahraini government had long been conferring with the other Gulf Arab states about the course of the uprising, and the intervention of a thousand Saudi army and national guard troops, five hundred police from the UAE, and some Qatari soldiers indicated that other GCC states felt action needed to be taken quickly in order to prevent any further spread, both within the country and regionally.[40] The country's immense strategic importance greatly informed the severity of this crackdown, which was conducted with the open collusion of Western governments. A three-month emergency law was declared on March 15, 2011, shutting down demonstrations and leading to the deaths and arrests of protesters. Nonetheless, despite the severe repression unleashed by the government and GCC troops, the movement has continued to organize—including targeting high-profile events (such as the Bahraini Grand Prix in April 2012) in an attempt to build solidarity with activists overseas, as well as mobilizing around the ongoing detention and torture of activists in the country.

Libya

The Libyan revolt that erupted in mid-February 2011 became a defining moment of the Arab uprisings. At the time of the escalating protests in Egypt and Tunisia, Libyan leader Muammar al-Qaddafi lent his unequivocal support to the tottering dictatorial regimes, claiming that the popular movements had been duped by propaganda spread through the Internet and the released cache of Wikileaks documents. Qaddafi castigated Tunisian demonstrators—at that point Ben Ali had just been ousted—for falling prey to "empty talk" scripted by "any liar, any drunkard, anyone under the influence."[41] These comments confirmed the essential solidarity between the various autocratic leaders across North Africa, despite their contrasting historical trajectories and foreign policy alliances.

Qaddafi's regime had undergone a profound transformation over the previous two decades. In 1969, he had been at the head of a movement deeply inspired by the Nasserist example in Egypt, leading a band of soldiers to overthrow the colonially backed regime of King Idris. Under Idris, Libya had been little more than a parking lot for British and US military bases—with the indifferent monarch receiving rental payments and wheat shipments in return for allowing Western troops basing rights in the desert and on the Mediterranean coast. The country had suffered brutally under colonialism, as the Italian government viewed the Libyan coast as its best chance of gaining a foothold in the region. Hundreds of thousands of Libyans were killed or deported as a result of the Italian occupation, with up to one-quarter of the 225,000-strong population of the city of Cyrenica massacred during the Italian "pacification" between 1928 and 1932.[42] Mass prisons and concentration camps were also established across Libya by the occupying power; in just one of these prisons, al-Barayka Camp, no fewer than eighty thousand people were interred, of which more than one-third died between 1930 and 1932, according to Italian estimates.[43]

With formal independence declared in 1951, Idris became a reluctant ruler over a fractured country. Indeed, at the time of his overthrow in 1969, the country had been a unified state for only six years. Idris had ruled through a system of patronage that rested upon a tiny group of favored individuals, tribes, and families; the nation had never developed a broader national identity.[44] For much of Idris's reign the country's main export was scrap metal left over from World War II air battles. The weakness of class consciousness or other social identities that might have extended across the national space meant that the only group with the cohesiveness to overthrow the monarchy was found in the military.

Qaddafi and his military comrades tapped into a widespread disdain of the Idris regime to seize power in a coup in September 1969. At the time Idris was overthrown, Libya was exporting three million barrels of oil per day.[45] Much like the Gulf states, the break with the structures of colonialism saw a nationalization of the oil fields (in 1972) and an increase in the oil rents charged to foreign multinationals. There were significant improvements in many social indicators, as the Qaddafi regime used these revenues to develop programs in literacy, health, and housing. Farmers were given land confiscated from Italian colonizers or wealthy landowners connected to the Idris monarchy and its tribal base, the Sa'adi in eastern Libya.[46]

For all these reasons, the military coup of 1969 heralded a significant break from the preceding era. Qaddafi's infamous Green Book, widely distributed in Libya, laid out a vision of society that claimed to abolish class differences and political disputes, dispensing with formal systems of parliamentary democracy in exchange for the supposed direct rule of the people. In reality, what developed was a bifurcated political system. A formal structure was established, consisting of a pyramidal system of popular committees that culminated in the General People's Congress (GPC), which was—at least in theory—elected from the bottom up and in which the sovereignty of the people was invested. But, simultaneously alongside this structure lay a second set of political institutions, the Revolutionary Committees (RC), which were outside of the purview of the people and controlled by Qaddafi and a small clique of loyal followers and family. Through the RCs, Qaddafi controlled all the repressive apparatus of the state as well as the judiciary and key economic levers of Libyan society—notably the oil industry. Over time, Qaddafi was able to gradually extend his control over the decisions and leadership of the GPC itself. Under laws passed in the mid-1970s, anyone guilty of founding a political party could be executed. Likewise, despite the rapid growth in the size of the Libyan military—from seven thousand in 1969 to eighty-five thousand in 1988—the effective armed bodies of the state were concentrated in a complex network of security forces that were directly controlled by Qaddafi and his family.[47] As this structure unfolded through the 1980s and 1990s, Qaddafi also sought to integrate members of important tribes (notably the Qadafha, Warfalla, and Maqarha) into the structures of the RCs—leading some to speak of a "retribalization" of Libyan society.[48]

The forms of rule established under Qaddafi were highly repressive and aimed at eliminating any form of political activity or independent mobilization outside of the structures sanctioned by the regime itself. At the same time, although some social gains followed in the immediate wake of the coup, the country's working class was sharply stratified, with a very large proportion of the working class in Libya composed of migrant workers from Egypt, Tunisia, and neighboring African countries such as Niger, Chad, and Ghana. By the late 2000s, the number of migrant workers in Libya was estimated to make up around 20 to 25 percent of the country's population (and thus an even higher proportion of the labor force).[49] Anti-migrant racism was deliberately stoked by the regime, which was to have important ramifications through the uprising that led to Qaddafi's overthrow. Indeed, in the autumn of 2000, 130 sub-Saharan migrants were killed during anti-African riots—with Qaddafi and the official Libyan press referring to African migrants as drug dealers, murderers, and carriers of infectious diseases.[50]

During the 1980s, Libya was largely isolated from world markets in response to Qaddafi's support for assorted guerrilla groups, the country's chemical weapons program, its pursuit of nuclear weapons, and the bombing of a Pan Am airplane over Lockerbie, Scotland, in 1988. Sanctions and the lower price of oil through the 1990s hit the regime hard. By the early 2000s, however, this isolation began to end as the regime swung toward a rapprochement with the West. (Qatar, it should be noted, played a major role in bringing Qaddafi in from the cold). Qaddafi gave his vigorous endorsement to the US invasion of Afghanistan and closely collaborated with the US "War on

Terror," including assisting in CIA rendition flights and torture programs.[51] With the lifting of UN sanctions on Libya in 2003 (in place since 1992), key figures around Qaddafi—most notably his son Saif el-Islam Qaddafi, a recent London School of Economics graduate—pushed strongly for adopting neoliberal reforms. The ascent of this neoliberal wing within the Libyan state was captured in Saif's strident insistence that "everything should be privatized" in a speech before the Libya Youth Forum in 2008.[52]

Libya's neoliberal trajectory through the late 2000s was strongly supported by US and European leaders, who saw the potential prize represented by the opening up of Libya's vast oil and gas reserves to foreign ownership. The country holds the largest proven oil reserves in Africa and is ranked among the top ten largest reserves in the world.[52] It also has significant amounts of natural gas, the fourth largest in Africa. In this context, the neoliberal shift championed by Saif el-Islam and other figures close to Qaddafi was met with a lifting of sanctions on the country and an embrace of the Qaddafi regime. A rapid succession of official visits by politicians, advisers, and assorted academics—including Condoleezza Rice, Tony Blair, Silvio Berlusconi, Benjamin Barber, Anthony Giddens, Joseph Nye, and Michael Porter—found the visitors only too willing to endorse the Libyan government despite its ongoing political repression.

Although Libya's steps toward neoliberal reform were hesitant, subject to competing factions within the ruling elite and the capricious whims of Qaddafi himself, there is little doubt as to which direction economic policy was moving. This was neoliberalism overlaid on the highly fragmented, depoliticized, and patrimonial structures of Libyan society under Qaddafi—but it was neoliberalism nonetheless. It acted to widen inequalities—particularly in the wake of the 2008 crisis and the drop in oil prices. Statistical evidence on Libya is scant and notoriously unreliable, but oft-quoted figures referred to 20 percent unemployment and one-third of Libyans living below the poverty line in the period immediately preceding the 2011 rebellion. At the same time, international financial institutions were enthusiastic about the neoliberal trajectory of the country. A report issued by the IMF on February 15, 2011, applauded the Libyan government, noting that "An ambitious program to privatise banks and develop the nascent financial sector is underway. Banks have been partially privatized, interest rates decontrolled, and competition encouraged . . . ongoing efforts to restructure and modernize the Central Bank of Libya are under way with assistance from the Fund."[54]

Just two days after the IMF released this upbeat report, however, activists in Benghazi called for a *yawm al-ghadab* (day of rage)—borrowing the stock phrase that all the Arab uprisings were to employ. The demonstrators were protesting the arrest of a prominent human rights lawyer, Fathi Tarbil, who had represented families of prisoners killed in a notorious Libyan prison massacre in 1996.[55] But the movement soon expanded to encompass wider grievances against the regime. Despite arrests and killing of protesters by the security forces, the rebellion spread rapidly throughout the east of the country, which had been relatively neglected by Qaddafi. Protests also resonated in some neighborhoods of the capital, Tripoli. Although Qadaffi amassed large numbers of troops and firepower against the rebels, there were defections of important tribes, such as the Warfallah, as well as important regime figures, including the country's interior minister and army leaders such as Major General al-Fattah Younis.[56]

By the last week of February, the momentum of the demonstrations was superseded by increasing calls from rebel leaders—particularly those who had defected from the highest ranks of the Qaddafi regime—for some form of foreign intervention. This call was soon embraced by powers such as Britain, France, Germany, and the United States, which—deploying the language of "genocide" and "massacre"—passed UN Resolution 1973 on March 17, 2011. The resolution called for a "no fly zone" and authorized all necessary means to "protect civilians and civilian-populated areas." Despite an explicit disavowal of any "foreign occupation force" in the text of the resolution, it essentially opened up the space for Western powers to act as arbiter of the conflict—any no-fly zone or "protection" of civilians clearly required a military force and coordination with the rebel troops. From that moment onward, NATO came to play the leading role in determining the pace and orientation of the revolt against Qaddafi.

The NATO intervention in Libya represented a clear attempt to coopt the direction and leadership of the rebellion itself. As the history of the region makes only too clear, Western powers had few issues with Qaddafi or any other dictatorial regime, or with the loss of civilian life. Their primary concern was to get ahead of the wider movement across the region; the intervention in Libya presented an opportunity to do this in a way that would cut off the possibility of a contiguous liberated territory across North Africa. Undoubtedly, the possibility of accessing the country's lucrative energy supplies provided further motivation for intervention. Over the subsequent months, NATO—backed by the Gulf Arab states, particularly Qatar and Saudi Arabia—moved incrementally to shift the character of the Libyan uprising toward cultivating a leadership that was satisfactory in the eyes of the West. This leadership came to be embodied in the National Transitional Council (NTC), an institution largely made up of ex-regime figures and others beholden to the West. After a period of military stalemate and various attempts at negotiated solutions, the final assault on Tripoli in August 2011 saw the overthrow of Qaddafi. On September 16, 2011, the NTC was recognized by the United Nations as the legal representative of Libya.[57] In July 2012, elections occurred for the General National Congress (GNC), which subsequently took over legislative powers from the NTC. Although the political terrain remains highly fragmented and fluid, the dominant parties appear to be strongly oriented toward a neoliberal economic program and a continuation of the Qaddafi-era rapprochement with the West.[58]

Syria

Many of the same factors that underlay the revolts in nearby countries could also be found in Syria. Similar to the Libyan case, the regime of Hafez al-Assad, father of the current Syrian ruler, Bashar al-Assad, had stayed largely outside the orbit of US power through the 1970s and 1980s. Assad had cultivated an image of anti-imperialism, although—again like Qaddafi—this was frequently more a case of rhetoric than reality. A coup against a left-wing faction of the Ba'ath Party brought Assad to power in 1970. Following this seizure of power, Assad institutionalized a form of leadership that was to remain a consistent feature of Syrian politics up to the current day. On the one hand, he moved consciously to incorporate a layer of the majority Sunni population (particularly its urban bourgeoisie) into the apparatus of the state and, most significantly, its commercial operations. Simultaneously, on the other, he ensured that members of his Alawite sect controlled the key levers of the army and security apparatuses. Family members directly commanded strategic elite army divisions such as the Republican Guard. In this manner, the country's state and commercial bourgeoisies were fully dependent on (and complicit with) Assad's rule, while simultaneously he was shielded from any potential coup by an Alawite minority that had a powerful stake in the continuation of the regime.

Prior to Assad's 1970 coup, Ba'athist governments had implemented a series of state-centered economic policies that echoed those of the Arab nationalist governments discussed in earlier chapters. The country had seen significant extension in state support for many basic social needs, with levels of education, health, and literacy improving considerably in these earlier years. By the mid-1980s, however, Hafez al-Assad had embarked on a gradual liberalization of the economy that would gather pace through the 1990s and culminate in a deep neoliberal reform program under his son, who succeeded his father in 2000. One of the most astute observers of Syria's political economy, Bassam Haddad, has tracked this process in detail. Haddad notes that Bashar al-Assad's policies of privatization, opening up to foreign direct investment, and removal of state control led to key industrial sectors such as metallurgy, chemicals, and textiles coming under private sector control.[59] By 2007, the private sector represented around 60.5 percent of GDP, up from 52.3 percent in 2000.[60] A tightly knit group of business conglomerates were nurtured through their close contacts with the regime and benefited from the liberalization process. Two major holding companies collected the most prosperous of these business groups, fed through state contracts, other links to the Assad regime, and joint investments with the Gulf.[61]

These processes led to a sharpening of social schisms within Syria, with rural areas, in particular, severely affected by the changes. One of the significant drivers of the rising inequality was the elimination of state farms and the shift to private ownership of land in a manner strikingly similar to that described for North Africa in chapter 4. Agrarian reform had been a key policy of the Syrian government through the 1970s, and its reversal led to the emergence of large private farms that appropriated much of the underground water. This was an important factor behind a developing water crisis through the mid-2000s, with agriculture falling from 7.8 percent of GDP in 2005 to 2.2 percent in 2010.[62] Coupled with the effects of climate change and drought, the water crisis meant that many Syrian families could no longer survive on the land—it was estimated by the UN Office for the Coordination of Humanitarian Affairs that more than three hundred thousand Syrian families moved to urban areas as a consequence of this rural crisis in one of the "largest internal displacements in the Middle East in recent years."[63]

This social polarization was given an even stronger push following the Syrian withdrawal from Lebanon in 2005. Lebanon had been a critical adjunct to Syria's economy—helping provide banking and financial services for the country's elite (and plenty of opportunities for criminal activities) while absorbing large numbers of poor workers from the Syrian countryside. Syrian migrant workers formed the bulk of Lebanon's unskilled workforce and were employed in the construction, agriculture, and cleaning sectors, or as peddlers and porters. They did not require visas to enter Lebanon and, as a result, almost the entire Syrian workforce in Lebanon—estimated at between four hundred thousand and one million people—was unregistered. Remittances from Syrian workers in Lebanon made up 8 percent of Syrian GDP in the mid-2000s.[64] With Syrian withdrawal from Lebanon, the employment pressures—as well as the situation on the land—deteriorated even further. From 2005 to 2010, the country witnessed a 10 percent increase in poverty, geographically concentrated in the northeast and south of the country. Growing poverty was exacerbated by the flight of more than 1.2 million people from the land (according to the most conservative estimates) as a result of drought and economic crisis.

The political economy backdrop to the Syrian revolt thus resembles that of other countries in the region and—like Egypt, Tunisia, and elsewhere—the Syrian regime was also marked by autocratic rule and violent repression of domestic dissent.[65] The emergence of protests in March 2011 confronted these factors in the same manner as the protests in other states. Much of the dynamic of the uprising has also been similar—with some forces pushing for nonsectarian, community-based mobilizations (including armed defense against the regime), on the one hand, and, on the other, self-appointed elites (and some defectors from the regime) attempting to impose a pro-imperialist direction on the uprising.[66]

The divisions among the opposition to the regime are further shaped by geopolitical rivalries. Precisely because of Syria's relatively recent neoliberal opening—coinciding with the global crisis and the growing weight of other powers in the world market—international rivalries over the Middle East have been sharply condensed in the country. In the most recent period, Russia and China have been the main allies of the Assad regime and have viewed the country as an important position from which to build a counterweight to US power (see chapter 2). This has been reinforced through the Syrian government's alliances with Iran and the armed resistance group Hizbullah in Lebanon.

Despite these rivalries, however, it would be wrong to assess the struggle in Syria solely through the lens of geopolitics—this simply ignores the political economy of class and state formation in the country, reducing the Syrian people to a classless mass of rival "sects" and "tribes." The roots of the Syrian uprising lie in an attempt to overthrow an autocratic regime presiding over a highly polarized neoliberal economy. Yet, as was the case with Libya, Western governments—acting in conjunction with regional allies such as the Gulf and Turkey—will clearly attempt to push the course of the uprising in a direction amenable to their long-term interests. At the time of writing these efforts have not been successful. The Western-backed Syrian National Council (SNC) finds little support inside the country itself, and activists on the ground have largely denounced calls for Western military intervention. Indeed, in March 2012, following the second meeting of the so-called Friends of Syria, attended by eighty-three countries, and which acknowledged the SNC as representative and central leadership of the Syrian opposition, Syrian activists decried

> the open and clear support from countries like the US, Saudi Arabia, EU, Qatar and Turkey [for the SNC]. These are the countries that support it, and provide political, financial and media support. But despite this support and extensive media exposure, it cannot hide the reality that the SNC is closer to a ghost without soul. It is protected by these countries because it is used as the entry card into the Syrian opposition.[67]

Compounded by the specific nature of Syrian state and society—the deep linkages of the country's bourgeoisie with the Assad regime, the distinctive sectarian characteristics that underpin its mode of rule, and the particular geopolitical rivalries that surround the country—Syria is enduring a tragic and very bloody conflict. As of late 2012, at least forty thousand people had been killed and 1.2 million displaced.[68]

Common Themes, Contrasting Paths

No country in the Middle East has been left untouched by the rebellions that began in Tunisia in December 2010. In Jordan, protests began on January 14, 2011, around issues of unemployment, high food and energy prices, corruption, and poverty. Protesters demanded the resignation of Jordanian prime minister Samir Rifai, whose well-established neoliberal credentials (and close relationship with Gulf capitalism) were highlighted by his position as CEO and founder of a leading Jordanian investment firm, Jordan Dubai Capital. Demonstrations continued on a monthly basis throughout 2011, which Jordan's King Abdullah II met with repression as well as the granting of various concessions—including the sacking of Rifai and his cabinet in October 2011. Although Abdullah has managed to remain in power throughout the protests—partly due to the specific role of the monarchy and the nature of political rule in Jordan—they have gradually escalated from protests about specific policies to calls for an abdication by the king himself.[69] Large, regular protests have also taken place in Algeria, Morocco, Kuwait, Oman, Lebanon, the Palestinian West Bank, and Saudi Arabia. All these protests have addressed issues of unemployment, high prices (particularly food), and political exclusion. They have borrowed extensively from the language and discourse of the uprisings in other parts of the Middle East and utilized many of the same tactics such as mass gatherings in central squares, strikes, and sit-ins—Algeria even saw a repeat of Mohammed Bouazizi's self-immolation by dozens of people outside government buildings, four of whom eventually died from their burns. None of these protests has yet produced a fundamental change in government policies or leadership, but they confirm the profound manner in which the same types of issues resonate deeply across the region.

The speed and scale of these protests has fed the fashionable interpretation that they were "leaderless" and "unorganized"—a spontaneous outburst of an inchoate mass. Yet while these movements certainly drew into action millions of people who had never before mobilized in political action—and it is true to say that they were generally not led by single, clearly identifiable organizations—their successes and failures were nonetheless strongly connected to previous waves of struggle. Earlier political battles provided an indispensable network of activists as well as the hard-fought lessons of experience that made it possible to confront autocratic regimes. Not only did these earlier struggles provide organizational networks and lessons, they also contributed to undermining the all-pervasive sense of fear on which these regimes so heavily rested—making it possible for people to move onto the streets when they did.

In Tunisia, one of the most important examples of these preexisting social forces was the left wing of the Tunisian labor movement, which had fought doggedly for years to resist the capitulation of the general secretariat of the UGTT (the official union federation) to the Ben Ali regime. Trade union rank-and-file committees, for example, had played a central role in the momentous 2008 Revolt of the Gafsa Mining Basin, which has been described as the "most important protest movement seen in Tunisia since the Bread Revolt of January 1984."[70] The Gafsa Revolt drew together the unemployed, workers on temporary contracts, high school students, and families of those who worked in the region's phosphate mines.[71] Employing a range of tactics, including hunger strikes, sit-ins, and street protests—the movement was principally aimed at tackling the labor market deregulation and precariousness that were core features of Tunisian neoliberalism. The significance of this powerful strike wave lay in the manner in which it drew together those most impacted by the reform process—notably the unemployed and temporary workers—and brought them up against the structures of the regime, including the official trade union federation.[72] Despite the state repression that eventually ended this 2008 strike, it helped to lay the ground for the 2010–11 uprising.[73]

Likewise, in Egypt, the protests that erupted in January 2011 had their antecedents in earlier waves of mass struggle. Between 2004 and 2009, more than 1,900 protests had taken place, involving more than 1.7 million workers in strike action.[74] Western diplomats well understood the significance of this earlier strike wave, as Vijay Prashad has documented, describing US ambassador Francis Riccardione's remarks in a secret cable to Washington that the protests "demonstrated it was possible to tear down a poster of Mubarak and stomp on it, to shout obscene anti-regime slogans, to burn a minibus and hurl rocks at riot police."[75] This mid-2000s strike wave intersected with and built upon earlier phases of struggle in the country, most notably solidarity with the Second Intifada in Palestine, in which university and high school students confronted the regime's close alliance with Israel. These demonstrations of 2000–2002 helped politicize both students and the wider population, developing networks that were later critical to the demonstrations that culminated in January 2011.[76] The earlier mobilizations in many ways served as a "proxy for domestic dissent," bringing together a wide range of different political forces in street demonstrations that inevitably culminated with chants against the regime.[77] The message of these protests reverberated throughout the silent majority of Egyptian society, revealing the fact that it was possible (at least in the moment) to shake off fear of the regime.

In Tunisia and Egypt, the strength and prominence of labor movements, expressed through strikes, demonstrations, and the emergence of new workers' organizations, provided a social force capable of decisively confronting the old regime. In other cases, where this earlier history of struggle was largely absent and movements had faced much sharper repression, the uprisings took on a more mixed character. This opened them up to being diverted by Western powers, often exploiting and encouraging preexisting ethnic, sectarian, tribal, or parochial divisions. In the case of Libya, this took the form of direct military intervention, in which large parts of the previous state elite simply switched sides. In Yemen, competing demands came from social movements, tribal elites, secessionist forces in the south, Islamic fundamentalist movements, and the Houthi groups in the north of the country. The extreme concentration of the country's resources in the hands of a tiny number of families, with wealth distributed through patronage networks centered on the Saleh regime and state apparatus, also made the emergence of an autonomous opposition much more difficult. In this case, the regime remained essentially intact, with the process steered by the GCC and the West. In other cases, the weaknesses of working-class organization—particularly in those states where a large proportion of the working class was composed of migrant workers who faced exclusion and racism from the "citizen" population—helped to reinforce this process (e.g., Libya, Bahrain, and the other Gulf states).

Crises at the top of the state itself, typically generated by an imminent transition to a new generation of leaders, also shaped the relative success of movements by weakening the cohesiveness of ruling regimes. In Egypt and Tunisia, the potential overthrow of regime figureheads (such as Mubarak and Ben Ali) presented the military and capitalist class with the challenge of taking charge of the transition, as opposing the movement might lead to its deepening radicalization. For this reason, the military in both cases essentially deserted the autocrats, attempting to steer the direction of transition in a manner that would ensure the continued stability of capitalist relations. In contrast, in the case of Syria, where the accumulation of the elite was so closely bound up and interpenetrated with the regime itself, the division at the top of the state has been a much more protracted affair. In Yemen and Bahrain, the deep political influence of the Gulf states (particularly Saudi Arabia) acted to reinforce and strengthen state structures, shaping the eventual outcome.

Despite these specificities, however, one overriding theme emerges from these uprisings. The popular movements that erupted in 2011 represented much more than the overthrow of despised dictators. Of course the protesters were centrally united around demands for authoritarian regimes to end, and the demonstrations encompassed a very wide variety of social layers (including, in some cases, elements of the upper classes). But to concentrate on the surface appearances of these demonstrations obscures their real content. These mobilizations indicate that "politics" and "economics," which are typically conceived as separate spheres, are fused and part of the same struggle. The battle against political despotism is inevitably intertwined with the dynamic of class struggle. These uprisings reflected not just a crisis of regime legitimacy or a concern with political freedom, but were—at their root—confronting the outcomes of capitalist development itself.

The Counterrevolutionary Moment

This fusion of the political and economic spheres is strongly confirmed in the nature of the counterrevolutionary response. The initial reaction of world leaders was one of prevarication, indicated in the anxious comments emanating from Washington and its allies. On January 18, 2011, US secretary of state Hillary Clinton remarked in an interview with the Saudi-owned Arabiya channel that she was concerned about the impact of the "unrest and instability" on the "very positive aspects of our relationship with Tunisia," confirming that the United States was "not taking sides" and that it would "wait and see."[78] Saudi Arabia's disapproval was underlined more frankly by the Saudi monarch's revilement of Egyptian and Tunisian protesters as "infiltrators" who "in the name of freedom of expression . . . spew out their hatred in destruction . . . inciting a malicious sedition."[79] Likewise, the former Israeli ambassador in Cairo described the potential fall of the Mubarak regime as "a horrible scenario" and "a disaster for Israel, Jordan, Saudi Arabia, the Gulf states, Europe and the U.S."[80] Other Arab leaders—notably Palestinian president Mahmoud Abbas, Jordan's King Abdullah, and Sheikh Nahyan of the United Arab Emirates—openly extended their support to both Ben Ali and Mubarak. It was a stark demonstration of the patterns of shared interests shaping the Middle East political system.

Following Mubarak's overthrow in February 2011, however, the language of these leaders shifted. From a position that had oscillated between passive and open support for Ben Ali and Mubarak, the dominant narrative moved toward a call for "orderly transition" and acclamations about the need for "democracy." US president Barack Obama and other government spokespeople expressed their approval of the "spirit of peaceful protest and perseverance" and declared that the United States would "continue to be a friend and partner . . . ready to provide whatever assistance is necessary . . . to pursue a credible transition to a democracy."[81] In numerous statements such as these, the uprisings were recast as a simple struggle for political democracy, concerned only with ending the long years of autocracy. The focus of Western powers shifted to the question of "orderly transition"—a phrase repeated ad nauseam by all those who had previously supported the old authoritarian regimes.

The real content of this appeal to order was an attempt to demobilize the new political and social forces unleashed in the course of uprisings and to restore the legitimacy of the state structures and previous patterns of rule. A prominent feature of this was a reassertion of the neoliberal program itself, initially expressed through an ideological reframing that attempted to render the uprisings within a pro-market discourse. Perhaps the most glaring example of this discursive shift was the statement made by World Bank president Robert Zoellick at a World Bank meeting on the Middle East in mid-April 2011. Referring to Mohammed Bouazizi, Zoellick remarked,

> The key point I have also been emphasizing and I emphasized in this speech is that it is not just a question of money. It is a question of policy . . . keep in mind, the late Mr. Bouazizi was basically driven to burn himself alive because he was harassed with red tape . . . one starting point is to quit harassing those people and let them have a chance to start some small businesses.[82]

This same fundamental message was repeatedly emphasized by US and European spokespeople in the months following the uprisings: this was not a revolt against several decades of neoliberalism, but rather a movement against an intrusive state that had obstructed the pursuit of individual self-interest through the market. Ne-oliberal ideology was attempting to resorb dissent and fashion it in its own image.

In this discursive reframing of the uprisings, the massive protests that overthrew Mubarak and Ben Ali occurred due to the absence of capitalism rather than to its normal functioning. In an ideological sense, this reframing directly attacked the popular aspirations that arose through the course of the struggles themselves—to reclaim wealth that was stolen from the people, offer state support and services to the poor, nationalize those industries that were privatized, and place restrictions on foreign investment. These were the alternatives that, in the words of the Egyptian economist Wael Gamal, "were wide open and clear, but meant a departure from the old policies and therefore would explode the new political compromise."[83] Precisely because in these uprisings the political and economic demands were inseparable and intertwined, this effort to recast the struggle as "pro-market" was, in a very real sense, directly aimed at undercutting and weakening the revolutionary impulse that drove these movements—an attempt to ensure that the Middle East would not deviate from either the neoliberal trajectories or foreign alliances established in the previous period. Coupled with the direct military interventions in Libya and Bahrain, and increasingly overt attempts to steer the course of the Syrian up-rising, Western powers and their local allies began a concerted attempt to curtail and demobilize the popular awakening that unfolded during 2011.

The Deceptive Promise of Aid

One of the key elements of this strategy was the well-tested weapon of financial aid. Shortly after Ben Ali and Mubarak were overthrown, a series of financial aid packages was hastily promised to new governments by leading international in-stitutions and Western rulers.[84] The press releases accompanying these financial packages spoke grandly of "the transition to democracy and freedom," but in re-ality they espoused an identical logic to the economic strategies that had been in place for decades. The Institute of International Finance (IIF), a policy and lobby organization that brings together the largest financial institutions in the world, candidly noted this in early May 2011, stating:

> As momentous as the current security and political restructuring challenges may be, it is absolutely critical that the transition authorities . . . place a high priority on deepening and accelerating structural economic reforms . . . transi-tion and subsequent governments must articulate a credible medium-term re-form and stabilization framework . . . [and] need to focus on creating the legal and institutional environment for fostering entrepreneurship, investment, and market-driven growth.[85]

Echoing the conditionality requirements of earlier loan packages, the IIF went on to bluntly identify this acceleration of structural adjustment as the "context" in which aid would be provided.[86] These same sentiments were confirmed by the IMF in a report to the May 26–27, 2011, G8 Summit, which spoke of the key role of the private sector, attracting FDI, and supporting "an enabling environment in which the private sector flourishes" as the necessary priorities of the region.[87]

Moreover, in much the same way as IFIs viewed the debt crises of the 1970s and 1980s as a useful moment of opportunity, the uprisings of 2011 were also seen as presenting a chance to consolidate the neoliberal trajectory. Indeed, in May 2011, the EIB made exactly this point in a report outlining the centrality of PPPs to their economic strategy for the region. Noting the revolts had produced a sense of "increased uncertainty and instability," the EIB went on to conclude that "moments of political change can also represent an opportunity to reinforce or improve already existing institutional frameworks."[88] Comparing the region to 1990s Poland and South Africa—two cases where the language of "orderly transition" was also widely deployed—the EIB commented that "[these countries] effectively maintained and reinforced the institutional framework for investment."[89]

The comparison with Eastern Europe was not merely rhetorical. In early 2011, the European Bank for Reconstruction and Development (EBRD) announced that it was planning to enter the Middle East. Its foray into North Africa in 2011 was a watershed moment—the institution had been established in 1991 with the goal of transitioning Eastern Europe to capitalism through a program of deep-seated privatization, and it had never before been active outside of Europe. The implications of the EBRD's entry into the region were highly significant, signaling a renewed emphasis on neoliberal reform by Western states (particularly in the infrastructure sector through the use of PPPs).[90] As the EBRD's president, Thomas Mirow, put it in the lead-up to the bank's discussions on opening headquarters in Egypt, "The EBRD was created in 1991 to promote democracy and market economy, and the historic developments in Egypt strike a deep chord at this bank."[91]

In the immediate wake of the uprisings in Tunisia and Egypt, the EBRD quickly placed itself at the center of European intervention in the uprisings, predicting that its funding would reach up to €2.5 billion annually by 2015.[92] In October 2011, EBRD shareholders voted to allow Egypt, Morocco, Tunisia, and Jordan to become recipients of the organization's funds, and, in January 2012, Jordan and Tunisia became members—joining Morocco and Egypt as the only shareholders from the Arab world. A series of conferences in 2011 and 2012 culminated in an announcement in September 2012 that the EBRD had agreed to fund three projects in Tunisia, Morocco, and Jordan, aimed at deepening trade with Europe and supporting private equity investments in the region. Simultaneously, the EBRD's new loans were accompanied by feverish attempts by the World Bank, the IMF, and the African Development Bank to induce governments in the region to borrow, thereby locking in the economic status quo. [93] All these financial initiatives were aimed at turning the movements that had erupted in 2011 away from any deep-seated change to the patterns of capitalist development characterized by earlier regimes. In the words of one Tunisian activist, "Foreign debt is not a secondary question to the ongoing social struggles confronting the current Tunisian revolution, it is at the heart of the struggle. It raises economical, political, and social questions that relate to popular sovereignty and foreign control, and how we divide the wealth of the country and achieve rights for all Tunisians."[94]

The Muslim Brotherhood and the Counterrevolution

This strategic orientation of Western states was soon faced, however, with the ongoing aspirations of revolutionary movements, particularly in the paradigmatic example of Egypt. Despite the fanfare that accompanied promised Western financial aid, loan packages to Egypt did not seriously materialize during 2011–12. A major factor in this delay was the recognition by popular forces that these aid packages simply represented a reconstitution of the chains of debt that had been such a prominent feature of the ousted regimes. The question of the IMF and World Bank loans to Egypt became a topic of heated debate among wide layers of the Egyptian population—even the country's finance minister was forced to respond on national TV to the concerns around conditionality raised by activist groups against the debt. This intense popular debate reflected the shift in power unleashed by the revolutionary movements; the millions of people who had entered the political stage sought real change, not just a new face on the old ways.

The explosion of different social struggles through 2011 confirms this increased confidence and combativeness of wide swaths of the Egyptian populace. Wildcat strikes and worker actions began immediately after the overthrow of Mubarak in February 2011. A statement on February 19, 2011, signed by representatives of independent workers' organizations in more than forty factories and workplaces, noted the "strikes, occupations, and demonstrations by hundreds of thousands of workers across Egypt during the current period" and the importance of reaffirming the "social aspect of this revolution and to prevent the revolution being taken away from those at its base who should be its beneficiaries."[95] The statement listed a range of demands around minimum (and maximum) wage, job security, renationalization of privatized enterprises, and the right to take industrial action. Most significantly, the statement called for the dissolution of the Egyptian Trade Union Federation (ETUF) as "one of the most important symbols of corruption under the defunct regime."[96]

In September 2011, another major strike wave erupted, involving teachers, doctors, and workers in public transport, sugar refineries, and the postal sector. This wave of workers' actions was particularly important because it spread across entire industrial sectors (unlike the strikes in February, which had been more localized to particular workplaces). A nationwide teachers' strike at this time, for example, encompassed nearly half a million workers at its peak, demanding the resignation of the minister of education, more investment in schools, and better educational conditions. The doctors' strike raised the question of improved health care and better hospitals. A major theme in all these strikes was the notion of *tathir*—the "cleansing" of public institutions of remnants of the old regime. Workers' actions took place alongside a myriad of other social struggles—including protests against military courts (more than twelve thousand people faced military trials in the period immediately following Mubarak's demise), student strikes against fees and draconian administrative regulations, demonstrations to confront the increasing attacks against women, and campaigns to abolish the debt incurred under Mubarak's regime. This unprecedented flowering of social mobilization profoundly illustrated the linkages between the day-to-day economic interests of workers around wages and conditions and broader social and political questions.

In this context, Western powers and their local allies were compelled to turn to other means to vitiate the heightened political consciousness. Any continuation of capitalism as usual required the rehabilitation of the Mubarak-era mechanisms of control (both repressive and ideological) as a means to ensure a pacified and depoliticized population. In this they faced an immense challenge—many of the structures of the state, which previously had ensured the political passivity of the population, had partially disintegrated during the uprisings. The police and security apparatuses, for example, had largely disappeared from the streets during the early part of 2011—indeed, a major turning point in the ousting of Mubarak occurred in late January 2011, when protesters burned down police stations across the country. Mubarak's ruling party, the National Democratic Party (NDP), had been disbanded (and its imposing headquarters on the Nile River set ablaze). In workplaces, one of the state's most important mechanisms of control, the ETUF, also lost influence as new, independent trade unions began to emerge amid the burgeoning strike movements.

One attempted solution to this challenge of restoring the old patterns of rule focused upon parties coming out of the tradition of political Islam, most notably the once-outlawed Muslim Brotherhood (MB). Much like Mubarak's NDP, the organization had a deep penetration across the country, including in rural areas, and was thereby able to play an important ideological and mobilizational role. It had taken a pernicious position in the February and September 2011 strike waves, repeatedly acting to undermine independent workers' actions and demobilize movements on the streets. The September 2011 teachers' strike, for example, eventually collapsed after the MB refused to support the ongoing mobilizations and channeled control of the sector back into the old ETUF-affiliated teacher's union. Likewise, among doctors, the MB was able to call off actions because of its domination of the doctor's union.[97] Its close linkages with important sections of the Egyptian bourgeoisie, its willingness to accommodate with the military and with US imperialism, and its strong connections with regional powers in the Gulf meant that it presented an attractive model for restoration of the status quo.

Accomplishing this process took most of 2012. Following a complex series of electoral contests, the MB's Mohammed Morsi came to power as Egypt's president on June 30, 2012.[98] Immediately following the election of Morsi and the swearing-in of his cabinet in early August 2012, a new series of strikes broke out. This strike wave included textile workers, ceramic workers, doctors, university workers, postal workers, and health workers from across the entire country. Its epicenter was the industrial city of Mahalla al-Kubra, where twenty-five thousand textile workers at the state-owned Mahalla Misr Spinning and Weaving Company had struck in mid-July 2012. These workers played a leading role in Mubarak's overthrow, as well as in the earlier strike waves of 2006–2008 that helped delegitimize the Mubarak regime and build new centers of labor militancy. In response to this strike, the MB sent representatives to the factories to convince workers to end the action, only for them to be chased away by the strikers.

These actions point to the class orientation of the MB itself. In early December 2012, the organization agreed in principle to an IMF loan—although the request was later stalled following popular opposition. It also passed a series of highly repressive laws against labor and other social movements and brought the military back into a position of strength.[99] Morsi's cabinet appointments demonstrated the clear continuity with the old patterns of rule. His finance minister, Mumtaz al-Said, remained from the previous military-appointed cabinet. Al-Said is an ardent proponent of neoliberal policies and strongly pushed for the international loans from the IMF and World Bank. As minister of investment, Morsi appointed Osama Saleh, who had been chosen by Mubarak as chairman of Egypt's General Authority for Free Zones and Investment, an institution that led the drive to market Egypt as a low-wage platform for foreign investors. The minister for trade and industry was Hatem Saleh, CEO of Gozour Food Industry Group, a subsidiary of the Gulf-linked Citadel Capital (see chapter 6). For the position of interior minister, Morsi appointed Ahmed Gamal Eddin, deputy interior minister during 2011, who was responsible for much of the repression directed against protesters over that year. On the day of his appointment, the Arabic edition of the newspaper *Al-Masry Al-Youm* reported that Eddin promised to "restore security [as the] highest priority of the Ministry of Interior."[100] He particularly identified protests and demonstrations as "obstacles to achieving security and economic stability" and pledged to punish "citizens who block roads and disable railways" (the head of the Egyptian National Railways Authority had complained about the more than 870 protests and strikes since the overthrow of Mubarak).[101] In addition to his record in the repressive apparatus of the state, Eddin is the nephew of the former leader of Mubarak's now dissolved NDP parliamentary bloc.

The MB, as with most Islamist movements in the region, clearly draws upon support from some layers of the rural and urban poor, as well as the urban "middle class" (indicated by the MB's historically strong showing in elections for associations of lawyers, doctors, engineers, and other professionals). At the same time, the leadership is openly pro-capitalist and has explicitly embraced a neoliberal economic program. Central leaders of the organization, such as Khairat Al-Shater and Hassan Malek, are millionaire businessmen. Other key business leaders associated with the MB include Safwan Thabet of the Juhayna Group, Egypt's largest dairy and juice company (see chapter 6); Mohamed Moamen of Mo'men Group, which operates a large Egyptian fast food chain; and Abdel Rahman Seoudi, who runs a supermarket chain and agricultural export company. These individuals completely control the organization's decision-making process (through the so-called Guidance Bureau) as well as its economic program. This class fraction was able to develop a massive financial empire under Mubarak, while simultaneously facing periodic repression from the state and Mubarak-allied elites. The conflicts between the MB leadership, the military, and the old Mubarak allies remain, but these are best seen as competitive struggles within and between fractions of the same Egyptian capitalist class and state apparatus. At root, they represent similar class interests and are united against the popular movement.[102]

This class character of the MB is intimately connected to the regional patterns traced throughout this book—most specifically the role of the Gulf Arab states. The Gulf states, particularly Saudi Arabia and Qatar, have taken a lead role in supporting Islamist movements in Egypt (and elsewhere) throughout the course of the uprisings. Concurrently, these states (notably Saudi Arabia, Kuwait, and the UAE) have also maintained extremely close relationships with the leadership of the Egyptian military. One of the conclusions to be drawn from this book is that this aid is not solely due to religious fidelity but is rather a key element to a further deepening of the Gulf's political penetration of the state apparatus. It is one expression, in other words, of the internationalization of the Egyptian state, a means through which Gulf capitalism ensures that Egypt will continue to maintain the patterns of accumulation that characterized the preceding decades.

At the same time, the conservative brand of Islam promoted by the Gulf and articulated by Islamist movements such as the MB is a key component of the counterrevolutionary dynamic. The spread of reactionary ideas toward women, religious minorities, Shi'a, and so forth is an essential feature of the ideological battle against the revolutionary movements—one that acts to splinter and weaken solidarities. Central to this is the war against women's involvement in and leadership of political struggles. The rev-

olutionary movements in Egypt (and elsewhere) have necessarily had many women activists at their core—in large part due to the patterns of capitalist development traced
throughout this book—and a decisive feature of the attempt to restore the status quo is
to shut down women's visibility in the public sphere, removing women as active participants on the front lines of resistance. In this sense, conservative strictures on the
role of women are an integral component of broader counterrevolutionary goals. It is
an attempt to "put bodies back in their place," as the insightful work of Paul Amar has
pointed out.[103] The position of women is thus a key barometer for the health of the revolutionary process, and the movements that have arisen around this question, notably
in Egypt, are essential.

For all of these reasons, much like its cousin the AKP (Adalet ve Kalkınma Partisi;
Justice and Development Party) in Turkey, the Egyptian Islamist movement can be understood as the political expression of a segment of the country's bourgeoisie, which
rests upon support from middle and poorer layers of society, and seeks to maintain the
previously existing patterns of capital accumulation at both the national and regional
scales. It is an organization that supports continued privatization, increased exposure
to global financial markets, further deregulation of labor markets, and more reliance
on loans from international financial institutions such as the IMF and World Bank. The
role of the MB in Egypt is a powerful indication of how Islamist politics have emerged as
a useful instrument of political elites and Western powers in their attempt to reconstitute
the power of capital over Egyptian society, particularly in the context of the partial disintegration of the old modes of rule.[104] This orientation may well generate contradictions
with the rhetoric and practices of the organization but, as with the Turkish AKP, the MB
should not be seen as an anticapitalist or progressive alternative to authoritarian rule.

Nonetheless, within this context, it is essential to remember that the state should
not be reduced to the MB or whichever political party may hold a majority in the government. These parties are organizational representations of various social forces, but
the state remains a much broader institutional expression of capitalist class power that
extends beyond the immediate reins of governmental power. Most significantly, as
this book has repeatedly emphasized, military and security forces hold a particularly
critical position within Arab state structures. While the form that this takes differs
across the region—from the sharply sectarian character of armies in Bahrain and Syria
to elite units led directly by ruling families in Qaddafi's Libya and Saleh's Yemen—the
security apparatus remains the core element of class power in all countries. This observation is singularly important in the Egyptian case, as the leading ranks of the Egyptian military not only are deeply connected to the capitalist class itself (through their
multiple business interests) but also form the main interlocutor with the United States
and other Western powers (evidenced by the massive levels of US aid that flow directly

to the military). At all serious junctures over the last two years, beginning with the overthrow of Mubarak himself, the armed forces have interceded in an attempt to shut down and demobilize the independent self-organization of the Egyptian people. This role will undoubtedly continue into the future.

Yet despite the best efforts of Arab militaries, Western powers, and political forces such as the MB, it would be wrong to judge the enormous changes that have ensued in the Middle East as aborted or in terminal decline. The root causes of the uprisings remain unaddressed, and the potential for a renewal of struggle is ever present. The key reason for such guarded optimism is the growing clarity of the social and class dynamics that have propelled these movements, and the undaunted mobilizations that continue to take place. The millions of people who took to the streets for the first time in 2011 have themselves been radically transformed. The implications of this are often overlooked—the results of these uprisings cannot be judged solely on the basis of the to-and-fro of political succession and the temporary alliances that may have been formed at the top of the state. These uprisings have irrevocably changed the political consciousness of an entire generation. This is their primary legacy. This is not an issue of which individual or party happens to hold the position of president but a struggle for real change that cannot be solved through cosmetic alterations at the top. A profound growth of self-awareness and political confidence now permeates the consciousness of millions of people; it is a genie that old and new elites, foreign and regional powers alike, are desperately attempting to put back in the bottle. The revolutionary process must either continue to push forward to tackle capitalism itself or be silenced for another generation.

Conclusion: The Anticipation of Freedom

These two poles of revolution and counterrevolution remain the defining feature of the region's political battles and confirm the significance of processes of class and state formation to any coherent understanding of the region. As this book has emphasized, imperialism, the nature of neoliberal transformation, and the pervasiveness of autocracy are all internally related aspects of capitalism in the Middle East. All these aspects shaped the form that the 2008 financial crisis took and its specific ramifications for the region. Seen from this perspective, the roots of the 2011 uprisings are certainly not to be found in a single factor (such as authoritarianism, poverty, food prices, unemployment, and so forth) but, just as importantly, the roots are not "multicausal." All the various factors typically proffered to explain the revolts are bound up in the way that capitalism has formed in the region. The connections that exist between these factors are essential to how they themselves are constituted; it is not possible to separate or divide them from one another as different "things."

As integral and essential parts of a totality they exist through their interrelationship with the whole. Without confronting and overcoming this totality—capitalism itself—there can be no long-term solutions to the region's problems.

This book has presented some of the broad outlines of capitalism in the Middle East through tracing the historically structured processes of class and state formation and their interlinkages across different spaces and scales—rural and urban; national, regional, and global. It has shown that, over the last few decades, the development of capitalism in the region has produced highly polarized outcomes—a tiny layer of the population benefits from its control over key moments of accumulation and is linked closely to international capital, alongside a growing mass of poor, dispossessed populations across rural and urban areas. Networks of production and consumption are integrated into the world market to varying degrees but have consistently produced high levels of dependence on imports and an exposure to the vicissitudes of the global economy. Authoritarian state structures—distinguished by the dialectic of centralization and decentralization discussed in chapter 3—have been the essential midwife of this lopsided capitalist development.

Class formation during the neoliberal era has seen the growing interpenetration of the region's capitalist classes such that it makes little sense to identify a "national" bourgeoisie whose interests are somehow counterposed to those of large international or regional capital. Rather, the region's capitalist classes have been integrated into the patterns and mechanisms of imperialist rule, with their accumulation fully dependent upon the movement of capital across the various regional and international circuits examined throughout this book. Ownership structures reflect this process, with other "foreign" capital interiorized within the structures of class and state across the region. The state form in the Middle East has thus become internationalized alongside the internationalization of capital, oriented toward ensuring the conditions of accumulation for all capital, regardless of any apparent nationality. The region's immense strategic significance, the manner of its integration into the world market, and the fusion of economic and political power all preclude any form of capitalism that is not highly autocratic and that does not exclude the population from any effective control over social processes. For these reasons, it is a fantasy to hold out the possibility of convincing a "patriotic bourgeoisie" to act in the interests of the majority and build "social democratic" capitalist states in the Middle East. These capitalist classes are part of the problem, not the solution.

Any fundamental change in the region necessarily requires not only confronting capitalism at the national scale but also tackling the regional configurations that sustain these patterns of exploitation. The latter means being absolutely clear on the ways that imperialism has continued to dominate the region over the last few decades. As chapter

2 concluded, a persistent theme of this has been the accentuating of regional hierarchies through mechanisms such as debt and aid, the activities of institutions such as the World Bank and IMF, and—of course—the continued reality of direct military intervention. The activities of Western powers—and, more recently, states such as China and Russia—are crucially dependent on maintaining ongoing control of the region. For this reason, the starting point of real liberation will entail exposing and confronting all the myriad forms of this intervention.

Essential to this process is an understanding of the specificity of two poles of imperialist power in the region—Israel and the Gulf Arab states. As this book has emphasized, Israel's special place in the projection of Western power stems directly from its character as a settler-colonial state dependent on the dispossession of the Palestinian people, which means that its alliance with imperialism is an existential part of the state itself, uniquely insulated from the domestic pressures within Israeli society. This alliance is not solely military in nature; the country has also been deeply connected to the way that neoliberalism developed across the region. One of the central conclusions that can be drawn from this is that the Palestinian struggle holds immense strategic weight in the political struggles of the region as a whole. Confronting Western domination of the region must necessarily pass through the question of Palestine.

This book has also focused upon the particular role of the Gulf Arab states in the regional political economy. The Gulf's dramatic political ascendancy in the post-2011 moment reflects this and bears important consequences for the nature of future political struggles. It means, for example, that struggles to reverse the neoliberal policies outlined in this book inevitably come up against the entrenched interests of the Gulf states themselves. This has been confirmed in various strikes and protests that have continued throughout 2011 and 2012 (most visibly in the Egyptian context).[105] To be clear, this may not yet be expressed formally in the political content of the mass struggles, but it is necessarily present in the essence of these movements and the social forces with which they must grapple.

The specific role of the Gulf in the Middle East political economy means that any effective confrontation of capitalism requires a pan-regional approach. There are no long-term, nationally based solutions to the problems facing the Middle East that leave the control of such immense wealth in the hands of a tiny layer of the region's population. This is not meant to imply, of course, that revolutionary movements will immediately start from the regional scale without passing through a confrontation with national ruling classes. But the point is to see these different scales of struggle as inseparable. Without a regional orientation that points strategically to tackling the position and power of the Gulf monarchies, there will be no fundamental change in the region. From the vantage point of 2012 the notion of a pan-regional struggle might seem like a utopian vision, but the events of the last two years confirm its acute possibility—it is the reality and attainability of this endpoint that has provoked such great fear in the corridors of power in Washington, Riyadh, and Doha.

The Middle East remains a core zone of the world market, and the successes and failures of its social struggles will be a major factor in determining the nature of global capitalism in the years to come. The uprisings that unfolded during 2011 and 2012 are the property of all concerned with building a postcapitalist future. In their best sense, the Arab uprisings represent an essential link in the inspiring chain of struggles that have erupted across the globe over the last two years. And, in much the same way, the creeping spread of counterrevolution across the region is part of the common attempt of all capitalist states to beat back and pacify resistance to crisis and austerity. The Arab uprisings point to the hope, necessity, and potential that rebellion holds. This promise of revolt remains ever-present in the political moment—it extends beyond the Middle East and belongs to all who seek a different world.

Appendix 1: Export/Import Trade Patterns for the Middle East

	Exports to EU/US as % of total export trade			Imports from EU/US as % of total import trade			Top five export partners (2010), %	Top five import partners (2010), %
	1996–1999	2000–2003	2004–2007*	1996–1999	2000–2003	2004–2007*		
Algeria	EU: 63.5 US: 15.2	EU: 63.0 US: 15.6	EU: 56.2 US: 23.4	EU: 60.3 US: 9.9	EU: 61.5 US: 8.9	EU: 54.7 US: 6.9	EU (49.5) US (24.5) Canada (5.2) Turkey (4.8) Brazil (4.3)	EU (50.6) China (11.0) US (5.2) South Korea (4.9) Japan (3.8)
Egypt	EU: 41.9 US: 12.2	EU: 36.2 US: 9.5	EU: 33.2 US: 7.79	EU: 39.9 US: 15.0	EU: 32.4 US: 14.1	EU: 24.5 US: 9.2	EU (30.5) Saudi Arabia (6.1) US (5.9) Libya (4.8) India (4.6)	EU (32.6) US (9.4) China (9.4) Saudi Arabia (4.0) Turkey (3.6)
Libya	EU: 82.9 US: 0	EU: 83.3 US: 0	EU: 77.8 US: 5.1	EU: 63.9 US: 0.4	EU: 64.9 US: 0.27	EU: 53.3 US: 2.6	EU (76.5) China (9.3) US (4.6) India (1.6) Tunisia (1.5)	EU (41.6) China (10.4) Turkey (9.7) South Korea (7.1) Egypt (6.3)

Appendix 1: Export/Import Trade Patterns for the Middle East (cont.)

	Exports to EU/US as % of total export trade			Imports from EU/US as % of total import trade			Top five export partners (2010), %	Top five import partners (2010), %
	1996–1999	2000–2003	2004–2007*	1996–1999	2000–2003	2004–2007*		
Morocco	EU: 60.6 US: 3.6	EU: 75.0 US: 3.3	EU: 73.4 US: 2.7	EU: 54.9 US: 6.1	EU: 58.2 US: 4.4	EU: 53.7 US: 4.4	EU (59.1) India (6.0) US (3.6) Brazil (3.3) Switzerland (1.9)	EU (50.2) China (8.0) US (7.1) Saudi Arabia (5.9) Russia (3.6)
Tunisia	EU: 80.1 US: 0.78	EU: 80.9 US: 0.77	EU: 82.4 US: 1.4	EU: 73.5 US: 3.7	EU: 72.0 US: 3.6	EU: 67.1 US: 2.9	EU (74.1) Libya (6.3) US (2.5) Algeria (2.3) India (1.8)	EU (66.9) China (4.7) Turkey (3.3) Libya (3.1) US (2.7)
Bahrain	EU: 3.6 US: 2.5	EU: 4.4 US: 2.2	EU: 3.6 US: 2.7	EU: 24.9 US: 9.3	EU: 26.1 US: 12.6	EU: 27.1 US: 7.0	Saudi Arabia (2.9) EU (2.5) India (2.1) Japan (2.0) UAE (1.9)	Saudi Arabia (24.2) EU (17.6) US (12.0) China (7.7) Brazil (5.8)

Appendix 1: Export/Import Trade Patterns for the Middle East (cont.)

	Exports to EU/US as % of total export trade			Imports from EU/US as % of total import trade			Top five export partners (2010), %	Top five import partners (2010), %
	1996–1999	2000–2003	2004–2007*	1996–1999	2000–2003	2004–2007*		
Lebanon	EU: 26.6 US: 5.4	EU: 21.2 US: 7.05	EU: 14.4 US: 3.6	EU: 48.9 US: 9.4	EU: 51.2 US: 6.1	EU: 48.7 US: 5.4	Syria (27.1) UAE (13.6) EU (9.4) Saudi Arabia (6.5) Turkey (5.3)	EU (32.8) US (10.3) Syria (10.2) China (7.4) Ukraine (5.8)
Iran	EU: 41.3 US: 0.0	EU: 23.4 US: 0.6	EU: 22.0 US: 0.3	EU: 39.7 US: 0.2	EU: 39.7 US: 0.4	EU: 38.2 US: 0.3	EU (17.8) China (17.1) Japan (10.4) India (10.4) Turkey (7.2)	UAE (34.0) EU (21.5) China (8.7) Turkey (5.8) South Korea (5.6)
Jordan	EU: 8.7 US: 0.9	EU: 4.9 US: 13.1	EU: 3.4 US: 25.6	EU: 34.0 US: 9.7	EU: 29.9 US: 8.1	EU: 24.3 US: 5.5	US (15.7) Iraq (15.4) India (13.3) Saudi Arabia (10.8) UAE (4.3)	EU (20.1) Saudi Arabia (20.0) China (11.0) US (5.7) Egypt (4.6)

Appendix 1: Export/Import Trade Patterns for the Middle East (cont.)

	Exports to EU/US as % of total export trade			Imports from EU/US as % of total import trade			Top five export partners (2010), %	Top five import partners (2010), %
	1996–1999	2000–2003	2004–2007*	1996–1999	2000–2003	2004–2007*		
Syria	EU: 44.1 US: 0.6	EU: 57.2 US: 3.0	EU: 39.0 US: 2.3	EU: 37.6 US: 5.8	EU: 35.5 US: 3.8	EU: 23.3 US: 2.3	Iraq (30.2) EU (27.7) Lebanon (11.8) Saudi Arabia (5.0) Turkey (3.9)	EU (18.0) Saudi Arabia (11.4) China (10.3) Turkey (7.7) UAE (5.6)
Saudi Arabia	EU: 18.5 US: 16.3	EU: 16.3 US: 19.1	EU: 14.4 US: 16.8	EU: 34.3 US: 21.2	EU: 33.2 US: 17.0	EU: 32.8 US: 13.8	Japan (14.7) China (13.5) US (13.5) South Korea (11.0) EU (8.6)	EU (29.4) US (12.4) China (11.2) Japan (6.9) South Korea (4.9)
Oman	EU: 1.9 US: 2.2	EU: 2.0 US: 2.2	EU: 2.3 US: 2.4	EU: 26.3 US: 7.2	EU: 21.3 US: 6.2	EU: 21.8 US: 5.5	China (23.8) Japan (13.2) South Korea (12.0) UAE (11.9) India (10.6)	UAE (25.8) EU (18.0) Japan (16.0) US (5.6) China (4.8)

Appendix 1: Export/Import Trade Patterns for the Middle East (cont.)

	Exports to EU/US as % of total export trade			Imports from EU/US as % of total import trade			Top five export partners (2010), %	Top five import partners (2010), %
	1996–1999	2000–2003	2004–2007*	1996–1999	2000–2003	2004–2007*		
Kuwait	EU: 11.7 US: 12.1	EU: 11.8 US: 12.8	EU: 9.8 US: 9.9	EU: 32.0 US: 14.5	EU: 34.6 US: 13.1	EU: 33.5 US: 13.6	South Korea (17.6) Japan (10.9) India (16.7) China (14.7) US (9.2)	EU (22.7) US (13.6) China (9.0) India (8.0) Saudi Arabia (6.9)
UAE	EU: 5.5 US: 2.4	EU: 6.2 US: 2.4	EU: 8.0 US: 1.3	EU: 31.8 US: 10.2	EU: 34.4 US: 7.5	EU: 32.5 US: 8.4	India (16.4) Japan (15.5) Iran (11.9) South Korea (6.4) Thailand (4.7)	EU (21.2) India (19.1) China (13.8) US (7.5) Japan (4.7)
Qatar	EU: 2.1 US: 3.7	EU: 1.5 US: 2.7	EU: 3.1 US: 0.9	EU: 40.7 US: 12.0	EU: 36.1 US: 12.3	EU: 37.2 US: 10.6	Japan (30.1) South Korea (16.6) EU (13.8) India (8.6) Singapore (7.6)	EU (34.2) US (16.9) UAE (8.0) Japan (6.1) Saudi Arabia (5.9)

Appendix 1: Export/Import Trade Patterns for the Middle East (cont.)

	Exports to EU/US as % of total export trade			Imports from EU/US as % of total import trade			Top five export partners (2010), %	Top five import partners (2010), %
	1996–1999	2000–2003	2004–2007*	1996–1999	2000–2003	2004–2007*		
Israel	EU:33.2 US: 33.5	EU:28.4 US:38.4	EU: 28.8 US: 36.7	EU: 50.4 US: 19.7	EU: 42.5 US: 18.1	EU: 38.6 US: 13.7	US (32.1) EU (26.6) Hong Kong (6.8) India (5.0) China (3.5)	EU (34.9) US (11.5) China (8.1) Switzerland (5.5) India (3.2)

* Lebanon figures for 2004 only. Data calculated by author from IMF Direction of Trade Statistics and European Commission Trade Statistics (http://ec.europa.eu/).

Appendix 2: Trade Relationships between MENA and EU/US blocs

	Relationship with European Union			Relationship with United States		
	Status of EU Association Agreement	Exports to EU (2010)	Imports from EU (2010)	Status of trade agreements with the US	Exports to US (2010)	Imports from US (2010)
Saudi Arabia	(not part of EMP), EU–GCC FTA under negotiation since 2002	Total value 18.6 billion, of which: oil 82.6%; chemicals 13.9%	Total value 19.9 billion, of which: machinery and transport equipment 48.8%; chemicals 12.3%	Trade and Investment Framework 2003	Total value 45 billion, of which: oil and gas 89%	Total value 12.8 billion, of which: machinery, equipment, vehicles, and aircraft 64%
Kuwait	(not part of EMP), EU–GCC FTA under negotiation since 2002	Total value 3.8 billion, of which: oil and petrochemicals 96.6%	Total value 4.8 billion, of which: machinery and equipment 52.5%	Trade and Investment Framework 2004	Total value 7.4 billion, of which: oil and petrochemicals 86.8%	Total value: 2.5 billion, of which: machinery, equipment, vehicles, and aircraft 64%
UAE	(not part of EMP), EU–GCC FTA under negotiation since 2002	Total value 5.97 billion, of which: oil and gas 41.4%; pearls, gold, and precious stones 24.4%	Total value 30.9 billion, of which: machinery and equipment: 53.9%	Trade and Investment Framework 2004	Total value 2.4 billion, of which: aluminium 27.7%; oil and gas 11.8%; iron and steel 8.2%	Total value 14.2 billion, of which: machinery, equipment, vehicles, and aircraft 62%

Appendix 2: Trade Relationships between MENA and EU/US blocs (cont.)

	Relationship with European Union			Relationship with United States		
	Status of EU Association Agreement	Exports to EU (2010)	Imports from EU (2010)	Status of trade agreements with the US	Exports to US (2010)	Imports from US (2010)
Qatar	(not part of EMP), EU–GCC FTA under negotiation since 2002	Total value 6.88 billion, of which: oil and gas 78%; chemicals 11.8%	Total value 1.7 billion, of which: machinery and equipment 69.6%	Trade and Investment Framework 2004	Total value 1.2 billion, of which: oil and gas 60.7%; aluminium 13.6%; fertilizers 13.5%	Total value 2.6 billion, of which: machinery, equipment, vehicles and aircraft 85%
Oman	(not part of EMP), EU–GCC FTA under negotiation since 2002	Total value 329 million, of which: oil and gas 35.7%; chemicals 35.2%	Total value 2.4 billion, of which: machinery and transport equipment 63.7%	FTA signed 2009	Total value 2.2 billion, of which: oils and fuels 76%; plastics and fertilizers 13%	Total value 1.4 billion, of which: machinery, equipment, vehicles and aircraft 67%
Bahrain	(not part of EMP), EU–GCC FTA under negotiation since 2002	Total value 811 million, of which: oil, petroleum products, iron ores 41.4%; aluminium and aluminium products 49.9%	Total value 1.6 billion, of which: machinery 57.1%; agricultural products 10.2%	FTA signed 2005	Total value 518 million, of which: fertilizers 29.3%; aluminium 18.9%	Total value 1.2 billion, of which: machinery, vehicles, aircraft and equipment 80%

Appendix 2: Trade Relationships between MENA and EU/US blocs (cont.)

	Relationship with European Union			Relationship with United States		
	Status of EU Association Agreement	Exports to EU (2010)	Imports from EU (2010)	Status of trade agreements with the US	Exports to US (2010)	Imports from US (2010)
Morocco	Signed February 1996 Entry into Force March 2000	Total value 8.1 billion, of which: textiles and clothing 33.2%; agricultural products 25.6%; fuels and chemicals 9.0%	Total value 12.4 billion, of which: machinery and equipment 37.6%; agricultural products 9.9%	FTA January 2006	Total value 990.7 million, of which: textiles and clothing 8.3%; agricultural products 16.8%; fertilizers and phosphates 41.9%	Total value 2.8 billion of which: machinery and equipment 21.5%; agricultural products 50% (corn oil, soybeans, and cereals)
Tunisia	Signed July 1995 Entry into Force March 1998	Total value 8.1 billion, of which: textiles and clothing 32.0%; agricultural products 6.9%; fuels and chemicals 18.3%	Total value 10.4 billion, of which: machinery and equipment 34.9%; agricultural products 6.4%	Trade and Investment Framework signed 2002	Total value 357 million, of which: textiles and clothing 23.6%; agricultural products 23.1%; fertilizers and mineral fuels 16.6%	Total value 575 million, of which: machinery and equipment 12%; agricultural products 48% (corn oil, soybeans, and cereals)

Appendix 2: Trade Relationships between MENA and EU/US blocs (cont.)

	Relationship with European Union			Relationship with United States		
	Status of EU Association Agreement	Exports to EU (2010)	Imports from EU (2010)	Status of trade agreements with the US	Exports to US (2010)	Imports from US (2010)
Egypt	Signed June 2001 Entry into Force June 2004	Total value 6.4 billion, of which: textiles and clothing 10.4%; agricultural products 8.6%; fuels and chemicals (natural gas) 52.9%	Total value 11.4 billion, of which: machinery and equipment 44.3%; agricultural products 9.2%	Trade and Investment Framework Agreement signed 1999; QIZ Agreement February 2005	Total value 2.1 billion, of which: textiles and clothing 48%; agricultural products 1.5%; fuels and chemicals 25.4% (mostly fertilizers and natural gas)	Total value 6.2 billion, of which: machinery and equipment 27%; agricultural products 32% (mostly cereals and soybeans)
Lebanon	Signed June 2002 Entry into Force April 2006	Total value 281 million, of which: fuels and mining products (cement) 23.3%; chemicals (fertilizers, phosphoric chemicals) 9.4%; semi-manufactured goods (precious stones) 15.1%	Total value 3.6 billion, of which: fuels and mining products 25.6%; machinery and equipment 23.6%	Trade and Investment Framework November 2006	Total value 79.4 million, of which: precious stones 15%; food and beverages 25%	Total value 1.7 billion, of which: fuels 48.8%; vehicles 22%; cereals 4%

Appendix 2: Trade Relationships between MENA and EU/US blocs (cont.)

	Relationship with European Union			Relationship with United States		
	Status of EU Association Agreement	Exports to EU (2010)	Imports from EU (2010)	Status of trade agreements with the US	Exports to US (2010)	Imports from US (2010)
Jordan	Signed November 1997 Entry into Force May 2002	Total value 132 million, of which: mining products (mostly cement, potash, and phosphates) 23.3%; chemicals (fertilizers) 27.3%; textiles and clothing 4.7%	Total value 2.4 billion, of which: machinery and transport 50.6%	QIZ Agreement 1996; FTA October 2000	Total value 1.06 billion, of which: textiles and clothing (85%).	Total value 1.4 billion, of which: vehicles 20%; cereals 18%; machinery 20%
Libya	(not in ENP), has observer status in EMP	Total value 24.9 billion, of which: oil 90.5%	Total value 4.6 billion, of which: machinery and equipment 39.3%; agricultural products 11.1%	Trade and Investment Framework signed May 2010	Total value 686 million, of which: oil 98%	Total value 276 million, of which: machinery and equipment 28%; agricultural products 60% (mostly cereals)

Appendix 2: Trade Relationships between MENA and EU/US blocs (cont.)

	Relationship with European Union			Relationship with United States		
	Status of EU Association Agreement	Exports to EU (2010)	Imports from EU (2010)	Status of trade agreements with the US	Exports to US (2010)	Imports from US (2010)
Israel	Signed November 1995 Entry into Force June 2000	Total value 11.7 billion, of which: chemicals 20.1%; machinery and mechanical appliances 21.7%; precious and semiprecious stones 12.1%	Total value: 15.07 billion, of which: machinery and transport equipment 33.6%; chemicals 15.3%; other semi-manufactures 26.9%; fuels and mining products 24.6%	FTA September 1985 (also covers goods from West Bank and Gaza Strip)	Total value 23 billion, of which: diamonds 40.6%; pharmaceutical products 24.5%	Total value 8.1 billion, of which: machinery and electrical equipment 41%; cereals 4.2%
Syria	AA initialed December 2008, but not signed	Total value: 3.1 billion, of which: oil 88.5%	Total value 3.5 billion, of which: machinery and equipment 35%		Total value 407 million, of which: oil 88.2%	Total value 245 million, of which: cereals and soybean products 90%
Algeria	Signed April 2002 Entry into Force September 2005	Total value 12.4 billion, of which: oil and gas 72.3%	Total value 18.9 billion, of which: machinery and equipment 41.4%; agricultural products 16.4%		Total value 14.67 billion, of which: oil and gas 91.5%	Total value 1.57 billion, of which: machinery and equipment 60%; agricultural products 6% (mostly soybean oil)

Source: US Trade Representative Office and European Commission Trade Statistics.

Appendix 3: Selected World Bank Lending to Morocco, Jordan, Egypt, and Tunisia, 1984–2010

Country	Selected World Bank Projects*
Morocco	US$6.1 billion from 1990–2011, total of 175 loans

Morocco (continued)

1984–n.a.: Industry and Trade Policy Adjustment Loan, $150.4 million (export-oriented production; lower tariffs; liberalize prices)

1985–n.a.: Agricultural Sector Adjustment Loan, $100 million (open agriculture sector to private investment; liberalize prices of inputs; privatize agricultural services)

1985–n.a.: Industry and Trade Policy Adjustment Loan, $200 million (decrease industry protection; privatization; financial sector reform)

1986–1989: Education Sector Reform Program, $150 million (shift education spending away from higher education to basic education; lower spending of education by making teachers work longer hours; reduce teacher recruitment)

1987–n.a.: Telecommunications Project, $125 million (expand and restructure telecommunications sector with a view to privatization)

1987–1990: Public Enterprise Rationalization Loan, $240 million (increase competitiveness of public sector; privatization).

1987–1992: Agricultural Sector Adjustment Loan, $225 million (continue price liberalization; privatization; shift to export-oriented agriculture).

1989–n.a.: Structural Adjustment Loan, $200 million (fiscal cuts; trade liberalization; privatization)

1989–n.a.: National Agricultural Credit Programme, $190 million (extend credit to private farmers)

1989–n.a.: Industrial Finance Project, $170 million (encourage export-oriented private sector loans from banking system)

1990–1998: Health Sector Investment Project, $180 million (restructure health sector; increase involvement of private sector health insurance)

1990–1998: Port Sector Project, $251 million (develop port for export-oriented production; increase private sector involvement in port management)

1991–1998: Financial Sector Development Project, $235 million (liberalize the financial sector)

1993–1997: Telecommunications Sector Restructuring Project, $1.2 billion (prepare telecommunications sector for privatization)

1994–1998: Agricultural Sector Investment Project, $850 million (liberalize agricultural markets)

1995–1996: Financial Markets Development Loan $250 million (privatize banking sector; develop capital markets)

1996–2004: Railway Restructuring Project, $614 million (restructure railways in preparation for privatization)

1999: Policy Reform Support Loan, $250 million (privatization and reduce government wage bill)

2005–2008: Housing Sector Development Policy Loan $150 million (introduce market-based finance into the housing market)

Appendix 3: Selected World Bank Lending to Morocco, Jordan, Egypt, and Tunisia, 1984–2010 (cont.)

Country	Selected World Bank Projects*
Jordan	US$2 billion over 104 projects 1993–1997: Energy Sector Adjustment Loan Project, $80 million (reduce subsidies for energy prices and prepare sector for private involvement) 1994–1997: Agricultural Sector Adjustment Loan $80 million (reduce agricultural subsidies and liberalize the land market) 1994–2000: Jordan Telecommunications Project, $222 million (prepare telecommunications sector for privatization) 1995–1996: Economic Reform and Development Loan $80 million (liberalize trade and investment; prepare for privatization) 1996–1997: Economic Reform and Development Loan II $120 million (trade liberalization, reduction in tariffs, removal of investment barriers; privatization) 1999–2006: Amman Water & Sanitation Management Project, $136 million (prepare water and wastewater services for privatization) 2001–2002: Public Sector Reform Loans I and II, $240 million (restructure public sector; implement performance-oriented budgeting)
Egypt	US$14.3 billion over 160 projects 1992: Structural Adjustment Loan $300 million (liberalize of rural rents; privatization; reduce price subsidies) 1993–2003: Private Sector Tourism Infrastructure and Environmental Management Project, $804 million (privatize the tourism sector) 2004–2009: Airports Development Project, $574 million (develop airport infrastructure in preparation for private-sector involvement/privatization) 2006–2007: Financial Sector Development Loan, $500 million (deepen financial markets; promote privatization of finance sector) 2007–2011: West Delta Water Conservation and Irrigation Rehabilitation Project $213 million (develop PPP in the irrigation sector) 2007–2012: Egypt-Alexandria Development Project $110 million (promote private sector involvement in Alexandria through increasing PPP provision of infrastructure; reduce barriers to investment in the city) 2008–2009: Financial Sector Development Loan, $500 million (deepen financial markets; promote privatization of finance sector) 2010–2015: EG-Giza North Power Project $1.4 billion (promote private sector involvement in the power industry through PPPs) 2010–2015: Egypt—Wind Power Development Project $796 million (promote private sector involvement in wind industry through PPPs)

Appendix 3: Selected World Bank Lending to Morocco, Jordan, Egypt, and Tunisia, 1984–2010 (cont.)

Country	Selected World Bank Projects*
Tunisia	$7.4 billion over 167 projects

Tunisia $7.4 billion over 167 projects

1986–1991: Agricultural Sector Adjustment Loan, $150 million (liberalization of agricultural prices and privatization)

1987–1989: Industrial and Trade Policy Adjustment Loan, $150 million (liberalization of investment climate, export-oriented development, labor market deregulation)

1988–1992: Structural Adjustment Loan Project, $130 million, (structural adjustment)

1991–1994: Economic & Financial Reforms Support Loan $250 million (liberalize external trade; liberalize prices; public sector reform)

1993–1999: Public Enterprise Reform Project, $130 million (prepare public enterprises for privatization)

1993–2000: Tunisia Private Investment Credit Project, $119 million (finance private sector companies)

1996–2007: Economic Competitiveness Loan, 4 loans, total $666 million (structural reforms, privatization, banking sector reform)

1997–2005: Greater Tunis Sewerage and Reuse Project, $103 million (develop private sector participation in the sewerage system)

1999–2001: Export Competitiveness Loan $376 million (labour market deregulation; privatization; liberalize telecommunications sector)

2009–2011: Integration and Competitiveness Development Policy Loan Project $250 million (enhance trade integration with Europe; increase openness to foreign investment; reduce tariff rates)

*World Bank figures shown are not necessarily total amount disbursed—figures are for the total cost of the project and thus include amounts provided by other bodies such as the ADB, EIB, and so forth; objectives may also not have been met. Data correct as of December 23, 2012. Data from World Bank project database. n.a. = not available.

Appendix 4: FDI Flows to Selected MENA Countries (2008–2010), in Millions of Euros

Country	Rank	Top Five FDI Sources (2008–2010)	FDI Total (2008–2010)	Top Three Projects Announced in 2010
Algeria	1	France	650	1. EEIC (UAE), urban park/tourism complex, 1805 2. Total (France), gas field, 680 3. Emiral (UAE), property development, 206
	2	Italy	147	
	3	US	134	
	4	Russia	83	
	5	GCC · Oman (67)	67	
Egypt	1	GCC · UAE (627) · Qatar (420) · Saudi Arabia (387) · Kuwait (193)	1627	1. BP (UK), gas development, 6573 2. RWE (Germany), gas development, 2800 3. BG (UK), pipelines, 1435
	2	UK	1297	
	3	US	688	
	4	Germany	294	
	5	India	203	
Jordan	1	GCC · UAE (719) · Kuwait (129) · Saudi Arabia (44) · Qatar (18)	910	1. Estia (Estonia), oil shale, 3540 2. Estia (Estonia), oil shale, 1000 3. Areva (France), uranium, 444
	2	France	197	
	3	Estonia	151	
	4	Switerzland	53	
	5	Netherlands	40	
Lebanon	1	GCC · Kuwait (287) · UAE (124)	411	1. Majd Al Futtaim (UAE), shopping mall, 580 2. EFG-Hermes (Egypt), bank, 395 3. Kempinski (Switzerland), hotel, 110

Country	Rank	Top Five FDI Sources (2008–2010)	FDI Total (2008–2010)	Top Three Projects Announced in 2010
	2	Egypt	132	
	3	Switzerland	43	
	4	US	27	
	5	Canada	27	
Libya	1	GCC • Bahrain (325) • UAE (157) • Qatar (111) • Oman (55)	648	1. Qatar Investment Authority (Qatar), real estate, 657.7 2. Al Maabar (UAE), real estate, 132 3. Dow (US), petrochemical, 73
	2	USA	244	
	3	Spain	190	
	4	France	122	
	5	Austria	122	
Morocco	1	France	1003	1. GDF Suez (France), power, 1130 2. Taqa (UAE), electricity, 877 3. France Telecom (France), telecommunications, 640
	2	GCC • Kuwait (327) • UAE (160) • Saudi Arabia (88)	575	
	3	Spain	339	
	4	UK	143	
	5	Libya	71	
Palestine	1	GCC • Qatar (58) • Saudi Arabia (12)	70	
	2	Jordan	32	
	3	US	8	
Syria	1	China	1077	1. CNPC (China), oil, 1000 2. Majd Al Futtaim (UAE), real estate, 719 3. MTN (South Africa), telecommunications, 403

Country	Rank	Top Five FDI Sources (2008–2010)	FDI Total (2008–2010)	Top Three Projects Announced in 2010
	2	GCC · Bahrain (83) · Kuwait (87) · UAE (82) · Qatar (68) · Saudi Arabia (44)	364	
	3	Egypt	111	
	4	Canada	107	
	5	France	92	
Tunisia	1	GCC · Qatar (386) · Bahrain (111) · UAE (92) · Kuwait (34)	623	1. Gulf Finance House (Bahrain), offshore financial center, 2100 2. Qatar Telecom (Qatar), Telecommunications, 1100 3. Global wood (Switzerland), wood export, 900
	2	France	260	
	3	UK	114	
	4	Switzerland	79	
	5	Italy	67	

Source: Data from ANIMA Investment Network, *Investments and Partnerships in MED Region, 2010* (Marseilles: ANIMA, 2011), 49–68.

Bibliography

Aarts, Paul, Pieter van Dijke, Iris Kolman, Jort Statema, and Ghassan Dahhan. *From Resilience to Revolt, Making Sense of the Arab Spring*. Wetenschappelijk Onderzoek- en Documentatiecentrum, University of Amsterdam Department of Political Science, July 2012.

Abdalla, Ahmed. *The Student Movement and National Politics in Egypt, 1923–1973*. London: al-Saqi, 1985.

Abdul-Fadil, Mahmoud. *The Political Economy of Nasserism: A Study in Employment and Income Distribution Policies in Urban Egypt, 1952–72*. Cambridge: Cambridge University Press, 1980.

Abou-El-Fadl, Reem. "The Road to Jerusalem through Tahrir Square: Anti-Zionism and Palestine in the 2011 Egyptian Revolution." *Journal of Palestine Studies* 41, no. 2 (Winter 2012): 6–26.

Abrahamian, Ervand. "The 1953 Coup in Iran." *Science and Society* 65, no. 2 (Summer 2001): 182–215.

Abu Jaber, Tayseer. "Jordanian Labor Migration: Social, Political and Economic Effects." In *Labor Migration: Palestine, Jordan, Egypt and Israel*, edited by Mohammad Shtayyeh. Jerusalem: Palestinian Center for Regional Studies, 1997.

Abu-Lughod, Janet. "Demographic Consequences of the Occupation." *MERIP Reports, The Palestinian Dilemma*, no. 115 (June 1983):13–17.

Achcar, Gilbert. *Clash of Barbarisms: September 11 and the Making of the New World Disorder*. New York: Monthly Review Press, 2002.

———. "The Strategic Triad: The United States, Russia, and China," *New Left Review* 1, no. 228 (March–April 1998): 91–126.

Adams, Jr., Richard. "Workers' Remittances and Inequality in Rural Egypt." *Economic*

Development and Cultural Change 38, no. 1 (1989): 45–71.

Adly, Amr Ismail. "Politically-Embedded Cronyism: The Case of Post-Liberalization Egypt," *Business and Politics* 11, no. 4 (2009).

African Development Bank. *Land Policy in Africa: North Africa Regional Assessment*, Addis Ababa, Ethiopia: AUC-ECA-AfDB Consortium, 2010.

African Development Bank. "The Political Economy of Food Security in North Africa," *AFDB Policy Brief*, 2012.

Agence France-Presse. "Leading Tunisia Union Calls for Dec. 13 Nationwide Strike," December 5, 2012.

Aghrout, Ahmed and Redha M. Bougherira, eds. *Algeria in Transition: Reforms and Development Prospects*. London: RoutledgeCurzon, 2004.

Ahmed, Akhter, Howarth Bouis, Tamar Gutner, and Hans Löfgren. *The Egyptian Food Subsidy System: Structure, Performance, and Options for Reform*, Research Report 119. Washington, DC: International Food Policy Research Institute, 2001.

Ahmed Al-Fayoumi, Nedal and Bana M. Abuzayed. "Assessment of the Jordanian Banking Sector within the Context of GATS Agreement," *Banks and Bank Systems* 4, no. 2 (2009).

Aizhu, Chen. "Despite Delays, China Seeks Full Iran Oil Volume for Third Month," Reuters, September 5, 2012.

'Al, Manwal Abdel. "Tajrabat kutla jabhat al-'amal al-niqabi [Experiences of the Progressive Workers Front]," in *Ashkaliya al'amal al-niqabi fi falastin* [Issues in Labour Organizing in Palestine]. Ramallah: Center for Human Rights and Democracy, 1999.

Al-Badri, Yasri. "Al-wazir al dakhaliyya: Morsi talab bi'tifael 'al amn al-watani'" [Interior Minister: Morsi demands we deal with "national security"], *Al-Masry Al-Youm*, August 3, 2012. www.almasryalyoum.com/node/1027176.

Albo, Greg. "Contemporary Capitalism," in *Elgar Companion to Marxist Economics*, edited by Ben Fine and Alfredo Saad-Filho. London: Elgar, 2012.

Albo, Greg. "Contesting the 'New Capitalism,'" in *Varieties of Capitalism, Varieties of Approaches*, edited by David Coates. New York: Palgrave Macmillan, 2005.

Albo, Greg. "The Old and New Economics of Imperialism," in *Socialist Register 2004: The New Imperial Challenge*, edited by Colin Leys and Leo Panitch. London: Merlin Press, 2003.

Albo, Greg, Leo Panitch, and Sam Gindin. *In and Out of Crisis: The Global Financial Meltdown and Left Alternatives*. Oakland, CA: PM Press, 2010.

Alexander, Justin and Colin Rowat. "A Clean Slate in Iraq: From Debt to Development," *Middle East Report* 228 (Autumn 2003): 32–36.

Al-Haq. *A Nation Under Siege, Annual Report on Human Rights in the Occupied Territories, 1989*. Ramallah: Al-Haq, 1990.

Ali, K. T. "Tatawwurat muqliqa li-awda' al-zira'a wa-al-ghitha' fi al-watan al-'arabi khilal al-sab'inat" [Disturbing Developments in the Conditions of Agriculture and Nutrition in the Arab Nation During the Seventies], in *Dirasat fi al-tanmiya waal-taka-mul al-iqtisadi al-'arabi* [Studies in Arab Economic Development and Integration]. Beirut: Centre for Arab Unity Studies, 1982: 405–43.

Allen, Theodore. *The Invention of the White Race: Racial Oppression and Social Control.* New York: Verso, 1994.

Allon, Yigal. *The Making of Israel's Army.* New York: Universe Books, 1970.

al-Shamkhy, Fathi. "al maduneeya al-kharajeeya wa al-thawra al-Tunisiyya" [Foreign Debt and the Tunisian Revolution], *al-thawra dai'ma* no. 2 (Spring 2012): 143–146.

Al Watan Daily. "Rate of suicide among migrant workers in Kuwait on the rise," August 8, 2010.

Amin, Samir. *Fi Naqd al-Khitab al-Arabi al-Rahen* [A Critique of the Current Arab Discourse]. Cairo: el-Ain, 2010.

Analysis for Economic Decisions (ADE). *Evaluation of Economic Co-operation between the European Commission and Mediterranean Countries,* Final Report, vol. 1. Louvain-la-Neuve: ADE, November 2003.

Anderson, Lisa. "Absolutism and the Resilience of Monarchy in the Middle East," *Political Science Quarterly* 106, no. 1 (Spring 1991): 1–15.

Anderson, Lisa. "Peace and Democracy in the Middle East: The Constraints of Soft Budgets," *Journal of International Affairs* 49 (Summer 1995): 25–44.

Anderson, Lisa. *The State and Social Transformation in Tunisia and Libya, 1830–1980.* Princeton, NJ: Princeton University Press, 1986.

Angrist, Michele. *Politics and Society in the Contemporary Middle East.* Boulder, CO: Lynne Rienner, 2010.

Angulo, A. M, N. Mtimet, B. Dhehibi, M. Atwi, O. Ben Youssef, J. M. Gil, and M. B. Sai. "A Revisited Gravity Equation in Trade Flow Analysis: An Application to the Case of Tunisian Olive Oil Exports," *Investigaciones Regionales,* no. 21 (2011): 225–239.

ANIMA Investment Network. *Investments and Partnerships in MED Region, 2010.* Marseilles: ANIMA, 2011.

Arnold, Wayne. "Private Equity Alive and Kicking in the Gulf," *The National,* September 24, 2008. www.thenational.ae.

Aryani, Lara. "Yemen's Turn: An Overview," in *The Dawn of the Arab Uprising,* edited by Bassam Haddad, Rosie Bsheer, and Ziad Abu-Rish. London: Pluto Press, 2011.

Augustin, Ebba, Ruby Assad, and Dalila Jaziri. *Women Empowerment for Improved Research in Agricultural Development, Innovation and Knowledge Transfer in the West Asia/North Africa Region.* Amman: Association of Agricultural Research Institutions in the Near East and North Africa, 2012.

Ayubi, Nazih. *Overstating the Arab State: Politics and Society in the Middle East*. London: I.B. Taurus, 2001.

Aziz, Maryam. "Ennahda Activists Attack Tunisian Union," December 5, 2012. english.nuqudy.com.

Baer, Gabriel. *Studies in the Social History of Modern Egypt*. Chicago: University of Chicago Press, 1969.

Bahour, Sam. "Economic Prison Zones," *Middle East Report Online*, November 19, 2010. www.merip.org/mero/mero111910.

Baldwin, Hanson. "Oil Strategy in World War II," *American Petroleum Institute Quarterly—Centennial Issue*. Washington, DC: American Petroleum Institute, 1959.

Banaji, Jairus. *Theory as History: Essays on Modes of Production and Exploitation*. Leiden: Brill, 2010.

Barkey, Henri. *Political Economy of Stabilization Measures in the Middle East*. New York: St. Martin's Press, 1992.

Bartram, David V. "Foreign Workers in Israel: History and Theory," *International Migration Review* 32, no. 2 (Summer 1998): 303–325.

Bayat, Asef and Eric Denis. "Who Is Afraid of Ashwaiyyat?" *Environment and Urbanization* 12, no. 2 (1990): 185–199.

BBC News. "Gaza—Humanitarian Situation," January 30, 2009. http://news.bbc.co.uk/1/hi/world/middle_east/7845428.stm.

BBC News. "Yemen Unrest: 'Dozens Killed' as Gunmen Target Rally," March 18, 2011, www.bbc.co.uk/news/world-middle-east-12783585.

Beinin, Joel. "Egyptian Textile Workers: From Craft Artisans Facing European Competition to Proletarians Contending with the State," in *The Ashgate Companion to the History of Textile Workers, 1650–2000*, edited by Lex Heerma Van Voss, Els Hiemstra-Kuperus, and Elise Van Nederveen Meerkerk. Surrey/Burlington: Ashgate Publishing, 2010.

Beinin, Joel. *Was the Red Flag Flying There? Marxist Politics and the Arab-Israeli Conflict in Egypt and Israel, 1948–1965*. Berkeley, CA: University of California Press, 1990.

Bellin, Eva. "The Robustness of Authoritarianism in the Middle East: Exceptionalism in Comparative Perspective," *Comparative Politics* 36, no. 2 (January 2004): 139–157.

Bencherifa, Abdellatif. "Migration internationale et developpement agricole au Maroc," in *Migration Internationale et Changements Sociaux dans le Maghreb Colloque internationale Hammamet*, 243–260. Université de Tunis: Tunis, 1997.

Benvinisti, Meron. *The West Bank Data Project: A Survey of Israel's Policies*. Washington, DC: American Enterprise Institute for Public Policy Research, 1984.

Bilgili, Özge and Silja Weyel. "Migration in Morocco: History, Current Trends and Future Prospects," Paper Series, Migration and Development Country Profiles. Maastricht Graduate School of Governance, December 2009.

Bill, James and Carl Leiden. *Politics in the Middle East*. Boston: Little Brown, 1984.

Birks, John and Clive Sinclair. *Arab Manpower: The Crisis of Development*. London: Croom Helm, 1980.

Bishara, Azmi. *Al mujtama'a al madani:dirassa naqdiyya*. [Civil Society: An Analytical Study]. Beirut: Markaz Dirassat al Wihda al A'arabiyya, 1998.

Botman, Selma. *The Rise of Egyptian Communism, 1939–1970*. Syracuse, NY: Syracuse University Press, 1988.

Bouillon, Markus E. *The Peace Business: Money and Power in the Palestine-Israel Conflict*. London: I.B. Taurus, 2006.

Bredeloup, Sylvie and Olivier Pliez. *The Libyan Migration Corridor*. Florence: European University Institute, Robert Schuman Centre for Advanced Studies, 2011.

Bromley, Simon. *American Hegemony and World Oil: The Industry, the State System and the World Economy*. Cambridge: Polity Press, 1991.

Brumberg, Daniel. "Authoritarian Legacies and Reform Strategies in the Arab World," in *Political Liberalization and Democratization in the Arab World, Vol. 1, Theoretical Perspectives*, edited by Rex Brynen, Bahgat Korany, and Paul Noble. Boulder, CO: Lynne Rienner, 1995.

Brusilovsky, Helen and Natalia Gitelson. *Israel's Foreign Trade 2000–2010*. Jerusalem and Tel Aviv: Israel Central Bureau of Statistics, 2011.

B'Tselem. *Forbidden Roads: Israel's Discriminatory Road Regime in the West Bank* Jerusalem: B'Tselem, 2004.

Bukharin, Nikolai. *Imperialism and World Economy*. London: Merlin Press, 1972.

Burki, Talha Khan. "Yemen's Hunger Crisis," *The Lancet* 380, no. 9842 (August 2012): 637–638.

Burns, William Joseph. *Economic Aid and American Policy Toward Egypt, 1955–1981*. Albany, NY: SUNY Press, 1985.

Bush, Ray. *Civil Society and the Uncivil State Land Tenure Reform in Egypt and the Crisis of Rural Livelihoods*. Programme Paper no. 9. United Nations Research Institute for Social Development, May 2004.

Bush, Ray. *Counter-revolution in Egypt's Countryside: Land and Farmers in the Era of Economic Reform*. London: Zed Books, 2002.

Callinicos, Alex. "Iraq: Fulcrum of World Politics," *Third World Quarterly* 26, nos. 4–5 (2005): 593–608.

Callinicos, Alex and Justin Rosenberg. "Uneven and Combined Development: The Social-Relational Substratum of 'the International'? An Exchange of Letters," *Cambridge Review of International Affairs* 21, no. 1 (2008): 77–112.

Carana Corporation. *Privatization in Egypt: Quarterly Review April–June 2002*. Report commissioned by USAID, Cairo: Privatization Coordination Support Unit, 2002.

Central Informatics Organisation. *Bahrain in Figures*. Kingdom of Bahrain, General Directorate of Statistic and Population Registry, no. 23, December 2006.

Chalcraft, John. "Subalternity, Material Practices, and Popular Aspirations: Syrian Migrant Workers in Lebanon," *Arab Studies Journal* 14, no. 2 (Fall 2006): 9–38.

Champion, Daryl. *The Paradoxical Kingdom: Saudi Arabia and the Momentum of Reform*. New York: Columbia University Press, 2003.

Chapman, Keith. *The International Petrochemical Industry: Evolution and Location*. Oxford: Blackwell, 1991.

Chatelard, Geraldine. "Jordan: A Refugee Haven," Migration Information Source, July 1, 2004. www.migrationinformation.org/feature/display.cfm?ID=794.

Chaudry, Kiren. *The Price of Wealth: Economies and Institutions in the Middle East*. New York: Cornell University Press, 1997.

Claessens, Stijn and Neeltje van Horen. "Foreign Banks: Trends, Impact and Financial Stability." International Monetary Fund Working Paper no. 12/10. IMF, January 2012.

Clarke, Simon. *Marx, Marginalism and Modern Sociology*. London: Macmillan, 1991.

Cobain, Ian. "CIA Working with Palestinian Security Agents," *Guardian*, December 17, 2009. www.guardian.co.uk/world/2009/dec/17/cia-palestinian-security-agents.

Cohen, Hillel. "The Matrix of Surveillance," in *Surveillance and Control in Israel/Palestine: Population, Territory and Power*, edited by Elia Zuriek, David Lyon, and Yasmeen Abu-Laban. New York: Routledge, 2011.

Colliers International. "Dubai Real Estate Overview," *Market Research*, Fourth Quarter. Abu Dhabi: Colliers International, 2007.

Collyer, Michael. "The Development Impact of Temporary International Labour Migration on Southern Mediterranean Sending Countries: Contrasting Examples of Morocco and Egypt," Working Paper T6. Sussex Centre for Migration Research, August 2004.

Commercial International Brokerage Company. "Arab Cotton Ginning Company (ACGC)," *Egypt Company Update*. June 12, 2007.

Commission of the European Communities. *Communication from the Commission to the Council and the European Parliament: Wider Europe—Neighbourhood: A New Framework for Relations with our Eastern and Southern Neighbours*. Brussels: CEC, 2003. http://ec.europa.eu/world/enp/pdf/com03_104_en.pdf.

Consortium for Applied Research on International Migration (CARIM). *Migration Profile, Egypt*. Robert Schuman Centre for Advanced Studies, April 2010. http://www.carim.org/public/migrationprofiles/MP_Egypt_EN.pdf.

Consortium for Applied Research on International Migration (CARIM). *Migration Profile, Morocco*. Robert Schuman Centre for Advanced Studies, November 2009. http://www.carim.org/public/migrationprofiles/MP_Morocco_EN.pdf.

Consortium for Applied Research on International Migration (CARIM). *Migration Profile, Tunisia*. Robert Schuman Centre for Advanced Studies, June 2010. www.carim.org/public/migrationprofiles/MP_Tunisia_EN.pdf.

Cruce, Fredrika. *Evaluating Value Added Tax in Morocco*, Minor Field Study Series no. 209, Lund University, 2010. www.nek.lu.se/Publ/mfs/209.pdf.

Crystal, Jill. *Oil and Politics in the Gulf: Rulers and Merchants in Kuwait and Qatar*. Glasgow: Cambridge University Press, 1995.

Cummins, Chip. "Saudi Arabia Voices Support for Mubarak," *Wall Street Journal*, January 29, 2011.

The Daily Star. "The Promises and Perils of Public Private Partnerships in Lebanon," November 17, 2011. www.albawaba.com/promises-and-perils-public-private-partnerships-401438.

Daoud, Zakya. "Agrarian Capitalism and the Moroccan Crisis," *MERIP Reports*, *Land and Labor*, no. 99 (September 1981): 27–33

Davidson, Neil. "The Necessity of Multiple Nation-States for Capital," *Rethinking Marxism: A Journal of Economics, Culture & Society* 24, no.1 (2012): 26-46.

Dayton, Keith. "Speech to The Washington Institute's 2009 Soref Symposium," Washington Institute for Near East Policy, May 7, 2009. www.washingtoninstitute.org/html/pdf/DaytonKeynote.pdf.

de Haas, Hein. "Migration, Remittances and Regional Development in Southern Morocco," *Geoforum* 37 (2006): 565–580.

de Haas, Hein. "Morocco's Migration Experience: A Transitional Perspective," *International Migration* 54, no. 4 (2007): 39–70.

Detrie, Megan. "Will Renationalisations Transform Egypt's Textile Sector?," *Just Style*, October 21, 2011. www.just-style.com/analysis/will-renationalisations-transform-egypts-textile-sector_id112514.aspx.

Deutsche Bank. "Egypt Real Estate: Time to Be Selective," *Global Markets Research*, July 5, 2010.

Dodd, Peter and Halim Barakat. *River Without Bridges*. Beirut: The Institute for Palestine Studies, 1969.

Dun and Bradstreet. "UAE Private Equity Report," *Industry Perspectives*. Dubai: Dun and Bradstreet, 2008.

Efrat, Elisha. *Geography and Politics in Israel since 1967*. London: Frank Cass, 1988.

Ehab, Maye. "Labor Market Flexibility in Egypt: With Application to the Textiles and Apparel Industry." Working Paper no. 170, Egyptian Centre for Economic Studies, June 2012.

el-Haddad, Amirah. *Effects of the Global Crisis on the Clothing Sector: A Blessing in Disguise?* Geneva: ILO, 2010.

El Hajoui, Mehdi, Aviel Marrache, Roman Rosenberg, and Kelly Spriggs. *Morocco*. Philadelphia: Wharton School Financial Institutions Center, University of Pennsylvania.

El Hajoui, Mehdi, Aviel Marrache, and Susan Keppelman. *Tunisia*. Philadelphia: Wharton School Financial Institutions Center, University of Pennsylvania.

Egyptian-British Chamber of Commerce. *Report on Banking Reform in Egypt*, 2008.

Egyptian-British Chamber of Commerce. *Tax Policies in Egypt*, May 2010. www.thee-bcc.com.

Entelis, John P. "Oil Wealth and the Prospects for Democratization in the Arabian Peninsula: The Case of Saudi Arabia," in *Arab Oil: Impact on the Arab Countries and Global Implications*, edited by Naiem A. Sherbiny and Mark A. Tessler. New York: Praeger, 1976.

European Commission, *The Barcelona Process, 5 Years On, 1995–2000*. Luxemburg: The Office for Official Publications of the European Communities, 2000.

European Investment Bank. *Study on PPP Legal & Financial Frameworks in the Mediterranean Partner Countries, vol. 1—A Regional Approach*. Facility for Euro-Mediterranean Investment and Partnership, 2011.

European Investment Bank. *FEMIP Study on PPP Legal & Financial Frameworks in the Mediterranean Partner Countries*, vol. 1. Facility for Euro-Mediterranean Investment and Partnership, May 2011.

Farah, Nadia. *Egypt's Political Economy: Power Relations in Development.* Cairo: American University of Cairo Press, 2009.

Fargues, Philippe. "Arab Migration to Europe: Trends and Policies." *International Migration Review* 38, no. 4 (Winter 2004).

Farazi, Subika, Erik Feyen, and Roberto Rocha. *Bank Ownership and Performance in the Middle East and North Africa Region*. World Bank Policy Research Working Paper, no. 5620. Washington, DC: World Bank, April 2011.

Farsakh, Leila. *Palestinian Labour Migration to Israel*. New York: Routledge, 2005.

Fergany, Nader. *Aspects of Labor Migration and Unemployment in the Arab Region*. Cairo: Almishkat Center for Research, 2001.

Fernandez-Stark, Karina, Penny Bamber, and Gary Gereffi. *The Fruit and Vegetables Global Value Chain: Economic Upgrading and Workforce Development*. Durham, NC: Duke University Center on Globalization, Governance and Competitiveness, November 2011.

Fielding-Smith, Abigail. "Yemenis Call for an End to Saleh Regime," *Financial Times*, January 27, 2011.

Foltz, Jeremy D. "Micro-Economic Perspectives on Tunisia's Agro-Export Strategy." In *Food, Agriculture, and Economic Policy in the Middle East and North Africa*; Research in Middle East Economics, vol. 5. Bingley, UK: Emerald Group Publishing Limited, 2003.

Food and Agriculture Organization of the United Nations. *Breaking Ground: Present and*

Future Perspectives for Women in Agriculture. Rome: Food and Agriculture Organization of the United Nations, 2005.

Food and Agriculture Organization of the United Nations. *Gender Dimensions of Agricultural and Rural Employment: Differentiated Pathways out of Poverty: Status, Trends and Gaps.* Rome: Food and Agriculture Organization of the United Nations, 2010.

Fornaji, Hadi. "Plight of Foreigners in Libya 'Worse Than under Qaddafi' Claims Amnesty International," *Libya Herald*, November 13, 2012.

Forte, David F. "Egyptian Land Law: An Evaluation," *American Journal of Comparative Law* 26 (1978).

Foundation for Middle East Peace. "Israeli Settlements in the Occupied Territories: A Guide," *Settlement Report* 12, no. 7 (March 2002).

Gabriel, Stuart A. and Eitan F. Sabatello. "Palestinian Migration from the West Bank and Gaza: Economic and Demographic Analyses," *Economic Development and Cultural Change* 34, no. 2 (January 1986): 245–262.

Gálvez-Nogales, Eva. "The Rise of Agrifood Technopoles in the Middle East and North Africa," Agricultural Management, Marketing and Finance Working Document, no. 30, FAO, 2011.

Gamal, Wael. "al waqa'a yurfid badilkum al-waheed" [Reality Rejects your single alternative], *Jadaliyya*, December 17, 2012. www.jadaliyya.com.

Gambard, Michelle. "Advocating for Sri Lankan Migrant Workers," *Critical Asian Studies* 41, no. 1 (2009): 61–88.

Garcia-Kilroy, Catiana and Anderson Caputo Silva. "Reforming Government Debt Markets in MENA." Policy Research Working Paper, no. 5611, World Bank, March 2011.

Gardner, Bruce L. "The Political Economy of U.S. Export Subsidies for Wheat," in *The Political Economy of American Trade Policy*, edited by Anne O. Krueger. Chicago: University of Chicago Press, 1996.

Geddes, Barbara. "Authoritarian Breakdown: Empirical Test of a Game Theoretic Argument," paper presented at the annual meeting of the American Political Science Association, Atlanta, September 2–5, 1999.

General Authority for Investment. *Invest in Egypt: Textiles and Ready Made Garments.* 2010. www.gafinet.org/English/SectorsValuePreposition/Textiles%20value%20proposition-2010.pdf.

Ghalyoun, Burhan. "Binaa al mujtamaa al madani: dawr al 'awamel el dakhiliyya wal kharijiyya" [The Construction of Civil Society: The Role of Interior and Exterior Factors]. in *Al Mujtama' al madani fil watan al 'arabi* [Civil Society in the Arab World]. Beirut: Markaz Dirassat al Wihda al A'arabiyya, 2000.

Glain, Stephen. "Egyptian Farmers Make Themselves Heard," *New York Times*, June 27, 2012.

Global Investment House. *Private Equity—Luring Regional and International Investors Alike*. Kuwait: Global Investment House, July 2007.

Global Investment House. *Qatar 2008*. Kuwait: Global Investment, 2008.

Global Investment House. *The Rise of Private Equity*. Kuwait: Global Investment House, July 2006.

Gobe, Eric. "The Gafsa Mining Basin between Riots and a Social Movement: Meaning and Significance of a Protest Movement in Ben Ali's Tunisia," *HAL-SHS*, January 20, 2011. http://halshs.archives-ouvertes.fr/halshs-00557826.

Goldberg, Esther. *Jewish Settlement in the West Bank and Gaza Strip*. Tel Aviv: International Center for Peace in the Middle East, 1993.

Goldstein, Andrea. "The Political Economy of Regulatory Reform: Telecoms in the Southern Mediterranean." Working Paper no. 216, OECD Development Centre, November 2003.

Graham-Brown, Sarah. "Agriculture and Labour Transformation in Palestine," in Kathy and Pandeli Glavanis, *The Rural Middle East: Peasant Lives and Modes of Production*. London: Zed Books, 1990.

Grimwade, Nigel. *International Trade: New Patterns of Trade, Production, and Investment*. New York: Routledge, 2000.

Gulf Venture Capital Association. *Private Equity in the MENA Region*. Annual Report 2009. Bahrain: GVCA, 2009.

Gvirtzman, Haim. *Maps of Israeli Interests in Judea and Samaria, Determining the Extent of the Additional Withdrawals*. Security and Policy Studies no. 34. Tel Aviv: BESA Center for Strategic Studies, 1997.

Haddad, Bassam. *Business Networks in Syria: The Political Economy of Authoritarian Resilience*. Palo Alto, CA: Stanford University Press, 2011.

Haddad, Bassam. "The Political Economy of Syria: Realities and Challenges," *Middle East Policy* 18, no. 2 (Summer 2011): 46–61.

Halliday, Fred. *Arabia Without Sultans*. London: Saqi Books, 2001.

Hanieh, Adam. *Capitalism and Class in the Gulf Arab States*. New York: Palgrave-Macmillan, 2011.

Hanieh, Adam. "'Democracy Promotion' and Neo-Liberalism in the Middle East," *State of Nature* 3 (Spring 2006). www.stateofnature.org/democracyPromotion.html.

Hanieh, Adam. "Palestine in the Middle East: Opposing Neoliberalism and US Power," *MRzine*, July 19, 2008. www.monthlyreview.org/mrzine.

Hanieh, Adam. "The Politics of Curfew in the Occupied Territories." In *The Struggle for Sovereignty in Israel/Palestine, 1993–2005*, edited by Joel Beinin and Rebecca Stein, 324–337. Palo Alto, CA: Stanford University Press, 2006,

Harrigan, Jane, Chengang Wang, and Hamed El-Said. "The Politics of IMF and World

Bank Lending: Will It Backfire in the Middle East and North Africa?" in *The IMF, World Bank and Policy Reform*, edited by Alberto Paloni and Maurizio Zanardi. London and New York: Routledge, 2006.

Harvey, David. *A Brief History of Neoliberalism*. Oxford: Oxford University Press, 2005.

Harvey, David. "The Geopolitics of Capitalism," in *Social Relations and Spatial Structures*, edited by D. Gregory and J. Urry. London: Macmillan, 1985.

Harvey, David. *The Limits to Capital*. London: Verso, 1999.

Hazbun, Waleed. *Beaches, Ruins, Resorts: The Politics of Tourism in the Arab World*. Minneapolis, MN: University of Minnesota Press, 2008.

Heikal, Mohammed. *The Sphinx and the Commissar*. New York: Harper and Row, 1978.

Henry, Clement Moore and Robert Springborg. *Globalization and the Politics of Development in the Middle East*. Cambridge: Cambridge University Press, 2010.

Hever, Shir. *The Political Economy of Israel's Occupation: Repression Beyond Exploitation*. London; Pluto Press, 2010.

Hibou, Béatrice. "The Tunisian Revolution Did Not Come out of Nowhere," interview with Sadri Khiari, translation by Stefan Kipfer, *Politique Africaine* (April 2011). www.decolonialtranslation.com/english/the-tunisian-revolution-did-not-come-out-of-nowhere.html.

Hilal, Jamil. "Civil Society in Palestine: A Literature Review," *Research Papers for the Regional Conference on Research on Civil Society Organisations: Status and Prospects*. Foundation for Future, January 2010.

Hilal, Jamil. *A Dangerous Decade: The 2nd Gender Profile of the Occupied West Bank and Gaza (2000—2010)*. Birzeit: Institute for Women's Studies, Birzeit University, 2010.

Hill, Allan G. "The Palestinian Population of the Middle East," *Population and Development Review* 9, no. 2 (June 1983): 293–316.

Hinnebusch, Raymond. *The International Politics of the Middle East*. Manchester and New York: Manchester University Press, 1988.

Hirsch, Joachim. "The State Apparatus and Social Reproduction: Elements of a Theory of the Bourgeois State." In *State and Capital: A Marxist Debate*, edited by John Holloway and Sol Picciotto. London: Edward Arnold, 1979.

Honig-Parnass, Tikva. *False Prophets of Peace: Liberal Zionism and the Struggle for Palestine*. Chicago: Haymarket Books, 2011.

Honig-Parnass, Tikva. "Zionist Principles of Separation and Ethnic Cleansing on Both Sides of the Green Line." In *Between the Lines: Readings on Israel, the Palestinians and the US "War on Terror,"* edited by Tikva Honig-Parnass and Toufic Haddad. Chicago: Haymarket Books, 2007.

Hudgins, Edward L. *The Middendorf Plan's Strategy for Central America's Economic Growth*. Washington DC: Heritage Foundation, 1987. www.policyarchive.org/handle/10207/

bitstreams/12485.pdf.

Hudson, Michael. *Arab Politics: The Search for Legitimacy*. New Haven, CT: Yale University Press, 1977.

Human Rights Watch. *"As If I Am Not Human": Abuses against Asian Domestic Workers in Saudi Arabia*. New York: Human Rights Watch, July 2008.

Human Rights Watch. *Building Towers, Cheating Workers*. New York: Human Rights Watch, 2006.

Human Rights Watch. *For a Better Life: Migrant Worker Abuse in Bahrain and the Government Reform Agenda*. New York: Human Rights Watch, 2012.

Huwaydi, Fahmi. "Al-Islam wa 'l-dimuqratiyya" [Islam and Democracy], *Al-Mustaqbal al-'arabi*, no. 166, December 1992.

Industrial Modernization Centre (IMC). Food Export Strategy, Final Report. Cairo: Egyptian Government, May 2006. www.imc-egypt.org.

Institute of International Finance. *The Arab World in Transition: Assessing the Economic Impact*. Washington, DC: Institute of International Finance, May 2011.

Internal Displacement Monitoring Centre. *Yemen: Internal Displacement Continues amid Multiple Crises*. Geneva: IDMC, December 2012. www.unhcr.org/refworld/docid/50d0343b2.html.

International Crisis Group. "Popular Protest in North Africa and the Middle East (VI): The Syrian People's Slow-motion Revolution," *Crisis Group Middle East/North Africa Report*, July 6, 2011.

International Crisis Group. "Popular Protest in North Africa and the Middle East (III): The Bahrain Revolt," *Crisis Group Middle East/North Africa Report*, April 6, 2011.

International Food Policy Research Institute. *Middle East and North Africa Strategy*. Washington, DC: IFPRI, February 2010. www.ipfri.org.

International Labour Organization. *Global Employment Trends for Youth: 2011 Update* Geneva: ILO, 2011. www.ilo.org/wcmsp5/groups/public/—-ed_emp/—-emp_elm/—-trends/documents/publication/wcms_165455.pdf.

International Labour Organization. *Tunisia: A New Social Contract for Fair and Equitable Growth*. Geneva: International Institute for Labour Studies, 2011.

International Monetary Fund. *Arab Republic of Egypt: 2006 Article IV Consultation—Staff Report*. Public Information Note. Washington, DC: IMF, 2006.

International Monetary Fund. *Arab Republic of Egypt—2010 Article IV Consultation Mission, Concluding Statement*. Washington, DC: IMF, February 16, 2010. www.imf.org/external/np/ms/2010/021610.htm.

International Monetary Fund. *Economic Transformation in MENA: Delivering on the Promise of Shared Prosperity*. IMF Staff Report to the G8 Summit. Washington, DC: May 27, 2011. www.imf.org/external/np/g8/pdf/052711.pdf.

International Monetary Fund. *Government Finance Statistics*, edition July 2012. Washington DC: IMF, 2012.

International Monetary Fund. "IMF Executive Board Concludes 2010 Article IV Consultation with the Socialist People's Libyan Arab Jamahiriya." Public Information Notice (PIN) no. 11/23. February 15, 2011. www.imf.org/external/np/sec/pn/2011/pn1123.htm.

International Monetary Fund. "Letter of Intent and Memorandum of Economic and Financial Policies from the Jordanian Government to the IMF," June 15, 2004.

International Monetary Fund. *Regional Economic Outlook: Middle East and Central Asia*. World Economic and Financial Surveys. Washington, DC: IMF, April 11, 2011. www.imf.org/external/pubs/ft/reo/2011/mcd/eng/pdf/mreo0411.pdf.

International Organization for Migration. *Migrants Caught in Crisis*. Geneva: IOM, 2011.

Invest in Morocco. *Emerging Morocco: A Gate to Opportunities*. Royaume du Maroc—Agence Marocaine de Développement des Investissements, 2011. www.unido.or.jp/download/AMDI_Tokyo_Dec2011.pdf.

Iqbal, Farrukh. *Sustaining Gains in Poverty Reduction and Human Development in the Middle East and North Africa*. Washington, DC: World Bank, 2006.

Ismail, Abdel-Mawla. "Drinking Water Protests in Egypt and the Role of Civil Society." *Transnational Institute*, July 17, 2012. www.tni.org/article/drinking-water-protests.

Jbili, Abdelali, Klaus Enders, and Volker Treichel. "Financial Sector Reforms in Algeria, Morocco and Tunisia: A Preliminary Assessment." IMF Working Paper WP/97/81. Washington, DC: IMF, 1997.

Jones, Geoffrey. "Banking in the Gulf Before 1960." In *The Gulf in the Early 20th Century: Foreign Institutions and Local Responses*, edited by J. Dewdney and H. Bleaney. London: University of Durham, 1986.

JP Morgan. *MENA Equity Research—Talaat Mostafa Group*. New York: JP Morgan, June 7, 2010.

Kapiszewski, Andrzej. "Arab Labour Migration to the GCC States." In *Arab Migration in a Globalized World*, vol. 2003. Geneva: IOM and League of Arab States, 2004.

Katzman, Kenneth. *The Persian Gulf States: Issues for U.S. Policy*. Washington, DC: Congressional Research Service, 2006.

Kazim, Aqil. *The United Arab Emirates AD 600 to the Present: A Socio-Discursive Transformation in the Arabian Gulf*. Dubai: Gulf Book Centre, 2000.

Khalidi, Raja and Sobhi Samour. "Neoliberalism as Liberation: The Statehood Program and the Remaking of the Palestinian National Movement," *Journal of Palestine Studies* 40, no. 2 (Winter 2011): 6–25.

King, Stephen. *Liberalization Against Democracy: The Local Politics of Economic Reform in Tunisia*. Bloomington, IN: Indiana University Press, 2003.

Kotschwar, Barbara and Jeffrey J. Schott. *Reengaging Egypt: Options for US-Egypt Eco-*

nomic Relations. Washington, DC: Peterson Institute for International Economics, 2010.

Kydd, Jonathan and Sophie Thoyer. *Structural Adjustment and Moroccan Agriculture: An Assessment of the Reforms in the Sugar and Cereal Sectors*. Working Paper no. 70, Paris: OECD, 1992.

Lachaal, Lassaad, Boubaker Dhehibi, Ali Chebil, Aymen Frija, and Chokri Thabet. "National Agricultural Situation Report for Tunisia." *Market and Trade Policies for Mediterranean Agriculture: The Case of Fruit/Vegetable and Olive Oil*. Chania, Greece: MEDFROL, 2002.

Laroui, Abdallah. "African Initiatives and Resistance in North Africa and the Sahara," in *Africa Under Colonial Domination, 1880–1935*: vol. 7, edited by Albert Adu Boahen. London: Heinemann Educational Books, 1985.

Lazaar, Mohamed. "International Migration and Its Consequences in the Central Rif (Morocco)." *European Review of International Migration* 3 (1987): 97–114.

Lefebvre, Henri. *The Production of Space*. Oxford: Basil Blackwell, 1991.

Lewin-Epstein, Noah and Moshe Semyonov. "Occupational Change in Israel: Bringing the Labor Market Back." *Israel Social Science Research* 2, no. 2 (1984): 3–18.

Lindsey, Brink. "The Trade Front: Combating Terrorism with Open Markets." *Trade Policy Analysis*, no. 24 (2003).

Litani, Yehuda. "Village Leagues: What Kind of Carrot," *Journal of Palestine Studies* 11, no. 3 (Spring 1982): 174–178.

Lopez-Acevedo, Gladys and Raymond Robertson, *Sewing Success, Employment, Wages, and Poverty following the End of the Multi-Fibre Arrangement*. Washington, DC: World Bank, 2012.

Lucas, Russell. "Monarchical Authoritarianism: Survival and Political Liberalization in a Middle Eastern Regime Type." *International Journal of Middle East Studies* 36, no. 1 (2004): 103–119.

Lynfield, Ben. "Israel Worried as Mubarak Teeters." *GlobalPost*, Jaunary 29, 2011. www.globalpost.com/dispatch/israel/110129/egypt-mubarak-netanyahu.

Machover, Moshe. *Israelis and Palestinians: Conflict and Resolution*. Chicago: Haymarket Books, 2012.

Madi, Amer, Hassan Abu Hassan, Nabil Al Ghool, and Omar Abu Ghosh. *The Impact of Closure and High Food Prices on Performance of Imported Staple Foods and Vegetable and Fruits Market in the oPt*. Rome: UN World Food Programme, December 2009.

Majid, Nomaan. *Reaching Millennium Goals: How Well Does Agricultural Productivity Growth Reduce Poverty?* Employment Strategy Paper 2004/12, Geneva: International Labor Organization, 2004.

Mandel, Ernest. *Late Capitalism*. London: Verso, 1983.

Mann, Michael. *The Dark Side of Democracy: Explaining Ethnic Cleansing*. Cambridge: Cambridge University Press, 2004.

Marx, Karl. *Grundrisse*. Harmondsworth: Penguin, 1973.

Masalha, Nur. *Expulsion of the Palestinians: The Concept of "Transfer" in Zionist Political Thought*. Washington, DC: Institute for Palestine Studies, 1992.

Massey, Doreen. *Spatial Divisions of Labour: Social Structures and the Geography of Production*. London: MacMillan Education, 1984.

McKinsey Global Institute. *The New Power Brokers: How Oil, Asia, Hedge Funds, and Private Equity Are Shaping Global Capital Markets*. New York: McKinsey & Company, 2007. www.mckinseyquarterly.com.

Meiksins Wood, Ellen. *Democracy against Capitalism*. Cambridge: Cambridge University Press, 1995.

Meiksins Wood, Ellen. "Logics of Power: A Conversation with David Harvey," *Historical Materialism* 14, no. 4 (2006): 9–34.

Miller, Greg. "White House Approves Broader Yemen Drone Campaign." *Washington Post*, April 26, 2012.

Mitchell, Timothy. *Rule of Experts: Egypt, Techno-Politics, Modernity*. Berkeley, CA: University of California Press, 2002.

Mohieldin, Mahmoud. *Neighborly Investments—Finance and Development*. Washington, DC: IMF, 2008.

Mundlak, Yair. *Agricultural Productivity and Economic Policy: Concepts and Measures*. OECD Working Paper no. 75. Paris: OECD, 1992.

Naisse, Ghayath. "mulahathat naqdiyya hawl al-muw'aradda al-Suriyya wa darourat binaa qiyada thawriyya jamaharriyya badila" [Critical notes around the Syrian opposition and the necessity to build an alternative popular revolutionary leadership], *al-thawra dai'ma* no. 2 (Spring 2012).

Nakhleh, Emile. *Bahrain: Political Development in a Modernizing Society*. Lexington, MA: Lexington Books, 1976.

Namatalla, Ahmed A. "SODIC Approves LE1.1 Billion Capital Increase." *Daily Star Egypt*, October 18, 2006.

Nasser, Gamal Abdul. *Falsafat al-thawrah* [Philosophy of the Revolution]. Beirut: Dar al-Qalam, 1970.

Nassur, Adib. *Al-Naksa wal-khata*. Beirut: Dar al-katib al-'arabi, n.d.

Naufal, George and Carlos Varga-Silva. "Migrant Transfers in the MENA Region: A Two-Way Street in Which Traffic Is Changing." In *Migration and Remittances during the Global Financial Crisis and Beyond*, edited by Ibrahim Sirkeci, Jeffrey H. Cohen, and Dilip Rath. Washington, DC: World Bank Publications, 2012.

Negotiations Affairs Department. "Israel's Wall in the Qalqilya District, September

2004." www.nad-plo.org.

Nexant Chem Systems. *Outlook for the Petrochemical Industry: Good Times Ahead*. Buenos Aires: Instituto Petroquimico Argentino, 2004.

Nitzan, Jonathan and Shimshon Bichler. *The Global Political Economy of Israel*. London: Pluto Press, 2002.

Norton, Augustus Richard. *Civil Society in the Middle East, vol. 2*. Social, Economic and Political Studies of the Middle East Series. Leiden: Brill, 2001.

Norton-Taylor, Richard. "Libyan Dissident Offered Money to Avoid MI6 Appearing in Open Court." *Guardian Weekly*, April 10, 2012. www.guardian.co.uk/world/2012/apr/10/libyan-dissident-compensation-uk-rendition.

O'Donnell, Guillermo, Philippe Schmitter, and Lawrence Whitehead, eds. *Transitions from Authoritarian Rule: Prospects for Democracy*. Baltimore, MD: Johns Hopkins University Press, 1986.

OECD. *Progress in Public Management in the Middle East and North Africa: Case Studies on Policy Reform*. Paris: OECD, 2010.

Office of Trade Policy Analysis, Manufacturing and Services, International Trade Administration. *US Morocco Free Trade Agreement, Key Market Access Results and Benefits*. Washington, DC: International Trade Administration, November 2004.

Ollman, Bertell. *Dance of the Dialectic: Steps in Marx's Method*. Urbana, IL: University of Illinois Press, 2003.

Otman, Waniss and Erling Karlber. *The Libyan Economy: Economic Diversification and International Repositioning*. Berlin: Springer Books, 2007.

Oxford Business Group. *The Report: Emerging Morocco, 2007*. Oxford: Oxford Business Group, 2007.

Oxford Business Group. *Syria: A Year in Review, 2010*. Oxford: Oxford Business Group, 2010. www.oxfordbusinessgroup.com/economic_updates/syria-year-review-2010.

Palestinian Central Bureau of Statistics. *Poverty in the Palestinian Territory: Main Findings 2009–2010*. Ramallah: PCBS, 2011.

Palestinian National Authority. *Building a Palestinian State: Towards Peace and Prosperity*. Paris: PNA, 2007. http://imeu.net/engine2/uploads/pna-full-report.pdf.

Palestinian National Authority. *Palestine Reform and Development Plan (PRDP)*. Ministry of Planning, 2007.

Palloix, Christian. "Conceptualizing the Internationalization of Capital." *Review of Radical Political Economics* (1977): 3–17.

Panitch, Leo and Sam Gindin. "Finance and American Empire." In *Socialist Register 2005: The Empire Reloaded*, edited by Leo Panitch and Colin Leys. London: Merlin Press, 2004.

Panitch, Leo and Sam Gindin. "Global Capitalism and American Empire." In *Socialist*

Register 2004: The New Imperial Challenge, edited by Leo Panitch and Colin Leys. London: Merlin Press, 2003.

Pappé, Ilan. *The Ethnic Cleansing of Palestine*. London: Oneworld Publications, 2006.

Perard, Edouard. *Private Sector Participation and Regulatory Reform in Water Supply: The Middle East and North African (MEDA) Experience*. Milan: Fondazione Eni Enrico Mattei, 2007.

Poulantzas, Nicos. *Classes in Contemporary Capitalism*. London: New Left Books, 1979.

Prashad, Vijay. *Arab Spring, Libyan Winter*. Oakland, CA: AK Press, 2012.

Prime Holding and Talaat Mostafa Group Holding Co. (TMG). *Real Estate & Tourism Sectors Report*. Giza: TMG, January 3, 2008.

Przeworski, Adam. *Democracy and the Market: Political and Economic Reforms in Eastern Europe and Latin America*. Cambridge: Cambridge University Press, 1991.

Qatamesh, Ahmad. "al-taghirat al-bunyawiya al'ati istajadat ala al-kuwa al-a'mila fi daffa wa gaza ma ba'ad Oslo" [The structural changes that have occurred to the labour force in the West Bank and Gaza after Oslo], in *Ashkaliya al'amal al-niqabi fi falastin* [Issues in Labour Organizing in Palestine]. Ramallah: Center for Human Rights and Democracy, 1999.

Radwan, Samir, Vali Jamal, and Ajit Kumar Ghose. *Tunisia: Rural Labour and Structural Transformation*. London: Routledge, 1991.

Rahman, Saifur. "Dubai Represents 23% of Gulf's Retail Sector." *Gulf News*, April 18, 2006.

RDI Policy Brief. "Land Title Registry: Recommendations to Improve the Land Registration Process Towards a Formal Rural Land Market." *Land Title Registry*, issue 22. Giza: RDI, June 2000. http://pdf.usaid.gov/pdf_docs/PNACS209.pdf.

Reichert, Christoph. "Labour Migration and Rural Development in Egypt—A Study of Return Migration in Six Villages." *Sociologia ruralis* 33, no. 1 (1993): 42–60.

Retzky, Allan. "Peace in the Middle East: What Does It Really Mean for Israeli Business?" *The Columbia Journal of World Business* 30, no. 3 (1995): 26–32.

Reuters. "EBRD Aims to Complete Egypt Inclusion Study by Spring," February 15, 2011.

Reuters. "Sofiproteol Buys 41 Pct of Moroccan Cook-Oil Maker," July 13, 2011.

Reuters. "Up to 335,000 People Have Fled Syria Violence: UNHCR," October 9, 2012.

Richards, Alan and John Waterbury. *A Political Economy of the Middle East: Third Edition*. Boulder, CO: Westview Press, 2008.

Robbins, Philip. *A History of Jordan*. Cambridge: Cambridge University Press, 2004.

Roccu, Roberto. "Gramsci in Cairo: Neoliberal Authoritarianism, Passive Revolution and Failed Hegemony in Egypt under Mubarak, 1991-2010," PhD thesis, Department of International Relations of the London School of Economics, January 2012.

Ron, James. *Frontiers and Ghettos: State Violence in Serbia and Israel*. Berkeley, CA: University of California Press, 2003.

Rosen, Nir. "How It Started in Yemen: From Tahrir to Taghyir," in *The Dawn of the Arab Uprisings*, edited by Bassam Haddad, Rosie Bsheer, and Ziad Abu-Rish. London: Pluto Press, 2011.

Ross, Michael. "Does Oil Hinder Democracy?" *World Politics* 53, no. 3 (2001): 235–61.

Roy, Sara. "De-development Revisited: Palestinian Economy and Society Since Oslo." *Journal of Palestine Studies* 28, no. 3 (April 1, 1999): 64–82.

Russell, Sharon. "International Migration and Political Turmoil in the Middle East." *Population and Development Review* 18, no. 4 (1992): 719–728.

Saad-Filho, Alfredo and Deborah Johnston. *Neoliberalism: A Critical Reader*. London: Pluto Press, 1995.

Saad-Filho, Alfredo. "Value, Capital and Exploitation." In *Anti-Capitalism: A Marxist Introduction*, edited by Alfredo Saad-Fildo. London: Pluto Press, 2003.

Saghir, Jamal. "Privatization in Tunisia." *World Bank Cofinancing and Financial Advisory Services Discussion Paper Series*, no. 101 (1993): 1–27.

Saif, Ibrahim and Thoraya El-Rayyes. "Labour Markets Performance and Migration Flows in Jordan." In *Labour Markets Performance and Migration Flows in Arab Mediterranean Countries: Determinants and Effects*, European Commission Occasional Paper 60, vol. 3. Brussels: European Commission, 2010.

Sales-i-Campos, Albert and Eloisa Pineiro-Orge. *Made in Morocco*. Barcelona: Network Wear, 2011. www.achact.be/upload/files/MadeinMaroc_rapport_ENGL.pdf.

Samara, Adel. *The Political Economy of the West Bank 1967–1987: From Peripheralization to Development*. London: Khamsin Publications, 1988.

Sanghvi, Sunil, Rupert Simons, and Roberto Uchoa. "Four Lessons for Transforming African Agriculture," *McKinsey Quarterly*, April 2011.

Saudi Arabia British Bank. *Saudi Arabia—Thinking Big*. Fourth Quarter Report. Riyadh: SABB, 2007.

Saudi Arabia General Investment Authority. *Annual Report of FDI into Saudi Arabia 2010*. Riyadh: SAGIA, 2011. www.sagia.gov.sa/PageFiles/4132/Annual_Report_FDI%20_SAUDI_ARABIA.pdf.

Saudi Arabia Ministry of Economy and Planning. *Employment and Wages Survey 1996 and 2000*. www.mep.gov.sa.

Saudi Gazette. "Aramco: China Overtakes US as Largest Customer," April 6, 2010.

Savas, Emanuel. *Privatization in the City*. Washington, DC: CQ Press, 2005.

Schiff, Benjamin. *Refugees Unto the Third Generation—UN AID to Palestinians*. Syracuse,

NY: Syracuse University Press, 1995.

Schlumberger, Oliver. *Debating Arab Authoritarianism: Dynamics and Durability in Nondemocratic Regimes*. Palo Alto, CA: Stanford University Press, 2007.

Semyonov, Moshe and Noah Lewin-Epstein. *Hewers of Wood and Drawers of Water: Noncitizen Arabs in the Israeli Labor Market*. Ithaca, NY: ILR Press, 1987.

Shaaban, Abdul Hussein. "mafhoum al mujtama' al-madani: bayn al-tanweer wa al-tash'heer" [The Concept of Civil Society: Between Enlightenment and Slander]. Al Hewar, March 16, 2008. www.ahewar.org/debat/show.art.asp?aid=128248.

Shah, Nasra. "The Management of Irregular Migration and its Consequences for Development: Gulf Co-operation Council." Working Paper no. 19. ILO Asian Regional Program on Governance of Labour Migration, Regional Office for Asia and the Pacific, 2009.

Shah, Samira. "On the Road to Apartheid: The Bypass Road Network in the West Bank." *Columbia Human Rights Law Review* 29 (Fall 1997): 221–90.

Shaikh, Anwar. "Foreign Trade and the Law of Value—Part One." *Science and Society* 43 (1979): 281–302.

Shaikh, Anwar. "Foreign Trade and the Law of Value—Part Two." *Science and Society* 44 (1980): 27–57.

Shaikh, Anwar and Ahmet Tonak. *Measuring the Wealth of Nations*. Cambridge: Cambridge University Press, 1994.

Shamsi, Maitha. *Ta'qiym siyassay al hijra f'il dawla majlis attawan alkhaleeji* [Evaluation of Labour Policies in the GCC]. United Nations Expert Group Meeting on International Migration and Development in the Arab Region. Beirut: Department of Economic and Social Affairs, United Nations Secretariat, 2006.

Sharp, Jeremy M. *Egypt: Background and U.S. Relations*. Washington, DC: Congressional Research Service, September 13, 2012. www.fas.org/sgp/crs/mideast/RL33003.pdf.

Shaw, R. Paul. *Mobilizing Human Resources in the Arab World*. London: Kegan Paul International, 1983.

Shehadi, Kamal. *Lessons in Privatization: Considerations for Arab States*. Geneva: United Nations Development Programme, January 2002.

Sherbiny, Naiem. *Oil and the Internationalization of Arab Banks*. Oxford: Oxford Institute for Energy Studies, 1985.

Skees, Jerry. "Developing Rainfall-Based Index Insurance in Morocco." Policy Research Working Paper no. 2577. Washington, DC: World Bank, 2001.

Smith, Dan. *The Seventh Fire: The Struggle for Aboriginal Government*. Toronto: Key Porter Books, 1993.

Solh, Karim. *The Emergence of Regional and Global Investment Leaders Out of Abu Dhabi*. Paper presented on behalf of Gulf Capital to the Abu Dhabi Economic Forum 2008, Emirates Palace, Abu Dhabi, February 3–4, 2008.

Spitz, Peter. *Petrochemicals: The Rise of an Industry*. New York: John Wiley, 1988.

State of Qatar. *Al Nashra Sanawiyya Al Ihsayaht Al Taq'a wa al San'aeya* [Annual Statistical Bulletin on Energy and Industry], vol. 23. Doha: General Secretariat for Development Planning, 2004.

Stop the Wall. "Development or Normalization? A Critique of West Bank Development Approaches and Projects," May 20, 2008. http://stopthewall.org.

Stork, Joe. "Bailing out Sadat." *MERIP Reports*, no. 56 (April 1977).

Stork, Joe. "The Carter Doctrine and US Bases in the Middle East." *MERIP Reports*, no. 90 (September 1980).

Stork, Joe. "US Strategy in the Gulf." *MERIP Reports*, no. 36 (April 1975).

Suskind, Ron. *The Price of Loyalty*. New York: Simon & Schuster, 2004.

Swearingen, Will. "Agricultural Development and Environmental Constraints in Northwest Africa," in *Rural Development in Eurasia and the Middle East: Land Reform, Demographic Change, and Environmental Constraints*, edited by Kurt E. Engelmann and Vjeran Pavlaković. Seattle, WA: University of Washington Press, 2001.

Swearingen, Will. *Moroccan Mirages: Agrarian Dreams and Deceptions, 1912–1986*. London: I.B. Taurus, 1988.

Takriti, Abdel Razzaq. *Monsoon Revolution: Republicans, Sultans, and Empires in Oman, 1965–76*. Oxford: Oxford University Press, 2012.

Tal, Lawrence. "Britain and the Jordan Crisis of 1958." *Middle Eastern Studies* 31, no. 1 (January 1995): 39–57.

Tamari, Salim. "In League with Zion: Israel's Search for a Native Pillar." *Journal of Palestine Studies* 12, no. 4 (Summer 1983): 41–56.

Tarabisbi, George. *Al-Dawlah al-qutriyya wa al-nazariyyah al-qawmiyya* [The Regional State and the Nationalist Theory]. Beirut: Dar al-Tali'a, 1982.

Tatom, John A. "Is Tax Policy Retarding Growth in Morocco?" Networks Financial Institute, Working Paper no. 27, Indiana State University, November 2007.

Tohami, Ahmed. "Al-Dustour wa al-Sara al-Ijtimayyi al-siyyasi ba'ad al-thawra fi misr" [The Constitution and the Political Social Struggle After the Revolution in Egypt]. *Jadaliyya*, December 5, 2012.

True, Warren. "Global Ethylene Capacity Continues Advance in 2011." *Oil and Gas Journal* 110, no. 7 (July 2, 2012). www.ogj.com.

United Nations Conference on Trade and Development. *Report on UNCTAD Assistance to the Palestinian People: Developments in the Economy of the Occupied Palestinian Territory*. Geneva: UNCTAD, July 15, 2011. http://unctad.org/en/Docs/tdb58d4_en.pdf.

United Nations Development Programme. *Arab Human Development Report, The Challenge to Human Security*. New York: UNDP, 2009.

United Nations Development Programme. *Focus—Qalqilya and Tulkarem*, 2003, vol.1, Jerusalem: UNDP, 2003.

UN Habitat. *Cairo: A City in Transition*. Nairobi, Kenya: UN Human Settlements Programme, 2011.

USAID. Country Profile, Egypt, Property Rights and Resource Governance. Washington, DC: USAID, September 2010. http://usaidlandtenure.net/egypt.

USAID. *Manual for the Formation of an Employee Share Ownership Plan for the Alexandria Tire Company and Other Companies in Egypt*. Washington, DC: Center for Privatization, 1988. http://pdf.usaid.gov/pdf_docs/pnabc466.pdf40.

USAID. *Private Enterprise Development*. Policy Paper. Washington, DC: Bureau for Program and Policy Coordination, USAID, March 1985.

USAID. *USAID Assistance in Fiscal Reform: Comprehensive Tax Reform in Egypt*. Project Document, June 2006. Washingon, DC: USAID, 2006.

US Department of State. *Trafficking in Persons Report 2010*. Washington, DC: State Department Printing Office, 2010.

US Department of State. "Hillary Rodham Clinton, interview with Taher Barake of *Al Arabiya*." January 11, 2011. www.state.gov/secretary/rm/2011/01/154295.htm.

US Embassy, Israel. Text of Cairo Conference Declaration, November 14, 1996. www.usembassy-israel.org.il/publish/press/summit/es11115.htm.

Usher, Graham. *Palestine in Crisis: The Struggle for Peace and Political Independence after Oslo*. London: Pluto Press, 1995.

Van der Linden, Marcel. Workers of the World: Essays in Global Labor History, Leiden: Brill, 2008.

Vandewalle, Dirk. *A History of Modern Libya*. Cambridge: Cambridge University Press, 2012.

Vassiliev, Alexei. *The History of Saudi Arabia*. London: Saqi Books, 1998.

Vitalis, Robert. *America's Kingdom: Mythmaking on the Saudi Oil Frontier*. Palo Alto, CA: Stanford University Press, 2007.

Vitalis, Robert. *When Capitalists Collide: Business Conflict and the End of Empire in Egypt*. Berkeley, CA: University of California Press, 1995.

Vitullo, Anita. "Uprising in Gaza." In *Intifada: The Palestinian Uprising*, edited by Zachary Lockman and Joel Beinin. Boston: South End Press, 1989.

Wahba, Jackline. "Labour Markets Performance and Migration Flows in Egypt," in *Labour Markets Performance and Migration Flows in Arab Mediterranean Countries: Determinants and Effects*, European Commission Occasional Paper no. 60, vol. 3. Brussels: European Commission, 2010.

Waterbury, John. *Exposed to Innumerable Delusions: Public Enterprise and State Power in Egypt*. New York: Cambridge University Press, 1993.

Wegren, Stephen. *Land Privatization: Why Russia Is Indeterminate and What Is to Be Done.* Washington, DC: National Council for Eurasian and East European Research, 2003.

Weir, Fred. "Why Russia Is Willing to Sell Arms to Syria." *Christian Science Monitor,* January 19, 2012. www.csmonitor.com/World/Europe/2012/0119/Why-Russia-is-willing-to-sell-arms-to-Syria.

White House Office of the Press Secretary. "Remarks by the President on Egypt." February 11, 2011. www.whitehouse.gov/the-press-office/2011/02/11/remarks-president-egypt.

Williams, Daniel. "Water Crisis Grips Syria." *New York Times.* March 2, 2010.

Wimmer, Andreas and Nina Glick Schiller. "Methodological Nationalism and Beyond: Nation-State Building, Migration and the Social Sciences." *Global Networks* 2, no. 4 (2002):301–334.

World Bank. *Agricultural Growth for the Poor: An Agenda for Development.* Washington, DC: World Bank, 2005.

World Bank, *Agricultural Innovation Systems: An Investment Sourcebook.* Washington, DC: World Bank, 2012.

World Bank. *Building the Palestinian State: Sustaining Growth, Institutions, and Service Delivery.* Washington, DC: World Bank, April 2011.

World Bank. *Bureaucrats in Business.* Washington, DC: World Bank, 1995.

World Bank. *Country Assistance Strategy for the Republic of Egypt.* World Bank Report no. 32190-EG. Washington, DC: 2005.

World Bank. *Country Assistance Strategy, Jordan.* Washington, DC: World Bank, 2011.

World Bank. *Doing Business 2010: Comparing Regulation in 183 Economies.* Washington, DC: World Bank, 2011.

World Bank. *The "Door to Door" Movement of Goods.* Washington, DC: World Bank, July 5, 2005.

World Bank. *The Economic Effects of Restricted Access to Land in the West Bank.* Washington, DC: World Bank, 2008. www.worldbank.org.

World Bank. *From Privilege to Competition: Unlocking Private-Led Growth in the Middle-East and North Africa.* Washington, DC: World Bank, 2009.

World Bank. *Loan Document for Economic Development Policy Loan.* Washington, DC: World Bank, May 26, 2010.

World Bank. *Morocco Social and Integrated Agriculture.* Project Information Document, Concept Note. Washington, DC: World Bank, March 4, 2012.

World Bank. *Morocco, Tunisia, Egypt and Jordan after the End of the Multi-Fiber Agreement: Impact, Challenges and Prospects.* Washington, DC: World Bank, 2006.

World Bank. *Project Appraisal Document on a Proposed Grant of $2 Million to the West Bank* *and Gaza for a Palestinian-NGO Project*. Washington, DC: World Bank, May 27, 2010.

World Bank. *Report and Recommendation on Proposed Public Enterprise Loan to the Republic of Tunisia*.Washington, DC: World Bank, June 12, 1989.

World Bank. Robert Zoellick, Remarks at the Opening Press Conference. Washington, DC: World Bank, April 14, 2011. http://go.worldbank.org/92JDBZXKL0.

World Bank. *Rural Development: From Vision to Action*. Environmentally and Socially Sustainable Development Studies and Monographs, series 12. Washington, DC: World Bank, 1997.

World Bank. *Trade, Investment, and Development in the Middle East and North Africa: Engaging with the World*. Washington, DC: World Bank, 2003.

World Bank. "Trade Options for the Palestinian Economy." Working Paper no. 21 (English), March 2001.

World Bank. *Tunisia: Agricultural Policy Review*. Report no. 35239-TN. Washington, DC: World Bank, 2006.

World Bank. *Tunisia Governance and Opportunity Development Policy Loan*. Washington, DC: World Bank, May 26, 2011.

World Bank. *The Underpinnings of the Future Palestinian State: Sustainable Growth and Institutions, Economic Monitoring Report to the Ad Hoc Liaison Committee*. Washington, DC: World Bank, 2010.

World Bank. *Unlocking the Employment Potential in the Middle East and North Africa: Toward a New Social Contract*. Washington, DC: World Bank, 2004.

World Investment News. Interview with Mohammed Taymour, December 20, 1998. www.winne.com/egypt/toe110.html.

Wright, Steven. *Fixing the Kingdom: Political Evolution and Socio-Economic Challenges in Bahrain*. Center for International and Regional Studies, Georgetown University School of Foreign Service in Qatar, Occasional Paper no. 3. Doha: CIRS, 2008.

Zahlan, Antoine and Rosemarie Zahlan, "The Palestinian Future: Education and Manpower," *Journal of Palestine Studies* 6, no. 4 (Summer 1977).

Zahlan, Rosemary. *The Making of the Modern Gulf States*. Reading: Garnet Publishing, 1998.

Zgheib, Niqal. "Major Step forward as Shareholders Approve Three Projects." *EBRD Press Release*, September 18, 2012. www.ebrd.com/english/pages/news/press/2012/120918.shtml.

Zoellick, Robert. "Global Trade and the Middle East: Reawakening a Vibrant Past," Remarks at the World Economic Forum Amman, Jordan, June 23, 2003. www.usinfo.state.gov.

Zoellick, Robert. "Our Credo: Free Trade and Competition." *Wall Street Journal*, July 10, 2003.

Zohry, Ayman. "The Place of Egypt in the Regional Migration System as a Receiving Country." *Revue Européenne des Migrations Internationales* 19, no. 3 (2003): 129–149.

Zohry, Ayman and Barbara Harris-Bond. "Contemporary Egyptian Migration: An Overview of Voluntary and Forced Migration." Working Paper C3. Development Research Centre on Migration, Globalisation and Poverty, University of Sussex, December 2003.

Notes

Chapter 1: Theories and Perspectives

1. Another Arabic term is sometimes used to convey the meaning of civil society, *al-mujtama' al-ahli*, which describes more the activities of traditional kin-based and religious charities. There is a wide-ranging debate in the Arabic literature on whether something akin to the sphere of civil society predates contemporary times. Some authors contend that in the Islamic period, self-organized nonstate institutions mediating the connection with the ruler existed prior to the emergence of the modern notion of civil society, and thus the term does not fit the Arab world in the same way as it does in the West (Fahmi Huwaydi, "Al-Islam wa 'l-dimuqratiyya," [Islam and Democracy], in *Al-Mustaqbal al-'arabi*, no. 166 [December 1992]). From this perspective, Burhan Ghalyoun, the Syrian scholar and currently head of the Syrian National Council (see chapter 7), has argued modern states need to incorporate these traditional Islamic forms into modern structures (Burhan Ghalyoun, "Binaa al mujtamaa al madani: dawr al 'awamel el dakhiliyya wal kharijiyya" [The Construction of Civil Society: The Role of Interior and Exterior Factors], in *Al Mujtama' al madani fil watan al 'arabi* [Civil Society in the Arab World], [Beirut: Markaz Dirassat al Wihda al A'arabiyya, 2000, 733–755]. Palestinian intellectual Azmi Bishara has criticized these conceptions for their ahistorical and static views of social structures, which tend to divorce political structures from their historical context (Azmi Bishara, *Al mujtama'a al madani: dirassa naqdiyya*. [Civil Society: An Analytical Study], [Beirut: Markaz Dirassat al Wihda al A'arabiyya, 1998]). Regardless of internal differences, all these perspectives adopt the basic division of state/civil society as the starting point for analysis.

2. Augustus Richard Norton, *Civil Society in the Middle East*, vol. 2, Social, Economic and Political Studies of the Middle East Series (Leiden: Brill, 2001), x.

3. Abdul Hussein Shaaban, "mafhoum al mujtama' al-madani: bayn al-tanweer wa al-tash'heer" [The Concept of Civil Society: Between Enlightenment and Slander], Al Hewar, March 16, 2008, www.ahewar.org/debat/show.art.asp?aid=128248.

4. Ibid.

5. Alan Richards and John Waterbury, *A Political Economy of the Middle East: Third Edition* (Boulder, CO: Westview Press, 2008), 5.

6. Michele Angrist, *Politics and Society in the Contemporary Middle East* (Boulder, CO: Lynne Rienner, 2010), 4. Nazih Ayubi, *Overstating the Arab State: Politics and Society in the Middle East* (London: I.B. Taurus, 2001) presents a comprehensive survey of both Arabic and English literature on the Middle East state.

7. Oliver Schlumberger, *Debating Arab Authoritarianism: Dynamics and Durability in Nondemocratic Regimes* (Palo Alto, CA: Stanford University Press, 2007), 5.

8. Angrist, *Politics and Society*, 5.

9. Ibid., 7.

10. Ibid.

11. Two classic examples of this perspective are Samuel Huntington, *The Clash of Civilizations and the Remaking of World Order* (New York: Simon & Schuster, 1991), and Raphael Patai, *The Arab Mind* (New York: Scribner, 1973). Patai's book was apparently the inspiration for US torture and sexual abuse of Iraqi prisoners in the Abu Ghraib prison in 2004.

12. James Bill and Carl Leiden, *Politics in the Middle East* (Boston: Little Brown, 1984), 133.

13. Michael Hudson, *Arab Politics: The Search for Legitimacy* (New Haven, CT: Yale University Press, 1977), 166.

14. Guillermo O'Donnell, Philippe Schmitter, and Lawrence Whitehead, eds., *Transitions from Authoritarian Rule: Prospects for Democracy* (Baltimore, MD: Johns Hopkins University Press, 1986).

15. Russell Lucas, "Monarchical Authoritarianism: Survival and Political Liberalization in a Middle Eastern Regime Type," *International Journal of Middle East Studies* 36, no. 1 (2004): 103–119; Lisa Anderson, "Absolutism and the Resilience of Monarchy in the Middle East," *Political Science Quarterly* 106, no. 1 (Spring 1991): 1–15.

16. Michael Ross, "Does Oil Hinder Democracy?" *World Politics* 53, no. 3 (2001): 235–61.

17. Barbara Geddes, "Authoritarian Breakdown: Empirical Test of a Game Theoretic Argument," paper presented at the annual meeting of the American Political Science Association, Atlanta, September 2–5, 1999.

18. The literature on this is extensive, but representative examples of this debate in the Middle East context can be found in Henri Barkey, *Political Economy of Stabilization Measures in the Middle East* (New York: St. Martin's Press, 1992). For a more general argument, see Adam Przeworski, *Democracy and the Market: Political and Economic Reforms in Eastern Europe and Latin America* (Cambridge: Cambridge University Press, 1991).

19. Eva Bellin, "The Robustness of Authoritarianism in the Middle East: Exceptionalism in Comparative Perspective," *Comparative Politics* 36, no. 2 (January 2004), 139.

20. Ibid., 148.

21. See John P. Entelis, "Oil Wealth and the Prospects for Democratization in the Arabian Peninsula: The Case of Saudi Arabia," in *Arab Oil: Impact on the Arab Countries and Global Implications*, eds. Naiem A. Sherbiny and Mark A. Tessler (New York: Praeger, 1976) for this argument in the case of Saudi Arabia; Lisa Anderson, "Peace and Democracy in the Middle East: The Constraints of Soft Budgets," *Journal of International Affairs* 49 (Summer 1995) for the more general argument.

22. Clement Moore Henry and Robert Springborg, *Globalization and the Politics of Development in the Middle East* (Cambridge: Cambridge University Press, 2010), 13.

23. Ibid., xiv.

24. Ibid. Some authors would argue that there was a new type of authoritarianism developing in the region, which has been dubbed a "liberalized autocracy" (Daniel Brumberg, "Authoritarian Legacies and Reform Strategies in the Arab World," in Rex Brynen, Bahgat Korany, and Paul Noble, eds., *Political Liberalization and Democratization in the Arab World*, vol. 1, Theoretical Perspectives

(Boulder, CO: Lynne Rienner, 1995). Nonetheless, all approaches shared a basic normative assumption that liberalization was the appropriate and desired goal of policy.

25. This link is explicitly made by one of the most oft-cited measures of "democracy" in the Arab world—the rankings provided annually by the think tank Freedom House (FH). Although FH rankings are almost always mentioned in the literature on "democracy," the methodological basis of these rankings is rarely questioned by those who cite them. A key measure used by FH to rank a country's "freedom" is the presence of state control over industrial sectors, trade, and prices. This is codified in the question, "Does the government exert tight control over the economy, including through state ownership and the setting of prices and production quotas?" as one of its measures of democratic practice: www.freedomhouse.org/report/freedom-world-2011/checklist-questions-and-guidelines.

26. "President Bush Discusses Importance of Democracy in Middle East—Remarks by the President on Winston Churchill and the War on Terror," Library of Congress, Washington, DC, February 4, 2004. http://merln.ndu.edu/archivepdf/nss/WH/20040204-4.pdf.

27. See Adam Hanieh, "'Democracy Promotion' and Neo-Liberalism in the Middle East," *State of Nature* 3 (Spring 2006), www.stateofnature.org/democracyPromotion.html, for a detailed discussion of this orientation in the case of Iraq and the wider Middle East.

28. This argument does not mean that international financial institutions did not see the capitalist state as *necessary* for the development of market conditions. In the late 1990s and through the 2000s, in particular, there was a renewed emphasis on the state's role in strengthening markets—codified most notably in the World Bank's 1997 World Development Report. The 1997 WDR called for "bringing the state back in" and utilizing the state to create an "enabling environment" for the growth of the private sector. Western governments and international financial institutions began to use notions such as good governance, decentralization, and accountability—terms that will be discussed in further detail later in the book. The underlying logic, however, would remain the same—providing the conditions for capitalist growth was the key function of the state and Middle East authoritarianism blocked the development of markets. Moreover, the basic conceptual division between state and civil society ran through all these perspectives.

29. White House Office of the Press Secretary, Remarks by the President on the Middle East and North Africa, May 19, 2011, www.whitehouse.gov/the-press-office/2011/05/19/remarks-president-middle-east-and-north-africa.

30. Zoellick's comments are discussed further in chapter 7.

31. The literature on this is of course vast. See Simon Clarke, *Marx, Marginalism and Modern Sociology* (London: Macmillan, 1991), 97–110, for an excellent discussion of Marx's conception of class in contrast to standard sociological approaches.

32. This is the basis of Marx's labor theory of value. See Alfredo Saad-Filho, "Value, Capital and Exploitation," in *Anti-Capitalism: A Marxist Introduction* (London: Pluto Press, 2003), 27–41, for a concise introduction; Clarke, *Marx, Marginalism and Modern Sociology*, especially chapter 4; Anwar Shaikh and Ahmet Tonak, *Measuring the Wealth of Nations* (Cambridge: Cambridge University Press, 1994).

33. Karl Marx, *Grundrisse* (Harmondsworth: Penguin, 1973), 176.

34. See Theodore Allen, *The Invention of the White Race: Racial Oppression and Social Control* (New York: Verso, 1994) for an illustration of this approach in regards to race in the United States.

35. David Harvey, *The Limits to Capital* (London: Verso, 1999); Doreen Massey, *Spatial Divisions of Labour: Social Structures and the Geography of Production* (London: MacMillan Education, 1984).

36. Karl Marx, *Capital*, vol. 1 (Harmondsworth: Penguin, 1976), 272.

37. Jairus Banaji, *Theory as History: Essays on Mode of Production and Exploitation* (Leiden: Brill, 2010), 154.

38. Ellen Meiksins Wood, *Democracy against Capitalism* (Cambridge: Cambridge University Press, 1995), 244.

39. Ibid., 245.

40. Neil Davidson, "The Necessity of Multiple Nation-States for Capital," *Rethinking Marxism: A Journal of Economics, Culture & Society*, 24, no.1 (2012): 27.

41. Bertell Ollman, *Dance of the Dialectic: Steps in Marx's Method* (Urbana, IL: University of Illinois Press, 2003), 202.

42. Ibid.

43. Davidson, "The Necessity of Multiple Nation-States for Capital," 28.

44. Joachim Hirsch, "The State Apparatus and Social Reproduction: Elements of a Theory of the Bourgeois State," in *State and Capital: A Marxist Debate*, eds. John Holloway and Sol Picciotto (London: Edward Arnold, 1979), 58.

45. Greg Albo, "Contesting the 'New Capitalism,'" in *Varieties of Capitalism, Varieties of Approaches*, ed. D. Coates (New York: Palgrave Macmillan, 2005), 74. These approaches to the state are typically inspired by Max Weber, the German sociologist whose approach to social science emphasized the construction of "ideal types"—of the state, bureaucracy, and so forth—to which actually existing forms could be compared and measured.

46. Marx, *Grundrisse*, 539.

47. Christian Palloix, "Conceptualizing the Internationalization of Capital," *Review of Radical Political Economics* (1977): 9, 20.

48. Greg Albo, "Contemporary Capitalism," in *Elgar Companion to Marxist Economics*, eds. Ben Fine and Alfredo Saad-Filho (London: Elgar, 2012), 86.

49. Leo Panitch and Sam Gindin, "Finance and American Empire," in *Socialist Register 2005: The Empire Reloaded*, eds. L. Panitch and C. Leys (London: Merlin Press, 2004), 64.

50. Greg Albo, "The Old and New Economics of Imperialism," in *Socialist Register 2004: The New Imperial Challenge*, eds. C. Leys and L. Panitch (London: Merlin Press, 2003), 91.

51. Ibid., 94.

52. Leo Panitch and Sam Gindin, "Global Capitalism and American Empire," in *Socialist Register 2004: The New Imperial Challenge*, eds. C. Leys and L. Panitch (London: Merlin Press, 2003), 17. A similar argument is offered by Ellen Meiksins Wood, who has emphasized that "Global capital is served . . . by a global system of multiple territorial states." Ellen Meiksins Wood, "Logics of Power: A Conversation with David Harvey," *Historical Materialism* 14, no. 4 (2006): 12.

53. Andreas Wimmer and Nina Glick Schiller, "Methodological Nationalism and Beyond: Nation-State Building, Migration and the Social Sciences," *Global Networks* 2, no. 4 (2002): 301-334.

54. Marcel van der Linden, *Workers of the World: Essays in Global Labor History* (Leiden: Brill, 2008), 7.

55. Ibid. The existence (and persistence) of the states system within global capitalism is the subject of an important and interesting debate among Marxists, but one beyond the scope of this book. A useful contribution to this debate has recently been made by Neil Davidson (2012), who argues that this system should be seen as neither a historically contingency nor the result of a fusion of separate logics of capital and territory. In contrast to these two widely held positions, Davidson puts forth the perspective that the state system is an inescapable product of competitive accumulation between capitals. In particular, he emphasizes the role of nation-states in generating an ideology of nationalism that can be used to tie working-class interests to the state and hence to capital. Many thanks to Jeff Webber for pointing me to this article.

56. Nicos Poulantzas, *Classes in Contemporary Capitalism* (London: New Left Books, 1979).

57. Ibid., 46–47.

58. Sabahi received a particularly strong showing in working-class urban areas. It was widely alleged

that the results were tampered with in order to edge him out of the second-round run-off. For further description of the election, please see chapter 7, note 99.

59. Hamdeen Sabahi, *al-barnamaj al-intikhabi* [Electoral Program], http://hamdeensabahy.com.

60. Ibid.

61. Nikolai Bukharin, *Imperialism and World Economy* (London: Merlin Press, 1972), 41.

62. Albo, "The Old and New Economics of Imperialism," 90.

63. The concept of combined and uneven development originated with Leon Trotsky, and was then developed by a range of authors including Ernest Mandel and Michael Lowy. For an interesting contemporary view of this issue, see Alex Callinicos and Justin Rosenberg, "Uneven and Combined Development: The Social-Relational Substratum of 'the International'? An Exchange of Letters," *Cambridge Review of International Affairs* 21, no. 1 (2008): 77–112.

64. Alex Callinicos, "Iraq: Fulcrum of World Politics," *Third World Quarterly* 26, nos. 4–5 (2005): 599.

65. See Alfredo Saad-Filho, and Deborah Johnston, *Neoliberalism: A Critical Reader* (London: Pluto Press, 1995).

66. David Harvey, *A Brief History of Neoliberalism* (Oxford: Oxford University Press, 2005), 19.

67. Adam Hanieh, *Capitalism and Class in the Gulf Arab States* (New York: Palgrave-Macmillan, 2011), 87–90.

68. The phrase "Middle East" has been widely noted for its Eurocentrism in that it automatically sets the frame of reference as Europe (indeed, it was first coined by a British military officer). The term "Arab world" is also problematic, however, given the widespread presence of non-Arab populations throughout all states of the region.

Chapter 2: Framing the Region

1. Nigel Grimwade, *International Trade: New Patterns of Trade, Production, and Investment* (New York: Routledge, 2000), 119.

2. The petrochemical industry depended upon petroleum and natural gas as the primary feedstock, in contrast to prewar production, which had utilized coal. See Peter Spitz, *Petrochemicals: The Rise of an Industry* (New York: John Wiley, 1988) and Keith Chapman, *The International Petrochemical Industry: Evolution and Location* (Oxford: Blackwell, 1991), for detailed histories.

3. Simon Bromley, *American Hegemony and World Oil: The Industry, the State System and the World Economy* (Cambridge: Polity Press, 1991), 82.

4. Hanson Baldwin, "Oil Strategy in World War II," *American Petroleum Institute Quarterly—Centennial Issue* (Washington, DC: American Petroleum Institute, 1959).

5. United States Department of State, *Foreign Relations of the United States: Diplomatic Papers 1945: Vol. 8, The Near East and Africa* (Washington, DC: Government Printing Office, 1945), 45. http://bit.ly/9z8FFF.

6. See Adam Hanieh, *Capitalism and Class in the Gulf Arab States* (New York: Palgrave-Macmillan 2011), chapter 2, for further discussion of this period.

7. Joe Stork, "The Carter Doctrine and US Bases in the Middle East," *MERIP Reports*, no. 90 (September 1980) 14.

8. Ervand Abrahamian, "The 1953 Coup in Iran," *Science and Society* 65, no. 2 (Summer 2001).

9. For accounts of Nasserism and this early period, see Mahmoud Abdul-Fadil, *The Political Economy of Nasserism: A Study in Employment and Income Distribution Policies in Urban Egypt, 1952–72* (Cambridge: Cambridge University Press, 1980); Ahmed Abdalla, *The Student Movement and National Politics in Egypt, 1923–1973* (London: al-Saqi, 1985); Joel Beinin, *Was the Red Flag Flying There? Marxist Politics and the Arab-Israeli Conflict in Egypt and Israel, 1948–1965* (Berkeley, CA: University

of California Press, 1990); Selma Botman, *The Rise of Egyptian Communism, 1939–1970* (Syracuse, NY: Syracuse University Press, 1988); Robert Vitalis, *When Capitalists Collide: Business Conflict and the End of Empire in Egypt* (Berkeley, CA: University of California Press, 1995).

10. Dwight Eisenhower, "Special Message to the Congress on the Situation in the Middle East," January 5, 1957. Online by Gerhard Peters and John T. Woolley, *The American Presidency Project.* www.presidency.ucsb.edu/ws/index.php?pid=11007.

11. Ibid.

12. Lawrence Tal, "Britain and the Jordan Crisis of 1958," *Middle Eastern Studies* 31, no. 1 (January 1995), 39.

13. Ibid., 40.

14. Raymond Hinnebusch, *The International Politics of the Middle East* (Manchester and New York: Manchester University Press, 1988), 26.

15. The UAR eventually fell apart in 1961 following a military coup in Syria. Rivalries between Iraq and Egypt also emerged with the refusal of the former to join the UAR.

16. Tal, "Britain and the Jordan Crisis," 46.

17. In 1954, Bahrain was the site of the Gulf's first political party, the Higher Executive Committee, which demanded the expulsion of the British political resident, Charles Belgrave. Demonstrators met a visit of the British foreign secretary, Selwyn Lloyd, in 1956, by stoning his car and chanting anticolonial slogans. See Simon Smith, *Britain's Revival and Fall in the Gulf: Kuwait, Bahrain, Qatar, and the Trucial States, 1950–71* (London: Routledge, 2004), 9. Later that year, workers at the Bahrain Petroleum Company agitated for the right to form unions. Britain aided the al-Khalifa monarchy in suppressing these protests by, among other actions, supplying helicopters to drop tear gas and identify demonstrators (Smith, *Britain's Revival,* 22).

18. Emile Nakhleh, *Bahrain: Political Development in a Modernizing Society* (Lexington, MA: Lexington Books, 1976), 79. Several protesters were killed during the uprising, and the government instituted the 1965 Law of Public Security, which essentially gave it a free hand to issue any order deemed necessary for "security." Notwithstanding the repression, ongoing strikes and demonstrations meant that Bahrain was the site of the most sustained and powerful protests against British rule in the Gulf.

19. Fred Halliday, *Arabia Without Sultans* (London: Saqi Books, 2001).

20. Abdel Razzaq Takriti, *Monsoon Revolution: Republicans, Sultans, and Empires in Oman, 1965–76* (Oxford: Oxford University Press, 2012).

21. It is beyond the scope of this book to provide a full account of Arab nationalism. Interested readers are referred to Halim Barakat, *The Arab World: Society, Culture, and State* (Berkeley, CA: University of California Press, 1993) for a useful overview.

22. This point is made particularly forcefully in Samir Amin's important book *Fi Naqd al-Khitab al-Arabi al-Rahen* [A Critique of the Current Arab Discourse] (Cairo: el-Ain, 2010).

23. Adib Nassur, *Al-Naksa wal-khata'* (Beirut: Dar al-katib al-'arabi, n.d.).

24. Cited in Abbas Alnasrawi, *Arab Nationalism, Oil, and the Political Economy of Dependency* (Westport, CT: Greenwood Publishing Group, 1991), 40. Another important Syrian philosopher, George Tarabishi, has criticized Arab nationalism for overemphasizing unity without seriously considering the reality of *qutriyya* (the division of the Arab world into separate nation states); George Tarabisbi, *Al-Dawlah al-qutriyya wa al-nazariyyah al-qawmiyya* [The Regional State and the Nationalist Theory] (Beirut: Dar al-Tali'a, 1982), 8–10.

25. Gamal Abdul Nasser, *Falsafat al-thawrah* [Philosophy of the Revolution] (Beirut: Dar al-Qalam, 1970), 183–184.

26. For an excellent account of this process in relation to the Egyptian student movement, see Ahmed

Abdalla, *The Student Movement and National Politics in Egypt* (London: Saqi Books, 1985).

27. Gilbert Achcar, *Clash of Barbarisms: September 11 and the Making of the New World Disorder* (New York: Monthly Review Press, 2002).

28. Alexei Vassiliev, *The History of Saudi Arabia* (London: Saqi Books, 1998), 386.

29. US Senate, *Senate Documents*, 1966, 89th Congress, Issue 12716–1, 234.

30. Abrahamian, "The 1953 Coup in Iran."

31. Joe Stork, "US Strategy in the Gulf," *MERIP Reports*, no. 36 (April 1975), 19.

32. Ibid.

33. Iranian troops supported British intervention in Dhofar and were supplied with US helicopters and other weaponry. By 1976, the Dhofar rebellion had been crushed.

34. Stork, "US Strategy," 20.

35. Ilan Pappé, *The Ethnic Cleansing of Palestine* (London: Oneworld Publications, 2006).

36. See Tikva Honig-Parnass, *False Prophets of Peace: Liberal Zionism and the Struggle for Palestine* (Chicago: Haymarket Books, 2011), and Moshe Machover, *Israelis and Palestinians: Conflict and Resolution* (Chicago: Haymarket Books, 2012), for two recent books that analyze the role of Israel in the region from a Marxist perspective.

37. In the region, Iran (up until its 1979 revolution) was the main ally of Israel.

38. It also has a profound impact on the evolution of the Palestinian wing of the Arab nationalist movement. Suhair Salti al-Tal, *Harakat al- qawmiyeen al- Arab wa in itafatha al-fikriyah* [The Arab Nationalist Movement and Its Ideological Twists] (Beirut: Center for Arab Studies, 1996) discusses the different trends within the Palestinian movement, notably its conception of the "petit-bourgeoisie" in the Arab world, which attempted to make a distinction between the Palestinian petit-bourgeoisie and the wider Arab ruling classes (see pages 196–199).

39. Southern Yemen became independent as the People's Republic of South Yemen on November 30, 1967. In June 1969, a left-wing faction of the country's National Liberation Front gained control and renamed the country as the People's Democratic Republic of Yemen in 1970.

40. The defeat in 1967 had a contradictory effect on nationalist thought. Most significantly, it contributed to the rise of the Palestinian struggle, which moved away from a reliance on Arab regimes toward a strategy of national liberation based on Palestinians themselves. This was symbolized by the coming to power of Yasser Arafat and his Fatah faction as the leader of the Palestine Liberation Organization (PLO). The evolution of the PLO and the Palestinian struggle is discussed in further detail in chapter 5.

41. The centrality of aid and debt has continued through to the contemporary era and bears important implications for assessing Western responses to the contemporary situation—as later chapters will discuss in some detail.

42. US legislation required food to be sourced, packaged, and shipped by US producers, even if cheaper alternatives were available. These policies were an important feature of the rise of US agribusiness companies linked to the grain industry, notably ADM, Cargill, and Bunge.

43. William Joseph Burns, *Economic Aid and American Policy Toward Egypt, 1955–1981* (Albany, NY: SUNY Press, 1985), 126.

44. Cited in Burns, *Economic Aid*, 127.

45. Ibid.

46. Calculated by author from FAO statistics. Timothy Mitchell convincingly demonstrates that the increase in imports was not a consequence of population growth (domestic production generally rose at a faster rate than population over these two decades) nor of improved caloric intake for the majority of the population, noting that a "1988 survey found that 29 percent of [Egyptian] children suffered from mild undernutrition and another 31 percent from moderate or severe undernutri-

tion. Between 1978 and 1986 the prevalence of acute undernutrition may have more than doubled" (Timothy Mitchell, *Rule of Experts: Egypt, Techno-Politics, Modernity* [Berkeley, CA: University of California Press, 2002], 214). Moreover, growing cereal imports corresponded with a dietary change toward meat consumption, which was a reflection of the widening divide between rich and poor in Egyptian society—with Egypt's elite (and the country's tourists) consuming meat while the rest of the country experienced high levels of malnutrition. Changes in tenancy laws as a result of neoliberalism further encouraged this shift, as the larger farms that consolidated in the wake of the new regulations switched to the more profitable production of meat (see chapter 3).

47. From 1970 to 1979, wheat imports made up on average, 42 percent of domestic supply in Algeria, 33.5 percent in Morocco, and 32.4 percent in Tunisia. Over the following decade, this dependency would rise to 54.4 percent in Algeria, 43.5 percent in Morocco, and 49.8 percent in Tunisia. Average for 1980–89 calculated by author from FAO statistics.

48. Joe Stork, "Bailing out Sadat," *MERIP Reports*, no. 56 (April 1977), 9.

49. Ibid.

50. Volcker's decision to raise interest rates to double-digit figures was a key moment of consolidation of the neoliberal program—aimed at halting US inflation by precipitating a recession, thereby increasing unemployment and lowering wage levels. Concurrently, the Volcker Shock helped to strengthen the position of the US dollar vis-à-vis other currencies, as capital was attracted to the United States in search of high returns.

51. Jeremy M. Sharp, *Egypt: Background and U.S. Relations*, Congressional Research Service, September 13, 2012, 9. www.fas.org/sgp/crs/mideast/RL33003.pdf.

52. Ibid., 8. This military aid not only confirmed Egypt's paramount position in the projection of US power across the region but also acted to consolidate the strength of the military within the Egyptian state. Aid was also a form of Keynesian support for the US military industry, as funds were required to be spent on US hardware and support services. Through this period, US food aid also continued. The so-called largest flour sale in history, for example, saw the US government provide 30 million bushels of free wheat to US millers in 1983, who then sold around 1 million metric tons of flour to Egypt at an extremely low price (Bruce Gardner, "The Political Economy of US Export Subsidies for Wheat," in *The Political Economy of American Trade Policy*, ed. Anne O. Krueger [Chicago: University of Chicago Press, 1996], 304).

53. Mohammed Heikal, *The Sphinx and the Commissar* (New York: Harper and Row, 1978), 262.

54. Energy Information Authority, www.eia.gov.

55. The United States had encouraged the long-brewing conflict between Iraq and Iran, seeing war between the two states as an effective means to prevent either country from emerging as a challenger to US power.

56. Justin Alexander and Colin Rowat, "A Clean Slate in Iraq: From Debt to Development," *Middle East Report* 228 (Autumn 2003): 33.

57. Ibid.

58. Hussein also pointed to the fact that Kuwait itself had previously been a province of Ottoman-era Iraq, becoming an independent principality in the wake of World War I as Britain and France redrew borders in the region.

59. In 1972, American and British oil companies had been expelled from the country after the nationalization of the country's oil resources.

60. The war had further far-reaching implications for the politics of the region. It provided the pretext for the expulsion of much of the Arab migrant working population in the Gulf, which had important implications for the Gulf's class structure (see chapter 6). It also laid the basis for the political and economic isolation of the PLO, which supported Iraq during the attack. This weak-

ness made it more difficult for the Palestinian movement to resist the signing of the Oslo Accords in the early 1990s (see chapter 5).

61. A 1999 UNICEF study noted, "If the substantial reduction in child mortality throughout Iraq during the 1980s had continued through the 1990s, there would have been half a million fewer deaths of children under five in the country as a whole during the eight year period 1991 to 1998." UNICEF, "Iraq Surveys Show 'Humanitarian Emergency,'" August 12, 1999. www.unicef.org/newsline/99pr29.htm.

62. Jane Harrigan, Chengang Wang, and Hamed El-Said, "The Politics of IMF and World Bank Lending: Will It Backfire in the Middle East and North Africa?" in *The IMF, World Bank and Policy Reform*, eds. Alberto Paloni and Maurizio Zanardi (London and New York: Routledge, 2006), 79.

63. Ibid.

64. In 2010, just under half of all Israeli exports (excluding diamonds) were considered "'high tech." See Helen Brusilovsky and Natalia Gitelson, *Israel's Foreign Trade 2000–2010* (Jerusalem and Tel Aviv: Israel Central Bureau of Statistics, 2011), 5.

65. Hashemite Kingdom of Jordan, Foreign Ministry, Middle East and North African Summits, at www.mfa.gov.jo.

66. Waleed Hazbun, *Beaches, Ruins, Resorts: The Politics of Tourism in the Arab World* (Minneapolis, MN: University of Minnesota Press, 2008), 116.

67. Israel Ministry of Foreign Affairs, www.mfa.gov.il.

68. Ibid.

69. US Embassy of Israel, Text of Cairo Conference Declaration, November 14, 1996. www.usembassy-israel.org.il/publish/press/summit/es11115.htm.

70. Office of the United States Trade Representative (OUSTRA), Trade Policy Agenda, Section III, 2007, 5.

71. Barbara Kotschwar and Jeffrey J. Schott, *Reengaging Egypt: Options for US-Egypt Economic Relations* (Washington, DC: Peterson Institute for International Economics, 2010), 20.

72. Ibid.

73. In October 1998, US president Bill Clinton had openly called for "regime change" in Iraq with the signing of the so-called Iraq Liberation Act. In December of the same year he launched a four-day bombing campaign, Operation Desert Fox, with further attacks launched throughout 1999. These moves accelerated with the election of George W. Bush in 2000. According to the memoirs of former Bush treasury secretary Paul O'Neill, the first meeting of the National Security Council after Bush's election was headlined with a discussion of Iraq. At the January 30 meeting, defense secretary Donald Rumsfeld was reported to have said, "Imagine what the region would look like without Saddam and with a regime that's aligned with U.S. interests. . . . It would change everything in the region and beyond. It would demonstrate what U.S. policy is all about," cited in Ron Suskind, *The Price of Loyalty* (New York: Simon & Schuster, 2004), 85. The events of September 11, 2001, were to provide the official justification for bringing these plans to fruition. Despite later admissions that the evidence linking Iraq with the attacks and with weapons of mass destruction was fabricated, the United States used the opportunity to launch an invasion in 2003 in an attempt to finish the war that it had begun in January 1991. The US-led forces destroyed the country's political and social fabric and quickly passed a series of laws that opened the economy to foreign ownership. The war against Iraq had been preceded by the US-NATO invasion of Afghanistan in 2001, confirming the extreme significance of the entire geographical arc surrounding the Gulf states.

74. Robert Zoellick, "Global Trade and the Middle East: Reawakening a Vibrant Past," Remarks at the World Economic Forum, Amman, Jordan, June 23, 2003. www.usinfo.state.gov.

75. Ibid.

76. Zoellick said, "We could start to combine [FTAs], for example, we look towards the possibility of countries in the Gulf perhaps joining into the Bahrain Free Trade Agreement, making specialized arrangements for their goods and agriculture but following the basic rules, and that would have a benefit of encouraging regional integration, so that their products to qualify would not have just to come from Bahrain, but may come from Qatar or Oman or from UAE or a combination of that. So we can encourage regional integration in the process, whether in the Gulf, whether in the Maghreb or whether in other parts of the Arab world. And the ultimate goal, as the President said, would be to draw these into the Middle East Free Trade Area. That, of course, depends on the willingness of countries to undertake these reforms."

77. Robert Zoellick, "Our Credo: Free Trade and Competition," *Wall Street Journal*, July 10, 2003.

78. Brink Lindsey, "The Trade Front: Combating Terrorism with Open Markets," *Trade Policy Analysis*, no. 24 (August 5, 2003), 8.

79. Office of Trade Policy Analysis, Manufacturing and Services, International Trade Administration, "US Morocco Free Trade Agreement, Key Market Access Results and Benefits," November 2004. www.trade.gov. Accessed October 25, 2012.

80. Another major issue in the Morocco-US FTA was the restrictions it placed on Moroccan access to generic pharmaceuticals.

81. US Grains Council, "Global Update," January 6, 2006. http://thegrainsfoundation.org.

82. The text of the US-Bahrain FTA is available at www.fta.gov.bh.

83. Advisory Committee for Trade Policy and Negotiations (ACTPN), "The U.S.–Bahrain Free Trade Agreement (FTA)," July 14, 2004, www.ustr.gov.

84. In September 2005, the United States and Oman also agreed on the basic principles of an FTA and signed an agreement on January 19, 2006. In 2005, the United States began negotiations with its largest export market in the Middle East, the UAE, although these have yet to be concluded. Kuwait and Qatar have also expressed interest in obtaining an FTA with the United States. Kenneth Katzman, *The Persian Gulf States: Issues for U.S. Policy* (Washington, DC: Congressional Research Service, 2006), 28.

85. United States Census Bureau, "Trade in Goods with Israel," www.census.gov/foreign-trade/balance/c5081.html. Accessed October 20, 2012.

86. Saudi Arabia General Investment Authority (SAGIA), *Annual Report of FDI into Saudi Arabia 2010* (Riyadh: SAGIA, 2011), 3. www.sagia.gov.sa/PageFiles/4132/Annual_Report_FDI%20_SAUDI _ARABIA.pdf

87. There were three main reasons for Saudi Arabia's attraction of FDI during the 2000s: 1) the rise in oil prices from 1999 to 2008, which saw an expansion of the oil industry as well as other large-scale "mega projects"; 2) a change in the Foreign Investment Act in 2000, which considerably liberalized the environment for investment in the country by lifting prohibitions in a range of sectors (except for certain sectors that were given in a "negative list" designation), sped up the processing of investment licenses, gave equal rights to domestic and foreign investors, allowed 100 percent ownership of projects, and set corporate taxes to among the lowest in the world; and 3) the accession of Saudi Arabia to the WTO in 2005. These measures enabled a fivefold increase in FDI between 2005 and 2010 (SAGIA, *Annual Report*, 2).

88. ANIMA Investment Network, *Investments and Partnerships in MED Region, 2010* (Marseilles: ANIMA, 2011), 49–68.

89. EU-Mediterranean Partnership, *Barcelona Declaration*, 2005, 5. http://trade.ec.europa.eu/doclib/docs/2005/july/tradoc_124236.pdf.

90. Ibid., 5.

91. Ibid., 6.

92. Israel, Jordan, Morocco, Tunisia, Palestinian Authority, and Turkey between 1995 and 1997, and Egypt in 2004.

93. The term MEDA comes from the French, Mesures D'Accompagnement (accompanying measures).

94. The MEDA Programme.

95. European Commission, *The Barcelona Process, 5 Years On 1995–2000* (Luxemburg: The Office for Official Publications of the European Communities, 2000), 20.

96. Ibid., 22.

97. Ibid., 21.

98. Analysis for Economic Decisions (ADE), *Evaluation of Economic Co-operation between the European Commission and Mediterranean Countries*, Final Report, vol. 1 (Louvain-la-Neuve: ADE, November 2003), 24.

99. Ibid., 12.

100. Moreover, the ENP heavily emphasized the question of migration—with subsequent negotiations seeing an "externalization" of EU border control, through which Mediterranean countries took on a much more interventionist role in policing movement into the EU. This was particularly important given the coming into being of the Schengen Agreement, which essentially lifted internal border controls between EU countries. In this sense, European relationships with the Middle East thus became part of facilitating capitalist transformation within the EU itself.

101. Commission of the European Communities, *Communication from the Commission to the Council and the European Parliament: Wider Europe—Neighbourhood: A New Framework for Relations with our Eastern and Southern Neighbours* (Brussels: CEC, 2003), 8. http://ec.europa.eu/world/enp/pdf/com03_104_en.pdf.

102. European Commission, *Barcelona Process*, 16.

103. There are two types of cumulation—diagonal and bilateral. Bilateral cumulation allows EU-made inputs (e.g., a product produced in Germany) to be used in the production of EU-destined goods asembled in a particular EMP country (e.g., Egypt or Morocco). Under this rule, EU-made inputs are counted as originating in the exporting country for the purpose of qualifying under the trade preference program. Diagonal cumulation allows intermediary inputs from third countries that are not party to the FTA to be counted as being of domestic origin provided there is an FTA between the two cumulating countries. It thus can widen free trade areas by incorporating countries with established trade links.

104. European Commission, *Barcelona Process*, 5. The significance of this was seen in the Agadir Agreement, a free trade agreement signed in Rabat, Morocco, in February 2004, between Egypt, Jordan, Morocco, and Tunisia (Palestine joined in September 2011). The agreement came into force in March 2007 and meant that goods produced with inputs from any of the four countries could be treated as being from the same country for the purpose of export to the EU. The logic behind the Agadir Agreement was intended to more closely tie together productive activities (principally agriculture and textiles) across North Africa.

105. The discussion of the nature of these value transfers is beyond the scope of this book. Interested readers are referred to Anwar Shaikh, "Foreign Trade and the Law of Value—Part One," *Science and Society* 43 (1979): 281–302; Anwar Shaikh, "Foreign Trade and the Law of Value—Part Two," *Science and Society* 44 (1980): 27–57; and Ernest Mandel, *Late Capitalism* (London: Verso, 1983).

106. See appendix 3 for the data of FDI flows discussed in this paragraph.

107. See Gilbert Achcar, "The Strategic Triad: The United States, Russia, and China," *New Left Review* I/228 (March–April 1998): 91–126 for a discussion of these global rivalries. Achcar argues that

Russia and China's potential military weight is decisive within US calculations.

108. Chen Aizhu, "Despite Delays, China Seeks Full Iran Oil Volume for Third Month," *Reuters*, September 5, 2012.

109. Fred Weir, "Why Russia Is Willing to Sell Arms to Syria," *Christian Science Monitor*, January 19, 2012, www.csmonitor.com/World/Europe/2012/0119/Why-Russia-is-willing-to-sell-arms-to-Syria.

110. International Energy Agency, *World Energy Outlook* (Paris: OECD/IEA, 2007), 325.

111. *Saudi Gazette*, "Aramco: China Overtakes US as Largest Customer," April 6, 2010.

112. Nexant Chem Systems, *Outlook for the Petrochemical Industry: Good Times Ahead* (Buenos Aires: Instituto Petroquimico Argentino, 2004), 31.

113. The importance of unpacking these structures of ownership is indicated in the case of EMP countries that do manage to produce higher value-added goods for European markets—typically products such as cement, fertilizers, phosphates, and other chemicals (see appendix 2). While exports of these goods may be quite profitable, much of these profits often find their way back to Europe or further enrich domestic and regional elites because of the ownership structures that developed under neoliberalism.

Chapter 3: Mapping the Neoliberal Experience

1. The other major sectoral focus of neoliberal reform, agriculture, is not dealt with here but is discussed in detail in the following chapter.

2. The focus is on the period preceding the 2008 global economic crisis; the impact of this crisis on the region will be discussed more fully in chapter 7.

3. World Bank, *Trade, Investment, and Development in the Middle East and North Africa: Engaging with the World* (Washington, DC: World Bank, 2003), 19.

4. Ibid., 141.

5. Ibid., 4.

6. World Bank, *From Privilege to Competition: Unlocking Private-Led Growth in the Middle-East and North Africa* (Washington, DC: World Bank, 2009), 1.

7. World Bank, *Trade, Investment, and Development*, 23.

8. World Bank, *Bureaucrats in Business* (Washington, DC: World Bank, 1995), 45.

9. Kamal Shehadi, *Lessons in Privatization: Considerations for Arab States* (Geneva: United Nations Development Programme, January 2002), 17.

10. Tunisia was the first country to initiate a privatization program, in 1987, through the passage of Law 87–47, which established the institutional mechanisms for the process (the law was amended in 1989). Morocco followed the same path after the Royal Speech of April 8, 1988, which authorized the privatization process, and, in 1990, the Moroccan parliament passed a privatization law (no. 89–39). Egypt followed soon after with the launching of a privatization program in 1991 as part of a wider structural adjustment plan.

11. Privatization experiences in the GCC and elsewhere are taken up in subsequent chapters.

12. Calculated by author from the World Bank Privatization Database http://go.worldbank.org/W1ET8RG1Q0

13. Law 203 formally prevented mass layoffs from occurring after a firm was privatized, so from the perspective of potential buyers it was important that the shedding of workers preceded privatization itself.

14. Cited in John Waterbury, *Exposed to Innumerable Delusions: Public Enterprise and State Power in Egypt* (New York: Cambridge University Press, 1993), 142.

15. Edward L. Hudgins, *The Middendorf Plan's Strategy for Central America's Economic Growth* (Washington, DC: Heritage Foundation, 1987). www.policyarchive.org/handle/10207/bitstreams/12485.pdf.

16. USAID, *Private Enterprise Development*, Policy Paper (Washington, DC: Bureau for Program and Policy Coordination, USAID, March 1985), 15. A Commission on Privatization, initiated by US president Ronald Reagan in 1988, further recommended the use of employee stock ownership for "transferring state-owned enterprises to the private sector in developing countries."

17. USAID, *Manual for the Formation of an Employee Share Ownership Plan for the Alexandria Tire Company and Other Companies in Egypt* (Washington, DC: Center for Privatization, 1988), 40. http://pdf.usaid.gov/pdf_docs/pnabc466.pdf40.

18. Ibid., 1.

19. Ibid., 93.

20. Ibid., 4. Despite this optimistic scenario, workers repeatedly fought bitter strikes through the mid-1990s, particularly in the textile sector. Notable strikes occurred at Misr Fine Spinning and Weaving in 1994 and Misr Helwan Spinning and Weaving in 1998.

21. A full list is available at www.aucegypt.edu/src/wsite1/Pdfs/Privatization%20in%20Egypt%20-Quarterly%20Review.pdf.

22. Joel Beinin, "Egyptian Textile Workers: From Craft Artisans Facing European Competition to Proletarians Contending with the State," in *The Ashgate Companion to the History of Textile Workers, 1650–2000*, eds. Lex Heerma Van Voss, Els Hiemstra-Kuperus, and Elise Van Nederveen Meerkerk (Surrey/Burlington: Ashgate Publishing, 2010), 196.

23. International Monetary Fund (IMF), *Arab Republic of Egypt: 2006 Article IV Consultation—Staff Report, Public Information Note* (Washington, DC: IMF, 2006), 22.

24. Ibid., 8. The figure of a 50 percent drop in public sector workers is given in a report commissioned by USAID in 2002 (Carana Corporation, *Privatization in Egypt: Quarterly Review April–June 2002*, Report commissioned by USAID [Cairo: Privatization Coordination Support Unit, 2002], 10). The ILO statistical database records a fall from 1.13 million workers in public sector employment in 1994 to 678,100 in 2001 (http://laborsta.ilo.og).

25. Nadia Farah, *Egypt's Political Economy: Power Relations in Development* (Cairo: American University of Cairo Press), 50.

26. The World Bank wrote, for example, "Together with restrictions on dismissal, social protection costs force employers to reduce their labor costs by hiring fewer workers or by employing more workers on a temporary or illegal basis. Generous maternity leave provisions in the formal sector, which are required by many labor codes, further reduce female employment." World Bank, *Unlocking the Employment Potential in the Middle East and North Africa: Toward a New Social Contract* (Washington, DC: World Bank, 2004), 148.

27. World Bank, *Unlocking the Employment Potential*, 7.

28. Ibid., 6. These better conditions meant that "workers are attracted to such nonwage factors as job security, worker protections, and social allowances . . . as well as special provisions on work hours and maternity leave" (131).

29. Ibid., 7.

30. Ibid., 133.

31. World Bank, *Doing Business 2010: Comparing Regulation in 183 Economies* (Washington, DC: World Bank, 2011), vi.

32. In Egypt, where an interministerial committee utilized the *Doing Business* indicators to plan cuts to conditions, a 2003 law introduced indefinite temporary contracts and made it easier to hire and fire people. This was a watershed moment for Egyptian labor rights that increased the use of these contracts across the board. The singular importance of these issues was confirmed in the post-

2011 period, with workers in Egypt taking up the proliferation of temporary contracts as a central concern of strikes and other protest actions following the ousting of Mubarak (see chapter 7). Likewise, in Jordan, laws were passed that established no limits on the repeated use of fixed-term contracts and, even more generously, relieved companies from the requirement to pay severance in the case of dismissal. Notwithstanding these measures, however, the World Bank continued to recommend that the Jordanian government address "the burden of inefficient employment-related social safety net obligations borne by small and medium enterprises, and the market-distorting effects of the large public sector on wages and young people's employment expectations" (World Bank, *Country Assistance Strategy, Jordan* [Washington, DC: World Bank, 2011], 7). In Morocco, the IMF noted in 2001 that "labor market flexibility is essential for increasing the elasticity of employment" and welcomed the fact that a labor code was being discussed that would allow for a more "liberal system of hiring and labor shedding." (International Monetary Fund, *Morocco: 2001 Article IV Consultation*. Staff Report, IMF Country Report no. 01/205 [Washington, DC: IMF, 2001], 32.) Nevertheless, it recognized that the Moroccan government faced difficulties in implementing such a reform due to trade union opposition—negotiations for the labor code had indeed been ongoing for twenty years. In Morocco, a 2003 Labor Code permitted nonagricultural firms that were new (or producing a new product) to set up one-year contracts, which could be renewed once. In Tunisia, the IMF praised the government in both 2004 and 2006 for including a policy aimed at "relax[ing] firing restrictions" as one of four key elements within the Tunisian medium-term development strategy. (International Monetary Fund, *Tunisia: 2006 Article IV Consultation*. Staff Statement, IMF Country Report no. 06/207 [Washington, DC: IMF, 2006], 6.) The World Bank's Country Partnership Strategy (CPS) for 2009 specifically highlighted the role that the Bank would play in "support[ing] the reform of the labor market" so as to achieve "greater flexibility in hiring and firing" (World Bank, *Country Partnership Strategy for the Republic of Tunisia*. Report no. 50223-TUN [November 23, 2009], 30) One way this was to occur was through a Development Policy Loan, which would work with the Tunisian government (and the European Union) to develop new regulations that reduced labor rights within the public sector (Ibid., 30).

33. World Bank, *Loan Document for Economic Development Policy Loan* (Washington, DC: World Bank, May 26, 2010), 40–41. www.worldbank.org.

34. Emanuel Savas, *Privatization in the City* (Washington, DC: CQ Press, 2005), 16.

35. Edouard Perard, *Private Sector Participation and Regulatory Reform in Water Supply: The Middle East and North African (MEDA) Experience* (Milan: Fondazione Eni Enrico Mattei, 2007), 14. The main companies offering water services in the MENA region are SUEZ and Veolia. Of the thirty-three private water contracts in Algeria, Morocco, Egypt, Tunisia, Jordan, Syria, Lebanon, and the West Bank/Gaza between 1999 and 2006, twenty of them were won by either Suez or Veolia (Ibid., 26–27.)

36. *Daily Star*, "The Promises and Perils of Public Private Partnerships in Lebanon," November 17, 2011. www.albawaba.com/promises-and-perils-public-private-partnerships-401438.

37. European Investment Bank, *Study on PPP Legal & Financial Frameworks in the Mediterranean Partner Countries, Vol. 1—A Regional Approach* (Facility for Euro-Mediterranean Investment and Partnership, 2011), 14. www.eib.org/attachments/med/ppp-study-volume-1.pdf.

38. The European Investment Bank (EIB) acts through its financial arm, the Facility for Euro-Mediterranean Investment and Partnership (FEMIP). FEMIP focuses on nine Mediterranean countries—Algeria, Egypt, West Bank/Gaza, Israel, Jordan, Lebanon, Morocco, Syria, and Tunisia—and its main remit is encouraging "the modernisation and opening-up of the economies of the partner countries . . . focused on two priority areas: development of the private sector and the creation of an investment-friendly environment." To fulfill this aim, FEMIP has over €8.7 billion at its disposal to encourage the development of projects including PPPs (Ibid., 3).

www.eib.europa.eu/attachments/country/femip_ppp_2011_en.pdf.

39. World Bank, *Trade, Investment, and Development*, 4.

40. Ibid.

41. Ibid., 2.

42. Ibid., 124.

43. Morocco's simple average customs duty dropped from 33.4 percent in 2002 to 18.1 percent in 2010. Egypt, 26.8 percent in 1998 to 17 percent in 2009; Tunisia, 31 percent in 1994 to 16.5 percent in 2010; Jordan, 14.7 percent in 2000 to 10 percent in 2010. Source: WTO database.

44. In Egypt, the exceptions to this liberalization were the upstream oil and gas sector, for which joint ventures are required; in Jordan, investment in printing or publishing companies, or aircraft and maritime vessel maintenance, is limited to 50 percent ownership; in Morocco, no private investment—domestic or foreign—is permitted in phosphates, wholesale fruit and vegetable distribution, or water and electricity supplies (PPPs in distribution of these utilities have been permitted).

45. World Bank, *Trade, Investment, and Development*, 5.

46. Calculated by author from ILO data.

47. Amirah el-Haddad, *Effects of the Global Crisis on the Clothing Sector: A Blessing in Disguise?* (Geneva: ILO, 2010), 3.

48. Ibid.

49. Gladys Lopez-Acevedo and Raymond Robertson, *Sewing Success, Employment, Wages, and Poverty Following the End of the Multi-Fibre Arrangement* (Washington, DC: World Bank, 2012), 399; Albert Sales-i-Campos and Eloisa Pineiro-Orge, *Made in Morocco* (Barcelona: Network Wear, 2011), 8, www.achact.be/upload/files/MadeinMaroc_rapport_ENGL.pdf.

50. World Bank, *Morocco, Tunisia, Egypt and Jordan after the End of the Multi-Fiber Agreement: Impact, Challenges and Prospects* (Washington, DC: World Bank, 2006), vii.

51. Ibid., 27.

52. World Bank, *Trade, Investment, and Development*, 62.

53. Ibid., 55, 64.

54. Maye Ehab, "Labor Market Flexibility in Egypt: With Application to the Textiles and Apparel Industry," Working Paper no. 170, Egyptian Centre for Economic Studies, June 2012, 9.

55. ILO, *Tunisia: A New Social Contract for Fair and Equitable Growth* (Geneva: International Institute for Labour Studies, 2011), 45.

56. Sales-i-Campos and Pineiro-Orge, *Made in Morocco*, 10.

57. US Department of State, *Trafficking in Persons Report 2010* (Washington, DC: State Department, 2010), 191.

58. General Authority for Investment, "Invest in Egypt: Textiles and Ready Made Garments," 2010, 3, www.gafinet.org/English/SectorsValuePreposition/Textiles%20value%20proposition-2010.pdf.

59. Calculated by author from CAPMAS (2008) and ILO data (2000).

60. Megan Detrie, "Will Renationalisations Transform Egypt's Textile Sector?" *Just Style*, October 21, 2011, www.just-style.com/analysis/will-renationalisations-transform-egypts-textile-sector_id112514.aspx.

61. el-Haddad, *Effects of the Global Crisis*, 26.

62. A good example of this is the Arabia Cotton Ginning Company (ACGC), which is the largest textile firm by market value in Egypt and produces about 25 percent of the country's cotton. A Saudi private equity company, Amwal Al Khaleej, came to control ACGC after the company was privatized in 1995. In addition to producing cotton, manufacturing textiles and garments, and owning retail outlets, the company also owns a major stake in a flour mill, Upper Egypt Flour Mills (privatized in 2008).

ACGC had been state owned and was privatized in 1995 (see chapter 6 for further discussion).

63. Calculated by author from World Bank Data Set.

64. Amr Ismail Adly, "Politically-Embedded Cronyism: The Case of Post-Liberalization Egypt," *Business and Politics* 11, no. 4 (2009), 11.

65. Ibid., 12.

66. Subika Farazi, Erik Feyen, and Roberto Rocha, "Bank Ownership and Performance in the Middle East and North Africa Region," World Bank Policy Research Working Paper, No. 5620, 2011, 35.

67. Stijn Claessens and Neeltje Van Horen, "Foreign Banks: Trends, Impact and Financial Stability," International Monetary Fund Working Paper no. 12/10, January 2012, 30.

68. Ibid., 33.

69. Nedal Ahmed Al-Fayoumi and Bana M. Abuzayed, "Assessment of the Jordanian Banking Sector within the Context of GATS Agreement," *Banks and Bank Systems* 4, no. 2 (2009): 71; Morocco figures are from 2006. Mehdi El Hajoui, Aviel Marrache, Roman Rosenberg, and Kelly Spriggs, *Morocco* (Philadelphia: Wharton School Financial Institutions Center, University of Pennsylvania), 3.

70. Mehdi El Hajoui, Aviel Marrache, and Susan Keppelman, *Tunisia* (Philadelphia: Wharton School Financial Institutions Center, University of Pennsylvania), 4.

71. Egyptian British Chamber of Commerce, *Report on Banking Reform in Egypt*, 2008.

72. Al-Fayoumi and Abuzayed, "Assessment of the Jordanian Banking Sector," 71; El Hajoui, Marrache, Rosenberg, and Spriggs, *Morocco*, 3.

73. Abdelali Jbili, Klaus Enders, and Volker Treichel, "Financial Sector Reforms in Algeria, Morocco and Tunisia: A Preliminary Assessment," IMF Working Paper WP/97/81, 1997, 9.

74. Egyptian Stock Exchange, *Annual Report 2005* and *Annual Report 2010*.

75. Tunisia Stock Exchange, *Annual Report 2010*, 24.

76. Amman Stock Exchange, *Annual Report 2007*, 79; Oxford Business Group, *The Report: Emerging Morocco, 2007* (Oxford: Oxford Business Group, 2007), 77.

77. Roberto Roccu, "Gramsci in Cairo: Neoliberal Authoritarianism, Passive Revolution and Failed Hegemony in Egypt under Mubarak, 1991-2010," PhD thesis, Department of International Relations of the London School of Economics, January 2012, 146.

78. An IPO is a process whereby a company is listed on the stock market, opening shareholdership to a wider audience.

79. Jamal Saghir, "Privatization in Tunisia," *World Bank Cofinancing and Financial Advisory Services Discussion Paper Series*, no. 101 (1993): 10.

80. World Bank, *Unlocking the Employment Potential*, xvii.

81. Saghir, *Privatization in Tunisia*, 10.

82. The committee also included a handful of government ministers and a representative from the Central Bank.

83. Saghir, *Privatization in Tunisia*, i.

84. Ibid., 25.

85. Waniss Otman and Erling Karlber, *The Libyan Economy: Economic Diversification and International Repositioning* (Berlin: Springer Books, 2007), 200.

86. Saghir, *Privatization in Tunisia*, 20.

87. World Bank, *Report and Recommendation on Proposed Public Enterprise Loan to the Republic of Tunisia*, P-5055-N (Washington, DC: World Bank, June 12, 1989), 18.

88. Saghir, *Privatization in Tunisia*, 14.

89. Andrea Goldstein, "The Political Economy of Regulatory Reform: Telecoms in the Southern Mediterranean," Working Paper no. 216, OECD Development Centre, November 2003, 23.

90. In Egypt, for example, the World Bank has praised a particular scheme in the Qena governorate where "local administrations have negotiated the bureaucratic and legal space to tackle local development issues in a more flexible manner . . . health care workers can draw supplemental income from funds generated by co-payments on health services imposed under the authority of the local Executive Council, leading to improved morale and better staffing and utilization of health care facilities" (World Bank, *Country Assistance Strategy for the Republic of Egypt*, World Bank Report No. 32190-EG [Washington, DC: World Bank, 2005], 15). In other words, user fees could be implemented by the local government level as a result of the decentralization of the health sector.

91. International Monetary Fund, "Letter of Intent and Memorandum of Economic and Financial Policies from the Jordanian Government to the IMF," June 15, 2004. www.imf.org.

92. Abdel-Mawla Ismail, "Drinking Water Protests in Egypt and the Role of Civil Society," Transnational Institute, July 17, 2012, www.tni.org/article/drinking-water-protests. Accessed September 8, 2012.

93. OECD, *Progress in Public Management in the Middle East and North Africa: Case Studies on Policy Reform* (Paris: OECD, 2010), 288.

94. Ismail, "Drinking Water Protests."

95. Jordan, Egypt, and Morocco figures calculated by author from Ministry of Finance data; Tunisia from African Development Bank, *African Economic Outlook 2012* (Tunis-Belvedere: ADB, 2012), 6.

96. Akhter Ahmed, Howarth Bouis, Tamar Gutner, and Hans Löfgren, *The Egyptian Food Subsidy System: Structure, Performance, and Options for Reform*, Research Report 119 (Washington, DC: International Food Policy Research Institute, 2001), xi.

97. A cheaper bread baked with corn in addition to wheat that is a mainstay of diet for poorer Egyptians.

98. Ahmed, Bouis, Gutner, and Löfgren, *The Egyptian Food Subsidy System*, 9.

99. Farrukh Iqbal, *Sustaining Gains in Poverty Reduction and Human Development in the Middle East and North Africa* (Washington, DC: World Bank, 2006), 58.

100. Some of these subsidies were partially restored in the mid-2000s in response to social discontent from rising food prices, particularly following the global economic crisis in 2008. With the exception of Jordan, where subsidies dropped from 18.9 percent of government expenditure in 2005 to 3.9 percent in 2009, levels remained relatively high through to the end of the decade. Of particular note was Egypt, where government spending on food and fuel subsidies far exceeds that of any other country in the region—reaching 31 percent of current government expenditures in 2008. Despite these high rates, however, care needs to be taken in interpreting who benefits from these subsidies and what they mean for the nature of state expenditure. In the first place, 65 percent of Egypt's expenditures on subsidies are used for fuel, and the vast majority of this goes toward the energy consumption of large industries such as steel, cement, and fertilizer plants, rather than the household needs of poor Egyptian families. Thus, much of the high government expenditure on subsidies in Egypt actually reflects a transfer of wealth to the rich—not support for the poor. Moreover, increased expenditure on food subsidies is often a by-product of inflation of nonsubsidized foods. One example of this could be seen in early 2008, following a 37 percent annual increase in the price of nonsubsidized bread. Because of this price increase, many more people turned to the poorer-quality, subsidized baladi bread, and the length of bread lines grew—at least ten people died in the first two weeks of March 2008 from either exhaustion or the outbreak of fights as they waited in line. In this case, greater expenditures on subsidies did not indicate wider provision of food to the poor but were actually reflective of greater levels of immiseration in the broader population.

101. Calculated by author from central government budget statistics. These figures include spending on public security, taken from budget statements. It should be noted that the Egyptian trend is

often misstated in this regard, because analysts tend to only include "military" expenditure, which is around 5 percent of total government expenditure, while ignoring the internal security component of expenditure.

102. A VAT is an example of a regressive tax. It does not differentiate on the basis of wealth and the poor typically spend a greater share of their income on consumption goods.

103. USAID, *USAID Assistance in Fiscal Reform: Comprehensive Tax Reform in Egypt*, Project Document (Washington, DC: USAID, June 2006), 5.

104. Ibid., 6.

105. Egypt British Chamber of Commerce, "Tax Policies in Egypt," May 2010, www.theebcc.com.

106. Fredrika Cruce, *Evaluating Value Added Tax in Morocco*, Minor Field Study Series no. 209 (Lund, Sweden: Lund University, 2010), 39. www.nek.lu.se/Publ/mfs/209.pdf.

107. John A. Tatom, "Is Tax Policy Retarding Growth in Morocco?," Networks Financial Institute, Indiana State University, Working Paper no. 27, November 2007, 2.

108. In Jordan corporate tax rates dropped from 25 percent in 2005 to 14 percent in 2010; in Tunisia they fell from 35 percent to 30 percent over the same period.

109. Catiana Garcia-Kilroy and Anderson Caputo Silva, *Reforming Government Debt Markets in MENA*, Policy Research Working Paper, no. 5611 (Washington, DC: World Bank, March 2011), 9. The "debt to GDP" ratios in 2009 were: Egypt (73 percent), Jordan (65 percent), Morocco (47 percent), and Tunisia (47 percent). Lebanon is the other important country in this regard, with a 160 percent debt/GDP ratio.

110. International Monetary Fund, *Government Finance Statistics* (Washington, DC: IMF, July 2012). The expenditures on education, health, and food subsidies were 5.7 percent, 2.0 percent, and 12.9 percent of government expenditure, respectively (Egyptian Ministry of Finance, government budgets, various years).

111. World Bank database.

112. International Labour Organization, *Global Employment Trends for Youth: 2011 update* (Geneva: ILO, 2011), 10, www.ilo.org/wcmsp5/groups/public/—-ed_emp/—-emp_elm/—-trends/documents/publication/wcms_165455.pdf.

113. Jackline Wahba, "Labour Markets Performance and Migration Flows in Egypt," in *Labour Markets Performance and Migration Flows in Arab Mediterranean Countries: Determinants and Effects*, European Commission Occasional Paper 60, Volume III (Brussels: European Commission, 2010), 31.

114. Egypt 17.2 to 47.9 (2007); Syria 15.3 to 40.2 (2010); Jordan 22.6 to 45.9 (2009).

115. Ibrahim Saif and Thoraya El-Rayyes, "Labour Markets Performance and Migration Flows in Jordan," in *Labour Markets Performance and Migration Flows in Arab Mediterranean Countries: Determinants and Effects*, European Commission Occasional Paper 60, Volume III (Brussels: European Commission, 2010), 124.

116. One of the consequences of widespread graduate unemployment is the region's high level of international migration for individuals with tertiary education. World Bank data indicates that Morocco had 18.6 percent of its tertiary educated population residing in an OECD country in 2000, Tunisia 12.6 percent, Jordan 7.4 percent, and Egypt 4.7 percent. World Bank database, data.worldbank.org.

117. UNDP, *Arab Human Development Report, The Challenge to Human Security* (New York: UNDP, 2009), 111.

118. Wahba, *Labour Markets Performance*, 34.

119. In 2001, it was estimated that 42 percent of residents of Arab cities and towns lived in slums. UNDP, Arab Human Development Report, 116.

120. Wahba, *Labour Markets Performance*, 29.

121. Calculated by author from ILO wage statistics and World Bank data for CPI and GDP growth.

122. Saif and El-Rayyes, "Labour Markets Performance," 137.

123. Poverty line of PPP $2.70 per day. UNDP, *Arab Human Development Report*.

124. UNDP, *Arab Human Development Report*, 137.

125. World Bank Data, most recent years.

126. Calculated from data.worldbank.org. GDP per capita figures are as follows (2003/2008): Egypt ($1,188/$1,457), Jordan ($2,077/$2,728), Morocco ($1,841/$2,213), Tunisia ($2,973/$3,663). Figures in 2005 constant US dollars.

Chapter 4: Capitalism and Agrarian Change in North Africa

1. International Food Policy Research Institute (IFPRI), *Middle East and North Africa Strategy*. Washington, DC: IFPRI, February 2010). www.ipfri.org.

2. These rain-fed areas divide a narrow coastal strip that sees relatively high levels of rain from drier areas further inland that are typically used for sheep and pastoral activities, as well as for growing cereals (mostly wheat and barley).

3. Gabriel Baer, *Studies in the Social History of Modern Egypt* (Chicago: University of Chicago Press, 1969), 70.

4. USAID, *Country Profile, Egypt, Property Rights and Resource Governance* (Washington, DC: USAID, September 2010), 5. http://usaidlandtenure.net/egypt.

5. Will Swearingen, "Agricultural Development and Environmental Constraints in Northwest Africa," in *Rural Development in Eurasia and the Middle East: Land Reform, Demographic Change, and Environmental Constraints*, eds. Kurt E. Engelmann and Vjeran Pavlaković (Seattle, WA: University of Washington Press, 2001), 190.

6. See Ray Bush, *Counter-revolution in Egypt's Countryside: Land and Farmers in the Era of Economic Reform* (London: Zed Books, 2002) for a deeply incisive account of agriculture reform in Egypt.

7. The different paths to decolonization were in large part due to the guerrilla war against French rule in neighboring Algeria. In Algeria, French colonizers had displaced Algerian farmers en masse and transferred the most fertile land to European settlers during their 150-year occupation. As a result, around 60 percent of arable land in the country was held by either settlers or large Algerian landowners who supported French rule. During the War of Independence (1954–1962) more than one million Algerians were killed and more than two million farmers were forced into detention camps. Hundreds of villages and much of the most fertile land was destroyed through napalm attacks and bombing. With independence in 1962, the land controlled by European settlers was seized and converted into large state farms averaging one thousand hectares in size. Most of this land was concentrated in a narrow, fertile strip along the coast. In 1971, a further round of land reform saw limits placed on the size of privately held land (about eighty hectares per family) and any land over this amount was incorporated into state farms. See Ahmed Aghrout and Redha M. Bougherira, eds., *Algeria in Transition: Reforms and Development Prospects* (London: RoutledgeCurzon, 2004).

8. World Bank, *Rural Development: From Vision to Action*, Environmentally and Socially Sustainable Development Studies and Monographs Series 12 (Washington, DC: World Bank, 1997), 4.

9. Ibid., 5.

10. World Bank, *Agricultural Innovation Systems: An Investment Sourcebook* (Washington, DC: World Bank, 2012), 78.

11. Ibid. The theoretical framework for the Bank's argument draws heavily upon the work of the Nobel laureate Hernando de Soto. De Soto argues that an absence of property rights is akin to "dead capital." If legal title were provided to this property, credit would become accessible to the

poor, tax revenues would increase, and inflation would drop. The poor could use these property rights as collateral to access funds and finance. He claims that the unregistered, informal property in urban Egypt is worth about $241 billion, thirty times greater than the value of all companies registered on the Cairo Stock Exchange, with the vast majority of this property (70 percent) held by the poor. De Soto's argument is a thinly veiled excuse for privatization, and his prediction of "pro-poor" outcomes is nonsensical—the commodification of land leads inevitably to the concentration of ownership in fewer hands and the destitution of those forced to survive within market relations. This is exactly what has happened in the case of North African land markets.

12. World Bank, *Agricultural Innovation Systems: An Investment Sourcebook*, 77.

13. World Bank, *Rural Development: From Vision to Action*, 8.

14. Ibid., 84. Of course the Bank declines to note that this process led to the strengthening of large farm enterprises rather than an equitable redistribution of land. See Stephen Wegren, *Land Privatization: Why Russia Is Indeterminate and What Is to Be Done* (Washington, DC: National Council for Eurasian and East European Research, 2003), 2.

15. Zakya Daoud, "Agrarian Capitalism and the Moroccan Crisis," *MERIP Reports, Land and Labor*, No. 99 (September 1981), 30.

16. World Bank, *Tunisia: Agricultural Policy Review*, Report no. 35239-TN (Washington, DC: World Bank, 2006), 58.

17. Stephen King, *Liberalization Against Democracy: The Local Politics of Economic Reform in Tunisia* (Bloomington, IN: Indiana University Press, 2003), 26; Lisa Anderson, *The State and Social Transformation in Tunisia and Libya, 1830–1980* (Princeton, NJ: Princeton University Press, 1986), 240.

18. Samir Radwan, Vali Jamal, and Ajit Kumar Ghose, *Tunisia: Rural Labour and Structural Transformation* (London: Routledge, 1991), 40.

19. Radwan, Jamal, and Ghose, *Tunisia: Rural Labour*, 39.

20. Jeremy D. Foltz, "Micro-economic Perspectives on Tunisia's Agro-Export Strategy," *Food, Agriculture, and Economic Policy in the Middle East and North Africa, Research in Middle East Economics*, vol. 5 (Bingley, UK: Emerald Group Publishing Limited, 2003), 211.

21. Will Swearingen, *Moroccan Mirages: Agrarian Dreams and Deceptions, 1912–1986* (London: I.B. Taurus, 1988), 189.

22. Daoud, "Agrarian Capitalism and the Moroccan Crisis," 31.

23. Ibid.

24. Ibid.

25. David F. Forte, "Egyptian Land Law: An Evaluation," *American Journal of Comparative Law* 26, no. 273 (1978): 276.

26. One feddan=1.038 acres (0.42 hectare). This regulation was circumvented by many large landowners through giving the nominal title for land to relatives, thus fulfilling the conditions of the law but continuing to retain effective control.

27. In Egypt, for example, in 1987 the government eliminated the compulsory purchase of all crops except rice, cotton, and sugar cane. For wheat and corn crops, farmers were offered voluntary purchase at government-set floor prices. Rice marketing was liberalized in 1991 and subsidies for fertilizers were eliminated over 1991–1993. Likewise, other agricultural services such as land preparation and artificial insemination were charged at full cost to farmers. Similar policies were pursued in the rest of North Africa.

28. Jonathan Kydd and Sophie Thoyer, "Structural Adjustment and Moroccan Agriculture: An Assessment of the Reforms in the Sugar and Cereal Sectors," Working Paper no. 70, OECD, 25.

29. In Morocco, for example, at the time of these reforms, 80 percent of farmers were net purchasers of grain (Swearingen, "Agricultural Development," 194).

30. In Tunisia, after the coming to power of Ben Ali in 1987, remaining state land was essentially privatized through the offering of lengthy (up to forty-year) lease contracts. This took place as part of the adoption of the Tunisian government's Seventh Economic and Social Development Plan (1987–1991). The process was supported by the World Bank, which offered the country a $150 million loan, called the First Agricultural Sector Adjustment Loan (ASAL I), in 1987. In 1968, state farms had represented 40 percent of cultivable land, with more than half of the rural population living on such land. By 1985, following the transfer of much of this land to the rural bourgeoisie, the amount of state land had fallen by almost half: 1,078,000 hectares in 1968 to 600,000 hectares in 1985 (King, *Liberalization Against Democracy*, 35). By 2006, it had fallen to 500,000 hectares while 4.7 million hectares of land was privately held (World Bank, *Tunisia: Agricultural Policy Review*, 58). In Morocco, tribes collectively own approximately 42 percent of land with usufruct rights for tribal members; however, most agricultural land (nearly 78 percent) is privately owned (USAID, Morocco Property Rights and Governance Profile, 6).

31. See Ray Bush, "Civil Society and the Uncivil State Land Tenure Reform in Egypt and the Crisis of Rural Livelihoods," Program Paper no. 9, UNRISD, May 2004, for a detailed description of this process.

32. USAID, *Egypt Country Profile*, 6.

33. RDI Policy Brief, "Land Title Registry: Recommendations to Improve the Land Registration Process Towards a Formal Rural Land Market," *Land Title Registry*, no. 22 (June 2000): 1, http://pdf.usaid.gov/pdf_docs/PNACS209.pdf.

34. Bush, "Civil Society," 15.

35. Stephen Glain, "Egyptian Farmers Make Themselves Heard," *New York Times*, June 27, 2012.

36. A closely related corollary is that the population as a whole is subject to deepening and more frequent food crises in line with fluctuation of prices on the world market (see chapter 7). K. T. Ali, "Tatawwurat muqliqa li-awda' al-zira'a wa-al-ghitha' fi al-watan al-'arabi khilal al-sab'inat" [Disturbing Developments in the Conditions of Agriculture and Nutrition in the Arab Nation During the Seventies], in *Dirasat fi al-tanmiya waal-takamul al-iqtisadi al-'arabi* [Studies in Arab Economic Development and Integration] (Beirut: Centre for Arab Unity Studies, 1982), 405–43 provides an account of this process through the 1970s.

37. Yair Mundlak, "Agricultural Productivity and Economic Policy: Concepts and Measures," OECD Working Paper no. 75, 1992, 15.

38. Ibid., 15.

39. Nomaan Majid, *Reaching Millennium Goals: How Well Does Agricultural Productivity Growth Reduce Poverty?* Employment Strategy Paper no. 12 (Geneva: International Labor Organization, 2004), 17.

40. African Development Bank, *Land Policy in Africa: North Africa Regional Assessment* (Addis Ababa, Ethiopia: AUC-ECA-AfDB Consortium, 2010), 9.

41. World Bank, *Tunisia: Agricultural Policy Review*, 62.

42. African Development Bank, *Land Policy in Africa*, 10.

43. Roccu, "Gramsci in Cairo," 120.

44. FAO, *Breaking Ground: Present and Future Perspectives for Women in Agriculture* (Rome: FAO, 2005), 284. Likewise, in Morocco, the proportion of land owned by women is only 14 percent. Women have particularly lost out from the commodification of land when they are divorced, widowed, or have no male descendants. In Morocco, women from more than 4,631 tribes were denied the right to compensation for the sale of collectively owned tribal land during the privatization of land in the 1990s. Many of these women were forced into shantytowns near lands they once lived on, and since that time have continued to organize to gain access to compensation and land rights. The denial of their rights was justified on the basis of customary tribal law, known as *orf*, which predates Islam in Morocco. A grassroots movement, known as the Soulaliyate Women's Move-

ment, began organizing in Morocco in 2007 to win rights to compensation for the land.

45. USAID, *Egypt Country Profile*, 6.

46. Figures from World Bank database, http://data.worldbank.org.

47. Cited in UN Habitat, *Cairo: A City in Transition* (Nairobi, Kenya: UN Human Settlements Programme, 2011), 2. See also Asef Bayat and Eric Denis, "Who Is Afraid of Ashwaiyyat?" *Environment and Urbanization* 12, no. 2 (2000): 185–199.

48. See Ayman Zohry and Barbara Harris-Bond, "Contemporary Egyptian Migration: An Overview of Voluntary and Forced Migration," Working Paper C3, December 2003, Development Research Centre on Migration, Globalisation and Poverty, University of Sussex, 14–25, for a detailed mapping of rural to urban migration in the case of Egypt.

49. The term points to women's increasing presence in agricultural labor, whether as wage workers, small producers, or unpaid workers on a family farm. The statistics do not necessarily reveal whether the share of women in the agricultural labor force relative to men is increasing because more women are becoming economically active in general, or because fewer men are working in the sector. Statistics, particularly regarding hidden or unpaid labor of women, are also unreliable.

50. Ebba Augustin, Ruby Assad, and Dalila Jaziri, *Women Empowerment for Improved Research in Agricultural Development, Innovation and Knowledge Transfer in the West Asia/North Africa Region* (Amman: AARINENA 2012), 30–31. The report notes: "If the local culture permits, women have employment opportunities as seasonal laborers, but salaries are usually very low and protection is often non-existent . . . [women's] unpaid workload . . . can increase and the time women spend on their own plots (often for family consumption) can decrease. Women often have no access to the income generated from their farm labor . . . in small and medium sized farms, women have a much higher workload than their men-folk; they shoulder the heavy manual farm labor in addition to household and childcare duties. (It is on these farms that women lose out and their workload increases)" (310).

51. FAO, *Gender Dimensions of Agricultural and Rural Employment: Differentiated Pathways out of Poverty: Status, Trends and Gaps* (Rome: Food and Agriculture Organization of the United Nations, 2010), 3.

52. This does not mean that the majority of international migrants come from rural areas. Accurate statistical breakdown by place of origin is difficult to trace, particularly given that much migration may take place through a multiple series of journeys. Migration involves skilled and "unskilled" labor, and is often made by people who are not the poorest but have some ability to establish networks or pay for journeys. Changes in rural areas, however, have nonetheless been closely implicated in migration from the area. For empirical studies of rural to urban migration in the three countries, see Zohry and Harris-Bond, "Contemporary Egyptian Migration"; Richard Adams, Jr., "Workers' Remittances and Inequality in Rural Egypt," *Economic Development and Cultural Change* 38, no. 1 (1989): 45–71; Abdellatif Bencherifa, "Migration internationale et developpement agricole au Maroc," in *Migration Internationale et Changements Sociaux dans le Maghreb Colloque internationale Hammamet* (Tunis: Université de Tunis, 1997), 243–260; Christoph Reichert, "Labour Migration and Rural Development in Egypt—A Study of Return Migration in Six Villages," *Sociologia ruralis* 33, no. 1 (1993): 42–60; Mohamed Lazaar, "International Migration and Its Consequences in the Central Rif (Morocco)," *European Review of International Migration* 3 (1987): 97–114.

53. George Naufal and Carlos Varga-Silva, "Migrant Transfers in the MENA Region: A Two-way Street in Which Traffic is Changing," in *Migration and Remittances during the Global Financial Crisis and Beyond*, eds. Ibrahim Sirkeci, Jeffrey H. Cohen, and Dilip Rath (Washington, DC: World Bank Publications, 2012), 380.

54. Most of the Egyptian workers in Iraq were low-paid and played an important role in sustaining the country's economy during the 1980–1988 Iran-Iraq War. For Libya, around one-third of all

workers were migrants during the 1970s, and most were Egyptian (60 percent) and Tunisian (15 percent) (John Birks and Clive Sinclair, *Arab Manpower: The Crisis of Development* [London: Croom Helm, 1980], 135.) Until March 2007, the country embraced an open-borders policy for Arab and African states and no visas were required for migrant workers. This policy was aimed at securing Libya's labor-power needs as well as consolidating its political alliances with neighboring states.

55. 1976 figure from Michael Collyer, "The Development Impact of Temporary International Labour Migration on Southern Mediterranean Sending Countries: Contrasting Examples of Morocco and Egypt," Working Paper T6, Sussex Centre for Migration Research, August 2004, 11; Zohry and Harris-Bond, "Contemporary Egyptian Migration," 31, for the 1986 figure (citing CAPMAS statistics from 1989).

56. In 1985, it was estimated that 8.9 percent of Egyptian workers abroad were agricultural workers, 43 percent production workers, and 20.4 percent scientific and technical workers. In 2002, the figures were 8.6 percent, 33.8 percent, and 41 percent, respectively (Zohry and Harris-Bond, "Contemporary Egyptian Migration," 35). There was, however, significant variation between country of destination. Around one-third of Egyptian workers in Jordan and Iraq (in 2002) were working in the agricultural sector; in the Gulf monarchies, workers were concentrated in construction, teaching, and scientific/technical positions (Zohry and Harris-Bond, "Contemporary Egyptian Migration," 36).

57. Geraldine Chatelard, "Jordan: A Refugee Haven," Migration Information Source, July 1, 2004, www.migrationinformation.org/feature/display.cfm?ID=794. Accessed June 3, 2012.

58. Tayseer Abu Jaber, "Jordanian Labor Migration: Social, Political and Economic Effects," in Mohammad Shtayyeh, ed., *Labor Migration: Palestine, Jordan, Egypt and Israel* (Jerusalem: Palestinian Center for Regional Studies, 1997), 86.

59. Migration from Morocco since the end of colonial rule has gone through three main stages. The first, from 1960s to the early 1970s, saw young men from three main rural zones of the country—the Sous, the Rif Mountains, and the oases near the High Atlas Mountains—leave for Europe as cheap labor to feed the postwar boom. Many of these migrants were Berber and had been considered a political threat to the Moroccan government; migration was thus used as a means to remove them from the country. France had earlier used the same tactic against the Berber population. As migrants came generally from these three areas, village and family networks often re-created themselves in destination areas and helped to facilitate migration flows. The second stage took place after the end of the postwar boom and the onset of the oil crisis in the 1970s. European recruitment of workers ceased and migration became much more difficult. In this period, migration consisted mostly of family reunification. The third stage began in the 1990s and is typified by undocumented flows as well as the introduction of some limited temporary work programs in agriculture. See Özge Bilgili and Silja Weyel, "Migration in Morocco: History, Current Trends and Future Prospects," Paper Series: Migration and Development Country Profiles, Maastricht Graduate School of Governance, December 2009, 15; Hein de Haas, "Morocco's Migration Experience: A Transitional Perspective," *International Migration* 54, no. 4 (2007): 39–70 for detailed discussion.

60. One researcher was to note back in the 1970s that the province of Nador, in the Rif Mountains, "lives from emigration"; cited in Michael Collyer, "The Development Impact," 17. In another important agricultural area, the Todgha Valley, it was recently estimated that more than 40 percent of all households were connected to international migration in some way. Hein de Haas, "Migration, Remittances and Regional Development in Southern Morocco," *Geoforum* 37 (2006): 565–580, 569.

61. Figures calculated from statistics provided in Philippe Fargues, "Arab Migration to Europe:

Trends and Policies," *International Migration Review* 38, no. 4 (Winter 2004), 1348–1371. A large number of Tunisians are also present in Europe (349,000).

62. This process, of course, is not a new one; movement and migration of people has long been a feature of the region and was deliberately fostered through the colonial period. In the contemporary era, understanding this cross-scale nature of class formation, is critical to decoding the recent emphasis on migration in the Euro-Med agreements (see chapter 2). As this and earlier chapters have argued, the Euro-Med agreements have been an important constitutive element to neoliberalism in North Africa—they have thus been part of creating the conditions that compel people to leave their countries of origin in the first place. By explicitly incorporating the control and securing of borders into these agreements, the EU is now forcing North Africa to shoulder the responsibility for managing the consequences of this process in the interests of European capital.

63. For Morocco in 2001, remittances were more than $2 billion and constituted 40 percent of the remittances received across the entire continent of Africa (Philippe Fargues, "Arab Migration to Europe," 143). The country's remittances consistently exceed the value of tourism receipts and the export of phosphates. It should be noted that these figures are likely understated given the difficulties of measuring remittance flows.

64. Figures calculated by author from FAO data. The other major non-food agricultural export is cotton, which made up about 2 percent of Egypt's agricultural exports in 2009. About 8 percent of the rural population (according to a 1998 survey) is involved in cotton production. The Egyptian cotton industry is discussed more fully in the following chapter.

65. The other important agricultural crop in Morocco is hashish. Some reports claim that more than sixty thousand hectares of land are given over to cannabis cultivation, with the plants often hidden among other crops such as corn.

66. Lassaad Lachaal, Boubaker Dhehibi, Ali Chebil, Aymen Frija, Chokri Thabet, "National Agricultural Situation Report for Tunisia," in *Market and Trade Policies for Mediterranean Agriculture: The Case of Fruit/Vegetable and Olive Oil* (Chania, Greece: MEDFROL, 2002), 10.

67. Moreover, around 70 percent of these cereal farmers hold land under 5 hectares in size and represent only 23 percent of the total cereal cultivation. Jerry Skees, "Developing Rainfall-based Index Insurance in Morocco," Policy Research Working Paper 2577 (World Bank, 2001, 3). It should be noted that the expansion of Morocco's fruit and vegetable exports is closely connected to the occupation of the Western Sahara. In that area, nearly all fruits and vegetables are exported from crops grown on the land of Sahwaris who were expelled and now live in the Algerian desert.

68. IFPRI, *Middle East and North Africa Strategy*, 86–87.

69. Karina Fernandez-Stark, Penny Bamber, and Gary Gereffi, *The Fruit and Vegetables Global Value Chain: Economic Upgrading and Workforce Development* (Durham, NC: Duke University Center on Globalization, Governance, and Competitiveness, November 2011), 34. The process by which this concentration occurred is instructive and indicative of the impact of neoliberal reform. The first impetus was the introduction of a seasonal tariff by the European Community on Morocco in 1986, which meant producers had to shift toward high-cost greenhouse production in order to provide off-season produce for the European market. In the same year, the state-run Office de Commercialisation et d'Exportation lost its monopoly over the country's horticultural exports as a requirement of conditionalities connected to a 1985 World Bank loan. These two structural changes pushed small producers to consolidate, with seven corporate groups emerging (in partnership with French firms) to control production from the farm gate through to export and marketing. These companies include Maraissa and Rosaflor, which are joint ventures between the privately owned Groupe Tazi and the French company Soproma, and GEDA, which is controlled

by the Moroccan royal family. In addition to their farms elsewhere in the country, all these groups operate in occupied Western Sahara.

70. Citrus figures from World Bank, *Tunisia: Agricultural Policy Review*, 62; date exports are less concentrated, with four date exporters holding 36 percent. Olive oil data from A. M. Angulo, N. Mtimet, B. Dhehibi, M. Atwi, O. Ben Youssef, J. M. Gil, M. B. Sai, "A Revisited Gravity Equation in Trade Flow Analysis: An Application to the Case of Tunisian Olive Oil Exports," *Investigaciones Regionales* no. 21 (2011): 229.

71. The companies are Daltex for potatoes and Elgebaly for citrus. Export data from FAO and the Food Exporters Council (Egypt).

72. Industrial Modernization Centre (IMC), *Food Export Strategy, Final Report* (Cairo: Egyptian Government, May 2006), 37, www.imc-egypt.org.

73. Export-oriented production has also brought with it ecological concerns, as new export crops are often much more water hungry than traditionally grown crops. In Tunisia, for example, one researcher has estimated that a shift from onions and potatoes (traditional crops) to strawberries (a new export crop) would more than double a farmer's water usage. An agricultural strategy based on this type of production thus places great strain on water levels, particularly in the context of a region that faces immense challenges as a result of climate change. The ability to access and pay for water, moreover, particularly in the context of its price liberalization, acts to further widen the unevenness in power between large and small farmers. Jeremy Foltz, "Micro-Economic Perspectives on Tunisia's Agro-Export Strategy," 223.

74. World Bank, *Rural Development: From Vision to Action*, 69.

75. Ibid.

76. Ibid., 68–69.

77. World Bank, *Agricultural Innovation Systems: An Investment Sourcebook*, 4.

78. See the text of the PMV at Agency for Agricultural Development, Kingdom of Morocco, www.ada.gov.ma/en/Plan_Maroc_Vert/plan-maroc-vert.

79. World Bank, *Morocco Social and Integrated Agriculture*, Project Information Document, Concept Note (Washington, DC: World Bank, March 4, 2012), 1.

80. Sunil Sanghvi, Rupert Simons, and Roberto Uchoa, "Four Lessons for Transforming African Agriculture," *McKinsey Quarterly* (April 2011): 4.

81. Ibid., 10.

82. Foreign ownership of agricultural land in the key zones of the Nile Valley and Delta areas is still prohibited. In Morocco, foreign ownership of agricultural land for nonagricultural purposes is permitted.

83. Eva Gálvez-Nogales, "The Rise of Agrifood Technopoles in the Middle East and North Africa," Agricultural Management, Marketing and Finance Working Document, no. 30, FAO, 2011, 8.

84. Ibid., 8.

85. Reuters, "Sofiproteol Buys 41 Pct of Moroccan Cook-Oil Maker," July 13, 2011.

86. Capital Research, "Cairo Poultry Company," Company Note, May 12, 2009, 7.

87. NBK Capital, *Savola: The Power of Brands* (Kuwait: NBK Capital, June 3, 2010), 14.

88. Ibid.

89. Gálvez-Nogales, "The Rise of Agrifood Technopoles," 2.

90. Americana is part of the Al Kharafi Conglomerate, a massive Kuwaiti firm with interests in construction, real estate, banking, and petrochemicals in addition to its food operations. CPC had previously been government-owned but became a private company following the initial privatization wave under Sadat in the late 1970s.

91. The company provides food to foreign fast food chains such as KFC, Pizza Hut, and Burger King

as well as being the official supplier of poultry to the Egyptian military and the US Department of Defense in the Middle East. In addition to its poultry business, CPC also makes key food additives such as starch and glucose in a factory renovated with the help of a World Bank loan. CPC has a 25 percent market share in starch and 45 percent in glucose and exports both products around the MENA region from its factories in Egypt (Sigma Capital, *Cairo Poultry Company*, December 2011, 5).

92. Fernandez-Stark, Bamber, and Gereffi, *The Fruit and Vegetables Global Value Chain*, 34.

93. Gálvez-Nogales, "The Rise of Agrifood Technopoles," v, 6.

94. Invest in Morocco, *Emerging Morocco: A Gate to Opportunities* (Rabat: Royaume du Maroc—Agence Marocaine de Développement des Investissements, 2011). www.unido.or.jp/download/AMDI_Tokyo _Dec2011.pdf.

95. Other examples of large holding companies involved in agriculture include the TTS Groupe (owning 1,400 hectares of land for cattle, sheep, and cereal farming; hotels; tourism; air transport), Groupe Ellami (food processing, including 100 percent of the frozen fruits market for yogurt and ice cream; cable and electrical component manufacturing for the auto industry; industrial cable production; real estate; consulting), Groupe Loukil (agricultural machinery and seeds, engineering, trading, automobiles), Groupe Soroubat (1,000 hectares of vegetables, cattle, sheep and 550 hectares of fruit; real estate; transportation; concrete; construction).

96. The Ben Ali family itself has likely held a major stake in these companies although it is difficult to track these ownership relations due to the murkiness surrounding the former leader's business assets. Published material since the ousting of Ben Ali indicates, however, that their business interests were focused more on banking, real estate, automobiles, and transport.

97. Data from Tunisian Industry Portal, Government of Tunisia, Ministry of Industry. www.tunisianindustry.nat.tn/en/mixtes.asp.

98. One of the family members served on the central committee of Ben Ali's party, the RCD. In 2009, a member of the Ben Ayed family was the chief speaker at a gala event, attended by more than four thousand people, to celebrate the twenty-second anniversary of the coming to power of Ben Ali in 1987 (www.poulinagroupholding.com).

99. The World Bank, for example, noted in 2005: "Charging for water is a political issue, and it is difficult to get the price right. In many cases, user fees cover the costs of operating and maintaining the infrastructure, but this price is well below water's scarcity value in agricultural or nonfarm uses. . . . The long-term goal for managing water resources should be a market-based system that allocates water through tradable water rights." World Bank, *Agricultural Growth for the Poor: An Agenda for Development* (Washington, DC: World Bank, 2005), 80.

Chapter 5: Class and State in the West Bank

1. The South African model actually had its roots in European policies toward the indigenous population in Canada. The Canadian Indian Act (1876) established reserves for indigenous people and codified in law the separate legal status of Indians and Canadian citizens. Any person who wished to leave the reserves required a permit from the "Indian Agent"—an individual appointed by the Canadian state as its proxy on the reserve. This permit system was directly transferred to 1950s South African apartheid. Furthermore, the 1876 act made it illegal for native people to sell or produce goods without written permission of the Indian Agent and permitted Indian children to be removed from the reserves to missionary schools. Dan Smith, *The Seventh Fire: The Struggle for Aboriginal Government* (Toronto: Key Porter Books, 1993), 39.

2. For a recent extensive discussion of settler colonialism in the case of Palestine, see the special

issue of *Settler Colonial Studies* 2, no. 1 (2012).

3. Moreover, the patterns of control described in this chapter are not unique to the West Bank; see Tikva Honig-Parnass, "Zionist Principles of Separation and Ethnic Cleansing on Both Sides of the Green Line," in *Between the Lines: Readings on Israel, the Palestinians and the US "War on Terror,"* ed. Tikva Honig-Parnass and Toufic Haddad (Chicago: Haymarket Books, 2007).

4. It is revealing that much of the recent commentary on the Arab uprisings has tended to sidestep this critical point, acknowledging Palestine as essentially a moral issue that might stir the populations of neighboring countries but one with little relationship to the nature of the region's political economy.

5. Jordan annexed the West Bank and East Jerusalem on April 24, 1950, and gave all residents Jordanian citizenship. West Bank residents had already received the right to claim Jordanian citizenship in December 1949.

6. Adel Samara, *The Political Economy of the West Bank 1967–1987: From Peripheralization to Development* (London: Khamsin Publications, 1988), 89.

7. Philip Robbins, *A History of Jordan* (Cambridge: Cambridge University Press, 2004), 125.

8. Ibid.

9. Leila Farsakh, *Palestinian Labour Migration to Israel* (New York: Routledge, 2005), 100. These figures are from 1970 so very likely understate the weight of the large landowners in the pre-occupation period, given that much of the confiscated land came from large plots.

10. Samara, *The Political Economy of the West Bank*, 89.

11. Sarah Graham Brown, "Agriculture and Labour Transformation in Palestine," in Kathy and Pandeli Glavanis, *The Rural Middle East: Peasant Lives and Modes of Production* (London: Zed Books, 1990), 56.

12. The United Nations Refugee Works Association (UNRWA) estimates that around two hundred thousand Palestinians were driven from their homes and fled the West Bank to Jordan during and immediately after the 1967 war. UNRWA, *Report of the Commissioner-General 1966–1967*, UN General Assembly (A/6713), 1967, 11. Half of this number had already been made refugees in 1948, Benjamin Schiff, *Refugees Unto the Third Generation—UN AID to Palestinians* (Syracuse, NY: Syracuse University Press, 1995), 67. Various estimates have been made of the West Bank population, most based upon the 1961 Jordanian census. Abu-Lughod estimates a population of 820,000 (excluding Jerusalem) by downwardly revising the Jordanian census by 100,000 to take into account out-migration, with estimates of 220,000 Palestinians expelled based upon an Israeli census that took place immediately after the war, Janet Abu-Lughod, Demographic Consequences of the Occupation, *MERIP Reports, The Palestinian Dilemma*, no. 115 (June 1983): 13–17. Gabriel and Sabatello give the slightly higher estimate of 845,000 for the West Bank population. Stuart A. Gabriel and Eitan F. Sabatello, "Palestinian Migration from the West Bank and Gaza: Economic and Demographic Analyses," *Economic Development and Cultural Change* 34, no. 2 (January 1986): 245–262. Population transfer continued in the years following the war, and by September 1968 more than 400,000 Palestinian refugees from the West Bank and Gaza Strip were living in Jordan (Peter Dodd and Halim Barakat, *River Without Bridges* [Beirut: The Institute for Palestine Studies, 1969], 5). According to the Higher Ministerial Committee for Relief in Amman, the figure of refugees in Jordan from the West Bank and Gaza reached 428,669 in 1970 (398,000 of whom were from the West Bank). "Palestinian Emigration and Israeli Land Expropriation in the Occupied Territories," Research Study, *Journal of Palestine Studies* 3, no. 1 (Autumn 1973): 106–118.

13. Important exceptions to this include the work of Nur Masalha, who has documented the conscious manner in which this expulsion was carried out. See *Expulsion of the Palestinians: The Concept of*

"Transfer" in Zionist Political Thought (Washington, DC: Institute for Palestine Studies, 1992), and Dodd and Barakat, *River Without Bridges*.

14. Gush Emunim was a religious movement formally established in 1974 that argued the land occupied in 1967 was given by god to the Jewish people. They believed that by settling this land they would hasten the coming of the Messiah.

15. Farsakh, *Palestinian Labour Migration*, 33. This number includes Palestinians in East Jerusalem and the Gaza Strip.

16. James Ron, *Frontiers and Ghettos: State Violence in Serbia and Israel* (Berkeley, CA: University of California Press), 128.

17. Around one-quarter of the original Palestinian population living in historic Palestine remained on the land with the establishment of the state of Israel in 1948. These Palestinians gained Israeli citizenship, although they continue to be subject to laws that cast them as second-class residents. They were governed by military law until 1966.

18. Allon himself believed that no such thing as a Palestinian nationality existed although he entertained the possibility that one could arise. As a key Zionist military commander, he oversaw and directed the expulsion of the first wave of more than seven hundred thousand Palestinians from their homes and lands in 1948. Writing two years after the 1967 occupation, Allon made his support for population transfer clear, stating, "A Palestinian nation . . . if it exists, could therefore be created in Transjordan [the state of Jordan], either as a monarchy or republic." Yigal Allon, *The Making of Israel's Army* (New York: Universe Books, 1970), 103.

19. In some cases, such as the West Bank city of Hebron, Israeli settlements were built in the center of Palestinian towns.

20. Allon's plan was first presented in July 1967 with amended versions in June 1968, December 1968, January 1969, and September 1970.

21. Esther Goldberg, *Jewish Settlement in the West Bank and Gaza Strip* (Tel Aviv: International Center for Peace in the Middle East, 1993), 12.

22. See Elisha Efrat, *Geography and Politics in Israel since 1967* (London: Frank Cass, 1988), for a survey of these plans.

23. Haim Gvirtzman, *Maps of Israeli Interests in Judea and Samaria, Determining the Extent of the Additional Withdrawals*, Security and Policy Studies no. 34 (Tel Aviv: BESA Center for Strategic Studies, 1997), 7.

24. Samara, *The Political Economy of the West Bank*, 86.

25. Ibid., 91.

26. Graham Brown, "Agriculture and Labour Transformation," 68.

27. Labor and GDP figures: Farsakh, *Palestinian Labour Migration*, 41–42, 98. It should be emphasized that population figures in the West Bank and Gaza Strip are somewhat suspect given that, until 1997, the only census conducted in the area was one performed by the Israeli military in 1967 immediately after the occupation began.

28. Samara, *The Political Economy of the West Bank*, 88.

29. As this process of class formation was taking place internal to the West Bank, a concurrent but no less significant development was the growth of Palestinian capital connected to the Gulf states (see chapter 6).

30. Meron Benvinisti, *The West Bank Data Project: A Survey of Israel's Policies* (Washington, DC: American Enterprise Institute for Public Policy Research, 1984), 37–48.

31. Yehuda Litani, "Village Leagues: What Kind of Carrot," *Journal of Palestine Studies* 11, no. 3 (Spring 1982): 174–178.

32. Cited in Salim Tamari, "In League with Zion: Israel's Search for a Native Pillar," *Journal of Palestine*

Studies 12, no. 4 (Summer 1983): 41–56.

33. Hillel Cohen, "The Matrix of Surveillance," in *Surveillance and Control in Israel/Palestine: Population, Territory and Power*, eds. Elia Zuriek, David Lyon, and Yasmeen Abu-Laban (New York: Routledge, 2011), 108.

34. Noah Lewin-Epstein and Moshe Semyonov, "Occupational Change in Israel: Bringing the Labor Market Back," *Israel Social Science Research* 2, no. 2 (1984): 3–18.

35. Farsakh, *Palestinian Labour Migration*, 82 and 217, for labor figures.

36. Moshe Semyonov and Noah Lewin-Epstein, *Hewers of Wood and Drawers of Water: Noncitizen Arabs in the Israeli Labor Market* (Ithaca, NY: ILR Press, 1987), 29. Cheap Palestinian labor also enabled parts of the African and Arab Jewish population inside Israel, the so-called Mizrahim, who had formed the bulk of Israel's proletariat in the decades following the establishment of the state in 1948, to move up the social ladder. This helped to ameliorate the considerable tensions that had arisen during the 1970s between Mizrahim and European Jews, graphically symbolized in the emergence of a "Black Panther" movement among Mizrahim.

37. Farsakh, *Palestinian Labour Migration*, 88.

38. Ibid., 40.

39. The number of Palestinians working in the Gulf in 1981 was approximately the same as those working in Israel (Farsakh, *Palestinian Labour Migration*, 84).

40. Al-Haq, *Punishing a Nation: Human Rights Violations during the Palestinian Uprising, December 1987–1988* (Ramallah, West Bank: Al-Haq, 1989).

41. According to B'Tselem, the First Intifada claimed a total of 1,489 Palestinian lives and 185 Israeli lives. Of the Palestinians, 1,376 were killed by the Israeli military, while 113 were killed by Israeli civilians. These numbers include a total of 304 Palestinians classified as minors (under eighteen years).

42. According to the Palestinian Human Rights Information Center, around fifteen thousand curfews were placed on Palestinian areas with more than ten thousand people from the beginning of the First Intifada to December 31, 1993. Cited in Paul Findley, "Collective Acts of Complicity," Speaking Out, *Washington Report on Middle Eastern Affairs* (June 1994): 15, www.wrmea.com/backissues/0494/9404054.htm.

43. The Provisions Concerning the Suspension of the General Entry permit (residents of Administered Territories) (no. 5) (Temporary Provision)(Judea and Samaria), signed March 17, 1988, and The Provisions Concerning the Suspension of the General Entry permit (residents of Administered Territories) (no. 5) (Temporary Provision)(Gaza District Area), signed March 14, 1988.

44. See Al-Haq, *A Nation Under Siege, Annual Report on Human Rights in the Occupied Territories, 1989* (Ramallah: Al-Haq, 1990), 328.

45. The cards also aimed at discouraging political activity against the occupation. A personal interview with an Israeli soldier was required to get the card and although people at first tried to boycott them, curfews were imposed street by street with soldiers moving from house to house to confiscate the old cards. (Anita Vitullo, "Uprising in Gaza," in *Intifada: The Palestinian Uprising*, eds. Zachary Lockman and Joel Beinin (Boston: South End Press, 1989), 51.

46. These agreements were the Gaza Jericho Agreement (May 1994), the Interim Agreement (September 1995), the Hebron Accord (January 1997), and the Wye Memorandum (October 1998). An excellent account of the first few years of this process can be found in Graham Usher, *Palestine in Crisis: The Struggle for Peace and Political Independence after Oslo* (London: Pluto Press, 1995).

47. Allan Retzky, "Peace in the Middle East: What Does It Really Mean for Israeli Business?" *Columbia Journal of World Business* 30, no. 3 (1995): 26–32; see also Markus E. Bouillon, *The Peace Business: Money and Power in the Palestine-Israel Conflict* (London: I.B. Taurus, 2006).

48. See Jonathan Nitzan and Shimshon Bichler, *The Global Political Economy of Israel* (London: Pluto Press, 2002), for a description of the development of the Israeli capitalist class through this period.

49. Ibid.

50. The other component to this was the transformation of the PLO into an apparatus dependent upon the support of other Arab governments and funding from the Gulf region. The PLO's isolation following its backing of Saddam Hussein in the 1990–1991 war also played a major role in its support for the Oslo process.

51. Sharon was minister of Housing and Construction from June 1990 to July 1992 under the Likud-led government of Yitzhak Shamir. Labor came to power in the 1992 elections.

52. Foundation for Middle East Peace, "Israeli Settlements in the Occupied Territories: A Guide," *Settlement Report* 12, no. 7 (March 2002).

53. B'Tselem, *Forbidden Roads: Israel's Discriminatory Road Regime in the West Bank* (Jerusalem: B'Tselem, 2004).

54. Samira Shah, "On the Road to Apartheid: The Bypass Road Network in the West Bank," *Columbia Human Rights Law Review* 29 (Fall 1997): 221.

55. Gvirtzman, *Maps of Israeli Interests*, 9.

56. Ahmad Qatamesh, "al-taghirat al-bunyawiya al'ati istajadat ala al-kuwa al-a'mila fi daffa wa gaza ma ba'ad Oslo" [The structural changes that have occurred to the labor force in the West Bank and Gaza after Oslo], in *Ashkaliya al'amal al-niqabi fi falastin* [Issues in Labour Organizing in Palestine] (Ramallah: Center for Human Rights and Democracy, 1999), 7.

57. David V. Bartram, "Foreign Workers in Israel: History and Theory," *International Migration Review* 32, no. 2 (Summer 1998): 303–325.

58. Farsakh, *Palestinian Labour Migration*, 210.

59. World Bank, "Trade Options for the Palestinian Economy," Working Paper no. 21 (English), March 2001.

60. Farsakh, *Palestinian Labour Migration*, 209–210.

61. See Manwal Abdel 'al, "tajrabat kutla jabhat al-'amal al-niqabi" [Experiences of the Progressive Workers Front], in *Ashkaliya al'amal al-niqabi fi falastin* [Issues in Labour Organizing in Palestine] (Ramallah: Center for Human Rights and Democracy, 1999), 100–119, for a description of the challenges of organizing workers in this context as well as a description of the proletarianization process that accords with the analysis in this chapter.

62. Palestinian Central Bureau of Statistics (PCBS), www.pcbs.gov.ps.

63. Ibid.

64. For an analysis of the Paris Protocol, see Sara Roy, "De-development Revisited: Palestinian Economy and Society Since Oslo," *Journal of Palestine Studies* 28, no. 3 (April 1, 1999): 64–82.

65. Palestinian Central Bureau of Statistics (PCBS), www.pcbs.gov.ps.

66. PCBS, "Total Value of Exports from Remaining West Bank and Gaza Strip by Country of Destination and SITC (Standard International Trade Classification)"; "Total Value of Imports for Remaining West Bank and Gaza Strip by Country of Origin and SITC," 2005. This dependency was only to increase with time.

67. The Paris Protocol was signed in 1994 and gave precise expectations of which goods Palestinians were allowed to export and import, as well as tax regulations and other economic issues.

68. This ratio reached a remarkable 49 percent in 2002 and has remained very high since that time, Shir Hever, *The Political Economy of Israel's Occupation: Repression Beyond Exploitation* (London: Pluto Press, 2010), 31.

69. A 2008 study financed by USAID estimated around 1,200 local Palestinian NGOs in the West Bank alone (USAID, *The NGO Mapping Project* [Washington, DC: Center for the Study of the Pres-

idency, 2008]). A 2010 World Bank report estimated 2,100 NGOs registered in the West Bank and Gaza that received a total of $258 million in external funding in 2008 (World Bank, Project Appraisal Document on a Proposed Grant of $2 Million to the West Bank and Gaza for a Palestinian-NGO Project [Washington, DC: World Bank, May 27, 2010], 2). For a comprehensive critical overview of the sector, see Jamil Hilal, "Civil Society in Palestine: A Literature Review," *Research Papers for the Regional Conference on Research on Civil Society Organisations: Status and Prospects* (Amman: Foundation for Future, January 2010). The Palestine Economic Policy Research Unit (MAS) found that the number of NGOs active in the West Bank and Gaza Strip increased by an extraordinary 61.5 percent from 2000 to 2007 (MAS, "Mapping Palestinian Non-Governmental Organizations in the West Bank and the Gaza Strip" (Jerusalem: MAS, 2007).

70. Jamil Hilal notes that, according to a 2007 survey, Palestinian NGOs employed an average of twenty paid staff, "Civil Society in Palestine," 28. Extrapolating from this figure based on the size of the labor force (848,000) and an estimated 2,100 NGOs, approximately 5 percent of the labor force was directly employed in the NGO sector. To this needs to be added those Palestinians working for international NGOs and multilateral organizations.

71. Hever, *Political Economy of Israel's Occupation*, 36.

72. Ibid., 42–45.

73. An investigation into corruption by the Palestinian Legislative Council in 1997 documented all of these practices, including the involvement of Palestinian security forces in enforcing privileged routes of accumulation.

74. As he was a key leader of the Israeli right wing, Palestinians held Sharon responsible (among many other crimes) for the deaths of thousands of civilians during Israel's invasion of Lebanon in 1982 when he served as defense minister.

75. For a description of curfew during this period, see Adam Hanieh, "The Politics of Curfew in the Occupied Territories," in *The Struggle for Sovereignty in Israel/Palestine, 1993–2005*, eds. Joel Beinin and Rebecca Stein (Palo Alto, CA: Stanford University Press, 2006), 324–337.

76. Amer Madi, Hassan Abu Hassan, Nabil Al-Ghool, Omar Abu Ghosh, *The Impact of Closure and High Food Prices on Performance of Imported Staple Foods and Vegetable and Fruits Market in the oPt* (Rome: UN World Food Programme, December 2009), 19.

77. This economic deprivation had devastating effects upon the health of the population. A January 2003 study from CARE International reported that chronic malnutrition for children aged six to fifty-nine months stood at 17.5 percent in the Gaza Strip and 7.9 percent in the West Bank. The massive health problems facing the West Bank and Gaza Strip were further indicated by prevalence of anemia among children six to fifty-nine months of age, which stood at around 44 percent in both the West Bank and Gaza Strip. All aspects of daily life were affected. UNICEF reported that during the first term of the 2002–2003 school year more than 226,000 children and more than 9,300 teachers were unable to reach their regular classrooms. Over the same period, at least 580 schools were closed due to Israeli military curfews and closures.

78. United Nations Development Programme, *Focus—Qalqilya and Tulkarem*, vol. 1 (Jerusalem: UNDP, 2003), 3–4.

79. Negotiations Affairs Department, "Israel's Wall in the Qalqilya District," September 2004, www.nad-plo.org.

80. These three parties were Independent Palestine, Badil, and the Third Way, and were largely associated with Palestinian NGO figures.

81. While Israel's closure of the Gaza Strip has led to a disastrous humanitarian situation (maintained with the support of the Egyptian government), it is important not to overlook the nature of Hamas rule. Since gaining power in the area, Hamas has built a repressive and self-serving administra-

tion. It has tortured and killed members of opposing factions (including those of the Left) and has led the implementation of conservative social norms, particularly against women. Over time, Hamas's political vision has also narrowed, and it remains largely supportive of the status quo. A very important source of Hamas's power is the lucrative and extensive tunnel trade that exists in the Gaza Strip. The trade through these tunnels is highly regulated, with a government ministry that administers ownership, licensing and the movement of goods in and out of the Gaza Strip. All goods are weighed and taxed by Hamas officials. This trade provides the material basis for an emerging class of entrepreneurs linked to the Hamas administration. It also provides an incentive for Hamas to maintain the current arrangement. Israel appears to be largely happy with this quid pro quo arrangement. Despite periodic attempts to close some of the tunnels, Israel is satisfied as long as Hamas maintains a tight political grip on the population and any resistance activities.

82. BBC News, "Gaza—Humanitarian Situation," January 30, 2009, http://news.bbc.co.uk/1/hi/world/middle_east/7845428.stm. Accessed April 14, 2012.

83. Ibid.

84. Sharif Kanaana and Nabil Alqam, *al-hawajz al'askariyya al'israiliya* [Israeli Military Checkpoints] (Ramallah: Palestine Studies and Publishing Center, 2003) presents a detailed mapping of this system as it evolved through the 1990s and early 2000s.

85. The Middle East Quartet was established in 2002 and is a group composed of the United Nations, United States, European Union, and Russia. It is a permanent forum intended to follow up on the Oslo process, with Tony Blair as chief envoy.

86. See Adam Hanieh, "Palestine in the Middle East: Opposing Neoliberalism and US Power," in *MRzine*, July 19, 2008, www.monthlyreview.org/mrzine. For a recent critique of the PRDP, see Raja Khalidi and Sobhi Samour, "Neoliberalism as Liberation: The Statehood Program and the Remaking of the Palestinian National Movement," *Journal of Palestine Studies* 40, no. 2 (Winter 2011).

87. Palestinian National Authority (PNA), *Building a Palestinian State: Towards Peace and Prosperity* (Paris: PNA, 2007), 18. http://imeu.net/engine2/uploads/pna-full-report.pdf.

88. Palestinian National Authority, *Palestine Reform and Development Plan* (PRDP) (Ministry of Planning, 2007).

89. PNA, *Building a Palestinian State*, 13.

90. Jamil Hilal, *A Dangerous Decade: The 2nd Gender Profile of the Occupied West Bank and Gaza (2000–2010)* (Birzeit: Institute for Women's Studies, Birzeit University, 2010), 2.

91. In an environment of increasingly high dependency ratios (an average of 5.3 people were dependent on each employed person in 2007), nearly one million people relied upon wages garnered from public sector employment (Palestinian Central Bureau of Statistics).

92. Researchers at Bisan Center for Research and Development (www.bisan.org) have documented recent developments of industrial zones in some detail. See, for example, "Industrial Zone in Jalama . . . Sacrificing Agricultural Land in Exchange for Promises for Solving Unemployment Problem" in *Bada'el*, no. 2 (December 2010).

93. Stop the Wall, "Development or Normalization? A Critique of West Bank Development Approaches and Projects," May 20, 2008. http://stopthewall.org.

94. The al-Jalama zone, in the north near Jenin, supported by Germany and Turkey; the Bethlehem zone, led by France; the Jericho Agricultural Park in the Jordan Valley, led by Japan; the Tarqoumiyya Industrial Estate, in the south near Hebron, supported by the World Bank and Turkey. See Sam Bahour, "Economic Prison Zones," Middle East Report Online, November 19, 2010, www.merip.org/mero/mero111910.

95. Keith Dayton, "Speech to The Washington Institute's 2009 Soref Symposium," Washington In-

stitute for Near East Policy, May 7, 2009, www.washingtoninstitute.org/html/pdf/Dayton-Keynote.pdf.

96. Ian Cobain, "CIA Working with Palestinian Security Agents," *Guardian*, December 17, 2009, www.guardian.co.uk/world/2009/dec/17/cia-palestinian-security-agents. Accessed November 9, 2012.

97. See World Bank, "Trust Fund Details," http://go.worldbank.org/JJUOZ8HYIo.

98. Stop the Wall, "National BDS Steering Committee: Bethlehem Investment Conference: Development or Normalization?" May 20, 2008, http://stopthewall.org.

99. World Bank, *The Underpinnings of the Future Palestinian State: Sustainable Growth and Institutions, Economic Monitoring Report to the Ad Hoc Liaison Committee* (Washington, DC: World Bank, September 21, 2010), 30.

100. World Bank, *The Economic Effects of Restricted Access to Land in the West Bank* (Washington, DC: World Bank, 2008), viii.

101. World Bank, *Building the Palestinian State: Sustaining Growth, Institutions, and Service Delivery* (Washington, DC: World Bank, April 2011), 16.

102. The funding of these checkpoints was carried out with the familiar neoliberal justification of improving trade and speeding up the movement of goods throughout the area. See World Bank, *The "Door to Door" Movement of Goods* (Washington, DC: World Bank, July 5, 2005), 6; Stop the Wall, "Development or Normalization?

103. United Nations Conference on Trade and Development (UNCTAD), *Report on UNCTAD Assistance to the Palestinian People: Developments in the Economy of the Occupied Palestinian Territory* (Geneva: UNCTAD, July 15, 2011), http://unctad.org/en/Docs/tdb58d4_en.pdf.

104. Ibid., 3. GDP/per capita figures in 2004 dollars.

105. Ibid., 5.

106. Palestinian Central Bureau of Statistics (PCBS), *Poverty in the Palestinian Territory: Main Findings 2009–2010* (Ramallah: PCBS, 2011), 19 and 24, http://pcbs.gov.ps/Portals/_PCBS/Downloads/book1789.pdf.

107. Ibid., 18.

108. UNCTAD, *Report on UNCTAD Assistance to the Palestinian People*, 2.

109. Ibid., 2.

110. Palestine Monetary Authority, *Monthly Statistical Bulletin* (Ramallah: May 2011), 13.

111. Ibid., 17.

112. For further discussion of how finance-led neoliberalism has transformed forms of social solidarity and political struggle, see Greg Albo, Leo Panitch, and Sam Gindin, *In and Out of Crisis: The Global Financial Meltdown and Left Alternatives* (Oakland, CA: PM Press, 2010).

113. One recent example of this is the Prawer Plan, which was approved by the Israeli government in September 2011. If fully carried out, this plan will result in the expulsion of up to seventy thousand Palestinian Bedouin from their villages in the Naqab (Negev) Desert (these Palestinians hold Israeli citizenship). More than one thousand homes were demolished in 2011 as part of this plan.

Chapter 6: The Regional Scale

1. For further detail and development of many of the arguments made in this chapter, please see Adam Hanieh, *Capitalism and Class in the Gulf Arab States* (New York: Palgrave-Macmillan, 2011).

2. See Kiren Chaudry, *The Price of Wealth: Economies and Institutions in the Middle East* (Ithaca, NY: Cornell University Press, 1997); Jill Crystal, *Oil and Politics in the Gulf: Rulers and Merchants in Kuwait and Qatar* (Glasgow: Cambridge University Press, 1995); Rosemary Said-Zahlan, *The Mak-*

ing of the Modern Gulf States (Reading: Garnet Publishing, 1998); Alexei Vassiliev, *The History of Saudi Arabia* (London: Saqi Books, 1998); Aqil Kazim, *The United Arab Emirates AD 600 to the Present: A Socio-Discursive Transformation in the Arabian Gulf* (Dubai: Gulf Book Centre, 2000); Daryl Champion, *The Paradoxical Kingdom: Saudi Arabia and the Momentum of Reform* (New York: Columbia University Press, 2003) for surveys of individual Gulf states.

3.   Crystal, *Oil and Politics in the Gulf*.

4.   See Robert Vitalis, *America's Kingdom: Mythmaking on the Saudi Oil Frontier* (Palo Alto, CA: Stanford University Press, 2007) for a detailed account of these conditions in the case of Aramco, the (then US-owned) oil company that operated in Saudi Arabia.

5.   Maitha Shamsi, *Ta'qiym siyassay al hijra f'il dawla majlis attawan alkhaleeji* [Evaluation of Labour Policies in the GCC], United Nations Expert Group Meeting on International Migration and Development in the Arab Region (Beirut: Department of Economic and Social Affairs United Nations Secretariat, 2006), 61.

6.   The notion of "spatial structuring of class" originates in the work of the British geographer Doreen Massey. See Doreen Massey, *Spatial Divisions of Labour: Social Structures and the Geography of Production* (London: MacMillan Education, 1984); Henri Lefebvre, *The Production of Space* (Oxford: Basil Blackwell, 1991); and David Harvey, "The Geopolitics of Capitalism," in *Social Relations and Spatial Structures*, eds. D. Gregor and J. Urry (London: Macmillan, 1985) for further development of these ideas.

7.   For widely cited examples that follow this line of argument, see J.S. Birks and C.A. Sinclair, *International Migration and Development in the Arab Region* (Geneva: ILO, 1980); and, more recently, International Organization for Migration/League of Arab States, *Arab Migration in a Globalized World*, vol. 2003 (Geneva: International Organization for Migration and League of Arab States, 2004).

8.   Alfredo Saad-Filho, "Value, Capital and Exploitation," in *Anti-Capitalism: A Marxist Introduction*, ed. Alfredo Saad-Filho (London: Pluto Press, 2003).

9.   See chapter 18 of Karl Marx, *Capital*, vol. 1, for a discussion of this in further detail.

10.   Saad-Filho, "Value, Capital and Exploitation," 35.

11.   This is not to deny, of course, that individual families may not gain a *relative* benefit from remittances vis-à-vis others in their home countries; indeed, many families are highly dependent upon these remittances. This fact, however, should not obscure the deep exploitation that exists at the core of the system.

12.   Of course this does not mean that exploitation per se would disappear, as the capital-labor relationship would still exist.

13.   This fact reveals the weakness of strategies by the Gulf to reduce their reliance on temporary migrant labor through plans to increase the proportion of citizen labor in the private sector workforce. Mut'ab Jabir Al-Ahmad (1993) presents an extreme example of this when he makes the argument that GCC regional integration would allow the Gulf to reduce its reliance on foreign labor and thereby economize expenditure on the military and state apparatuses (Mut'ab al-Ahmad, *al-Nizam al-fikri wa-al-ijra'i lil-Ittihad al-Khaliji al-Fidirali* [Theoretical and Practical Organization of the GCC] (Kuwait: Cooperation Council of the Arab Gulf States, 1993).

14.   R. Paul Shaw, *Mobilizing Human Resources in the Arab World* (London: Kegan Paul International, 1983), 38.

15.   Antoine Zahlan and Rosemarie Zahlan, "The Palestinian Future: Education and Manpower," *Journal of Palestine Studies* 6, no. 4 (Summer 1977): 107.

16.   Allan G. Hill, "The Palestinian Population of the Middle East," *Population and Development Review* 9, no. 2 (June 1983): 310.

17.   Shaw, *Mobilizing Human Resources*, 5.

18. Ayman Zohry, "The Place of Egypt in the Regional Migration System as a Receiving Country," *Revue Européenne des Migrations Internationales* 19, no. 3 (2003): 129–149.

19. Another factor here was the massive level of construction set in train by remittance flows. These remittances helped to fuel urban growth that drew agricultural workers away from rural areas, creating further demand for construction labor and shortages in the rural sector.

20. Tayseer Jaber, "Jordanian Labor Migration: Social, Political, and Economic Effects," in *Labor Migration: Palestine, Jordan, Egypt and Israel*, ed. Mohammad Shtayyeh (Jerusalem: Palestinian Center for Regional Studies, 1997), 86.

21. Sharon Russell, "International Migration and Political Turmoil in the Middle East," *Population and Development Review* 18, no. 4 (1992): 719–728.

22. Nader Fergany, *Aspects of Labor Migration and Unemployment in the Arab Region* (Cairo: Almishkat Center for Research, 2001), 7; Jaber, "Jordanian Labour Migration," 86.

23. Géraldine Chatelard, "Jordan: A Refugee Haven," Migration Information Source, July 1, 2004, www.migrationinformation.org/feature/display.cfm?ID=794.

24. Andrzej Kapiszewski, "Arab Labour Migration to the GCC States," in *Arab Migration in a Globalized World*, vol. 2003 (International Organization for Migration and League of Arab States, 2004), 123. This shift should not be interpreted as diminishing the importance of the Gulf region for Arab workers. Many Egyptian, Lebanese, Yemeni, and Jordanian families are still reliant upon remittance flows from the Gulf region. It was estimated, for example, that in 2007, 30 percent of Lebanon's labor force resided in the Gulf.

25. ILO, *International Labour Migration and Employment in the Arab Region: Origins, Consequences and the Way Forward*, Thematic Paper, Arab Employment Forum (Geneva: ILO, 2009), 19.

26. Data on the Bangladeshi migrant workforce is drawn from the Ministry of Expatriates Welfare and Overseas Employment, Government of the People's Republic of Bangladesh, http://probashi.gov.bd/publication/publication.php. Retrieved November 15, 2010.

27. Ministry of Overseas Indian Affairs, *Annual Report 2007–2008* (New Delhi: Government of India, 2008), 62, www.moia.gov.in.

28. A large number of fake companies have sprung up in the Gulf to sell work permits for which there are no actual jobs attached. Migrants are then forced to find illegal work in precarious conditions. In 2004, it was estimated that 27 percent of the total workforce of the UAE were sponsored through these companies. The Saudi Ministry of Labour has said that 70 percent of the visas issued by the ministry are sold on the black market (Nasra Shah, "The Management of Irregular Migration and its Consequences for Development: Gulf Co-operation Council," Working Paper 19, 2009, ILO Asian Regional Program on Governance of Labour Migration, Regional Office for Asia and the Pacific, 8).

29. A Human Rights Watch investigation into the Dubai construction industry interviewed a number of construction workers and found that they "paid fees in a range of $2,000-$3,000 to local recruitment agencies in their home countries to obtain employment sponsorship in the UAE . . . [They] enter into employment contracts for a period of one to three years, subject to renewal, at a monthly wage ranging from $106 to $250; on average a migrant construction worker earns $175 a month (the average per capita income in the UAE is $2,106 a month)" (Human Rights Watch, *Building Towers, Cheating Workers*, [New York: Human Rights Watch, 2006], 24.

30. Saudi Arabia British Bank (SABB). *Saudi Arabia—Thinking Big*, Fourth Quarter Report (Riyadh: Saudi British Bank, 2007). 9; Global Investment House (GIH), *Qatar 2008* (Kuwait: Global Investment, 2008), 29.

31. Saudi Arabia Ministry of Economy and Planning, Employment and Wages Survey 1996 and 2000, www.mep.gov.sa.

32. State of Qatar, *Al Nashra Sanawiyya Al Ihsayaht Al Taq'a wa al San'aeya* [Annual Statistical Bulletin on Energy and Industry], vol. 23 (Doha: General Secretariat for Development Planning, 2004), 127.

33. Bahrain Centre for Human Rights, www.bahrainrights.org. Accessed December 3, 2011.

34. Human Rights Watch, *'As If I Am Not Human': Abuses against Asian Domestic Workers in Saudi Arabia* (New York: Human Rights Watch, July 2008), 73.

35. Ibid., 49.

36. Ibid., 60.

37. *Al Watan Daily*, "Rate of Suicide among Migrant Workers in Kuwait on the Rise," August 8, 2010, 3.

38. Human Rights Watch, *For a Better Life: Migrant Worker Abuse in Bahrain and the Government Reform Agenda* (New York: Human Rights Watch, 2012), 59.

39. In Kuwait, a national trade union federation exists, but for workers to form a union there must be at least fifteen Kuwaiti nationals in the workplace. This effectively prevents unions from forming in the private sector as most workers are migrant workers. In Qatar, non-Qataris are not permitted to form a union. While unions are permitted in Bahrain, strikes are banned in the hydrocarbon, health, education, pharmacy, security, civil defense, airport, port, and transport sectors.

40. Michelle Gambard, "Advocating for Sri Lankan Migrant Workers," *Critical Asian Studies* 41, no. 1 (2009): 65. A 2007 report by Human Rights Watch found that one-quarter of domestic workers they interviewed in the Gulf were forced to "sleep under stairs, in hallways, on living room floors, or in common living quarters" because they were not provided with adequate living quarters. www.hrw.org/reports/2007/srilanka1107/4.htm. Accessed October 7, 2012.

41. Kapiszewski, "Arab Labour Migration," 117.

42. Parts of this section draw upon Adam Hanieh, "Khaleeji-Capital: Class-Formation and Regional Integration in the Middle-East Gulf," *Historical Materialism* 18, no. 2 (2010): 35–76.

43. In Saudi Arabia, upstream production is controlled by the state-owned Saudi Aramco, which has been the largest oil company in the world for eighteen years. In Kuwait, the state-run Kuwait Oil Company (KOC) is responsible for the upstream sector and the constitution mandates that foreign companies may not control the country's oil resources. In the UAE, each of the Emirates has its own state-owned company but there is considerable foreign investment through the subsidiaries of these companies. For example, in Abu Dhabi, the Abu Dhabi Company for Onshore Oil Operations (ADCO) is 40 percent owned by foreign multinationals and 60 percent by the state-owned Abu Dhabi National Oil Company (ADNOC). In Qatar, foreign companies accounted for one-third of Qatar's oil production capacity in 2007. In Oman, more than 90 percent of oil exploration and production in Oman takes place through Petroleum Development Oman (PDO), which is a joint venture between the government (60 percent), Royal Dutch Shell (34 percent), Total (4 percent), and Partex (2 percent). In Bahrain, onshore oil production is controlled by the state-owned Bahrain Petroleum Company (BAPCO), while exploration concessions have been awarded to foreign investors in offshore areas.

44. In many cases, members of the royal family with high-level positions would use the distribution of construction and other contracts to privately enrich themselves or close family members.

45. In the case of aluminium, for example, energy represents around 30 percent of production costs. For steel and cement, energy can reach up to 40 percent of total costs.

46. Hanieh, *Capitalism and Class*, 118.

47. Ibid. See also Warren True, "Global Ethylene Capacity Continues Advance in 2011," *Oil and Gas Journal* 110, no. 7 (July 2, 2012).

48. Hanieh, *Capitalism and Class*, 74. Important figures measured in dollars

49. Geant is the fifth largest retail chain in the world. In the GCC, it operates in Saudi Arabia, Bahrain, the UAE, and Kuwait. The French-owned Carrefour is the second largest retail group in the world, with GCC stores located in the UAE (first opened in 1995), Saudi Arabia (first opened in 2004), Qatar, and Oman. Geant is operated by the UAE-based Ghurair Group in Bahrain, UAE, and Kuwait, and by the Saudi-based Fawaz Al Hokair Group in Saudi Arabia. Carrefour is operated by the UAE-based Majd Al Futtaim Group across the GCC.

50. The Saudi-based Fawaz Al Hokair Group provides an excellent illustration of these patterns. Hokair began in 1989 with two menswear stores and has expanded into one of the largest Saudi retail capital groups. The group owns franchise and agency rights for around sixty international commodities concentrated in clothing (including the brands Accessorize, Adams Kids, Aldo, Ann Harvey, La Senza, Le Chateau, Marks and Spencer, Massimo Dutti, Sports City, Vero Moda, Zara) and food (including Booster Juice, Cinnabon, London Dairy, and Seattle's Best Coffee). A central component of the Hokair Group's accumulation is the Geant Hypermarket chain (the fifth largest in the world), which it operates across Saudi Arabia. Geant acts as an anchor store for large Hokair-owned malls, of which there are six in Saudi Arabia, housing more than nine hundred stores between them. In addition to these activities centered on the commodity circuit, Hokair is also involved in luxury hotels, finance, construction, healthcare, and telecommunications and distributes the Chinese-made car the Chery.

51. Saifur Rahman, "Dubai Represents 23% of Gulf's Retail Sector," *Gulf News*, April 18, 2006.

52. Colliers International, Dubai Real Estate Overview," *Market Research*, 4th Quarter (Abu Dhabi: Colliers International, 2007), 4.

53. Naiem Sherbiny, *Oil and the Internationalization of Arab Banks* (Oxford: Oxford Institute for Energy Studies, 1985), 6. BBME eventually became part of the HSBC Group.

54. Geoffrey Jones, "Banking in the Gulf Before 1960," in *The Gulf in the Early 20th Century: Foreign Institutions and Local Responses*, eds. J. Dewdney and H. Bleaney. (London: University of Durham, 1986), 22.

55. With the exception of the Saudi market and two Omani banks, foreign financial capital is not heavily involved in the direct ownership of Gulf banks. This should not be taken to mean, however, that foreign banks have not penetrated the Gulf financial circuit. This penetration has taken place through the opening of foreign bank branches in Gulf states and activities in off-shore markets that hold few restrictions on foreign activities (such as Bahrain and the Dubai International Financial Centre).

56. The company is often restructured through a range of measures typical to neoliberalism (such as sharp cuts in staff, selling-off of assets, and debt refinancing) or by splitting it up into profitable sections such as real estate. In doing so, they will often take on debt from international banks. Once restructuring is complete, the companies are then offered for sale (typically through a stock market IPO).

57. Global Investment House, *The Rise of Private Equity* (Kuwait: Global Investment House, 2006), 8.

58. Karim Solh, "The Emergence of Regional and Global Investment Leaders Out of Abu Dhabi" (paper presented on behalf of Gulf Capital to the Abu Dhabi Economic Forum 2008, Emirates Palace, Abu Dhabi, February 3–4, 2008), 7.

59. The significance of privatization for the expansion of private equity was noted in 2007 by one of the large Gulf PE firms, Global Investment House: "It is expected that the privatization pipeline in the MENA region to reach [sic] US$900bn with approximately 147 privatization transactions either announced or planned in the next ten years. Such infrastructure assets include roads, airports, bridges, public transit systems, seaports, power stations, power lines, gas pipelines, and communications network. Private equity funds plays the role in filling in the gap of financing as

the burden becomes increasingly large for the governments to tolerate on a stand alone basis, in addition the added value that private equity plays in this industry [sic]. It is argued that private equity ensures effective corporate governance, provides financial engineering, growth capital, a clear strategic vision, creates incentives for efficiency, amongst others." Global Investment House, *Private Equity—Luring Regional and International Investors Alike* (Kuwait: Global Investment House, July 2007), 15.

60. Hanieh, *Capitalism and Class* provides a listing of many of these conglomerates with detailed business activities.

61. See Hanieh, "The Internationalisation of Gulf Capital and Palestinian Class Formation," for histories of these groups.

62. In the Palestinian case, the development of large Palestinian conglomerates took place alongside massive flows of Palestinian refugee labor to the Gulf. The Saudi oil company Aramco established an office in Beirut with the specific purpose of recruiting Palestinian refugees as workers.

63. Founding vision and strategy available in Fahd Abdallah al-Nafisi, *Majlis al-Taawun al-Khaliji: Al-Itar al-Siyasi wal-Istratiji* [The Gulf Cooperation Council: The Political and Strategic Framework] (London: Ta-Ha Publishers, 1982).

64. See Hanieh, *Capitalism and Class* for the details of this process. "Khaleeji capital" comes from the Arabic word *khaleej*, meaning "Gulf," conveying more than just a geographical connotation but also a sense of a unique pan-Gulf identity.

65. Growth Gate Capital, quoted in Dun and Bradstreet, *UAE Private Equity Report*, Industry Perspectives (Dubai: Dun and Bradstreet, 2008), 8.

66. ANIMA Investment Network defines the Mediterranean as Algeria, Egypt, Israel, Jordan, Lebanon, Morocco, Palestinian Authority, Syria, Tunisia, and Turkey.

67. It is important to note that the large bulk of the region's surplus capital continues to be invested in the United States and other advanced capitalist countries. See Hanieh, *Capitalism and Class* for a detailed discussion of these flows and their role in the maintenance of US power.

68. Mahmoud Mohieldin, "Neighborly Investments," *Finance and Development* (December 2008): 41.

69. Moreover, contrary to common misconceptions, a large proportion of these financial investments come from privately controlled Gulf capital and not from sovereign wealth funds or state-owned companies. This demarcates the Gulf's investments from earlier phases of petrodollar flows, such as the 1970s, which were focused more upon government-to-government loans rather than taking direct ownership stakes in the region's economies.

70. Calculated by author from World Bank data. Gulf involvement is defined here as full ownership of companies as well as involvement at the level of board of directors in companies that purchased privatized entities.

71. See Hanieh, *Capitalism and Class*, 155–157, for a list and breakdown of share ownership for these banks.

72. Gulf Venture Capital Association (GVCA), *Private Equity in the MENA Region*, Annual Report 2009 (Manama: GVCA, 2009), 32.

73. Key Gulf business groups invested in Abraaj and represented on the board of directors include al Turki (Saudi Arabia), Qassimi (UAE), Kanoo (Bahrain), NBK Group (Qatar), Nowais (UAE), and al Jaber (UAE). In addition to these privately held GCC conglomerates, management and ownership of Abraaj also involves state bodies such as the Public Institution for Social Security (Kuwait) and the General Retirement and Pension Authority (Qatar). See Abraaj website, www.abraaj.com.

74. Wayne Arnold, "Private Equity Alive and Kicking in the Gulf," *The National*, September 24, 2008, www.thenational.ae. Accessed July 20, 2012.

75. Al Borg Laboratories, Egypt (one of the largest private laboratory chains in the Middle East);

Orascom Construction Industries (a leading Egyptian construction company and one of the world's biggest producers of nitrogen-based fertilizers and ammonia); Spinney's supermarket chain; Agrocorp (agricultural company producing tomato paste, roasted peppers, and artichoke); OMS (regional IT company).

76. Capital groups involved in Amwal Al Khaleej include A K Al Muhaidib and Sons (Saudi Arabia); Al Fozan (Saudi Arabia); Amar Al Khudairy (Saudi Arabia); Fahad Al Mubarak (Saudi Arabia); Mohammed Ali Al Abbar (UAE).

77. Market share data from ACGC website, www.arabcot.com. The chair of ACGC, Amin Abaza, was appointed Egypt's minister of agriculture in 2006 by Mubarak. In May 2012, he was jailed for corrupt land dealings during his time as minister.

78. Mohammed Taymour, chair of EFG-Hermes, noted in an interview in 1998: "I think that we have been instrumental in helping the government with the privatization activities. Many of the large privatization activities that were undertaken were marketed by EFG-Hermes through our brokers and investment banking activities, like the cement factories, tobacco, real estate, etc. I think that we benefited as a firm from the privatization program and we like to think that we contributed to the program at the same time." World Investment News, "Interview with Mohammed Taymour," December 20, 1998, www.winne.com/egypt/toe110.html. Accessed January 20, 2012.

79. Commercial International Brokerage Co., "Arab Cotton Ginning Company (ACGC)," *Egypt Company Update*, June 12, 2007, 2.

80. The Citadel-owned Wafra holds more than five hundred thousand feddans of agricultural land in Sudan and a second company, Nile Valley Petroleum, holds oil and gas exploration rights in Sudan and South Sudan. Citadel also holds Africa Railways, whose primary investment is a 51 percent stake in Rift Valley Railways (RVR), which holds a twenty-five-year concession to operate 2,352 kilometers of track linking the Indian Ocean port of Mombasa to the interiors of Kenya and Uganda, including the Ugandan capital of Kampala. Beltone owns Mahaseel, an agro-industrial company based in Sudan.

81. Prime Holding and Talaat Mostafa Group Holding Co. (TMG), *Real Estate & Tourism Sectors Report* (Giza: TMG, January 3, 2008), 20.

82. Figures in this paragraph calculated on January 3, 2012, by author from project list are publicly available at www.zawya.com.

83. Deutsche Bank, *Egypt: Real Estate*, Global Markets Research (London: Deutsche Bank, July 15, 2010), 17.

84. Ibid., 68.

85. JP Morgan, *MENA Equity Research—Talaat Mostafa Group* (London: JP Morgan/Cazenove, June 7, 2010), 33.

86. Deutsche Bank, *Egypt Real Estate: Time to Be Selective*, Global Markets Research (London: Deutsche Bank, July 5, 2010), 45.

87. Ahmed A. Namatalla, "SODIC Approves LE1.1 Billion Capital Increase," *Daily Star* (Egypt), October 18, 2006.

88. In 2009, the Middle East as a whole was acclaimed by the World Bank as the region with the largest jump in neoliberal reforms of any in the world, with seventeen out of nineteen countries recording advances in this regard.

89. Nicos Poulantzas, *Classes in Contemporary Capitalism* (London: Verso, 1978), 72.

Chapter 7: Crisis and Revolution

1. International Monetary Fund (IMF), "Arab Republic of Egypt—2010 Article IV Consultation Mis-

sion, Concluding Statement," February 16, 2010, www.imf.org/external/np/ms/2010/021610.htm. Accessed July 5, 2012.

2. African Development Bank, *The Political Economy of Food Security in North Africa*, AFDB Policy Brief (Tunis: AFDB, 2012), 6.

3. Calculated by author from FAO data.

4. Poor people in the region spend a very large proportion of their income on food (estimated by ESCWA as ranging from 35 percent to 65 percent of income for the MENA region).

5. African Development Bank, *The Political Economy of Food Security*, 9.

6. International Monetary Fund, *Regional Economic Outlook: Middle East and Central Asia*, World Economic and Financial Surveys (Washington, DC: IMF, April 11, 2011), 39, www.imf.org/external/pubs/ft/reo/2011/mcd/eng/pdf/mreo0411.pdf.

7. Ibid., 40.

8. Ibid., 39.

9. World Bank database (http://data.worldbank.org/).

10. Ibid.

11. Consortium for Applied Research on International Migration (CARIM), *Migration Profile, Tunisia* (Florence: Robert Schuman Centre for Advanced Studies, June 2010), 1. www.carim.org/public/migrationprofiles/MP_Tunisia_EN.pdf. These figures understate the true numbers, as they are drawn from consulate records and thus do not record most of the undocumented flows of migration.

12. Ibid., 1.

13. According to the latest figures, from 2000, 3.9 percent. Consortium for Applied Research on International Migration (CARIM), *Migration Profile, Egypt* (Florence: Robert Schuman Centre for Advanced Studies, April 2010), 1. www.carim.org/public/migrationprofiles/MP_Egypt_EN.pdf.

14. Ibid., 3.

15. For Morocco, for example, 61.7 percent of Moroccans in Spain, 55.1 percent in Italy, and 45.5 percent in France are employed in low-skilled occupations. Consortium for Applied Research on International Migration (CARIM), *Migration Profile, Morocco* (Florence: Robert Schuman Centre for Advanced Studies, November 2009), 1. www.carim.org/public/migrationprofiles/MP_Morocco_EN.pdf.

16. It is necessary to point out that a great deal of care needs to be taken in estimating remittance flows. They often fail to capture the large flows of unrecorded money across borders, or in-kind transfers in the form of gifts.

17. Twenty percent of GDP in 2009 was made up of remittances in Jordan. Consortium for Applied Research on International Migration (CARIM), *Migration Profile, Jordan* (Florence: Robert Schuman Centre for Advanced Studies, November 2010), www.carim.org/public/migrationprofiles/MP_Jordan_EN.pdf.

18. Oxford Business Group, "Syria: A Year in Review 2010," www.oxfordbusinessgroup.com/economic_updates/syria-year-review-2010. Accessed November 12, 2012.

19. McKinsey Global Institute, *The New Power Brokers: How Oil, Asia, Hedge Funds, and Private Equity Are Shaping Global Capital Markets* (New York: McKinsey & Company, 2007), 6, http://www.mckinseyquarterly.com. Accessed June 8, 2011.

20. Jordan (37 percent), Syria (63 percent), Tunisia (28 percent), Morocco (21 percent), and Lebanon (25 percent).

21. Rising commodity prices did have a contradictory impact. Some countries, such as Morocco and Jordan, experienced a partial rebound in exports following a rise in the price of phosphate rock of about 80 percent from the end of 2009 to 2011 (International Monetary Fund, *Regional Economic Outlook: Middle East and Central Asia*, 31). However, as noted in earlier chapters, these ben-

efits did not necessarily translate into an improvement in the situation of workers, as companies were either foreign-owned (Jordan) or linked to the monarchy (Morocco).

22. Abigail Fielding-Smith, "Yemenis Call for an End to Saleh Regime," *Financial Times*, January 27, 2011.

23. Saleh ruled Yemen from May 22, 1990, to February 27, 2012. Prior to this, he had been president of North Yemen from 1978 until its unification with South Yemen in 1990.

24. Talha Khan Burki, "Yemen's Hunger Crisis," *The Lancet* 380, no. 9842 (August 18, 2012): 637.

25. Ibid., 637.

26. Lara Aryani, "Yemen's Turn: An Overview," in *The Dawn of the Arab Uprisings*, eds. Bassam Haddad, Rosie Bsheer, and Ziad Abu-Rish (London: Pluto Press, 2011), 177.

27. Internal Displacement Monitoring Centre (IDMC), *Yemen: Internal Displacement Continues amid Multiple Crises* (Geneva, IDMC: December 17, 2012), www.unhcr.org/refworld/docid/50d0343b2.html.

28. Nir Rosen, "How It Started in Yemen: From Tahrir to Taghyir," in *The Dawn of the Arab Uprisings*, eds. Bassam Haddad, Rosie Bsheer, and Ziad Abu-Rish (London: Pluto Press, 2011), 184.

29. The deep and transformative participation of women in the Yemeni uprising is powerfully captured in the 2012 film *The Scream* by Yemeni filmmaker Khadija al-Salami.

30. The Hashid is the strongest tribal federation in Yemen and is led by the al-Ahmar family. Saleh is a member of the small Sanhan tribe that is also part of the Hashid.

31. BBC News, "Yemen Unrest: 'Dozens Killed' as Gunmen Target Rally," March 18, 2011, www.bbc.co.uk/news/world-middle-east-12783585. Accessed December 20, 2012.

32. The Muslim Brotherhood branch in Yemen is organized through Islah. Other GCC states also provide funds to social movements and a variety of economic projects in Yemen.

33. Bureau of Investigative Journalism, "Yemen: Reported US Covert Action 2012," May 8, 2012. www.thebureauinvestigates.com/2012/05/08/yemen-reported-us-covert-action-2012. Accessed December 20, 2012. In April 2012, Obama authorized a new set of rules regarding drone strikes in the country—allowing the US military to fire at targets even if the identity of those who could be killed was unknown. Greg Miller, "White House Approves Broader Yemen Drone Campaign," *Washington Post*, April 26, 2012.

34. This issue had been particularly prominent following allegations made in 2006 by a British Sudanese consultant to the government called Salah Al Bander. Bander produced documents that indicated government officials were deliberately stoking sectarian tensions through supporting pro-government NGOs, gerrymandering elections, and supporting families that "converted" from Shi'a to Sunni. The allegations became known as "Bandergate," and despite an initial promise to investigate, the government subsequently banned all discussion of the accusations.

35. Central Informatics Organisation, "Bahrain in Figures," *Kingdom of Bahrain, General Directorate of Statistic and Population Registry*, no. 23 (December 2006): 2.

36. Bahrain holds the least amount of oil in the GCC (only 0.03 percent of proven GCC reserves), all extracted from one field, Awali. With less revenue from oil, Bahrain has, since the 1970s, consciously decided to promote itself as a financial center modeled on Singapore and the Cayman Islands. In 1975, the Bahraini government introduced regulations to allow banks to operate "offshore banking units," which were exempt from all corporate taxes and were only required to pay a small fee to establish themselves on the island. This process coincided with the beginning of restrictions on foreign banks in Saudi Arabia and the decline of Lebanon as the banking capital of the Middle East due to the country's prolonged civil war. For these reasons, the country quickly developed into the key financial intermediary between the Gulf's petrodollar flows and financial markets in Europe and elsewhere. Over the last decade the government has moved to allow foreign

companies, particularly those based in other GCC states, open access to financial and real estate markets through a sustained program of privatization and liberalization (Ahmed Yusha', *Awlamat al-iqtisad al-Khaliji: qira'ah lil-tajribah al-Bahrayniyah* [Globalizing the Gulf Economies—the Case of Bahrain] [Beirut: al-Mu'assasah al-'Arabiyah lil-Dirasat wa-al-Nashr, 2003.)]

37. Steven Wright, "Fixing the Kingdom: Political Evolution and Socio-Economic Challenges in Bahrain," Occasional Paper no. 3, Center for International and Regional Studies, Georgetown University School of Foreign Service in Qatar, 2008, 10.

38. International Crisis Group (ICG), *Popular Protests in North Africa and the Middle East (III): The Bahrain Revolt*, MENA Report no. 105 (April 6, 2011): 5.

39. Bahrain Centre for Human Rights (BCHR), "Half of Bahraini Citizens are Suffering from Poverty and Poor Living Conditions," September 24, 2004, www.bahrainrights.org/node/199. A very significant aspect of this polarization has been the question of real estate. The government has refused to regulate the distribution of state-owned land, meaning that privatized land ends up being subject to speculation and extraordinary price rises, with high-end real estate projects out of the reach of most Bahrainis. These problems are compounded by a rapidly growing population, with more than one-quarter of the population under the age of fourteen. Bahraini activists have explicitly linked the question of housing and land inequality to the recent uprisings.

40. On March 10, protests had occurred among the Shi'a populations in Saudi Arabia just across the causeway connecting the country with Bahrain. Protests are banned in the country. Likewise, in Oman protests had taken place in the industrial city of Sohar throughout February and March. Protests were also called in Kuwait on March 8. Another side to shutting down the protests was financial inducement. In early March, the GCC announced a $20 billion aid package for Bahrain and Oman.

41. Cited in Vijay Prashad, *Arab Spring, Libyan Winter* (Oakland, CA: AK Press, 2012), 76.

42. Michael Mann, *The Dark Side of Democracy: Explaining Ethnic Cleansing* (Cambridge: Cambridge University Press, 2004), 309.

43. Abdallah Laroui, "African Initiatives and Resistance in North Africa and the Sahara," in *Africa Under Colonial Domination, 1880–1935*, vol. 7, ed. Albert Adu Boahen (London: Heinemann Educational Books, 1985), 100. Libya had also been the site of the first aerial bombardment from a plane in history—with the Italian pilot Giulio Gavotti dropping a bomb on Ain Zara and three more on Tajura on November 1, 1911.

44. Dirk Vandewalle, *A History of Modern Libya* (Cambridge: Cambridge University Press, 2012), 72–73.

45. Ibid., 62.

46. Ibid., 87.

47. Ibid., 145.

48. Ibid., 149.

49. The precise number of migrant workers is difficult to obtain, as up to two-thirds of these migrants were estimated to be undocumented. In 2010, the official stock of migrant workers was estimated by the United Nations Department of Economic and Social Affairs to be 682,482, 10.4 percent of Libya's total resident population. Human Rights Watch estimated an additional 1–1.2 million irregular migrants. Other sources suggested a total of 2–2.5 million migrants. International Organization for Migration (IOM), *Migrants Caught in Crisis* (Geneva: IOM, 2011), 8.

50. Sylvie Bredeloup and Olivier Pliez, *The Libyan Migration Corridor* (Florence: Robert Schuman Centre for Advanced Studies, 2011), 7.

51. The latter was strikingly confirmed in April 2012, when the British government offered the Libyan dissident Abdel Hakim Belhaj 1 million GBP in compensation in order to avoid appearing in a public court to explain Britain's cooperation with the Qaddafi regime in the kidnapping and tor-

ture of Belhaj. A letter from an officer in Britain's MI6 to the Qaddafi government in 2004 (subsequently discovered in a bombed building in Tripoli following the ousting of Qaddafi) said, "I congratulate you on the safe arrival of Abu Abdullah al-Sadiq [a name used by Belhaj]. This was the least we could do for you and for Libya to demonstrate the remarkable relationship we have built over the years." A few days later, Britain's prime minister, Tony Blair, visited Qaddafi in a highly publicized meeting between the two governments. Richard Norton-Taylor, "Libyan Dissident Offered Money to Avoid MI6 Appearing in Open Court," *Guardian Weekly*, April 10, 2012, www.guardian.co.uk/world/2012/apr/10/libya-dissident-compensation-uk-rendition. Accessed December 10, 2012.

52. Prashad, *Arab Spring, Libyan Winter*, 111.
53. Energy Information Administration, "Libya," Country Analysis Briefs, 2. www.eia.gov/cabs/libya/pdf.pdf. Accessed December 10, 2012.
54. International Monetary Fund, "IMF Executive Board Concludes 2010 Article IV Consultation with the Socialist People's Libyan Arab Jamahiriya," Public Information Notice (PIN) no. 11/23, February 15, 2011, www.imf.org/external/np/sec/pn/2011/pn1123.htm. Accessed November 3, 2012.
55. This event has been called the Abu Salim Prison Massacre, for which there has yet to be any independent inquiry. Human Rights Watch estimated 1,270 deaths in the prison at the hands of prison security.
56. Prashad, *Arab Spring, Libyan Winter*, 124.
57. One of the worst features of the situation in Libya is the treatment of African migrant workers. Indeed, Amnesty International was to note that the situation was worse than under Qaddafi (Hadi Fornaji, "Plight of Foreigners in Libya 'Worse Than under Qaddafi' Claims Amnesty International," *Libya Herald*, November 13, 2012). Another terrible indictment of the NTC was the treatment of the thirty thousand residents of the town of Tawergha, mostly populated by Black Libyans (descendents of slaves) who were ethnically cleansed from the town in October 2011.
58. The party that won the largest number of seats in the GNC was the National Forces Alliance, a loose grouping that brings together some of the country's most prominent families and other individuals. The NFA is headed by Mahmoud Jibril, who was head of the National Economic Development Board of Libya and reported directly to Qaddafi. In this position, which he held until 2011, Jibril was a strong advocate of liberalization.
59. Bassam Haddad, "The Political Economy of Syria: Realities and Challenges," *Middle East Policy* 18, no. 2 (Summer 2011): 46–61.
60. Haddad, "The Political Economy of Syria," 53.
61. Bassam Haddad, *Business Networks in Syria: The Political Economy of Authoritarian Resilience* (Palo Alto, CA: Stanford University Press, 2011), 26.
62. International Crisis Group, "Popular Protest in North Africa and the Middle East (VI): The Syrian People's Slow-motion Revolution," *Crisis Group Middle East/North Africa Report*, no. 108 (July 6, 2011): 15.
63. Daniel Williams, "Water Crisis Grips Syria," *New York Times*, March 2, 2010.
64. John Chalcraft, "Subalternity, Material Practices, and Popular Aspirations: Syrian Migrant Workers in Lebanon," *Arab Studies Journal* 14, no. 2 (Fall 2006): 10.
65. Perhaps the most notorious example of this was a massacre perpetrated by the regime in February 1982 of up to forty thousand people in Hama following an uprising by the Muslim Brotherhood against Hafez al-Assad.
66. In the former camp of popular forces are activists who were part of the struggle against the regime before the uprising, notably around the "Damascus spring" of 2001. This bloc also includes the Local Coordination Committees (LCCs), grassroots networks that are organizing the regular

demonstrations, civil disobedience, and strikes. In the pro-Western camp is the Syrian National Council, mostly composed of exiled regime opponents and dominated by the Muslim Brotherhood and other liberal forces close to Western governments and the Gulf. The SNC is supportive of Western intervention, despite the fact that it has little support inside the country itself.

67. Ghayath Naisse, "mulahathat naqdiyya hawl al-muw'aradda al-Suriyya wa darourat binaa qiyada thawriyya jamaharriyya badila" [Critical notes around the Syrian opposition and the necessity to build an alternative popular revolutionary leadership], al-thawra dai'ma, no. 2 (Spring 2012): 68–69. Unsurprisingly, the Gulf Arab states, headed by Qatar and Saudi Arabia, have led this attempt to find an "entry card into the Syrian opposition" through means such as financial support and the limited arming of various Islamist groups. Despite the fact that these groups represent a very small minority of the movement against Assad, their access to foreign funds and weapons has accentuated a dangerous sectarian discourse that threatens to undermine the Syrian uprising.

68. Reuters, "Up to 335,000 People Have Fled Syria Violence: UNHCR," October 9, 2012, www.reuters.com. Accessed December 16, 2012.

69. In Jordan, the monarchy has long played a balancing game between different tribal groups and social forces in the country. In this manner, the monarchy has been able to rely upon the allegiance of trans-Jordanian tribes, as well as Jordanians of East Bank origin. The country has a majority Palestinian population, and by privileging East Bank Jordanians, the king has managed to secure their loyalty. At the same time, the king has incorporated the wealthiest layers of the Palestinian community into Jordan's economic elites—dividing any potential challenge from that community. Finally, the king retains tight control over a network of security forces.

70. Algeria's devastating experience of an eight-year civil war, following a military coup against an elected Islamist government in 1992, remains a clear obstacle to the emergence of new social struggles in the country. Some estimates claim that up to two hundred thousand people were killed during the war.

71. Eric Gobe, "The Gafsa Mining Basin between Riots and a Social Movement: meaning and significance of a protest movement in Ben Ali's Tunisia," HAL-SHS, January 20, 2011, http://halshs.archives-ouvertes.fr/halshs-00557826. Accessed December 9, 2012.

72. The Gafsa Phosphate Company (GPC) is the largest employer in the area. Following the 1986 SAP in Tunisia, over three-quarters of the workforce lost their jobs. Gobe, "The Gafsa Mining Basin," 6.

73. Indeed, the secretary general of the regional branch of the UGTT was complicit in the process of outsourcing and deregulation—owning three of the companies that provided subcontracted labor to the mines. Gobe, "The Gafsa Mining Basin," 6.

74. According to Sadri Khiari, a Tunisian activist exiled in France since early 2003, the Gafsa Revolt and various other social movements that had emerged in Tunisia through the 2000s "helped foment an atmosphere laden with protest, an accumulation of experiences and the construction of informal activist networks of which the Tunisian revolution is a product." Béatrice Hibou, "The Tunisian Revolution Did Not Come Out of Nowhere," interview with Sadri Khiari, Politique africaine (April 2011). Translation by Stefan Kipfer, www.decolonialtranslation.com/english/the-tunisian-revolution-did-not-come-out-of-nowhere.html.

75. Paul Aarts, Pieter van Dijke, Iris Kolman, Jort Statema, and Ghassan Dahhan, From Resilience to Revolt, Making Sense of the Arab Spring (Amsterdam: Wetenschappelijk Onderzoek-en Documentatiecentrum, University of Amsterdam Department of Political Science, July 2012), 34.

76. Prashad, Arab Spring, Libyan Winter, 13.

77. Reem Abou-El-Fadl, "The Road to Jerusalem through Tahrir Square: Anti-Zionism and Palestine in the 2011 Egyptian Revolution," Journal of Palestine Studies 41, no. 2 (Winter 2012).

78. Ibid., 6.

79. US Department of State, "Hillary Rodham Clinton, Interview with Taher Barake of Al Arabiya," January 11, 2011, www.state.gov/secretary/rm/2011/01/154295.htm. Accessed December 5, 2012.

80. Chip Cummins, "Saudi Arabia Voices Support for Mubarak," *Wall Street Journal*, January 29, 2011.

81. Ben Lynfield, "Israel Worried as Mubarak Teeters," *GlobalPost*, January 29, 2011, www.globalpost.com/dispatch/israel/110129/egypt-mubarak-netanyahu. Accessed December 3, 2012.

82. White House Office of the Press Secretary, "Remarks by the President on Egypt," White House, February 11, 2011, www.whitehouse.gov/the-press-office/2011/02/11/remarks-president-egypt. Accessed May 9, 2011.

83. World Bank Group, "Remarks at the Opening Press Conference," Robert Zoellick, April 14, 2011, http://go.worldbank.org/92JDBZXKL0. Accessed May 9, 2011.

84. Wael Gamal, "al waqa'a yurfid badilkum al-waheed" [Reality Rejects Your Single Alternative], *Jadaliyya*, December 17, 2012, www.jadaliyya.com. Accessed December 17, 2012.

85. On May 19, 2011, US President Obama gave his first formal speech on the uprisings in which he offered the promise of financial aid. Obama's speech devoted much space to the question of economic policies in the new situation—indeed, the *sole* concrete policy advanced in his talk concerned US economic relationships with Egypt. A G8 meeting in France held on May 26–27 continued this trend, announcing that up to $20 billion would be offered to Egypt and Tunisia. When support from the Gulf Arab states was factored into these figures, Egypt alone appeared to be on the verge of receiving around $15 billion in loans, investment, and aid from governments and the key international financial institutions (IFI).

86. Institute of International Finance (IIF), *The Arab World in Transition: Assessing the Economic Impact* (Washington, DC: Institute of International Finance, May 2, 2011), 2.

87. Ibid.

88. "Overcoming high unemployment [in MENA] will require a substantial increase in the pace of economic growth.... Achieving such growth rates will entail both additional investment and improved productivity ... the key role will have to be played by the private sector, including by attracting foreign direct investment. Thus, government policies should support an enabling environment in which the private sector flourishes." International Monetary Fund, *Economic Transformation in MENA: Delivering on the Promise of Shared Prosperity*, IMF Staff Report to the G8 Summit (Washington, DC: IMF, May 27, 2011), 6, www.imf.org/external/np/g8/pdf/052711.pdf.

89. European Investment Bank, *FEMIP Study on PPP Legal & Financial Frameworks in the Mediterranean Partner Countries*, vol. 1 (Luxembourg: EIB, May 2011), 12.

90. Ibid.

91. Bluntly indicated by the *EBRD 2010 Transition Report*, which presents a detailed assessment of the East European and ex-Soviet republics, measuring their progress on a detailed set of indicators: 1) private sector share of GDP; 2) large-scale privatization; 3) small-scale privatization; 4) governance and enterprise restructuring; 5) price liberalization; 6) trade and foreign exchange system; 7) competition policy; 8) banking reform and interest rate liberalization; 9) securities markets and non-bank financial institutions; 10) overall infrastructure reform. Only countries that score well on these indicators are eligible for EBRD loans. www.ebrd.com/pages/research/publications/flagships/transition.shtml.

92. Reuters News, "EBRD Aims to Complete Egypt Inclusion Study by Spring," February 15, 2011.

93. Niqal Zgheib, "Major Step Forward as Shareholders Approve Three Projects," *EBRD Press Release*, September 18, 2012, www.ebrd.com/english/pages/news/press/2012/120918.shtml. Accessed October 20, 2012.

94. Tunisia was the recipient of the equivalent of $500 million from the World Bank in May 2011, aimed at fostering "deeper global integration ... reducing protection at home to enhance resource

allocation and efficiency . . . reforms to increase efficiency and attract private investment, [and improving] the business environment by removing red tape." The World Bank noted that one of the aims of the loan was to "send a strong signal" to private investors that "Tunisia is now open for business." World Bank, *Tunisia Governance and Opportunity Development Policy Loan* (Washington, DC: May 26, 2011), 5. Morocco, Jordan, and Yemen also received World Bank loans in 2011 and 2012. The African Development Bank extended loans to Tunisia and Morocco.

95. Fathi al-Shamkhy, "al maduneeya al-kharajeeya wa al-thawra al-Tunisiyya" [Foreign Debt and the Tunisian Revolution], *al-thawra dai'ma*, no. 2 (Spring 2012): 143–146.

96. "Egyptian Independent Trade Unionists' Declaration," www.arabawy.org.

97. Ibid.

98. Significantly, however, an independent ticket of rank-and-file activist groups won around a quarter of the seats on the General Council of the Doctors Union after the strike—an important challenge to the Brotherhood's monopoly on the union's affairs.

99. The first step in this process was the election for parliament held from November 28, 2011, to January 11, 2012, which saw the electoral bloc dominated by the Muslim Brotherhood's Freedom and Justice Party (FJP) obtain about 38 percent of the vote with voter turnout of around 54 percent. Another Islamist grouping, the Salafist bloc, led by the Al Nour Party, won around 28 percent to become the second largest force in the parliament. A coalition of Left and Socialist parties, united in the Revolution Continues Bloc, received a little under 3 percent and won seven seats in the Assembly. The strong showing of the MB in these elections was not surprising. Under Mubarak, the MB was—despite being banned—a semi-legal organization with relatively deep implantation across the country. For many years it was seen as the principal opposition to the Mubarak regime. Many other parties (including some of the parties of the Left) had only recently formed or begun to operate openly, and it was impossible to expect them to have the reach and organizational capacity of the MB. The Islamist parties were also well funded, both from domestic sources and the Gulf states, which made a significant difference in their ability to run national campaigns. Furthermore, in the rural areas, other parties had a much weaker presence than the MB, which had built established patronage and support networks over many years. These parliamentary elections were followed on May 23–24, 2012, by the first round of presidential elections. Turnout was below 50 percent, and the election came down to a three-way split between the MB's Mohammed Morsi (24.78 percent); Ahmed Shafiq (23.66 percent), the military's preferred candidate, who was a former commander of the Egyptian air force and the last prime minister under Mubarak; and Hamdeen Sabahi, a Nasserist candidate supported by much of the Left, who won 20.72 percent of the vote. The high vote for Sabahi—particularly in the key urban centers of Cairo, Alexandria, and Port Said, which he won—was a partial indication that areas often said to be dominated by Islamist supporters were not as monolithic as many analysts assumed. Sabahi's strong result in these governorates also confirmed the primarily urban character of the revolution. The second round of the presidential elections, held on June 16–17, pitted Morsi and Shafiq against one another in a run-off vote. Two days before the elections took place, however, the military leadership moved to dissolve the parliament that had been elected in January and institutionalize the military's control over the political process. They did this through a set of decrees that permitted military and state intelligence to arrest protesters, and gave themselves authority over drafting a new constitution and the right to assume the responsibilities of Parliament until a new one was elected. These actions led to public protests and some political forces issued a call for a boycott of the second round of the presidential elections. Turnout, however, was greater than the first round (51.85 percent compared to 46.42 percent), although over 3 percent of voters spoiled their ballots. Following a week's delay in announcing the result, during which time frenzied closed-door negoti-

ations took place between the MB and the military, Mohammed Morsi was declared the winner, with 51.73 percent of the votes to Shafiq's 48.27 percent. Morsi was inaugurated as president on June 30, 2012.

100. Ahmed Tohami, "Al-Dustour wa al-Sara al-Ijtimayyi al-siyyasi ba'ad al-thawra fi misr" [The Constitution and the Political Social Struggle After the Revolution in Egypt], *Jadaliyya*, December 5, 2012, www.jadaliyya.com. Accessed December 6, 2012.

101. Yasri Al-Badri, "Al-wazir al dakhaliyya: Morsi talab bi'tifael 'al amn al-watani'" [Interior Minister: Morsi Demands We Deal with "National Security"], *Al-Masry Al-Youm*, August 3, 2012, www.almasryalyoum.com/node/1027176. Accessed August 4, 2012.

102. Ibid.

103. Thus, while there may well develop tensions between the rank-and-file base of the MB and its leadership (shown, for example, in the split of a significant wing of the MB youth in mid-2011 that left to form the Egyptian Current Party), and there is undoubtedly a contradiction between the rhetoric of the organization around social justice and its economic program, it is incorrect to describe the MB as a "reformist" organization as some on the Left have done. While the MB draws support from all layers of Egyptian society, and this support has been fostered through the organization's apparent anti-imperialist and antimilitary rhetoric (although this is frequently overstated), the trajectory of the MB is one of compromise with the counterrevolution.

104. Paul Amar, "Old State, New Rules: New Logics of Popular Sovereignty and Subaltern Alternatives to the Egyptian 'Baltagi State,'" paper presented at Oxford University Conference, The Egyptian Revolution One Year On, Causes, Characteristics and Fortunes, May 25, 2012, Oxford University.

105. This process has not been limited to Egypt. In Tunisia, elections for a constitutional assembly on October 23, 2011, brought the Islamist Ennahda Party to power, which has similarly moved against unions and other social movements, including violent suppression and arrests of striking workers amid a general strike in early December 2012. Agence France-Presse, "Leading Tunisia Union Calls for Dec 13 Nationwide Strike," December 5, 2012; Maryam Aziz, "Ennahda Activists Attack Tunisian Union," December 5, 2012, english.nuqudy.com. In Syria, the MB dominated Syrian National Council has been at the forefront of pushing for Western intervention in the country.

106. There have been numerous examples of this over the last period: attempts to reclaim land purchased by Dubai's Damac Properties Co. and Al-Futtaim Group under the Mubarak regime at below market prices; the Toshka case, in which one hundred thousand hectares of agricultural land was sold at less than $10 a hectare to Saudi Arabia's Prince Alwaleed Bin Talal (postrevolution, Alwaleed was compelled to return seventy-five thousand hectares); the case of the aforementioned EFG-Hermes, which is under investigation for its connections to the Mubarak regime (the company has said that Gamal Mubarak, son of the former president, held an 18 percent stake in an EFG-Hermes subsidiary); the militant and long-standing labor actions by workers at Tanta Flax and Oils in demanding the renationalization of their factory, which was privatized and sold to a Saudi investor, Abdel Elah el-Kaaki, in 2005; the demand to renationalize the eighty-two-branch Egyptian department store, Omar Effendi, that was privatized in 2006 and sold to the Saudi-based Anwal Company.

Index

Abaza, Amin, 257n77
Abbas, Mahmoud. *See* Abu Mazen
Abdullah II, King of Jordan, 162, 165, 262n69
Abraaj Capital, 92, 139, 140, 141, 256n73
Abu Dhabi, 130–31, 135, 254n43
Abu Mazen, 113, 114, 115, 165
Advisory Committee for Trade Policy and
    Negotiations (ACTPN), 38
Afghanistan, 153, 156, 227n73
Aflaq, Michel, 25
AFL-CIO, 5
African Development Bank, 167–68
Agadir Agreement, 229n104
Ahmad, Mut'ab Jabir al-, 252n13
Alexandria Tire Company, 51–52
Al Furat Petroleum Company, 44
Algeria, 3, 23; civil war, 262n70; debt servicing,
    31–32; decolonization, 237n7; EMP
    involvement, 39, 42; exports and imports,
    30, 42, 188, 226n47; FDI, 137, 192; MEDA
    and, 40–41; privatization, 50; protests,
    162; US trade, 38, 188
Allon, Yitzhak, 103, 246n18
Allon Plan, 103, 107–8, 113, 246n20
Alwaleed, Bin Talal, Prince, 265n106
Amar, Paul, 172
Amwal Al Khaleej (AAK), 139, 140, 141, 233n62
Anglo-Iranian Oil Company (AIOC), 22
Apartheid Wall, 113, 119
Arabia Cotton Ginning Company (ACGC), 140,

233–34n62, 257n77
Arab Union, 24
Arafat, Yasser, 112, 114, 225n40
Aramco, 44, 256n62
Armenia, 41
Assad, Bashar al-, 43, 159
Assad, Hafez al-, 159
Austria, 193
Azerbaijan, 41

Bahrain, 24, 124, 125, 129–32 passim, 152–54,
    164; aid to, 260n40; alliances/joint
    projects, 11; army, 172; bank regulation,
    259n36; Britain in, 224nn17–18; exports
    and imports, 43, 178, 184; FDI, 193, 194;
    free trade agreements, 37–38, 228n76;
    immigrant workers, 129, 130, 131, 164;
    land inequality, 260n39; military
    interventions, 154, 166; oil, 132, 224n17,
    254n43, 259n36; poverty, 153; protests and
    revolts, 152–54, 164, 224nn17–18; stock
    market, 136–37; unemployment, 153;
    unions, 224n17, 254n39; US relations,
    37–38, 228n76; wages, 130
Bahrain Petroleum Company (BAPCO), 24,
    254n43
Bander, Salah Al, 259
Bangladesh, 59, 129, 130
Barak, Ehud, 112
Barcelona Process. *See* Euro-Mediterranean

Partnership (EMP)
Belarus, 41
Belhaj, Abdel Hakim, 260–61n51
Ben Ali, Zine El Abidine, 1, 26, 64, 65, 95, 149–50, 154, 162–66 passim, 244n96, 244n98
Bishara, Azmi, 219n1
Blair, Tony, 115, 157, 261n51
Bouazizi, Mohammed, 149, 162
Brazil, 43, 177, 178
Britain. *See* Great Britain
British Mandate, 22
Bromley, Simon, 21
Bush, George H. W., 33–34
Bush, George W., 5, 36, 227n73

Cairo: "Battle of the Camels," 150; land development, 142
Cairo Poultry Company (CPC), 92, 94, 243–44nn90–91
Cairo Stock Exchange, 63, 238n11
Canada, 110, 117, 177, 193, 194
Canadian Indian Act (1876), 244n1
Capital (Marx), 7
Carrefour, 91, 92, 93, 134, 139, 255n49
Cato Institute, 37
Center for International Public Enterprise (CIPE), 5
Central Intelligence Agency (CIA), 157
Chad, 156
Chamoun, Camille, 24
China, 14, 134, 175, 255n50; emigrant workers, 59; exports and imports, 43–44, 46, 58, 177–82 passim; FDI, 193; Jordanian relations, 23; Syrian relations, 43–44, 46, 161
Christopher, Warren, 35
Clinton, Bill, 112, 227n73
Clinton, Hillary, 164–65
Cyprus, 39

Danone, 91, 93, 94
Davidson, Neil, 222n55
Dayton, Keith, 117
Desert Fox. *See* Operation Desert Fox
De Soto, Hernando, 237–38n11
Dina Farms, 92, 94, 138
Dow, 20, 193
Dubai, 125, 131, 135, 137, 141, 143, 148, 150, 265n106; construction industry, 253n29

Eastern Europe, 109, 167, 263n91
Eddin, Ahmed Gamal, 170–71
EFG-Hermes, 140–41, 192, 257n78, 263n106

Egypt, 1, 3, 12, 17, 22–26 passim, 47–73 passim, 125; agriculture, 75–77 passim, 81–94 passim, 140, 238n27, 242n64; aid to, 30–31, 32; centralization/decentralization, 67, 235n90; counterrevolution, 168–73; customs duties, 233n43; debt, 31–32, 34, 70, 236n109; deregulation, 54; EBRD funding, 167; elections, 12, 170, 264n99; emigration and emigrant workers, 85, 126–28 passim, 147, 156, 236n116, 240–41n54, 241n56; EMP involvement, 39, 42; exports and imports, 42, 43, 58, 60, 86–87, 88, 186, 229n104; FDI, 137–43, 147, 192, 194, 265n106; finance, 61–63, 140–41, 145; food prices, 146, 148; food subsidies, 69, 235n100; foreign agribusiness, 89–90, 92; GDP growth, 73; government spending, 68–69, 72; IMF loans, 168, 170, 172; informal sector, 59, 72, 85; Israeli relations, 107; labor laws, 231–32n32; malnutrition, 72, 83, 225–26n46; Muslim Brotherhood in, 169–73, 264n99, 265n103; Palestinian relations, 113; poverty, 72, 83, 84, 146; PPPs, 55; privatization, 49–51, 59, 63, 66, 138, 140, 230n10, 233–34n62, 243n90, 263n106; protests, 163, 164, 165, 170–71; revolt of 2011, 150, 167, 168; QIZs, 36, 45, 117; Saudi relations, 28; strikes, 168–69, 170, 171; taxation, 70; textiles/garment industry, 38, 42, 57–60 passim, 140, 233–34n62, 242n64; tourist spending, 147; in UAR, 24; unemployment, 71–72, 146; US relations, 26, 29–34 passim, 51, 58, 170, 226n52, 263n85; US trade, 38, 42, 58, 60, 186; wages, 60, 69, 72; wars, 29, 30–31; water services, 68, 232n35; World Bank relations, 31, 32, 50, 52, 172, 190, 235n90; WTO membership, 56
Egyptian Mortgage Refinance Company (EMRC), 63
Egyptian Trade Union Federation (ETUF), 168, 169, 170
Eisenhower, Dwight, 23
Emirate of Transjordan. *See* Transjordan
Estonia, 192
Euro-Mediterranean Partnership (EMP), 39–42 passim, 45, 46, 56, 242n62
Europe, 21, 27, 31, 32; Moroccans in, 86, 258n15. *See also* Eastern Europe; European Union
European Bank for Reconstruction and Development (EBRD), 56, 167, 263n91
European Commission, 42

European Investment Bank (EIB), 40, 55–56, 167, 232n38
European Neighborhood Policy (ENP), 41, 187, 229n100
European Union (EU), 34, 39–43, 73; Association Agreements, 47, 56; border control, 229n100; exports and imports, 38, 42, 58, 60, 177–88, 229nn103–4; Palestinian relations, 110, 113

Facility for Euro-Mediterranean Investment and Partnership (FEMIP), 232n38
Faisal II, King of Iraq, 24
Farouk I, King of Egypt, 22
Fatah, 113, 114, 115, 225n40
Fawaz Al Hokair Group, 255nn49–50
Fayyad, Salam, 115, 118
France, 21–23 passim, 29, 41–42, 52, 59, 226n58; in Algeria, 237n7; FDI, 39, 42, 91–94 passim, 192–94 passim; immigrant workers, 86, 241n59, 258n15; joint ventures, 242n69; Libyan relations, 158; Palestinian relations, 115
Freedom House, 221n25
French Mandate, 22
Front for the Liberation of Occupied South Yemen (FLOSY), 24

Gafsa Revolt, 162, 262n74
Gamal, Wael, 166
Gaza Strip and West Bank. See Palestine
Geant, 93, 134, 254–55nn49–50
General Agreement on Tariffs (GATT), 58
General Agreement on Trade in Services (GATS), 61
Georgia (country), 41
Germany, 42, 59, 158, 192
Ghana, 156
Great Britain, 4, 21–29 passim, 77, 124, 125, 226n58; in Bahrain, 224nn17–18; Dayton force support, 117; FDI, 192–94; Libyan relations, 155, 158, 260–61n51; Palestinian aid, 110
Greece, 1, 22, 42
Green Morocco Plan. See Plan Maroc Vert (PMV)
Gulf Cooperation Council (GCC), 11, 17, 45, 63, 124, 136–40 passim, 148–54 passim, 252n13; aid to Bahrain and Oman, 260n40; FDI, 192–94 passim; regional integration, 252n13
Gulf Organization for the Development of Egypt (GODE), 31, 32

Gulf States. See Persian Gulf States
Gulf War (1990–1991), 85, 107, 129, 226–27n60, 227n73, 248n50

Haddad, Bassam, 159
Hamad bin Isa Al Khalifa, King of Bahrain, 152
Hamas, 114, 115, 249–50n81
Harvey, David, 14
Hassan II, King of Morocco, 64, 66
Hizbullah, 161
Hokair Group. See Fawaz Al Hokair Group
Hong Kong, 182
Hussein, Saddam, 33, 226n589
Hussein I, King of Jordan, 23, 24, 64

Idris I, King of Libya, 22, 155
India, 43, 59, 124, 126, 129, 144, 177–82 passim
Institute of International Finance (IIF), 166–67
International Monetary Fund (IMF), 15, 27, 32, 40, 61, 167; Egyptian relations, 31, 50, 52, 64, 82, 145, 168, 170, 172; Libyan relations, 157; Palestinian relations, 116, 118; Structural Adjustment Packages, 47, 50, 66; Tunisian relations, 66
International Republican Institute (IRI), 5
Iran, 3, 16, 22, 27, 28, 33–34, 154; Chinese/Russian relations, 43; in Dhofar rebellion, 225n33; oil, 21, 22; Syrian relations, 161; war with Iraq, 33, 226n55; working class, 127
Iraq, 3, 22, 23, 29, 75, 85, 146, 153; in Arab Union, 24; immigrant workers, 240n54, 241n56; invasion of Kuwait, 33, 129, 226n58; oil, 21; second US invasion of, 36; war with Iran, 33, 226n55; working class, 127. See also Gulf War (1990–1991)
Iraq Liberation Act, 227n73
Israel, 16, 27, 28–29, 45–46, 99–122 passim, 128, 246nn17–20; EMP involvement, 39; exports and imports, 38, 45, 188; Gaza Strip closure, 249n81; Mizrahim, 247n36; Mubarak ouster and, 165; Oslo Accords, 34–35; Prawer Plan, 251n113; US relations, 32–39 passim, 45
Italy, 42, 51, 52, 59, 155, 192, 194, 258n15, 260n43

Japan, 39, 66, 177–81 passim
Jibril, Mahmoud, 261n58
Jordan, 3, 35, 262n69; in Arab Union, 24; centralization/decentralization, 67; customs duties, 233n43; debt, 31–32, 236n109; deregulation, 54; EBRD funding,

167; Egyptian workers in, 85; emigration and emigrant workers, 128, 129, 147, 148, 236n116, 258n15; EMP involvement, 39; exports and imports, 38, 42, 43, 58, 187, 229n104; FDI, 192, 193, 258–59n21; finance, 61–62; food prices, 146; food subsidies, 69, 235n100; GDP growth, 73; government spending, 68–69; immigrant workers, 241n56; independence, 22; investments, 137; Israeli relations, 107; labor laws, 232n32; MEDA and, 40–41; Mubarak ouster and, 165; oil expenditure, 148–49; Palestinian relations, 113; Palestinians in, 99, 106, 245n12, 262n69; poverty, 146; PPPs, 55; privatization, 50; protests, 161–62; QIZs, 36, 45, 59, 66, 117; taxation, 70; textiles/garment industry, 38, 42, 57, 58, 59; tourist spending, 147; unemployment, 71–72, 146; US relations, 34, 36, 38; US trade, 38, 42, 56, 58, 59, 187; wages, 72; West Bank rule, 101–2, 245n5; World Bank projects, 190; WTO membership, 56
Juhayna Group, 92, 94, 139, 171

Kazakhstan, 43
Kenya, 257n80
Khiari, Sadri, 262n74
King Abdullah II. See Abdullah II, King of Jordan
King Hamad. See Hamad bin Isa Al Khalifa, King of Bahrain
King Faisal II. See Faisal II, King of Iraq
King Farouk. See Farouk I, King of Egypt
King Hassan II. See Hassan II, King of Morocco
King Hussein. See Hussein I, King of Jordan
King Idris. See Idris I, King of Libya
King Mohammed VI. See Mohammed VI, King of Morocco
King Saud. See Saud, King of Saudi Arabia
Kuwait, 124, 125, 129–39 passim, 243n90; Abraaj relations, 256n73; alliances/joint projects, 11, 31; exports and imports, 181, 183; FDI, 139, 192–94 passim; immigrant workers, 129, 130, 131; invasion by Iraq, 33, 129, 226n58; investments in Saudi Arabia, 39; oil, 21, 132, 254n43; Palestinians in, 128, 129; protests, 162, 260n40; unions, 254n39; US relations, 228n84; worker movements, 24
Kyrgyzstan, 43

Lebanon, 3, 24; banking, 259n36; emigrant

workers, 128; EMP involvement, 39, 42; exports and imports, 42, 186; FDI, 137, 147; independence, 22; oil expenditure, 148–49; Palestinians in, 99, 106, 256n62; privatization, 50, 66; protests, 162; Syrian relations, 160, 161; wealthy families, 136
Libya, 29, 85, 261n58; army, 172; British relations, 55, 58, 260–61n51; exports and imports, 42, 187; FDI, 137, 193; immigrant workers, 156, 160, 164, 240–41n54, 260n49, 261n57; independence, 22; military intervention, 163, 166; poverty, 157; protests and revolts, 154–58; site of first aerial bombing, 260n43

Malek, Hassan, 171
Malta, 39
Marx, Karl, 6–9 passim, 126
MEDA I and MEDA II, 40
Mediterranean Union (proposed), 41–42
MENA Economic Summits, 35–36
Merkel, Angela, 42
Mexico, 58–59
Michelin, 52
Middle East Free Trade Area (MEFTA), 36, 37
Middle East Quartet, 250n85
Mirow, Thomas, 167
Misr Spinning and Weaving, 57, 170, 231n20
Mitchell, Timothy, 225–26n46
Moamen, Mohamed, 171
Mohammed VI, King of Morocco, 66
Moldova, 41
Morocco, 3; agriculture, 30, 76–95 passim, 242n65, 242n67, 242n69, 243n82; customs duties, 233n43; debt, 31–32, 34, 236n109; deregulation, 54; EBRD funding, 167; emigration and emigrant workers, 86, 147, 236n116, 241n59, 242n63, 258n15; EMP involvement, 39, 42; exports and imports, 30, 42, 43, 58, 59, 87–88, 147, 185, 226n47, 229n104, 242n67, 242n69, 258–59n21; FDI, 137, 147, 193; female and child workers, 59; finance, 61–62; food prices, 146, food subsidies, 69, 235n100; foreign agribusiness, 89, 91; free trade agreements, 37–38, 228n80, 229n104; GDP growth, 73; government spending, 68–69; hashish, 242n65; illiteracy, 72; independence, 23; informal sector, 59, 72; labor laws, 232n32; malnutrition, 72, 83; MEDA and, 40–41; oil expenditure, 148–49; poverty, 72, 83, 84; PPPs, 55; privatization, 49–51, 66, 79–82 passim,

230n10; protests, 162, 168, 169; state power, 64; taxation, 70; textiles/garment industry, 38, 42, 57, 58, 59; tourist spending, 147; unemployment, 71; US relations, 37–38; US trade, 38, 56, 185, 228n80; women's land rights, 239–40n44; World Bank projects, 189; WTO membership, 56

Morsi, Mohammed, 170, 264n99

Mossadegh, Mohammed, 22, 28

Mubarak, Gamal, 263n106

Mubarak, Hosni, 26, 64, 67, 82, 85, 94, 128, 142; allies, 61, 171; Muslim Brotherhood relations, 264n99; ouster, 55, 150, 168–69, 173; privatization by, 140; protests against, 150, 163, 164, 165

Multi Fibre Arrangement (MFA), 58

Muslim Brotherhood (MB), 169–73, 259n32, 264n99, 265n103

Nabulsi, Suleiman al-, 23

Nahyan, Sheikh, 165

Nasser, Gamal Abdel, 22–29 passim, 77, 79, 81, 82, 155

Nassur, Adib, 25

National Democratic Institute (NDI), 5

National Endowment for Democracy (NED), 5

National Liberation Front (South Yemen), 24, 225n39

NATO, 158

Nazif, Ahmad, 52

Nepal, 130

Nestle, 91

Netherlands, 192

Niger, 156

North Yemen, 28, 259n23

Norway, 115

Obama, Barack, 6, 165, 259n33, 263n85

Ollman, Bertell, 8, 10, 126

Oman, 124, 125, 131, 132, 148; aid to, 260n40; alliances/joint projects, 11; banks, 135, 255n55; Dhofar rebellion, 28, 225n33; exports and imports, 44, 180, 184; FDI, 192, 193; immigrant workers, 125, 129; oil, 254n43; protests, 162, 260n40; US relations, 228n84

O'Neill, Paul, 227n73

Operation Desert Fox, 227n73

Oslo Accords, 34–35, 106–15 passim, 121, 226–27n60, 248n50

Ottoman Empire, 21, 102, 226n58

Pahlavi, Mohammad Reza, 28, 33

Pakistan, 129, 152

Palestine, 16, 28–29, 34–36 passim, 46, 99–122, 125, 175, 246nn17–20; acknowledgment of, 245n4; al-nakba, 101, 120, 121; emigrant workers, 128, 129, 247n39, 256n62; FDI, 137, 193; First Intifada, 106, 247nn41–42; malnutrition, 249n77; NGOs, 110, 249n70; poverty, 146; protests, 162; Second Intifada, 111–13, 114, 120, 163; Six-Day War, 225; unemployment, 146; wealthy families, 136

Palestine Liberation Organization (PLO), 34, 105–11 passim, 120, 129, 225n40, 226n60, 248n50

Palestine Reform and Development Program (PRDP), 101, 115–18

Palestinian Authority (PA), 34–36 passim, 39, 101, 107–21 passim

Palestinian Legislative Council, 114

Palloix, Christian, 9

Paris Protocol, 110, 248n67

Patten, Chris, 41

People's Democratic Republic of Yemen. See South Yemen

Persian Gulf States, 24, 31–34 passim, 38–39, 43, 46, 123–44; agriculture, 76, 88, 94, 97. See also Bahrain; Kuwait; Oman; Qatar; Saudi Arabia; United Arab Emirates

Philippines, 59, 109, 129, 130, 144

Pirelli, 51, 52

Plan Maroc Vert (PMV), 89

Poland, 167

Popular Front for the Liberation of the Occupied Arabian Gulf (PFLOAG), 24, 28

Poulantzas, Nicos, 11, 143

Prashad, Vijay, 163

Prawer Plan, 251n113

Prince Alwaleed Bin Talal. See Alwaleed Bin Talal, Prince

Qaddafi, Muammar al-, 154–59 passim, 261n51, 261n58

Qatamesh, Ahmed, 108–9

Qatar, 124–32 passim; Abraaj relations, 256; alliances/joint projects, 11, 31; Bahraini relations, 154; exports and imports, 181, 184; FDI, 138, 141, 142, 192–94 passim; immigrant workers, 129, 130, 254n39; Islamist relations, 171; Libyan relations, 156, 158; oil, 132, 254n43; Syrian relations, 161, 262n67; unions, 254n39; US relations, 153, 228n84; wages, 130; Yemeni relations, 152

Rabin, Yitzhak, 35, 106
RAND Corporation, 28
Republic of Yemen. *See* Yemen
Riccardione, Francis, 163
Romania, 109
Rumsfeld, Donald, 227n73
Russia, 43, 44, 161, 175, 178, 192

Sabahi, Hamdeen, 12, 223n59, 264n99
Sadat, Anwar, 29, 85, 128, 243n90
Said, Mumtaz al-, 170
Saleh, Ahmed Abdullah, 150, 152
Saleh, Ali Abdullah, 150–52 passim, 259n23, 259n30
Saleh, Hatem, 170
Saleh, Osama, 170
Sarkozy, Nicolas, 41–42
Saud, King of Saudi Arabia, 27
Saudi Arabia, 27–28, 125, 129–43 passim, 148–54 passim, 158–65 passim; alliances/joint projects, 11, 31; Bahraini relations, 154; banks, 259n36; Egyptian relations, 28; exports and imports, 180, 183; FDI, 138–43 passim, 192–94 passim, 228n87, 233n62, 265n106; immigrant workers, 125, 192, 253n28, 256n62; Islamist relations, 171; Libyan relations, 158; oil, 21, 44, 132, 133–34, 254n43, 256n62, 228n87, 256n62; protests, 162, 260n40; retail, 140, 255n50, 263n106; Syrian relations, 161, 262n67; US relations, 39, 45; worker movements, 24; Yemeni relations, 152
Saudi Basic Industries Organization (SABIC), 44, 133–34
Savas, Emanuel, 54
Savola, 138, 139
Schengen Agreement, 229n100
Seoudi, Abdul Rahman, 171
Shaaban, Abdul Hussein, 3
Shafiq, Ahmed, 264n99
Shah of Iran. *See* Pahlavi, Mohammad Reza
Shanghai Cooperation Organization (SCO), 43
Sharon, Ariel, 103, 105, 108, 112, 248n51
Sharon Plan, 103, 108, 113
Shater, Khairat al-, 171
Shebin El-Kom Textile Company, 60
Singapore, 181
Sixth of October Development and Investment Company (SODIC), 142–43
Solidarity Center, 5
South Africa, 35, 100, 167, 193, 244n1
South Korea, 43, 65, 177, 181

South Sudan, 257n80
South Yemen, 24, 29, 225n39
Soviet Union, 14, 22, 23, 25, 31, 33, 79
Spain, 1, 42, 59, 93, 94, 193, 258n15
Sri Lanka, 59, 129, 130
Sudan, 23, 141, 257n80
Suez Canal, 23, 25, 128
Switzerland, 178, 182, 192, 193, 194
Syria, 3, 23–24; army, 172; Chinese relations, 43–44; emigrant workers, 128; EMP involvement, 39; exports and imports, 43, 147, 188; FDI, 137, 147, 193; food prices, 146; independence, 22; oil expenditure, 148–49; poverty, 146; revolts, 159–61, 164, 166, 262n67; Russian relations, 43; unemployment, 146; wars, 29
Syrian National Council, 161, 261–62n66

Taalat Mustafa Group (TMG), 142
Tajikistan, 43
Tarabishi, George, 224n24
Tarbil, Fathi, 157
Taymour, Mohammed, 257n78
Thabet, Safwan, 171
Thailand, 109, 181
Transjordan, 22
Transport and Engineering Company (TRENCO), 51–52
Trotsky, Leon, 223n63
Truman, Harry, 22
Tunisia, 1, 3; agriculture, 30, 76–89 passim, 93, 95, 243n73; customs duties, 233n43; debt, 31–32, 236n109; deregulation, 54; EBRD funding, 167; elections, 265n105; emigration and emigrant workers, 147, 156, 236n116, 240–41n54; EMP involvement, 39, 42; exports and imports, 30, 42, 59, 87–88, 147, 185, 226n47, 229n104, 243n73; FDI, 137, 194; finance, 61–62; food prices, 146; food subsidies, 69, 235n100; foreign agribusiness, 89, 93; GDP growth, 73; government spending, 68–69; illiteracy, 72; independence, 23; informal sector, 72; job loss, 58; labor policy, 232n32; landownership, 239n30; malnutrition, 83; MEDA and, 40–41; oil expenditure, 148–49; poverty, 72, 83, 84; PPPs, 55; privatization, 49–51, 65–66, 79, 81–82, 230n10, 239n30; protests and revolts, 149–50, 162–67 passim, 173, 262n74; state power, 64–66 passim; taxation, 70; textiles/garment industry, 38, 42, 57, 58, 59; tourist spending, 147;

unemployment, 71, 146; US relations, 164–65; US trade, 38, 185; World Bank loans and projects, 191, 263–64n94; WTO membership, 56; Zoellick on, 6

Turkey, 3, 16, 23, 58, 65; AKP, 172; Dayton force support, 117; EMP involvement, 39; exports and imports, 43, 177–80 passim; opposition to MU, 42; Soviet influence, 22; Syrian relations, 161

Uganda, 257n80

Ukraine, 41, 179

United Arab Emirates (UAE), 124, 126, 129–42 passim, 148; alliances/joint projects, 11, 31; exports and imports, 178–83 passim; FDI, 39, 138–42 passim, 192–94 passim; immigrant workers, 130, 131, 253n28–29; oil, 254n43; police force in Bahrain, 154; US relations, 228n84. *See also* Abu Dhabi; Dubai

United Arab Republic (UAR), 24

United Kingdom. *See* Great Britain

United Nations, 22, 157, 158

United Nations Conference on Trade and Development (UNCTAD), 119

United Nations Development Program (UNDP), 66, 110

United States, 13, 20–39 passim, 43–46 passim, 73, 107; agribusiness, 225n42; Arab Spring and, 6, 164–66 passim, 263n85; in Bahrain, 153; "democracy promotion programs," 5; Dhofar rebellion role, 225n33; drone strikes on Yemen, 152, 259n33; Egyptian relations, 26, 29–34 passim, 51, 58, 170, 226n52, 263n85; exports and imports, 36–38 passim, 43, 177–88; FDI, 192, 193, financial crisis, 148; Libyan relations, 155, 156–57, 158; Palestinian relations, 110, 113. *See also* Gulf War (1990–1991)

USAID, 51–52, 82, 110

US Central Command (CENTCOM), 153

Uzbekistan, 43

Van der Linden, Marcel, 11

Volcker, Paul, 31, 226n50

West Bank Wall. *See* Apartheid Wall

Western Sahara, 242–43n69

Wood, Ellen Meiksins, 7, 222n38

World Economic Forum, 36–37

World Bank, 6, 15, 27, 40, 49–67 passim, 175; Egypt and, 31, 32, 50, 52, 172, 190, 235n90;

list of funded projects, 189–91; Palestinians and, 101, 110, 116–19 passim; rural development strategy, 78–79, 82; sees crisis as opportunity, 49, 167–68; on "social protection costs," 231n26; Tunisian loans, 191, 263–64n94; view of water as commodity, 244n99; World Development Report (1997), 221n28

World Trade Organization (WTO), 47, 56, 57, 61, 228n87

World War II, 19–22 passim, 123, 155

Yemen, 3, 146–52 passim, 163–64, 172, 259n23, 259nn29–33 passim; army, 172; emigrant workers, 128, 147, 148; exports, 147; FDI, 147; food prices, 148; Iraq support, 129; malnutrition, 150; poverty, 146, 150–51; privatization, 50; revolts, 150–52, 163–64; World Bank loans, 264n94

Yemen Arab Republic. *See* North Yemen

Zoellick, Robert, 6, 36–37, 165, 228n76

About the Author

Adam Hanieh is a Senior Lecturer in Development Studies at the School of Oriental and African Studies (SOAS), University of London. Prior to joining SOAS, Adam taught at Zayed University, United Arab Emirates. From 1997 to 2003, he lived and worked in Ramallah, Palestine, where he completed an MA in regional studies at Al Quds University. He holds a PhD in political science from York University, Canada. Adam is an editorial board member of the journal *Historical Materialism: Research in Critical Marxist Theory*, a founding member of the SOAS Centre for Palestine Studies, and a member of the committee of management for the Council for British Research in the Levant. His most recent book is *Capitalism and Class in the Gulf Arab States* (Palgrave-Macmillan, 2011).

Printed in the USA
CPSIA information can be obtained
at www.ICGtesting.com
JSHW011402020824
67476JS00005B/168

9 781608 463251